SOCIAL WELFARE

ADDRESSING POVERTY
AND HOMELESSNESS

ISSN 1937-3295

SOCIAL WELFARE
ADDRESSING POVERTY AND HOMELESSNESS

Stephen Meyer

INFORMATION PLUS® REFERENCE SERIES
Formerly Published by Information Plus, Wylie, Texas

GALE
A Cengage Company

Farmington Hills, Mich • San Francisco • New York • Waterville, Maine
Meriden, Conn • Mason, Ohio • Chicago

Social Welfare: Addressing Poverty and Homelessness

Stephen Meyer

Kepos Media, Inc.: Steven Long and Janice Jorgensen, Series Editors

Project Editor: Laura Avery

Rights Acquisition and Management: Ashley M. Maynard, Carissa Poweleit

Composition: Evi Abou-El-Seoud, Mary Beth Trimper

Manufacturing: Rita Wimberley

Product Design: Kristin Julien

Gale
27500 Drake Rd.
Farmington Hills, MI 48331-3535

ISBN-13: 978-0-7876-5103-9 (set)
ISBN-13: 978-1-4103-2561-7

ISSN 1937-3295

This title is also available as an e-book.
ISBN-13: 978-1-4103-3271-4 (set)
Contact your Gale sales representative for ordering information.

Printed in the United States of America
1 2 3 4 5   22 21 20 19 18

TABLE OF CONTENTS

PREFACE

Social Welfare: Addressing Poverty and Homelessness is part of the *Information Plus Reference Series*. The purpose of each volume of the series is to present the latest facts on a topic of pressing concern in modern American life. These topics include the most controversial and studied social issues of the 21st century: abortion, animal rights, capital punishment, care of senior citizens, crime, the environment, health care, immigration, national security, water, women, youth, and many more. Although this series is written especially for high school and undergraduate students, it is an excellent resource for anyone in need of factual information on current affairs.

By presenting the facts, it is the intention of Gale, a Cengage Company, to provide its readers with everything they need to reach an informed opinion on current issues. To that end, there is a particular emphasis in this series on the presentation of scientific studies, surveys, and statistics. These data are generally presented in the form of tables, charts, and other graphics placed within the text of each book. Every graphic is directly referred to and carefully explained in the text. The source of each graphic is presented within the graphic itself. The data used in these graphics are drawn from the most reputable and reliable sources, such as from the various branches of the U.S. government and from private organizations and associations. Every effort was made to secure the most recent information available. Readers should bear in mind that many major studies take years to conduct and that additional years often pass before the data from these studies are made available to the public. Therefore, in many cases the most recent information available in 2017 is dated from 2014 or 2015. Older statistics are sometimes presented as well, if they are landmark studies or of particular interest and no more-recent information exists.

Although statistics are a major focus of the *Information Plus Reference Series*, they are by no means its only content. Each book also presents the widely held positions and important ideas that shape how the book's subject is discussed in the United States. These positions are explained in detail and, where possible, in the words of their proponents. Some of the other material to be found in these books includes historical background, descriptions of major events related to the subject, relevant laws and court cases, and examples of how these issues play out in American life. Some books also feature primary documents or have pro and con debate sections that provide the words and opinions of prominent Americans on both sides of a controversial topic. All material is presented in an evenhanded and unbiased manner; readers will never be encouraged to accept one view of an issue over another.

HOW TO USE THIS BOOK

Aid for the poor has long been a controversial topic in the United States. Most Americans agree that society should help those who have fallen on hard times, but there are many different opinions as to how this is best accomplished. The 1990s were a time of particularly heavy debate about this issue, and with the Great Recession (which officially lasted from December 2007 to June 2009) and the passage of comprehensive health care reform in 2010, the second decade of the 21st century may be another period of debate and change in means-tested assistance. This volume also describes those who make use of the welfare system, why they use it, and what they get out of it.

Social Welfare: Addressing Poverty and Homelessness consists of eight chapters and three appendixes. Each chapter is devoted to a particular aspect of social welfare. For a summary of the information that is covered in each chapter, please see the synopses that are provided in the Table of Contents. Chapters generally begin with an overview of the basic facts and background information on the chapter's topic, then proceed to examine subtopics of particular interest. For example, Chapter 3:

Public Programs to Fight Poverty commences with a brief history of the modern U.S. welfare system, from the 1930s through the passage of the Personal Responsibility and Work Opportunity Reconciliation Act (PRWORA) of 1996. An outline of key PRWORA provisions follows, along with an overview of eligibility requirements at the state level. The chapter proceeds with a discussion of government efforts to assist Temporary Assistance for Needy Families recipients in finding jobs, with a focus on the various barriers to employment that confront many low-income Americans. An evaluation of other major government initiatives, such as the Supplemental Nutrition Assistance Program and the Special Supplemental Nutrition Program for Women, Infants, and Children, follows. The chapter concludes with an assessment of efforts to ease the financial burdens on the working poor, with a focus on the fight to raise the federal minimum wage and to provide tax relief to low-income families. Readers can find their way through each chapter by looking for the section and subsection headings, which are clearly set off from the text. They can also refer to the book's extensive Index if they already know what they are looking for.

Statistical Information

The tables and figures featured throughout *Social Welfare: Addressing Poverty and Homelessness* will be of particular use to readers in learning about this topic. These tables and figures represent an extensive collection of the most recent and valuable statistics on social welfare, as well as related issues—for example, graphics cover the amount of money spent each year for various government welfare programs, the demographics of poverty, child poverty rates in high-income countries, and the number of people without health insurance in the United States. Gale, a Cengage Company, believes that making this information available to readers is the most important way to fulfill the goal of this book: to help readers understand the issues and controversies surrounding social welfare and reach their own conclusions.

Each table or figure has a unique identifier appearing above it for ease of identification and reference. Titles for the tables and figures explain their purpose. At the end of each table or figure, the original source of the data is provided.

To help readers understand these often complicated statistics, all tables and figures are explained in the text. References in the text direct readers to the relevant statistics. Furthermore, the contents of all tables and figures are fully indexed. Please see the opening section of the Index at the back of this volume for a description of how to find tables and figures within it.

Appendixes

Besides the main body text and images, *Social Welfare: Addressing Poverty and Homelessness* has three appendixes. The first is the Important Names and Addresses directory. Here, readers will find contact information for a number of government and private organizations that can provide further information on aspects of social welfare. The second appendix is the Resources section, which can also assist readers in conducting their own research. In this section the author and editors of *Social Welfare: Addressing Poverty and Homelessness* describe some of the sources that were most useful during the compilation of this book. The final appendix is the Index. It has been greatly expanded from previous editions and should make it even easier to find specific topics in this book.

COMMENTS AND SUGGESTIONS

The editors of the *Information Plus Reference Series* welcome your feedback on *Social Welfare: Addressing Poverty and Homelessness*. Please direct all correspondence to:

Editors
Information Plus Reference Series
27500 Drake Rd.
Farmington Hills, MI 48331-3535

CHAPTER 1
POVERTY AND HOMELESSNESS IN THE UNITED STATES

The U.S. government, like the governments of other developed nations, administers a number of programs that are intended to provide for the basic needs of poor and disadvantaged citizens. These programs are collectively called social welfare programs and can take a variety of forms, including direct financial payments, assistance with food purchases, housing aid, and free health care. Compared with other developed nations, the social welfare system in the United States is modest in scope, with eligibility requirements that frequently exclude all but the poorest of citizens and time limits that are meant to keep individuals and families from becoming permanently dependent on government aid.

Modern U.S. social welfare policy has its roots in the so-called English Poor Laws, which were first implemented during the late 16th century and then codified by Queen Elizabeth I (1533–1603) in the Act for the Relief of the Poor in 1601, which made local government authorities responsible for aiding the indigent. During the colonial period in U.S. history, social welfare policy represented an extension of the English Poor Laws, with programs and institutions created at the colonial level and with large variations in benefits and management from colony to colony. After U.S. independence, there remained questions about the constitutionality of the federal government's involvement in social welfare. It was only with establishment of the Freedmen's Bureau, which was created in 1865 to aid newly liberated slaves after the Civil War (1861–1865), that a precedent was established for the federal management of social welfare programs in emergency situations.

During the Great Depression (1929–1939) the U.S. national unemployment rate rose as high as 25%, and public opinion shifted markedly in favor of a federal social welfare system that would operate permanently, rather than only in emergency situations. President Franklin D. Roosevelt (1882–1945) laid the groundwork for the modern U.S. welfare system with his New Deal, which consisted of a set of laws that were passed between 1933 and 1938 to stabilize the country's economy and provide relief to the poor and unemployed. Among the most prominent New Deal programs were the Works Progress Administration, which employed many of those who had lost their jobs during the Depression in a wide variety of public works projects, and the Social Security Act, which established a permanent system of retirement benefits, unemployment insurance, and aid to poor and handicapped children. This last feature of the act, which established the federal Aid to Dependent Children program, was expanded during the 1960s, and the program was renamed Aid to Families with Dependent Children (AFDC). Roosevelt also established the first national Food Stamp Program, which provided assistance with food purchases. This program was later discontinued before being revived during the 1960s, when the U.S. welfare system was expanded.

Besides the expansion of the AFDC and the reestablishment of a federal food assistance program, the 1960s saw the establishment of Medicare, which provides health care to retirees, and Medicaid, which provides health care to the poor and disabled. These were crucial parts of President Lyndon B. Johnson's (1908–1973) War on Poverty, which consisted of a set of legislative initiatives that grew out of the concern for social justice mobilized during the civil rights movement.

The poverty rate in the United States decreased substantially in the wake of Johnson's antipoverty initiatives, but public support for social programs waned in the decades that followed. Increasing opposition to social welfare programs culminated with the Personal Responsibility and Work Opportunity Reconciliation Act of 1996 (PRWORA), which was passed by the Republican-controlled U.S. House of Representatives and signed into law by the Democratic President Bill Clinton (1946–). The PRWORA replaced the AFDC, which offered open-ended support to impoverished families, with Temporary Assistance for Needy Families

(TANF), which was intended to incentivize job-seeking by limiting the amount of time a recipient can participate in the program. Although most of the funding for TANF comes from the federal government, as did the funding for the AFDC, states were granted wide latitude in deciding how to allocate benefits.

A major addition to the U.S. social welfare system came with the passage of the Patient Protection and Affordable Care Act (commonly known as the Affordable Care Act [ACA] or Obamacare), which was signed by President Barack Obama (1961–) in 2010. Besides attempting to reform the market for health insurance and to control rapidly rising health care costs, the ACA was intended to provide health insurance to those who could not afford it. The law's provisions began to go into effect soon after its passage, and total implementation of the health care overhaul was achieved by 2014. Although subject to harsh criticism and characterized as a catastrophe by many right-leaning pundits and politicians, the law had by late 2014 significantly increased access to health care among low-income Americans.

THE FEDERAL DEFINITION OF POVERTY

Decisions about how to determine who is poor and deserving of government aid have inspired controversy at least since the time of the English Poor Laws. Many of the U.S. government's social welfare initiatives hinge on the official definition of poverty, with both the size of an individual's benefits and the overall scope of the programs hanging in the balance.

The federal government began measuring poverty in 1959. During President Johnson's national War on Poverty, researchers realized that few statistical tools were available to measure the number of Americans who continued to live in poverty in one of the most affluent nations in the world. To fight this so-called war, it had to be determined who was poor and why.

During the early 1960s Mollie Orshansky (1915–2006) of the Social Security Administration suggested that the poverty income level be defined as the income sufficient to purchase a minimally adequate amount of goods and services. The necessary data for defining and pricing a full market basket of goods were not available then, nor are they available now. Orshansky noted, however, that in 1955 the U.S. Department of Agriculture (USDA) had published the Household Food Consumption Survey, which showed that an average family of three or more people spent approximately one-third of its after-tax income on food. She multiplied the USDA's 1961 economy food plan (a no-frills food basket meeting the then-recommended dietary allowances) by three.

Basically, this defined a poor family as any family or person whose after-tax income was not sufficient to purchase a minimally adequate diet if one-third of the income was spent on food. Differences were allowed for size of family, gender of the head of the household, and whether it was a farm or nonfarm family. The threshold (the level at which poverty begins) for a farm family was set at 70% of a nonfarm household. (The difference between farm and nonfarm households was eliminated in 1982.)

The poverty thresholds set by the U.S. Census Bureau are still based on the theoretical food budget. These thresholds are updated each year to reflect inflation. People with incomes below the applicable threshold are classified as living below the poverty level.

The Census Bureau's poverty thresholds are used for statistical purposes, such as the calculation of the number of poor in the United States. The U.S. Department of Health and Human Services (HHS) uses a simplified version of the Census Bureau's thresholds to arrive at a separate measure of poverty each year. These HHS poverty guidelines are used for administrative purposes by many federal agencies. The HHS uses them to determine eligibility for TANF, Community Services Block Grants, Low-Income Home Energy Assistance Block Grants, and Head Start educational allotments. The guidelines are also the basis for funding the USDA's Supplemental Nutrition Assistance Program (SNAP; previously called the Food Stamp Program), the National School Lunch Program, and the Special Supplemental Nutrition Program for Women, Infants, and Children. The U.S. Department of Labor uses the guidelines to determine funding for the Job Corps and other employment and training programs under the Workforce Investment Act of 1998. Some state and local governments choose to use the federal poverty guidelines for some of their own programs, such as state health insurance programs and financial guidelines for child support enforcement.

The poverty guidelines vary by family size and composition. In 2017 a family of four living in the 48 contiguous states and the District of Columbia was considered impoverished if it earned $24,600 or less annually. (See Table 1.1.) A person living alone who earned less than $12,060 was considered poor, as was a family of eight members making less than $41,320. The poverty level is set higher for Alaska and Hawaii, in keeping with federal practices dating from the 1960s that reflect the higher cost of living in those states relative to the 48 contiguous states and the District of Columbia. (See Table 1.2 and Table 1.3.)

THE HISTORICAL EFFORT TO REDUCE POVERTY

Since the late 1950s Americans have seen some successes and some failures in the battle against poverty. Table 1.4 provides historical data on those living below the federally established poverty level, and Figure 1.1 provides a graphic representation of the changes in the poverty rate between 1959 and 2015. Of the total population of nearly 176.6 million in 1959, 22.4%, or 39.5 million people, lived

TABLE 1.1

Poverty guidelines for the 48 contiguous states and the District of Columbia, 2017

Persons in family/household	Poverty guideline
1	$12,060
2	16,240
3	20,420
4	24,600
5	28,780
6	32,960
7	37,140
8	41,320

Notes: For families/households with more than 8 persons add $4,180 for each additional person.

SOURCE: "2017 Poverty Guidelines for the 48 Contiguous States and the District of Columbia," in "Annual Update of the HHS Poverty Guidelines," *Federal Register*, vol. 82, no. 19, January 31, 2017, https://www.gpo.gov/fdsys/pkg/FR-2017-01-31/pdf/2017-02076.pdf (accessed August 2, 2017)

TABLE 1.2

Poverty guidelines for Alaska, 2017

Persons in family/household	Poverty guideline
1	$15,060
2	20,290
3	25,520
4	30,750
5	35,980
6	41,210
7	46,440
8	51,670

Note: For families/households with more than 8 persons, add $5,230 for each additional person.

SOURCE: "2017 Poverty Guidelines for Alaska," in "Annual Update of the HHS Poverty Guidelines," *Federal Register*, vol. 82, no. 19, January 31, 2017, https://www.gpo.gov/fdsys/pkg/FR-2017-01-31/pdf/2017-02076.pdf (accessed August 2, 2017)

TABLE 1.3

Poverty guidelines for Hawaii, 2017

Persons in family/household	Poverty guideline
1	$13,860
2	18,670
3	23,480
4	28,290
5	33,100
6	37,910
7	42,720
8	47,530

Note: For families/households with more than 8 persons, add $4,810 for each additional person.

SOURCE: "2017 Poverty Guidelines for Hawaii," in "Annual Update of the HHS Poverty Guidelines," *Federal Register*, vol. 82, no. 19, January 31, 2017, https://www.gpo.gov/fdsys/pkg/FR-2017-01-31/pdf/2017-02076.pdf (accessed August 2, 2017)

below the poverty level. After an initial decline through the 1960s and 1970s, the poverty rate began to increase during the early 1980s, coinciding with a downturn in household and family incomes for all Americans. The poverty rate rose steadily until it reached a 17-year high of 15.2% in 1983, a year during which the country was climbing out of a serious economic recession.

The percentage of Americans living in poverty then began dropping, falling to 12.8% in 1989. (See Table 1.4.) After that, the percentage increased again, reaching 15.1% in 1993. Thereafter, it dropped to 11.3% in 2000 and then rose to 15.1% in 2010 in the wake of the Great Recession, which officially lasted from December 2007 to June 2009, but which had negative effects on employment and incomes well into the following decade. In 2015 the poverty rate, at 13.5%, remained above its prerecession level.

One of the key factors driving the poverty rate at all times is the availability of jobs. When the overall economy falters, as it did during the Great Recession, employers typically cut costs by reducing the number of their employees. The labor market at the height of the Great Recession (in 2009) was weaker than at any time since World War II (1939–1945). As Table 1.5 shows, the nationwide unemployment rate (the percentage of all people who are looking for jobs but cannot obtain them) peaked at 10% in late 2009. Although the unemployment rate slowly declined over the following years, it remained high by historical standards through 2013 and only began to approach prerecession levels in mid-2016.

Analysts believe the overall decline in poverty between 1959 and 2015 was due to both the growth in the economy and the success of some of the antipoverty programs that were instituted during the 1960s. Nevertheless, not all demographic subcategories experienced the same level of change; in fact, for many groups the poverty rate rose between 1970 and 2015. Bernadette D. Proctor, Jessica L. Semega, and Melissa A. Kollar of the Census Bureau note in *Income and Poverty in the United States: 2015* (September 2016, https://www.census.gov/content/dam/Census/library/publications/2016/demo/p60-256.pdf) that the poverty rate for those aged 65 years and older, who enjoy guaranteed income and health care benefits through the Social Security and Medicare programs, was 8.8% in 2015, a dramatic decline from 35% in 1959. (See Figure 1.2.) For children under the age of 18 years and for adults aged 18 to 64 years, however, the situation was different. Although these groups also experienced a dramatic reduction in their poverty rate as the programs associated with the War on Poverty took effect between 1959 and 1970, the poverty rate for children and working-age adults fluctuated over the succeeding 43 years and showed an overall upward tendency. In 2015, 19.7% of children and 12.4% of working-age adults lived in poverty. These percentages were up substantially from their 1970 levels.

TABLE 1.4

Poverty status of people by family relationship, 1959–2015

[Numbers in thousands. People as of March of the following year.]

	All people			All families			People in families — Families with female householder, no husband present			Unrelated individuals		
		Below poverty			Below poverty			Below poverty			Below poverty	
Year	Total	Number	Percent	Total	Number	Percent	Total	Number	Percent	Total	Number	Percent
2015	318,454	43,123	13.5	258,121	29,893	11.6	48,497	14,719	30.4	58,988	12,671	21.5
2014	315,804	46,657	14.8	256,308	32,615	12.7	48,019	15,905	33.1	57,937	13,374	23.1
2013[a]	313,096	46,269	14.8	256,070	32,786	12.8	49,951	17,170	34.4	55,400	12,707	22.9
2013[b]	312,965	45,318	14.5	254,988	31,530	12.4	47,007	15,606	33.2	56,564	13,181	23.3
2012	310,648	46,496	15.0	252,863	33,198	13.1	47,085	15,957	33.9	56,185	12,558	22.4
2011	308,456	46,247	15.0	252,316	33,126	13.1	48,103	16,451	34.2	54,517	12,416	22.8
2010[c]	306,130	46,343	15.1	250,200	33,120	13.2	46,454	15,911	34.3	54,250	12,449	22.9
2009	303,820	43,569	14.3	249,384	31,197	12.5	45,315	14,746	32.5	53,079	11,678	22.0
2008	301,041	39,829	13.2	248,301	28,564	11.5	44,027	13,812	31.4	51,534	10,710	20.8
2007	298,699	37,276	12.5	245,443	26,509	10.8	43,961	13,478	30.7	51,740	10,189	19.7
2006	296,450	36,460	12.3	245,199	25,915	10.6	43,223	13,199	30.5	49,884	9,977	20.0
2005	293,135	36,950	12.6	242,389	26,068	10.8	42,244	13,153	31.1	49,526	10,425	21.1
2004[d]	290,617	37,040	12.7	240,754	26,544	11.0	42,053	12,832	30.5	48,609	9,926	20.4
2003	287,699	35,861	12.5	238,903	25,684	10.8	41,311	12,413	30.0	47,594	9,713	20.4
2002	285,317	34,570	12.1	236,921	24,534	10.4	40,529	11,657	28.8	47,156	9,618	20.4
2001	281,475	32,907	11.7	233,911	23,215	9.9	39,261	11,223	28.6	46,392	9,226	19.9
2000[e]	278,944	31,581	11.3	231,909	22,347	9.6	38,375	10,926	28.5	45,624	8,653	19.0
1999[f]	276,208	32,791	11.9	230,789	23,830	10.3	38,580	11,764	30.5	43,977	8,400	19.1
1998	271,059	34,476	12.7	227,229	25,370	11.2	39,000	12,907	33.1	42,539	8,478	19.9
1997	268,480	35,574	13.3	225,369	26,217	11.6	38,412	13,494	35.1	41,672	8,687	20.8
1996	266,218	36,529	13.7	223,955	27,376	12.2	38,584	13,796	35.8	40,727	8,452	20.8
1995	263,733	36,425	13.8	222,792	27,501	12.3	38,908	14,205	36.5	39,484	8,247	20.9
1994	261,616	38,059	14.5	221,430	28,985	13.1	37,253	14,380	38.6	38,538	8,287	21.5
1993[g]	259,278	39,265	15.1	219,489	29,927	13.6	37,861	14,636	38.7	38,038	8,388	22.1
1992[h]	256,549	38,014	14.8	217,936	28,961	13.3	36,446	14,205	39.0	36,842	8,075	21.9
1991[i]	251,192	35,708	14.2	212,723	27,143	12.8	34,795	13,824	39.7	36,845	7,773	21.1
1990	248,644	33,585	13.5	210,967	25,232	12.0	33,795	12,578	37.2	36,056	7,446	20.7
1989	245,992	31,528	12.8	209,515	24,066	11.5	32,525	11,668	35.9	35,185	6,760	19.2
1988	243,530	31,745	13.0	208,056	24,048	11.6	32,164	11,972	37.2	34,340	7,070	20.6
1987[j]	240,982	32,221	13.4	206,877	24,725	12.0	31,893	12,148	38.1	32,992	6,857	20.8
1986	238,554	32,370	13.6	205,459	24,754	12.0	31,152	11,944	38.3	31,679	6,846	21.6
1985	236,594	33,064	14.0	203,963	25,729	12.6	30,878	11,600	37.6	31,351	6,725	21.5
1984	233,816	33,700	14.4	202,288	26,458	13.1	30,844	11,831	38.4	30,268	6,609	21.8
1983[k]	231,700	35,303	15.2	201,338	27,933	13.9	30,049	12,072	40.2	29,158	6,740	23.1
1982	229,412	34,398	15.0	200,385	27,349	13.6	28,834	11,701	40.6	27,908	6,458	23.1
1981[l]	227,157	31,822	14.0	198,541	24,850	12.5	28,587	11,051	38.7	27,714	6,490	23.4
1980	225,027	29,272	13.0	196,963	22,601	11.5	27,565	10,120	36.7	27,133	6,227	22.9
1979[m]	222,903	26,072	11.7	195,860	19,964	10.2	26,927	9,400	34.9	26,170	5,743	21.9
1978	215,656	24,497	11.4	191,071	19,062	10.0	26,032	9,269	35.6	24,585	5,435	22.1
1977	213,867	24,720	11.6	190,757	19,505	10.2	25,404	9,205	36.2	23,110	5,216	22.6
1976	212,303	24,975	11.8	190,844	19,632	10.3	24,204	9,029	37.3	21,459	5,344	24.9
1975	210,864	25,877	12.3	190,630	20,789	10.9	23,580	8,846	37.5	20,234	5,088	25.1
1974[n]	209,362	23,370	11.2	190,436	18,817	9.9	23,165	8,462	36.5	18,926	4,553	24.1
1973	207,621	22,973	11.1	189,361	18,299	9.7	21,823	8,178	37.5	18,260	4,674	25.6
1972	206,004	24,460	11.9	189,193	19,577	10.3	21,264	8,114	38.2	16,811	4,883	29.0
1971[o]	204,554	25,559	12.5	188,242	20,405	10.8	20,153	7,797	38.7	16,311	5,154	31.6
1970	202,183	25,420	12.6	186,692	20,330	10.9	19,673	7,503	38.1	15,491	5,090	32.9
1969	199,517	24,147	12.1	184,891	19,175	10.4	17,995	6,879	38.2	14,626	4,972	34.0
1968	197,628	25,389	12.8	183,825	20,695	11.3	18,048	6,990	38.7	13,803	4,694	34.0
1967[p]	195,672	27,769	14.2	182,558	22,771	12.5	17,788	6,898	38.8	13,114	4,998	38.1
1966	193,388	28,510	14.7	181,117	23,809	13.1	17,240	6,861	39.8	12,271	4,701	38.3
1965	191,413	33,185	17.3	179,281	28,358	15.8	16,371	7,524	46.0	12,132	4,827	39.8
1964	189,710	36,055	19.0	177,653	30,912	17.4	(NA)	7,297	44.4	12,057	5,143	42.7
1963	187,258	36,436	19.5	176,076	31,498	17.9	(NA)	7,646	47.7	11,182	4,938	44.2
1962	184,276	38,625	21.0	173,263	33,623	19.4	(NA)	7,781	50.3	11,013	5,002	45.4
1961	181,277	39,628	21.9	170,131	34,509	20.3	(NA)	7,252	48.1	11,146	5,119	45.9
1960	179,503	39,851	22.2	168,615	34,925	20.7	(NA)	7,247	48.9	10,888	4,926	45.2
1959	176,557	39,490	22.4	165,858	34,562	20.8	(NA)	7,014	49.4	10,699	4,928	46.1

RATIO OF INCOME TO POVERTY LEVELS

For purposes of analysis, the Census Bureau uses income-to-poverty ratios that are calculated by dividing income by the respective poverty threshold for each family size. (For example, a family with an income-to-poverty ratio of 1.5 has an income that is 150% above the poverty threshold specific to that family's size.) The resulting number is then tabulated on a scale that includes three categories: poor, near-poor, and nonpoor. Poor people have a poverty ratio below 1.00. People above the poverty level are divided into

TABLE 1.4

Poverty status of people by family relationship, 1959–2015 [CONTINUED]

[Numbers in thousands. People as of March of the following year.]

NA—Not available.

[a]The 2014 Annual Social and Economic Supplement of the Current Population Survey (CPS ASEC) included redesigned questions for income and health insurance coverage. All of the approximately 98,000 addresses were eligible to receive the redesigned set of health insurance coverage questions. The redesigned income questions were implemented to a subsample of these 98,000 addresses using a probability split panel design. Approximately 68,000 addresses were eligible to receive a set of income questions similar to those used in the 2013 CPS ASEC and the remaining 30,000 addresses were eligible to receive the redesigned income questions. The source of data for this table is the portion of the CPS ASEC sample which received the redesigned income questions, approximately 30,000 addresses.

[b]Data are based on the CPS ASEC sample of 68,000 addresses. The 2014 CPS ASEC included redesigned questions for income and health insurance coverage. All of the approximately 98,000 addresses were eligible to receive the redesigned set of health insurance coverage questions. The redesigned income questions were implemented to a subsample of these 98,000 addresses using a probability split panel design. Approximately 68,000 addresses were eligible to receive a set of income questions similar to those used in the 2013 CPS ASEC and the remaining 30,000 addresses were eligible to receive the redesigned income questions. The source of the 2013 data for this table is the portion of the CPS ASEC sample which received the income questions consistent with the 2013 CPS ASEC, approximately 68,000 addresses.

[c]Implementation of Census 2010-based population controls.

[d]The 2004 data have been revised to reflect a correction to the weights in the 2005 ASEC.

[e]Implementation of Census 2000 based population controls and sample expanded by 28,000 households.

[f]Implementation of Census 2000 based population controls.

[g]Data collection method changed from paper and pencil to computer-assisted interviewing. In addition, the March 1994 income supplement was revised to allow for the coding of different income amounts on selected questionnaire items. Limits either increased or decreased in the following categories: earnings increased to $999,999; Social Security increased to $49,999; Supplemental Security Income and Public Assistance increased to $24,999; Veterans' Benefits increased to $99,999; Child Support and Alimony decreased to $49,999.

[h]Implementation of 1990 census population controls.

[i]CPS file for March 1992 (1991 data) was corrected after the release of the 1991 Income and Poverty reports. Weights for nine person records were omitted on the original file.

[j]Implementation of a new March CPS processing system.

[k]Implementation of Hispanic population weighting controls.

[l]Implemented three technical changes to the poverty definition.

[m]Implementation of 1980 census population controls. Questionnaire expanded to show 27 possible values from 51 possible sources of income.

[n]Implementation of a new March CPS processing system. Questionnaire expanded to ask eleven income questions.

[o]Implementation of 1970 census population controls.

[p]Implementation of a new March CPS processing system.

SOURCE: Adapted from "Table 2. Poverty Status of People by Family Relationship, Race, and Hispanic Origin: 1959 to 2015," in *Historical Poverty Tables—People*, U.S. Census Bureau, September 1, 2016, https://www2.census.gov/programs-surveys/cps/tables/time-series/historical-poverty-people/hstpov2.xls (accessed August 2, 2017)

FIGURE 1.1

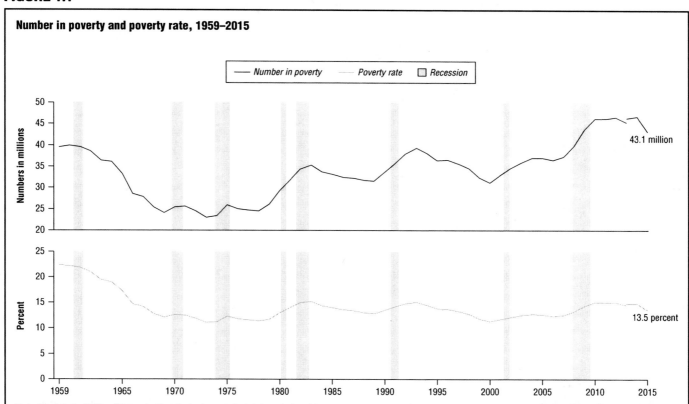

Number in poverty and poverty rate, 1959–2015

— Number in poverty ⋯⋯ Poverty rate ☐ Recession

43.1 million

13.5 percent

Note: The data for 2013 and beyond reflect the implementation of the redesigned income questions. The data points are placed at the midpoints of the respective years.

SOURCE: Bernadette D. Proctor, Jessica L. Semega, and Melissa A. Kollar, "Figure 4. Number in Poverty and Poverty Rate: 1959 to 2015," in *Income and Poverty in the United States: 2015*, U.S. Census Bureau, September 2016, https://www.census.gov/content/dam/Census/library/publications/2016/demo/p60-256.pdf (accessed August 2, 2017)

TABLE 1.5

Unemployment rate, 1948–September 2017

Year	Jan	Feb	Mar	Apr	May	Jun	Jul	Aug	Sep	Oct	Nov	Dec
1948	3.4	3.8	4.0	3.9	3.5	3.6	3.6	3.9	3.8	3.7	3.8	4.0
1949	4.3	4.7	5.0	5.3	6.1	6.2	6.7	6.8	6.6	7.9	6.4	6.6
1950	6.5	6.4	6.3	5.8	5.5	5.4	5.0	4.5	4.4	4.2	4.2	4.3
1951	3.7	3.4	3.4	3.1	3.0	3.2	3.1	3.1	3.3	3.5	3.5	3.1
1952	3.2	3.1	2.9	2.9	3.0	3.0	3.2	3.4	3.1	3.0	2.8	2.7
1953	2.9	2.6	2.6	2.7	2.5	2.5	2.6	2.7	2.9	3.1	3.5	4.5
1954	4.9	5.2	5.7	5.9	5.9	5.6	5.8	6.0	6.1	5.7	5.3	5.0
1955	4.9	4.7	4.6	4.7	4.3	4.2	4.0	4.2	4.1	4.3	4.2	4.2
1956	4.0	3.9	4.2	4.0	4.3	4.3	4.4	4.1	3.9	3.9	4.3	4.2
1957	4.2	3.9	3.7	3.9	4.1	4.3	4.2	4.1	4.4	4.5	5.1	5.2
1958	5.8	6.4	6.7	7.4	7.4	7.3	7.5	7.4	7.1	6.7	6.2	6.2
1959	6.0	5.9	5.6	5.2	5.1	5.0	5.1	5.2	5.5	5.7	5.8	5.3
1960	5.2	4.8	5.4	5.2	5.1	5.4	5.5	5.6	5.5	6.1	6.1	6.6
1961	6.6	6.9	6.9	7.0	7.1	6.9	7.0	6.6	6.7	6.5	6.1	6.0
1962	5.8	5.5	5.6	5.6	5.5	5.5	5.4	5.7	5.6	5.4	5.7	5.5
1963	5.7	5.9	5.7	5.7	5.9	5.6	5.6	5.4	5.5	5.5	5.7	5.5
1964	5.6	5.4	5.4	5.3	5.1	5.2	4.9	5.0	5.1	5.1	4.8	5.0
1965	4.9	5.1	4.7	4.8	4.6	4.6	4.4	4.4	4.3	4.2	4.1	4.0
1966	4.0	3.8	3.8	3.8	3.9	3.8	3.8	3.8	3.7	3.7	3.6	3.8
1967	3.9	3.8	3.8	3.8	3.8	3.9	3.8	3.8	3.8	4.0	3.9	3.8
1968	3.7	3.8	3.7	3.5	3.5	3.7	3.7	3.5	3.4	3.4	3.4	3.4
1969	3.4	3.4	3.4	3.4	3.4	3.5	3.5	3.5	3.7	3.7	3.5	3.5
1970	3.9	4.2	4.4	4.6	4.8	4.9	5.0	5.1	5.4	5.5	5.9	6.1
1971	5.9	5.9	6.0	5.9	5.9	5.9	6.0	6.1	6.0	5.8	6.0	6.0
1972	5.8	5.7	5.8	5.7	5.7	5.7	5.6	5.6	5.5	5.6	5.3	5.2
1973	4.9	5.0	4.9	5.0	4.9	4.9	4.8	4.8	4.8	4.6	4.8	4.9
1974	5.1	5.2	5.1	5.1	5.1	5.4	5.5	5.5	5.9	6.0	6.6	7.2
1975	8.1	8.1	8.6	8.8	9.0	8.8	8.6	8.4	8.4	8.4	8.3	8.2
1976	7.9	7.7	7.6	7.7	7.4	7.6	7.8	7.8	7.6	7.7	7.8	7.8
1977	7.5	7.6	7.4	7.2	7.0	7.2	6.9	7.0	6.8	6.8	6.8	6.4
1978	6.4	6.3	6.3	6.1	6.0	5.9	6.2	5.9	6.0	5.8	5.9	6.0
1979	5.9	5.9	5.8	5.8	5.6	5.7	5.7	6.0	5.9	6.0	5.9	6.0
1980	6.3	6.3	6.3	6.9	7.5	7.6	7.8	7.7	7.5	7.5	7.5	7.2
1981	7.5	7.4	7.4	7.2	7.5	7.5	7.2	7.4	7.6	7.9	8.3	8.5
1982	8.6	8.9	9.0	9.3	9.4	9.6	9.8	9.8	10.1	10.4	10.8	10.8
1983	10.4	10.4	10.3	10.2	10.1	10.1	9.4	9.5	9.2	8.8	8.5	8.3
1984	8.0	7.8	7.8	7.7	7.4	7.2	7.5	7.5	7.3	7.4	7.2	7.3
1985	7.3	7.2	7.2	7.3	7.2	7.4	7.4	7.1	7.1	7.1	7.0	7.0
1986	6.7	7.2	7.2	7.1	7.2	7.2	7.0	6.9	7.0	7.0	6.9	6.6
1987	6.6	6.6	6.6	6.3	6.3	6.2	6.1	6.0	5.9	6.0	5.8	5.7
1988	5.7	5.7	5.7	5.4	5.6	5.4	5.4	5.6	5.4	5.4	5.3	5.3
1989	5.4	5.2	5.0	5.2	5.2	5.3	5.2	5.2	5.3	5.3	5.4	5.4
1990	5.4	5.3	5.2	5.4	5.4	5.2	5.5	5.7	5.9	5.9	6.2	6.3
1991	6.4	6.6	6.8	6.7	6.9	6.9	6.8	6.9	6.9	7.0	7.0	7.3
1992	7.3	7.4	7.4	7.4	7.6	7.8	7.7	7.6	7.6	7.3	7.4	7.4
1993	7.3	7.1	7.0	7.1	7.1	7.0	6.9	6.8	6.7	6.8	6.6	6.5
1994	6.6	6.6	6.5	6.4	6.1	6.1	6.1	6.0	5.9	5.8	5.6	5.5
1995	5.6	5.4	5.4	5.8	5.6	5.6	5.7	5.7	5.6	5.5	5.6	5.6
1996	5.6	5.5	5.5	5.6	5.6	5.3	5.5	5.1	5.2	5.2	5.4	5.4
1997	5.3	5.2	5.2	5.1	4.9	5.0	4.9	4.8	4.9	4.7	4.6	4.7
1998	4.6	4.6	4.7	4.3	4.4	4.5	4.5	4.5	4.6	4.5	4.4	4.4
1999	4.3	4.4	4.2	4.3	4.2	4.3	4.3	4.2	4.2	4.1	4.1	4.0
2000	4.0	4.1	4.0	3.8	4.0	4.0	4.0	4.1	3.9	3.9	3.9	3.9
2001	4.2	4.2	4.3	4.4	4.3	4.5	4.6	4.9	5.0	5.3	5.5	5.7
2002	5.7	5.7	5.7	5.9	5.8	5.8	5.8	5.7	5.7	5.7	5.9	6.0
2003	5.8	5.9	5.9	6.0	6.1	6.3	6.2	6.1	6.1	6.0	5.8	5.7
2004	5.7	5.6	5.8	5.6	5.6	5.6	5.5	5.4	5.4	5.5	5.4	5.4
2005	5.3	5.4	5.2	5.2	5.1	5.0	5.0	4.9	5.0	5.0	5.0	4.9
2006	4.7	4.8	4.7	4.7	4.6	4.6	4.7	4.7	4.5	4.4	4.5	4.4
2007	4.6	4.5	4.4	4.5	4.4	4.6	4.7	4.6	4.7	4.7	4.7	5.0
2008	5.0	4.9	5.1	5.0	5.4	5.6	5.8	6.1	6.1	6.5	6.8	7.3
2009	7.8	8.3	8.7	9.0	9.4	9.5	9.5	9.6	9.8	10.0	9.9	9.9
2010	9.8	9.8	9.9	9.9	9.6	9.4	9.4	9.5	9.5	9.4	9.8	9.3
2011	9.1	9.0	9.0	9.1	9.0	9.1	9.0	9.0	9.0	8.8	8.6	8.5
2012	8.3	8.3	8.2	8.2	8.2	8.2	8.2	8.1	7.8	7.8	7.7	7.9
2013	8.0	7.7	7.5	7.6	7.5	7.5	7.3	7.3	7.2	7.2	6.9	6.7
2014	6.6	6.7	6.7	6.2	6.3	6.1	6.2	6.2	5.9	5.7	5.8	5.6
2015	5.7	5.5	5.4	5.4	5.5	5.3	5.2	5.1	5.0	5.0	5.0	5.0
2016	4.9	4.9	5.0	5.0	4.7	4.9	4.9	4.9	4.9	4.8	4.6	4.7
2017	4.8	4.7	4.5	4.4	4.3	4.4						

SOURCE: "Unemployment Rate (Series ID LNS14000000)," in *Labor Force Statistics from the Current Population Survey*, U.S. Department of Labor, Bureau of Labor Statistics, September 2017, http://data.bls.gov/timeseries/LNS14000000 (accessed August 2, 2017)

FIGURE 1.2

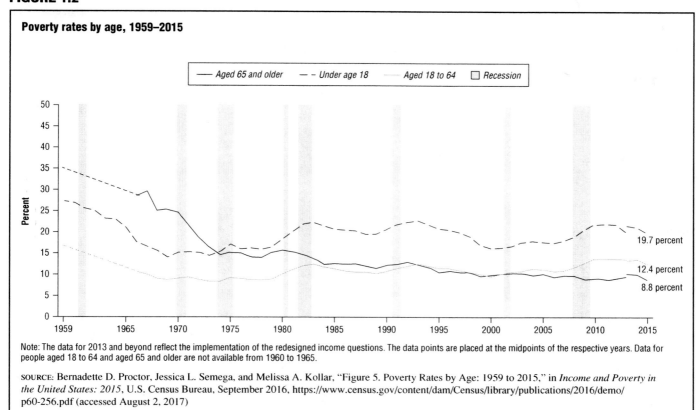

Poverty rates by age, 1959–2015

Note: The data for 2013 and beyond reflect the implementation of the redesigned income questions. The data points are placed at the midpoints of the respective years. Data for people aged 18 to 64 and aged 65 and older are not available from 1960 to 1965.

SOURCE: Bernadette D. Proctor, Jessica L. Semega, and Melissa A. Kollar, "Figure 5. Poverty Rates by Age: 1959 to 2015," in *Income and Poverty in the United States: 2015*, U.S. Census Bureau, September 2016, https://www.census.gov/content/dam/Census/library/publications/2016/demo/p60-256.pdf (accessed August 2, 2017)

two groups: the near-poor and the nonpoor. The near-poor have a poverty ratio between 1.00 and 1.24 (100% to 124% of the poverty level) and the nonpoor have an income-to-poverty ratio of 1.25 (125% of the poverty level) and above.

In 2015, 17.9% of the population, or 56.9 million people, were either poor or near-poor. (See Table 1.6.) Females were slightly more likely than males to be poor or near-poor. Poverty varied significantly by race and Hispanic origin. Whereas 12.3% of non-Hispanic whites and 14.5% of Asian Americans were poor or near-poor in 2015, 28.8% of Hispanics and 30.1% of African Americans had incomes below 125% of poverty. Within the poor and near-poor population, 19.4 million people had an income-to-poverty ratio under 0.5, or half of the poverty threshold. This was 6.1% of the total U.S. population in 2015.

Children are disproportionately likely to be poor. Although children under the age of 18 years made up 23.1% of the total U.S. population in 2015, they accounted for 33.6% of those living at half of the poverty threshold or below and for 33.7% of those living at between 50% and 99% of poverty. (See Figure 1.3.) By contrast, adults aged 18 to 64 years, at 61.9% of the U.S. population, made up 59.5% of those living at half of the poverty threshold and 54.2% of those at 50% to 99% of poverty. Meanwhile, those aged 65 years and older were the least likely to be poor or near-poor. At 14.9% of the U.S. population, the elderly accounted for only 6.9% of those living below half of the poverty threshold and 12.1% of those at 50% to 99% of poverty.

HOW ACCURATE IS THE POVERTY LEVEL?

Almost every year since the Census Bureau first defined the poverty level, observers have been concerned about its accuracy. Since the early 1960s, when Orshansky defined the estimated poverty level based on an average family's food budget, living patterns have changed and food costs have become a smaller percentage of family spending. As Table 1.7 shows, in 2015 the average consumer unit (defined as a family, an economically independent single person, or two or more unrelated people who live together but share expenses) spent $55,978. By far the largest portion of this spending was on housing, which accounted for $18,409 (32.9%) of total spending, followed by transportation, which accounted for $9,503 (17%) of average consumer spending. Food accounted for $7,023 (12.5%) of the average consumer unit's spending, which was slightly more than spending on personal insurance and pensions, $6,349 (11.3%).

The allocation of expenses for the lowest-earning 20% of American households, whose incomes are most directly relevant to the calculation of the poverty threshold,

TABLE 1.6

People with income below specified ratios of their poverty thresholds, by selected characteristics, 2015

[Numbers in thousands, margin of error in thousands or percentage points as appropriate. People as of March of the following year.]

| | | Income-to-poverty ratio | | | | | | | |
| | | Under 0.50 | | Under 1.25 | | Under 1.50 | | Under 2.00 | |
Characteristic	Total	Number	Percent	Number	Percent	Number	Percent	Number	Percent
All people	318,454	19,444	6.1	56,912	17.9	71,681	22.5	100,894	31.7
Age									
Under age 18	73,647	6,537	8.9	18,725	25.4	23,117	31.4	30,756	41.8
Aged 18 to 64	197,260	11,572	5.9	31,632	16.0	39,226	19.9	55,348	28.1
Aged 65 and older	47,547	1,335	2.8	6,556	13.8	9,338	19.6	14,789	31.1
Sex									
Male	156,009	8,484	5.4	25,208	16.2	31,989	20.5	45,868	29.4
Female	162,445	10,960	6.7	31,705	19.5	39,693	24.4	55,025	33.9
Race* and Hispanic origin									
White	245,536	12,555	5.1	38,504	15.7	49,245	20.1	71,104	29.0
White, not Hispanic	195,450	8,355	4.3	24,091	12.3	31,256	16.0	46,475	23.8
Black	41,625	4,549	10.9	12,538	30.1	15,180	36.5	19,843	47.7
Asian	18,241	1,133	6.2	2,638	14.5	3,275	18.0	4,465	24.5
Hispanic (any race)	56,780	4,839	8.5	16,328	28.8	20,278	35.7	27,921	49.2
Family status									
In families	258,121	12,464	4.8	40,272	15.6	51,477	19.9	74,400	28.8
Householder	82,199	3,666	4.5	11,603	14.1	14,822	18.0	21,812	26.5
Related children under age 18	72,558	6,121	8.4	18,106	25.0	22,399	30.9	29,927	41.2
Related children under age 6	23,459	2,341	10.0	6,296	26.8	7,747	33.0	10,291	43.9
In unrelated subfamilies	1,344	396	29.4	662	49.3	791	58.8	961	71.5
Unrelated individuals	58,988	6,585	11.2	15,978	27.1	19,414	32.9	25,532	43.3

*Federal surveys give respondents the option of reporting more than one race. Therefore, two basic ways of defining a race group are possible. A group such as Asian may be defined as those who reported Asian and no other race (the race-alone or single-race concept) or as those who reported Asian regardless of whether they also reported another race (the race-alone-or-in-combination concept). This table shows data using the first approach (race alone). The use of the single-race population does not imply that it is the preferred method of presenting or analyzing data. The Census Bureau uses a variety of approaches. Information on people who reported more than one race, such as White *and* American Indian and Alaska Native or Asian *and* Black or African American, is available from Census 2010 through American FactFinder. About 2.9 percent of people reported more than one race in Census 2010. Data for American Indians and Alaska Natives, Native Hawaiian and Other Pacific Islanders, and those reporting two or more races are not shown separately.

Note: Details may not sum to totals because of rounding.

SOURCE: Adapted from Bernadette D. Proctor, Jessica L. Semega, and Melissa A. Kollar, "Table 5. People with Income below Specified Ratios of Their Poverty Thresholds by Selected Characteristics: 2015," in *Income and Poverty in the United States: 2015*, U.S. Census Bureau, September 2016, https://www.census.gov/content/dam/Census/library/publications/2016/demo/p60-256.pdf (accessed August 2, 2017)

diverged somewhat from that of the average consumer unit in 2015. As Table 1.8 shows, this group's average (mean) annual expenditures totaled $24,470 in 2015, with 40.4% of that spending attributable to housing, 15.4% to food, 14.5% to transportation, and 7.9% to health care. Based on these changes in consumption patterns, many analysts ask: Should the amount spent on food be multiplied by a factor higher than three to arrive at a more accurate definition of poverty? Should the poverty level be based on housing, which is by far the most expensive need across all income brackets? Or should it be based on some other set of factors?

Other critics of the official poverty measure point to its insensitivity to geographical differences. Housing costs vary widely between rural and urban areas, as do costs for other basic necessities, including food, utilities, health care, and transportation. Even within one state, the differences between rural, suburban, and urban costs of living can diverge widely. A family of four with an income approaching the official poverty measure of $24,600 would clearly be able to purchase more with that amount of money in upstate New York (a predominantly rural area) than in New York City (an urban area), so why does the federal government define poverty identically for two such families?

Social changes, too, have altered the economic landscape in the 21st century, as critics of the official poverty measure point out. In families headed by two parents, both parents are far more likely to be working than they were a generation or two ago. There is also a much greater likelihood that a single parent, usually the mother, will be at the head of a family with children. Child care costs were of relatively little concern during the 1950s, when stay-at-home mothers were the norm, but have become a major issue for working parents in the 21st century. Moreover, family life has become more complicated, with complex financial consequences arising as parents living in one household may pay child support to another or receive support payments from another. Such incomes and expenses are not factored into the official poverty measure, therefore obscuring the overall portrait of the nation's poor.

FIGURE 1.3

Demographic makeup of the population at varying degrees of poverty, 2015

[In percent]

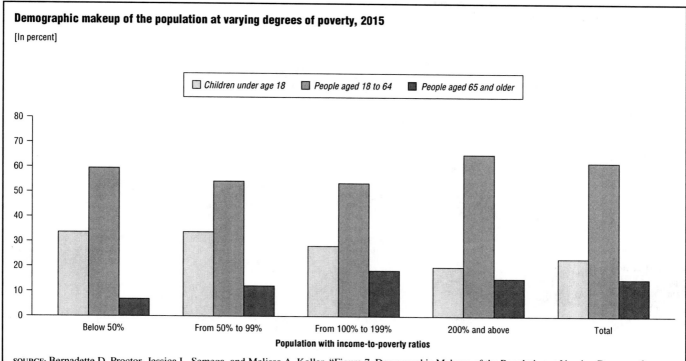

SOURCE: Bernadette D. Proctor, Jessica L. Semega, and Melissa A. Kollar, "Figure 7. Demographic Makeup of the Population at Varying Degrees of Poverty: 2015," in *Income and Poverty in the United States: 2015*, U.S. Census Bureau, September 2016, https://www.census.gov/content/dam/Census/library/publications/2016/demo/p60-256.pdf(accessed August 2, 2017)

TABLE 1.7

Average annual consumer expenditures, 2013–15

Item	2013	2014	2015	Percent change 2013–2014	Percent change 2014–2015
Average income before taxes	$63,784	$66,877	$69,629	4.8	4.1
Average annual expenditures	51,100	53,495	55,978	4.7	4.6
Food	6,602	6,759	7,023	2.4	3.9
Food at home	3,977	3,971	4,015	−0.2	1.1
Food away from home	2,625	2,787	3,008	6.2	7.9
Housing	17,148	17,798	18,409	3.8	3.4
Shelter	10,080	10,491	10,742	4.1	2.4
Utilities	3,737	3,921	3,885	4.9	−.9
Household furnishings and equipment	1,542	1,581	1,818	2.5	15.0
Apparel and services	1,604	1,786	1,846	11.3	3.4
Transportation	9,004	9,073	9,503	0.8	4.7
Vehicle purchases	3,271	3,301	3,997	0.9	21.1
Gasoline and motor oil	2,611	2,468	2,090	−5.5	−15.3
Healthcare	3,631	4,290	4,342	n/a	1.2
Health insurance	2,229	2,868	2,977	n/a	3.8
Entertainment	2,482	2,728	2,842	9.9	4.2
Education	1,138	1,236	1,315	8.6	6.4
Cash contributions	1,834	1,788	1,819	−2.5	1.7
Personal insurance and pensions	5,528	5,726	6,349	3.6	10.9
Life and other personal insurance	319	327	333	2.5	1.8
Pensions and Social Security	5,209	5,399	6,016	3.6	11.4
All other expenditures	2,129	2,311	2,530	8.5	9.5

Subcategories do not sum to 100%.

SOURCE: "Table A. Average Expenditures and Income of All Consumer Units and Percent Changes for Selected Components, 2013–2015," in "News Release: Consumer Expenditures—2015," U.S. Department of Labor, Bureau of Labor Statistics, August 30, 2016, https://www.bls.gov/news.release/pdf/cesan.pdf (accessed August 2, 2017)

Moreover, if the goal is to measure U.S. poverty accurately, these are not the only expenses and forms of income that many analysts believe should be included in the poverty guidelines. The official poverty thresholds

TABLE 1.8

Average annual consumer expenditures, by income quintile, 2015

Item	All consumer units	Lowest 20 percent	Second 20 percent	Third 20 percent	Fourth 20 percent	Highest 20 percent
Number of consumer units (in thousands)	128,437	25,672	25,562	25,700	25,730	25,773
Lower limit	n.a.	n.a.	$19,572	$37,638	$62,587	$103,057
Consumer unit characteristics:						
Income before taxes						
Mean	$69,627	$10,916	$28,343	$49,606	$80,813	$177,851
Average annual expenditures						
Mean	$55,978	$24,470	$35,063	$45,912	$63,671	$110,508
Food						
Mean	7,023	3,767	5,022	5,799	8,165	12,350
Share	12.5	15.4	14.3	12.6	12.8	11.2
Housing						
Mean	18,409	9,890	12,832	15,809	20,408	33,027
Share	32.9	40.4	36.6	34.4	32.1	29.9
Apparel and services						
Mean	1,846	776	1,139	1,303	1,984	4,025
Share	3.3	3.2	3.2	2.8	3.1	3.6
Transportation						
Mean	9,503	3,559	5,923	8,820	11,330	17,834
Share	17.0	14.5	16.9	19.2	17.8	16.1
Healthcare						
Mean	4,342	1,930	3,423	3,965	5,327	7,048
Share	7.8	7.9	9.8	8.6	8.4	6.4
Entertainment						
Mean	2,842	1,270	1,738	2,219	3,051	5,919
Share	5.1	5.2	5.0	4.8	4.8	5.4
Personal care products and services						
Mean	683	307	453	524	797	1,331
Share	1.2	1.3	1.3	1.1	1.3	1.2
Reading						
Mean	114	37	82	107	134	210
Share	0.2	0.1	0.2	0.2	0.2	0.2
Education						
Mean	1,315	689	494	614	986	3,779
Share	2.3	2.8	1.4	1.3	1.5	3.4
Tobacco products and smoking supplies						
Mean	349	308	360	376	372	332
Share	0.6	1.3	1.0	0.8	0.6	0.3
Miscellaneous						
Mean	871	439	550	674	982	1,706
Share	1.6	1.8	1.6	1.5	1.5	1.5
Cash contributions						
Mean	1,819	712	1,054	1,335	1,890	4,089
Share	3.2	2.9	3.0	2.9	3.0	3.7
Personal insurance and pensions						
Mean	6,349	592	1,740	3,980	7,667	17,699
Share	11.3	2.4	5.0	8.7	12.0	16.0

n.a. = Not applicable.

SOURCE: Adapted from "Table 1101. Quintiles of Income before Taxes: Annual Expenditure Means, Shares, Standard Errors, and Coefficients of Variation, Consumer Expenditure Survey, 2015," in *Consumer Expenditure Survey*, U.S. Department of Labor, Bureau of Labor Statistics, August 2016, https://www.bls.gov/cex/2015/combined/quintile.xlsx (accessed August 2, 2017)

take into account only gross income, neglecting to account for that portion of income that must be spent on taxes and is therefore unavailable for spending on basic necessities. Although many low-income Americans pay no federal income taxes, they are frequently still subject to state and payroll taxes. Additionally, the poverty guidelines do not take into account expenses that are accrued in the process of working or of out-of-pocket medical spending. Medical spending, too, is subject to another variable: age. The young spend far less money on health care than the elderly. Therefore, many critics argue that a poverty measure that does not take into account the burden of medical spending for the elderly does not accurately reflect economic realities.

Forms of income that are not factored into the official poverty thresholds include the various in-kind (or noncash) benefits that households receive from government sources, many of which can be used to meet basic expenses. Although some of these benefits, such as Medicaid, can be difficult to quantify, others, such as food assistance, have a more obvious cash value. Likewise, many poor and near-poor families benefit from the Earned Income Tax Credit, an Internal Revenue Service provision that allows working people to deduct certain dollar amounts from their tax bills if their incomes fall below annually updated thresholds. The deducted amounts function in the same way as government assistance, many analysts argue, and should therefore be included in poverty measurements.

THE SUPPLEMENTAL POVERTY MEASURE

Trudi Renwick and Liana Fox of the Census Bureau notes in *The Supplemental Poverty Measure: 2015* (September 2016, https://www.census.gov/content/dam/Census/library/publications/2016/demo/p60-258.pdf) that during the 1990s the widely publicized shortcomings in the official poverty measure led Congress to empower the National Academy of Sciences (NAS) to study the efficacy of the official measure and to recommend alternatives. The NAS assembled the Panel on Poverty and Family Assistance, and the panel's 1995 report, *Measuring Poverty: A New Approach*, recommended the creation of an alternate poverty measure to address many of the previously mentioned weaknesses in the official guidelines. During the late 1990s the Census Bureau began incorporating a number of experimental poverty measures in some of its reports and data sets. Taking into account various shortcomings of the official poverty measures, the data revealed different portraits of the poor population.

After continued research and discussion over the following decade, the U.S. Interagency Technical Working Group (ITWG) outlined the characteristics of a Supplemental Poverty Measure (SPM) that it proposed to begin using alongside the official measure. The new SPM specifies a poverty threshold that accounts not only for food expenses multiplied by three but also for the amount that is spent on a basic bundle of food, clothing, shelter, and utilities, as well as for additional household needs. The SPM further takes into account the needs of different family types and the needs of households in different geographic locations. In calculating income thresholds, the SPM includes not only cash income from all sources but also the value of various forms of government assistance and tax credits; and it takes into consideration necessary household expenses including income taxes, payroll taxes, child care, child support payments, and health care costs. (See Table 1.9.) There are no plans to use the SPM for the determination of funding for social welfare programs or as a replacement for the official measure in other contexts; rather, it is applied to Census Bureau data for the purpose of providing additional information about economic need to policy makers and analysts.

Renwick and Fox explain that the SPM poverty threshold differs from the official poverty threshold and that different SPM thresholds are provided depending on a household's housing status. (See Table 1.10.) These SPM thresholds, together with the additional variations in evaluating households, incomes, and expenditures, yield a different picture of the impoverished population than that rendered by use of the official measure. For example, 45.7 million people were poor in 2015 according to the SPM, whereas according to the official poverty measure 43.5 million people were poor. The SPM also shows a different distribution of the impoverished population by age. (See Figure 1.4.) Considerably fewer

TABLE 1.9

Official poverty measure vs. Supplemental Poverty Measure

	Official poverty measure	Supplemental poverty measure
Measurement units	Families or unrelated individuals	Families (including any coresident unrelated children, foster children, unmarried partners and their relatives) or unrelated individuals (who are not otherwise included in the family definition)
Poverty threshold	Three times the cost of a minimum food diet in 1963	The mean of expenditures on food, clothing, shelter, and utilities (FCSU) over all two-child consumer units in the 30th to 36th percentile range multiplied by 1.2
Threshold adjustments	Vary by family size, composition, and age of householder	Geographic adjustments for differences in housing costs by tenure and a three-parameter equivalence scale for family size and composition
Updating thresholds	Consumer Price Index: all items	5-year moving average of expenditures on FCSU
Resource measure	Gross before-tax cash income	Sum of cash income, plus noncash benefits that families can use to meet their FCSU needs, minus taxes (or plus tax credits), minus work expenses, out-of-pocket medical expenses, and child support paid to another household

SOURCE: Trudi Renwick and Liana Fox, "Poverty Measure Concepts: Official and Supplemental," in *The Supplemental Poverty Measure: 2015*, U.S. Census Bureau, September 2016, https://www.census.gov/content/dam/Census/library/publications/2016/demo/p60-258.pdf (accessed August 2, 2017)

TABLE 1.10

Official and supplemental poverty thresholds for a two-adult, two-child household, 2014 and 2015

[In dollars]

Measure	2014	2015
Official poverty measure	24,008	24,036
Research supplemental poverty measure		
Owners with a mortgage	25,844	25,930
Owners without a mortgage	21,380	21,806
Renters	25,460	25,583

Note: The thresholds, shares, and means were produced by Marisa Gudrais with assistance from Juan D. Munoz, and under the guidance of Thesia I. Garner. Gudrais, Munoz, and Garner work in the Division of Price and Index Number Research, Bureau of Labor Statistics (BLS). These thresholds and statistics are produced for research purposes only using the U.S. Consumer Expenditure Interview Survey. The thresholds are not BLS production quality. This work is solely that of the authors and does not necessarily reflect the official positions or policies of BLS, or the views of other staff members within this agency.

SOURCE: Adapted from Trudi Renwick and Liana Fox, "Table 1. Two Adult, Two-Child Poverty Thresholds: 2014 and 2015," in *The Supplemental Poverty Measure: 2015*, U.S. Census Bureau, September 2016, https://www .census.gov/content/dam/Census/library/publications/2016/demo/p60-258 .pdf (accessed August 2, 2017)

FIGURE 1.4

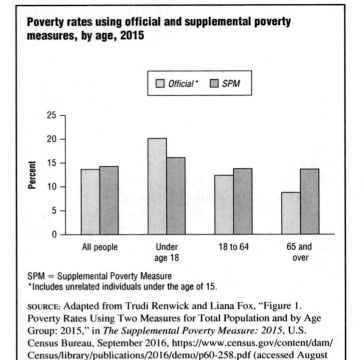

Poverty rates using official and supplemental poverty measures, by age, 2015

SPM = Supplemental Poverty Measure
*Includes unrelated individuals under the age of 15.

SOURCE: Adapted from Trudi Renwick and Liana Fox, "Figure 1. Poverty Rates Using Two Measures for Total Population and by Age Group: 2015," in *The Supplemental Poverty Measure: 2015*, U.S. Census Bureau, September 2016, https://www.census.gov/content/dam/ Census/library/publications/2016/demo/p60-258.pdf (accessed August 2, 2017)

children qualify as impoverished under the SPM, whereas more working-age adults and significantly more elderly adults do.

A number of policy experts have met the release of SPM data with skepticism. In "The Supplemental Poverty Measure: Is Child Poverty Really Less of a Problem Than We Thought?" (CEPR.net, August 3, 2012), Shawn Fremstad of the Center for Economic and Policy Research takes aim at the lower level of child poverty shown by the SPM. Arguing that the SPM accurately shows an increase in poverty among the elderly because of its inclusion of out-of-pocket medical expenses in its calculations, Fremstad maintains that comparable adjustments are needed in the calculation of child poverty to account for "children's basic needs for care and healthy development."

Mark Levinson of the Service Employees International Union makes a more fundamental case for the SPM's inadequacy in "Mismeasuring Poverty" (Prospect .org, June 25, 2012). Faulting the official poverty measure for "setting the poverty bar so low that tens of millions of poor Americans are not accounted for," Levinson maintains that the SPM fails to fix this basic shortcoming. Noting that the original intent of President Johnson's War on Poverty was to aid "those whose basic needs exceed their means to satisfy them," he laments the fact that tens of millions of Americans fit this description and yet do not qualify for government assistance. In place of either the official poverty measure or the SPM, Levinson suggests that a more reasonable alternative would be a definition of poverty such as those used in European countries, where families earning less than 50% or 60% of the national median income (depending on the country) are considered to be poor.

THE U.S. POVERTY LINE IN A GLOBAL CONTEXT

The poverty bar is indeed set lower in the United States than in other comparably developed countries. Martin Ravallion of the World Bank reports in "A Relative Question" (*Finance and Development*, vol. 49, no. 4, December 2012) that most high-income countries peg their poverty lines to average incomes, so that the poverty line rises as a country's economy grows. The rationale behind such systems is that one can feel poor in a rich country even when one's income is above the level required for basic subsistence and that poverty describes a condition of having too little money to participate in society.

To assess poverty, the World Bank uses a figure called purchasing power parity (PPP), which compares the ability of people to purchase basic necessities in different places and at different times. The poverty line is far lower in less-developed and developing countries than it is in the United States. According to the World Bank, in *2017: World Development Indicators* (2017, https://openknowledge.worldbank.org/ bitstream/handle/10986/26447/WDI-2017-web.pdf), the poverty line in the world's poorest countries was equivalent to $1.90 per day in 2011 PPP terms. This PPP threshold is significantly lower than that used in the world's most advanced economies. According to Ravallion, Luxembourg, the nation with the highest poverty line in the world in 2012, classified those living on less than the PPP equivalent of $43 per day as poor. Although U.S. citizens on average demonstrate consumption patterns similar to those in Luxembourg, meaning that participation in society would require roughly the same amount of income in both countries, the U.S. poverty line was equivalent to PPP of only $13 per day in 2012.

The World Bank reports in *2017: World Development Indicators* that 10.7% of people in the developing world lived on less than $1.90 per day in 2013, down dramatically from 34.8% in 1990. This was largely the result of rapid economic development in China and other countries. East Asia and the Pacific Rim experienced the most significant decline in poverty during this period, with the percentage of people living on less than $1.90 per day dropping from 60.2% in 1990 to 3.5% in 2013. By contrast, the nations of sub-Saharan Africa saw a relatively smaller decrease in poverty over this span, as the proportion of people living on less than $1.90 per day fell from 54.3% in 1990 to 41% in 2013.

INCOME INEQUALITY

Whether considered globally or nationally, there is no mistaking the relative nature of poverty. Although the official U.S. poverty measure does not account for an individual's or family's poverty in terms of the country's average income, researchers in the fields of anthropology, psychology, and economics have established that people judge their own level of welfare not in absolute terms but relative to the prosperity of their society as a whole. For this and other reasons, many policy experts are concerned about a growing body of evidence suggesting that the gap between the rich and the poor in the United States widened considerably at the end of the 20th century and the beginning of the 21st century.

Using Census Bureau data, Chad Stone et al. of the Center on Budget and Policy Priorities explain in *A Guide to Statistics on Historical Trends in Income Inequality* (September 25, 2017, https://www.cbpp.org/sites/default/files/atoms/files/11-28-11pov_0.pdf) that the gaps between the richest 1% of Americans and the middle and poorest fifths of Americans grew considerably between 1979 and 2013. During this period average after-tax incomes for the top 1% rose by 192%, whereas the lowest fifth of households saw their incomes increase by only 46% and the middle three-fifths of households saw their incomes increase by only 41%. In 2013, 12% of all after-tax income was earned by the wealthiest 1% of Americans.

Although the wealthiest Americans initially suffered significant financial setbacks during the Great Recession, income inequality continued to increase between 2010 and 2013. In the op-ed "Inequality, Unbelievably, Gets Worse" (NYTimes.com, November 16, 2014), Steven Rattner observes that according to the Federal Reserve System (the central banking and economic authority of the United States), incomes for the top 10% of earners rose 2% between 2010 and 2013, whereas incomes for the remaining 90% of earners declined. The declines varied by income strata. Those in the middle range of incomes (the 20th to the 60th percentiles) were hit the hardest: their incomes fell by 6% to 7%. Those just below the top 10%, in the 80th to 90th percentiles, saw their incomes fall 3%; those in the 60th to 80th percentiles saw their incomes fall 2%; and those in the bottom 20% saw their incomes fall 4%.

Census data on income and earnings, which report pretax earnings, support this picture of increasing inequality. According to *Income and Poverty in the United States: 2015*, the share of earnings going to the highest quintile of earners increased most significantly between 1977 and 2001, a period during which the richest 20% of Americans increased their share of all household income from 44% to 50.1%. (See Table 1.11.) This upper quintile's accumulation of wealth slipped slightly during the recession of the early 1990s, rebounded, then fell during the Great Recession, hitting 49.7% in 2007. After the recession, however, its share of total income rose, reaching 51.1% by 2015. The share of income going to the top 5% of earners increased even more, proportionally speaking, than that of the top 20%. In 1977 the top 5% of earners accounted for 16.8% of total household income; by 2015 this group accounted for 22.1% of all income.

These gains in the share of overall income by top earners naturally came at the expense of the remaining 80% of earners. The bottom four quintiles of income earners saw their shares of total income fall steadily. (See Table 1.11.) The lowest quintile's share of income was 4.2% in 1977 and 3.1% in 2015; the second-lowest quintile claimed 10.2% of all income in 1977 and 8.2% in 2015; the middle quintile of earners took home 16.9% of all income in 1977 and 14.3% in 2015; and the second-highest quintile's share was 24.7% in 1977 and 23.2% in 2015.

Why Is the Income Gap Growing?

Many reasons exist to explain the growing inequality, although observers disagree about which are more important. One reason is that the proportion of the elderly population, which is likely to earn less, is growing. According to the Census Bureau, 24.6% of all U.S. households (31 million out of 125.8 million), were headed by a householder 65 years of age or older in 2015. (See Table 1.12; a household may consist of a single individual or a group of related or unrelated people living together, whereas a family consists of related individuals.) The median (the middle value—half are higher and half are lower) household income

TABLE 1.11

Household income dispersion, selected years 1967–2015

[Income in 2015 CPI-U-RS adjusted dollars.]

Measures of income dispersion	2015	2014	2013[a]	2013[b]	2012	2007	1997	1987[c]	1977	1967[d]
Measure										
Household income at selected percentiles										
10th percentile limit	13,259	12,290	12,413	12,618	12,631	13,903	13,573	12,453	12,481	10,117
20th percentile limit	22,800	21,457	21,368	21,266	21,265	23,195	22,683	21,563	20,436	18,620
40th percentile limit	43,511	41,233	41,754	40,892	41,049	44,697	43,009	40,929	38,491	36,310
50th (median)	56,516	53,718	54,525	52,850	52,666	57,423	54,506	52,032	48,370	44,335
60th percentile limit	72,001	68,290	68,378	66,649	66,669	70,875	67,755	63,890	58,670	51,535
80th percentile limit	117,002	112,391	112,165	107,767	107,460	114,314	105,314	96,560	85,535	73,488
90th percentile limit	162,180	157,660	158,151	152,630	150,718	155,467	143,849	127,388	109,093	93,350
95th percentile limit	214,462	206,806	208,725	199,437	197,333	202,336	186,399	161,578	135,431	117,929
Household income ratios of selected percentiles										
90th/10th	12.23	12.83	12.74	12.10	11.93	11.18	10.60	10.23	8.74	9.23
95th/20th	9.41	9.64	9.77	9.38	9.28	8.72	8.22	7.49	6.63	6.33
95th/50th	3.80	3.85	3.83	3.78	3.79	3.54	3.43	3.11	2.80	2.70
80th/50th	2.07	2.09	2.06	2.04	2.07	2.00	1.94	1.86	1.77	1.68
80th/20th	5.13	5.24	5.25	5.07	5.05	4.93	4.64	4.48	4.19	3.95
20th/50th	0.40	0.40	0.39	0.40	0.41	0.41	0.42	0.42	0.42	0.43
Mean household income of quintiles										
Lowest quintile	12,457	11,689	11,797	11,855	11,861	13,204	13,019	12,243	11,886	9,931
Second quintile	32,631	31,123	31,352	31,044	30,656	33,656	32,549	31,114	29,257	27,515
Third quintile	56,832	54,103	54,683	53,239	52,833	57,120	54,759	52,020	48,395	43,925
Fourth quintile	92,031	87,935	87,989	84,983	84,751	90,435	84,814	78,631	70,909	61,459
Highest quintile	202,366	194,276	196,742	188,453	187,783	192,014	180,822	149,536	126,450	110,605
Top 5 percent	350,870	332,729	340,329	327,995	328,330	328,299	317,322	235,594	193,442	174,472
Shares of household income of quintiles										
Lowest quintile	3.1	3.1	3.1	3.2	3.2	3.4	3.6	3.8	4.2	4.0
Second quintile	8.2	8.2	8.2	8.4	8.3	8.7	8.9	9.6	10.2	10.8
Third quintile	14.3	14.3	14.3	14.4	14.4	14.8	15.0	16.1	16.9	17.3
Fourth quintile	23.2	23.2	23.0	23.0	23.0	23.4	23.2	24.3	24.7	24.2
Highest quintile	51.1	51.2	51.4	51.0	51.0	49.7	49.4	46.2	44.0	43.6
Top 5 percent	22.1	21.9	22.2	22.2	22.3	21.2	21.7	18.2	16.8	17.2
Summary measures										
Gini index of income inequality	0.479	0.480	0.482	0.476	0.477	0.463	0.459	0.426	0.402	0.397
Mean logarithmic deviation of income	0.596	0.611	0.606	0.578	0.586	0.532	0.484	0.414	0.364	0.380
Theil	0.420	0.419	0.428	0.415	0.423	0.391	0.396	0.311	0.276	0.287
Atkinson:										
e = 0.25	0.101	0.102	0.103	0.100	0.101	0.095	0.094	0.077	0.069	0.071
e = 0.50	0.199	0.200	0.202	0.196	0.198	0.185	0.183	0.155	0.139	0.143
e = 0.75	0.303	0.307	0.307	0.298	0.300	0.281	0.272	0.238	0.213	0.220

[a]The 2014 Annual Social and Economic Supplement of the Current Population Survey (CPS ASEC) included redesigned questions for income and health insurance coverage. All of the approximately 98,000 addresses were eligible to receive the redesigned set of health insurance coverage questions. The redesigned income questions were implemented to a subsample of these 98,000 addresses using a probability split panel design. Approximately 68,000 addresses were eligible to receive a set of income questions similar to those used in the 2013 CPS ASEC and the remaining 30,000 addresses were eligible to receive the redesigned income questions. The source of these 2013 estimates is the portion of the CPS ASEC sample which received the redesigned income questions, approximately 30,000 addresses.
[b]The source of these 2013 estimates is the portion of the CPS ASEC sample which received the income questions consistent with the 2013 CPS ASEC, approximately 68,000 addresses.
[c]Implementation of a new CPS ASEC processing system.
[d]Implementation of a new CPS ASEC processing system.

SOURCE: Adapted from Bernadette D. Proctor, Jessica L. Semega, and Melissa A. Kollar, "Table A-2. Selected Measures of Household Income Dispersion: 1967 to 2015," in *Income and Poverty in the United States: 2015*, U.S. Census Bureau, September 2016, https://www.census.gov/content/dam/Census/library/publications/2016/demo/p60-256.pdf (accessed August 2, 2017).

of households headed by a person aged 65 years or older was $38,515, compared with a median household income of $63,344 for households headed by someone under the age of 65 years.

In addition, more people than in previous years were living in nonfamily situations (either alone or with non-relatives). In 2015, 43.6 million of the 125.8 U.S. million households, or 34.7%, were nonfamily households. (See Table 1.12.) These nonfamily households earned a median income of $33,805, compared with the $72,165 median income of family households.

The increase in the number of households headed by females and the increased labor force participation of women have also contributed to growing income inequality in the United States. In 2015, 15.6 million of the 82.2 million U.S. family households, or 19%, were headed by

TABLE 1.12

Income and earnings summary measures, by selected characteristics, 2014 and 2015

[Income in 2015 dollars. Households and people as of March of the following year.]

Characteristic	2014 Number (thousands)	2014 Median income (dollars) Estimate	2015 Number (thousands)	2015 Median income (dollars) Estimate	Percentage change in real median income (2015 less 2014) Estimate
Households					
All households	124,587	53,718	125,819	56,516	5.2
Type of household					
Family households	81,716	68,504	82,184	72,165	5.3
Married-couple	60,010	81,118	60,251	84,626	4.3
Female householder, no husband present	15,544	36,192	15,622	37,797	4.4
Male householder, no wife present	6,162	53,746	6,310	55,861	3.9
Nonfamily households	42,871	32,084	43,635	33,805	5.4
Female householder	22,728	26,703	23,093	29,022	8.7
Male householder	20,143	39,226	20,542	40,762	3.9
Race[a] and Hispanic origin of householder					
White	98,679	56,932	99,313	60,109	5.6
White, not Hispanic	84,228	60,325	84,445	62,950	4.4
Black	16,437	35,439	16,539	36,898	4.1
Asian	6,040	74,382	6,328	77,166	3.7
Hispanic (any race)	16,239	42,540	16,667	45,148	6.1
Age of householder					
Under 65 years	94,640	60,531	94,820	63,344	4.6
15 to 24 years	6,370	34,645	6,361	36,108	4.2
25 to 34 years	20,075	54,305	20,047	57,366	5.6
35 to 44 years	21,121	66,770	21,222	71,417	7.0
45 to 54 years	23,566	70,913	23,294	73,857	4.2
55 to 64 years	23,509	60,649	23,896	62,802	3.5
65 years and older	29,946	36,938	30,998	38,515	4.3
Nativity of householder					
Native born	106,191	54,741	107,081	57,173	4.4
Foreign born	18,396	49,649	18,738	52,295	5.3
Naturalized citizen	9,735	59,329	9,856	61,982	4.5
Not a citizen	8,661	40,842	8,881	45,137	10.5
Region					
Northeast	22,179	59,278	22,347	62,182	4.9
Midwest	27,459	54,330	27,455	57,082	5.1
South	47,040	49,712	47,822	51,174	2.9
West	27,909	57,754	28,195	61,442	6.4
Residence[b]					
Inside metropolitan statistical areas	104,009	55,920	107,615	59,258	N
Inside principal cities	40,578	47,905	42,615	51,378	N
Outside principal cities	63,431	61,671	65,000	64,144	N
Outside metropolitan statistical areas[c]	20,578	45,534	18,204	44,657	N
Earnings of full-time, year-round workers					
Men with earnings	62,455	50,441	63,887	51,212	1.5
Women with earnings	46,226	39,667	47,211	40,742	2.7
Female-to-male earnings ratio	X	0.79	X	0.80	1.2

X Not applicable.

N Not comparable.

[a]Federal surveys give respondents the option of reporting more than one race. Therefore, two basic ways of defining a race group are possible. A group such as Asian may be defined as those who reported Asian and no other race (the race-alone or single-race concept) or as those who reported Asian regardless of whether they also reported another race (the race-alone-or-in-combination concept). This table shows data using the first approach (race alone). The use of the single-race population does not imply that it is the preferred method of presenting or analyzing data. The Census Bureau uses a variety of approaches. Information on people who reported more than one race, such as White **and** American Indian and Alaska Native or Asian **and** Black or African American, is available from Census 2010 through American FactFinder. About 2.9 percent of people reported more than one race in Census 2010. Data for American Indians and Alaska Natives, Native Hawaiians and Other Pacific Islanders, and those reporting two or more races are not shown separately.

[b]Once a decade, the CPS ASEC transitions to a new sample design and updates all metropolitan statistical area delineations. As a result, the metropolitan/nonmetropolitan estimates for 2014 and 2015 are not comparable. Users may want to use the American Community Survey estimates for metropolitan/nonmetropolitan comparisons.

[c]The "Outside metropolitan statistical areas" category includes both micropolitan statistical areas and territory outside of metropolitan and micropolitan statistical areas.

SOURCE: Adapted from Bernadette D. Proctor, Jessica L. Semega, and Melissa A. Kollar, "Table 1. Income and Earnings Summary Measures by Selected Characteristics: 2014 and 2015," in *Income and Poverty in the United States: 2015*, U.S. Census Bureau, September 2016, https://www.census.gov/content/dam/Census/library/publications/2016/demo/p60-256.pdf (accessed August 2, 2017).

women with no husband present, and 23.1 million of the 43.6 million U.S. nonfamily households, or 53%, were headed by women. (See Table 1.12.) Female-headed households typically earn significantly less than other types of households. In 2015 the earnings of female-headed family households in which no husband was present

($37,797) were only 67.7% of the earnings of male-headed family households in which no wife was present ($55,861) and only 44.7% of the earnings of married-couple households ($84,626). Meanwhile, female nonfamily householders had a median income ($29,022) that was 71.2% of the median income of male nonfamily householders ($40,762). On average, female full-time workers earned only 80% of what male full-time workers earned in 2015. (See Figure 1.5.)

Nevertheless, economists who study income and wealth inequality typically point to factors beyond these changes in the composition of households. Chrystia Freeland observes in "Income Inequality Sheds Its Taboo Status" (NYTimes.com, November 29, 2012) that most economists agree that the technology revolution and globalization that marked the late 20th and early 21st centuries, which have resulted in the loss of many of the best-paying jobs that were available to those in the lower income quintiles, are important drivers of inequality. While incomes have stagnated for the lower quintiles, those at the extreme top of the income scale have seen unprecedented gains in their earnings. Freeland notes that as of 2012, "the wealth of the 400 richest Americans has increased more than fivefold over the past 20 years."

In *Wealth Inequality in the United States since 1913: Evidence from Capitalized Income Tax Data* (October 2014, http://gabriel-zucman.eu/files/SaezZucman2014.pdf), Emmanuel Saez and Gabriel Zucman of the National Bureau of Economic Research focus on household wealth, as distinguished from household income, in an attempt to explain rising inequality. (Household wealth is the value of all of a household's assets minus its debts.) The researchers note that by 2012 the share of all U.S. wealth owned by the wealthiest 0.1% of Americans was higher than it had been since 1929, the year that the Great Depression began. After almost 50 years of increasing equality (1929 to 1978), the top 0.1% saw its share of total wealth rise from 7% in 1979 to 22% in 2012, while the share of overall wealth held by the bottom 90% of Americans steadily declined between the mid-1980s and 2012. According to Saez and Zucman, the increasing share of total wealth held by the richest 0.1% of Americans is a function both of ballooning incomes at the highest reaches of the economy and of the fact that the beneficiaries of such incomes in recent times are younger than in past eras. Thus, they have more years to accumulate returns on their astronomical wealth through savings and investment, thereby increasing the distance between their financial fortunes and those of the bottom 90%.

FIGURE 1.5

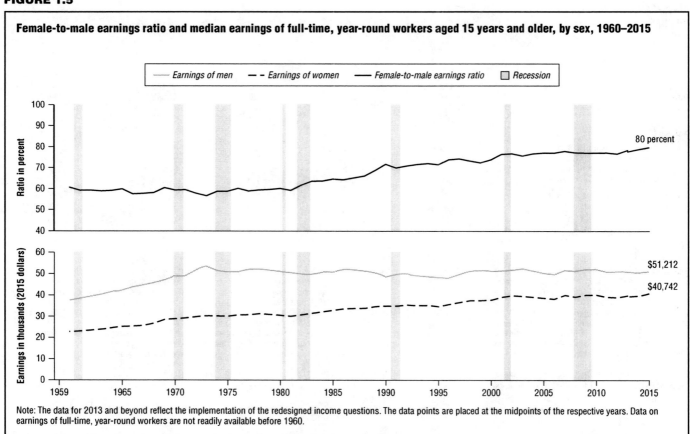

Female-to-male earnings ratio and median earnings of full-time, year-round workers aged 15 years and older, by sex, 1960–2015

Note: The data for 2013 and beyond reflect the implementation of the redesigned income questions. The data points are placed at the midpoints of the respective years. Data on earnings of full-time, year-round workers are not readily available before 1960.

SOURCE: Adapted from Bernadette D. Proctor, Jessica L. Semega, and Melissa A. Kollar, "Figure 2. Female-to-Male Earnings Ratio and Median Earnings of Full-Time, Year-Round Workers 15 Years and Older by Sex: 1960 to 2015," in *Income and Poverty in the United States: 2015*, U.S. Census Bureau, September 2016, https://www.census.gov/content/dam/Census/library/publications/2016/demo/p60-256.pdf (accessed August 2, 2017)

HOMELESSNESS

Homelessness is a complex social problem. Educators, sociologists, economists, and political scientists who have studied homelessness for decades agree that it is caused by a combination of poverty, misfortune, illness, and behavior. It is also evident that, for most people, homelessness is a temporary condition rather than a way of life and that the number of Americans who experience homelessness at some point in a given year has appreciably increased since the 1990s. Beyond these and other basic facts, however, the study of homelessness is complicated by methodological problems with counting the homeless and with disagreement over the definition of homelessness.

What Does It Mean to Be Homeless?

During a period of growing concern about homelessness in the mid-1980s, the first major piece of federal legislation aimed specifically at helping the homeless was adopted: the Stewart B. McKinney Homeless Assistance Act of 1987 (later renamed the McKinney-Vento Homeless Assistance Act). The act officially defines a homeless person as:

1. An individual who lacks a fixed, regular, and adequate nighttime residence; and

2. An individual who has a primary nighttime residence that is:

A. A supervised publicly or privately operated shelter designed to provide temporary living accommodations (including welfare hotels, congregate shelters, and transitional housing for the mentally ill);

B. An institution that provides a temporary residence for individuals intended to be institutionalized; or

C. A public or private place not designed for, or ordinarily used as, a regular sleeping accommodation for human beings.

The government definition of a homeless person focuses on whether a person is housed. Broader definitions of homelessness take into account whether a person has a home. For example, Martha Burt et al. report in *Helping America's Homeless: Emergency Shelter or Affordable Housing?* (2001) that as late as 1980 the Census Bureau identified people who lived alone and did not have a "usual home elsewhere"—in other words, a larger family—as homeless. In this sense the term *home* describes living within a family, rather than having a roof over one's head.

Burt et al. also state that homeless people themselves, when interviewed during the 1980s and 1990s, drew a distinction between having a house and having a home. Even when homeless people had spent significant time in a traditional shelter, such as an apartment or rented room, if they felt those houses were transitional or insecure, they identified themselves as having been homeless while living there. According to Burt et al., these answers "reflect how long they have been without significant attachments to people."

Burt et al. and other homeless advocates disagree with the narrow government definition of a homeless person, which focuses on a person's sleeping arrangements. They assert that the definition should be broadened to include groups of people who, while they may have somewhere to live, do not really have a home in the conventional sense. Considerable debate has resulted over expanding the classification to include people in situations such as the following:

- People engaging in prostitution who spend each night in a different hotel room, paid for by clients

- Children in foster or relative care

- People living in stable but inadequate housing (e.g., having no plumbing or heating)

- People "doubled up" in conventional dwellings for the short term (the Census Bureau defines doubled-up households as those including one or more person over the age of 18 years who is not enrolled in school and is not the householder, spouse, or cohabiting partner of the householder)

- People in hotels paid for by vouchers to the needy

- Elderly people living with family members because they cannot afford to live elsewhere

Official definitions are important because total counts of the homeless influence the levels of funding that Congress authorizes for homeless programs. With the availability of federal funds since the passage of the McKinney-Vento Homeless Assistance Act, institutional constituencies have formed that advocate for additional funding, an effort in which more expansive definitions are helpful.

Causes of Homelessness

In *The State of Homelessness in America: 2016* (2016, http://endhomelessness.org/wp-content/uploads/2016/10/2016-soh.pdf), the nonprofit National Alliance to End Homelessness reports that the leading causes of homelessness in the United States include lack of affordable housing, unemployment, and low incomes. In addition, the organization notes that mental illness and physical disabilities are leading factors in chronic homelessness, a condition defined as being homeless continuously for a year or longer, or of experiencing four or more incidences of homelessness over a three-year period.

Annie Lowery reports in "Homeless Rates in U.S. Held Level amid Recession, Study Says, but Big Gains Are Elusive" (NYTimes.com, December 10, 2012) that the U.S. Department of Housing and Urban Development (HUD) estimated that the overall number of the homeless did not rise over the course of the Great Recession and its aftermath, in spite of the large number of people who lost their home as a result of the housing crisis (the fall in real estate prices that, together with high unemployment, led many people to fall behind in their mortgage payments and often to lose their homes). In fact, the number of chronically homeless fell 19% between 2007 and 2012 as a result, most likely, of targeted government efforts to reduce that portion of the homeless population. It is further believed that the problem of temporary homelessness was alleviated during this period thanks to emergency stimulus funding passed by Congress to address the consequences of the Great Recession. Part of this funding aimed to identify those who were vulnerable to homelessness as a result of foreclosure and the lack of affordable housing, and to find new housing for them; HUD estimates that more than 1 million people avoided homelessness as a result of this program. However, given the decrease in the number of chronically homeless, the relative steadiness of the overall homeless count suggests that the ranks of those who were forced into temporary homelessness by the economic downturn increased appreciably between 2007 and 2012, in spite of the success of the government's homeless prevention efforts.

In any event, there is no disputing that millions of Americans lost their homes during the Great Recession. Rakesh Kochhar and D'Vera Cohn of the Pew Research Center observe in *Fighting Poverty in a Bad Economy, Americans Move In with Relatives* (October 3, 2011, http://www.pewsocialtrends.org/files/2011/10/Multigenerational-Households-Final1.pdf) that an unprecedented number of people left their own home and moved in with family members between 2007 and 2009. During that time the number of multigenerational households grew from 46.5 million to 51.4 million, for "the largest increase . . . in modern history." The National Alliance to End Homelessness notes in *The State of Homelessness in America: 2016* that the number of poor families living with relatives or friends remained elevated even after the Great Recession was over. There were 7 million such families in 2014, which was down 9% from 2013 but up 52% when compared with 2007. Although many advocates for the homeless would argue that such people should be counted among the homeless so that government aid might be more effective at meeting society's needs, these doubled-up families were not officially considered homeless.

Counting the Homeless

Crafting policies to combat homelessness depends heavily on the collection of reliable information regarding the number and attributes of the homeless population, but the very nature of homelessness makes accurate data collection difficult. Typically, researchers studying the U.S. population at large contact people in their homes using in-person or telephone surveys to obtain information regarding income, education levels, household size, ethnicity, and other demographic data. Homeless people cannot be counted at home, of course, and researchers have struggled to address this methodological shortcoming.

The Census Bureau, in particular, has encountered difficulties in counting the homeless, and objections to its methodology during the 1990s led it to discontinue its efforts to comprehensively assess the homeless population in the 21st century. In its most recent decennial census (2010), the bureau released homeless population figures only as they relate to one category: people living in "emergency and transitional shelters." In 2010, 209,325 Americans were counted as occupants of emergency and transitional shelters. (See Table 1.13.) This number, however, does not include everyone who is officially considered homeless by the federal government. An unspecified number of other people who met the federal definition of homelessness—such as people who were counted at domestic violence shelters, family crisis centers, soup kitchens, mobile food vans, and targeted nonsheltered outdoor locations (i.e., street people, car dwellers, and so on)—are included in the "other noninstitutional group quarters population" category along with some non-homeless populations (e.g., students living in college dormitories). As a result, the homeless portion of the category cannot be extracted.

In the 21st century HUD is widely seen as the sponsor of the most authoritative data on homelessness. The agency's attempts to collect data that accurately represent the U.S. homeless population at large center on its annual national point-in-time (PIT) studies of the homeless. These studies, which are undertaken in collaboration with local government officials and shelters across the United States, count the number of homeless people during a specific period and at specific places. The agency attempts to locate unsheltered as well as sheltered homeless people, and its yearly count is meant to provide a snapshot of the American homeless population on a given day.

HUD's assessment of the homeless population goes beyond PIT counts. The department also monitors the inventory of shelter beds to derive further information about the size of the homeless population and the nature of its needs. In addition, it collaborates with state and municipal governments in the collection of longitudinal data about specific homeless populations. These longitudinal data, which are collected over time in an attempt to determine long-term patterns among the homeless, are stored in a database called the Homeless Management Information Systems. PIT counts, shelter inventories, and Homeless Management Information Systems data represent the three main data sets that are used by local governments, in partnership with HUD, to build a yearly portrait of the American homeless population. Each year HUD submits its findings in the *Annual Homeless Assessment Report* to Congress.

According to Meghan Henry et al., in *The 2016 Annual Homeless Assessment Report (AHAR) to Congress—Part 1: Point-in-Time Estimates of Homelessness* (November 2016,

TABLE 1.13

Decennial Census count of group quarters and emergency and transitional shelter populations, 2010

Sex and selected age group	Total population		Group quarters population		Emergency and transitional shelter population		
	Number	Percent	Number	Percent	Number	Percent	Percent of group quarters population
Both sexes	308,745,538	100.0	7,987,323	100.0	209,325	100.0	2.6
Male	151,781,326	49.2	4,858,210	60.8	129,969	62.1	2.7
Female	156,964,212	50.8	3,129,113	39.2	79,356	37.9	2.5
Both sexes, all ages	308,745,538	100.0	7,987,323	100.0	209,325	100.0	2.6
Under 18 years	74,181,467	24.0	260,586	3.3	42,290	20.2	16.2
18 to 64 years	194,296,087	62.9	6,269,031	78.5	161,578	77.2	2.6
65 years and over	40,267,984	13.0	1,457,706	18.3	5,457	2.6	0.4
Median age	37.2	(X)	28.8	(X)	39.2	(X)	(X)
Male, all ages	151,781,326	100.0	4,858,210	100.0	129,969	100.0	2.7
Under 18 years	37,945,136	25.0	165,477	3.4	21,325	16.4	12.9
18 to 64 years	96,473,230	63.6	4,239,142	87.3	104,834	80.7	2.5
65 years and over	17,362,960	11.4	453,591	9.3	3,810	2.9	0.8
Median age	35.8	(X)	29.5	(X)	43.9	(X)	(X)
Female, all ages	156,964,212	100.0	3,129,113	100.0	79,356	100.0	2.5
Under 18 years	36,236,331	23.1	95,109	3.0	20,965	26.4	22.0
18 to 64 years	97,822,857	62.3	2,029,889	64.9	56,744	71.5	2.8
65 years and over	22,905,024	14.6	1,004,115	32.1	1,647	2.1	0.2
Median age	38.5	(X)	25.4	(X)	29.7	(X)	(X)

(X) Not applicable.

Note: Percentages may not sum to 100.0 due to rounding.

SOURCE: Amy Symens Smith, Charles Holmberg, and Marcella Jones-Puthoff, "Table 1. Total, Group Quarters, and Emergency and Transitional Shelter Populations by Sex and Selected Age Groups: 2010," in *The Emergency and Transitional Shelter Population: 2010*, U.S. Census Bureau, September 2012, http://www.census.gov/prod/cen2010/reports/c2010sr-02.pdf (accessed August 2, 2017)

https://www.hudexchange.info/resources/documents/2016-AHAR-Part-1.pdf), HUD conducted a PIT count on a single night in January 2016. On that night, HUD estimated that the U.S. homeless population was 549,928. (See Figure 1.6.) This was a 15% decline from the 2007 PIT estimate of 647,258. Most of this decline was due to a decrease in the number of unsheltered homeless. In 2007, 391,401 (60.5%) of the total homeless population of 647,258 was sheltered and 255,857 (39.5%) was unsheltered. By 2016, 373,571 (67.9%) of the total homeless population of 549,928 was sheltered and 176,357 (32.1%) was unsheltered.

The changes in total homelessness, as well as the decrease of unsheltered homelessness relative to sheltered homelessness, were likely influenced by an ongoing federal effort to retool the shelter system nationally to reduce chronic homelessness. As Figure 1.7 indicates, of the 549,928 homeless Americans counted on that January night in 2016, 36% were sheltered individuals and 32% were sheltered people in families. As in previous years, individuals were much more likely to be unsheltered than families. Of the total homeless count, 29% were unsheltered individuals and 3% were unsheltered people in families.

THE ONGOING FIGHT AGAINST POVERTY AND HOMELESSNESS

In the many media commemorations of the 50th anniversary of the War on Poverty in 2014, pundits routinely recalled President Ronald Reagan's (1911–2004) witticism: "We fought a war on poverty, and poverty won." Reagan's intent in voicing this idea was to suggest that the liberal safety-net policies of the New Deal and the War on Poverty, which required large amounts of federal spending and correspondingly high rates of taxation on people at the upper end of the income spectrum, were ineffective and should be reduced or abolished. During the years of his presidency (from 1981 to 1989), Reagan spearheaded reductions in the size of many government programs, and his understanding of the War on Poverty helped increase the activities to reduce the scope of the U.S. welfare system during the 1990s.

In the 21st century many conservatives continue to argue that government-funded safety-net programs keep poverty entrenched, whereas business-friendly attempts to expand the economy through low taxes and minimal regulation are the most successful means of lifting people out of poverty. Meanwhile, many left-leaning experts suggest that President Johnson's War on Poverty was in many ways a success and that the inability to generate greater reductions in the poverty level since that time are a direct result of the cuts to the safety net imposed during the Reagan years and beyond.

There are, of course, many variations on these positions as well as many positions that adopt neither of these basic left–right poles. For example, in "Actually, We

FIGURE 1.6

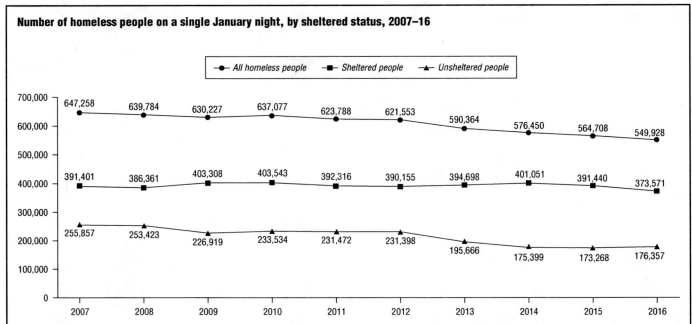

Number of homeless people on a single January night, by sheltered status, 2007–16

Legend: —●— All homeless people —■— Sheltered people —▲— Unsheltered people

All homeless people: 647,258 (2007), 639,784 (2008), 630,227 (2009), 637,077 (2010), 623,788 (2011), 621,553 (2012), 590,364 (2013), 576,450 (2014), 564,708 (2015), 549,928 (2016)

Sheltered people: 391,401 (2007), 386,361 (2008), 403,308 (2009), 403,543 (2010), 392,316 (2011), 390,155 (2012), 394,698 (2013), 401,051 (2014), 391,440 (2015), 373,571 (2016)

Unsheltered people: 255,857 (2007), 253,423 (2008), 226,919 (2009), 233,534 (2010), 231,472 (2011), 231,398 (2012), 195,666 (2013), 175,399 (2014), 173,268 (2015), 176,357 (2016)

SOURCE: Meghan Henry et al., "Exhibit 1.1. PIT Estimates of People Experiencing Homelessness by Sheltered Status, 2007–2016," in *The 2016 Annual Homeless Assessment Report (AHAR) to Congress—Part 1: Point-in-Time Estimates of Homelessness*, U.S. Department of Housing and Urban Development, Office of Community Planning and Development, November 2016, https://www.hudexchange.info/resources/documents/2016-AHAR-Part-1.pdf (accessed August 2, 2017)

FIGURE 1.7

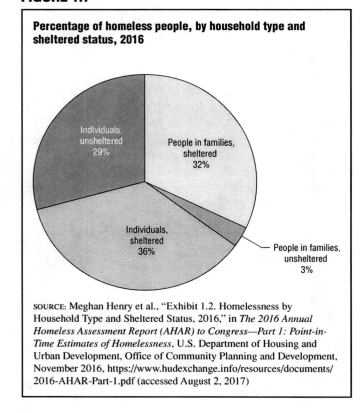

Percentage of homeless people, by household type and sheltered status, 2016

- People in families, sheltered 32%
- People in families, unsheltered 3%
- Individuals, sheltered 36%
- Individuals, unsheltered 29%

SOURCE: Meghan Henry et al., "Exhibit 1.2. Homelessness by Household Type and Sheltered Status, 2016," in *The 2016 Annual Homeless Assessment Report (AHAR) to Congress—Part 1: Point-in-Time Estimates of Homelessness*, U.S. Department of Housing and Urban Development, Office of Community Planning and Development, November 2016, https://www.hudexchange.info/resources/documents/2016-AHAR-Part-1.pdf (accessed August 2, 2017)

Won the War on Poverty" (Politico.com, January 24, 2014), Scott Winship updates the conservative interpretation of the War on Poverty. He argues that "the country has actually reduced poverty more than we often appreciate—and that decline in poverty has been less about the liberal programs of the New Deal and Great Society and more about economic growth and center-right welfare reforms than is widely recognized." He also suggests that the federal poverty line overstates the number of people in poverty because it fails "to account for food stamps, Medicaid, Medicare and public housing subsidies" as well as "for refundable tax credits that promote work." Winship maintains that the Census Bureau's techniques for adjusting for inflation overstate increases in the cost of living and thereby add to the overstatement of the size of the poor population. He cites the work of the economists Bruce Meyer and James Sullivan, who adjust for such statistical factors and find that the poverty rate fell from 32% in 1963 to 7% in 2000, before rising again to 8% in 2010.

By contrast, Jared Bernstein of the Center on Budget and Policy Priorities argues in "The War on Poverty at 50" (NYTimes.com, January 6, 2014) that the War on Poverty was a measured success but that structural changes in the economy stand in the way of eradicating poverty in the United States. In stark contrast to Winship, Bernstein argues that the official 2012 U.S. poverty rate of 15% undercounts the impoverished population and that the actual poverty rate that year was 16%. He further notes that in the absence of food stamps (now called SNAP), unemployment benefits, the Earned Income Tax Credit, and housing subsidies (among other government antipoverty programs), the 2012 poverty rate would have been 29%. Even so, these programs successfully lifted 40 million people, or 13% of the U.S. population, out of poverty in 2012. The inability of these programs to do more to fight poverty, according to Bernstein, stems from the fact that "they've had to work much harder in an economy that has made it a lot tougher for those at the bottom to get ahead." The major structural forces keeping people in poverty were, in his opinion, "inequality, globalization, deunionization, lower minimum wages, slack labor markets and decreasing returns to lower-end jobs."

Bernstein's conclusions are supported by data from the Economic Policy Institute, a nonpartisan think tank that is devoted to the interests of low- and middle-income workers. The institute particularly singles out income inequality as a driver of poverty. For example, the Economic Policy Institute (September 26, 2014, http://stateofworkingamerica.org/chart/swa-poverty-figure-7q-impact-econonic-demographic) claims that income inequality increased the poverty rate by 7.1 percentage points between 1979 and 2013, outpacing other economic and demographic factors that cut the poverty rate. These antipoverty factors included income growth, which accounted for a decline in poverty of 3.4 percentage points, and the educational composition of households, which accounted for a decline of 2.9 percentage points.

Those who maintain that structural economic forces must be addressed if poverty and homelessness are to be combated tend to support a strengthening of the safety net as well as new measures to support workers and low-income families. For example, in "Anti-poverty Leaders Discuss the Need for a Shared Agenda" (Nation.com, November 25, 2013), Greg Kaufmann suggests a coordinated antipoverty campaign premised on three main demands: raising the minimum wage above $10.10 per hour, which would be sufficient for a full-time worker to lift a family of three out of poverty; the introduction of paid sick and family leave for low-wage workers, which would allow them to care for themselves or family members without risking their job; and the creation of a system for affordable and adequate child care, which would enable single parents to work full time while still caring for their children.

The stories of low-income workers themselves often illuminate the challenges of escaping poverty and homelessness in ways that cannot be captured by expert analysis. For example, Linda Tirado states in "Why Poor People Stay Poor" (Slate.com, December 5, 2014), "I once lost a whole truck over a few hundred bucks. It had been towed, and when I called the company they told me they'd need a few hundred dollars for the fee. I didn't have a few hundred dollars.... I was working two jobs at the time. Both were part time. Neither paid a hundred bucks a day, much less two." Without her truck, Tirado had to walk 6 miles (10 km) every day to her jobs, and once she had been paid, she went to reclaim the vehicle, only to be told that it would now cost her over a thousand dollars to do so because of the fees for storing the vehicle that had been imposed in the meantime. Eventually, both Tirado and her husband lost their jobs because of their lack of transportation and, because they could not pay their rent, they soon lost their apartment as well. To avoid poverty and homelessness, explains Tirado, a low-income worker must either have good luck or substantial savings. "If I'm saving my spare five bucks a week, in the best-case scenario I will have saved $260 a year," Tirado writes. "If you deny yourself even small luxuries, that's the fortune you'll amass. Of course you will never manage to actually save it.... Something, I guarantee you, will happen in three months."

As Tirado's story illustrates, the poor are always at risk of becoming homeless. Thus, the fight against poverty is also a fight to prevent homelessness. However, once people have become homeless, they become the focus of a different set of aid efforts and government programs. Traditionally, private nonprofit groups that run shelters, soup kitchens, and other aid organizations have taken the lead in serving the needs of the homeless. These groups usually derive a large part of their funding from the federal government, often by applying for competitive grants awarded by HUD and other government agencies. Such efforts have been subject to many of the same criticisms as the larger safety-net programs that help the poor, and efforts to help the homeless have also sometimes run afoul of local residents who believe that feeding or helping the homeless encourages them to stay in the locality where they are being helped.

Whereas the predominant model for helping the homeless during the late 20th century involved a system of emergency shelters that housed the newly homeless and transitional shelters that put homeless individuals and families on a path toward self-sufficiency, a so-called housing-first approach increasingly characterizes the focus of government and nonprofit agencies in the 21st century. While funding remains in place for emergency shelters, the housing-first approach involves shifting government resources from transitional shelters to permanent housing. The chronically homeless are placed in permanent housing as quickly as possible and then matched with services to meet the health and behavioral needs that are often a primary cause of their having become homeless in the first place. Although this effort involves indefinitely subsidizing the housing costs of such individuals, it has been found to be more effective at helping the chronically homeless remain off the streets than any other previous aid effort. Furthermore, the housing-first approach has proven to be a fiscally responsible alternative to leaving chronically homeless people to fend for themselves on the streets. The federal funding that flows to state, local, and private groups implementing these efforts represents a reallocation of existing funds rather than an increase in overall funding, and the cost of permanent housing and services is significantly lower than the costs imposed by the chronically homeless on federal, state, and local governments, in the form of public funds spent on arrests, court fees, and emergency department bills.

Such programs, which combine fiscal priorities with effective aid to those in need, are more typical of the ongoing fight against poverty and homelessness than the simplistic left–right political debate might lead many ordinary citizens to believe. As the complexly interwoven social, economic, and political realities that drive poverty and homelessness change, the fight against poverty and homelessness will doubtless continue to change. However, contrary to Reagan's witticism, the fight is not over and it likely never will be.

CHAPTER 2
WHO ARE THE POOR?

CHARACTERISTICS OF THE POOR

Bernadette D. Proctor, Jessica L. Semega, and Melissa A. Kollar of the U.S. Census Bureau indicate in *Income and Poverty in the United States: 2015* (September 2016, https://www.census.gov/content/dam/Census/library/publications/2016/demo/p60-256.pdf) that 43.1 million people, or 13.5% of the 2015 U.S. population, had income-to-poverty ratios under 1.00 and were therefore officially considered poor. As is shown in Table 1.6 in Chapter 1, 56.9 million Americans, or 17.9% of the U.S. population, were poor or near-poor, meaning that they had income-to-poverty ratios of 1.25 or less.

Children under the age of 18 years are more likely than people of other ages to be poor. In 2015, 19.7% (14.5 million) of all American children were poor, compared with 12.4% (24.4 million) of adults aged 18 to 64 years and 8.8% (4.2 million) of adults aged 65 years and older. (See Table 2.1.) Children are also more likely than those in other age groups to experience income-to-poverty ratios of 1.25 or less. In 2015, 25.4% (18.7 million) of all children under the age of 18 years were either poor or near-poor, compared with 16% (31.6 million) of adults aged 18 to 64 years and 13.8% (6.6 million) of adults aged 65 years and older. (See Table 1.6 in Chapter 1.) Children were also disproportionately represented among the desperately poor (those whose incomes fall below half of the poverty line); 8.9% (6.5 million) of all children were in this category in 2015, compared with 5.9% (11.6 million) of adults aged 18 to 64 years and 2.8% (1.3 million) of adults over the age of 65 years.

Besides the previous statistics, which provide a yearly snapshot of poverty, the Census Bureau studies poverty longitudinally, surveying individuals at different points in time over multiple years. Publications based on these longitudinal studies provide additional insight into the experience of living in poverty. For example, Ashley N. Edwards of the Census Bureau reports in *Dynamics of Economic Well-Being: Poverty, 2009–2011* (January

2014, http://www.census.gov/prod/2014pubs/p70-137.pdf) that a much higher proportion of the U.S. population than that captured by the annual statistics experiences at least occasional poverty. In the three-year period from January 2009 to December 2011 nearly one-third (31.6%) of the total population lived below the poverty line for at least two months. Among those individuals who experienced poverty for at least two consecutive months, 44% lived below the poverty line for four months or less and 15.2% remained in poverty for more than two years. Some individuals exited and then reentered poverty during the survey period; overall, 35.4% of those individuals in poverty in 2009 were no longer in poverty in 2011. Nevertheless, roughly half of those who had exited poverty by the end of the study period had incomes of less than 150% of poverty, a threshold at which they remained at risk of falling below the poverty line given a change in their personal circumstances, such as the loss of a job, a health problem, or a major property loss.

RACE AND ETHNICITY

Historically, poverty rates have been consistently lower for whites than for minorities in the United States. According to Proctor, Semega, and Kollar, 28.5 million (18.1%) of whites lived below the poverty level in 1959. The proportion of whites living below the poverty level fell markedly during the 1960s and early 1970s, reaching a low of 8.4% in 1973. The poverty rate for whites remained between 9% and 12% from the 1980s through the early 21st century. In 2010 it reached its highest level (13%) since 1965. In 2015, 11.6% (28.6 million) of whites lived in poverty. (See Table 2.1.)

Proctor, Semega, and Kollar note that the poverty rate for African Americans started at a much higher level and has fallen more dramatically, but it has at all times been much higher than that for whites. In 1959, 55.1%

TABLE 2.1

People in poverty, by selected characteristics, 2014 and 2015

[Numbers in thousands. People as of March of the following year.]

Characteristic	2014 Total	2014 Below poverty Number	2014 Below poverty Percent	2015 Total	2015 Below poverty Number	2015 Below poverty Percent	Change in poverty (2015 less 2014)[a] Number	Change in poverty (2015 less 2014)[a] Percent
People								
Total	315,804	46,657	14.8	318,454	43,123	13.5	−3,534	−1.2
Family status								
In families	256,308	32,615	12.7	258,121	29,893	11.6	−2,722	−1.1
Householder	81,730	9,467	11.6	82,199	8,589	10.4	−879	−1.1
Related children under age 18	72,383	14,987	20.7	72,558	13,962	19.2	−1,025	−1.5
Related children under age 6	23,470	5,504	23.5	23,459	4,923	21.0	−582	−2.5
In unrelated subfamilies	1,558	668	42.9	1,344	559	41.6	−109	−1.3
Reference person	652	266	40.8	563	231	41.0	−35	0.1
Children under age 18	832	388	46.6	701	321	45.9	−67	−0.8
Unrelated individuals	57,937	13,374	23.1	58,988	12,671	21.5	−702	−1.6
Race[b] and Hispanic origin								
White	244,253	31,089	12.7	245,536	28,566	11.6	−2,523	−1.1
White, not Hispanic	195,208	19,652	10.1	195,450	17,786	9.1	−1,867	−1.0
Black	41,112	10,755	26.2	41,625	10,020	24.1	−735	−2.1
Asian	17,790	2,137	12.0	18,241	2,078	11.4	−59	−0.6
Hispanic (any race)	55,504	13,104	23.6	56,780	12,133	21.4	−971	−2.2
Sex								
Male	154,639	20,708	13.4	156,009	19,037	12.2	−1,671	−1.2
Female	161,164	25,949	16.1	162,445	24,086	14.8	−1,863	−1.3
Age								
Under age 18	73,556	15,540	21.1	73,647	14,509	19.7	−1,031	−1.4
Aged 18 to 64	196,254	26,527	13.5	197,260	24,414	12.4	−2,114	−1.1
Aged 65 and older	45,994	4,590	10.0	47,547	4,201	8.8	−389	−1.1
Nativity								
Native born	273,628	38,871	14.2	275,398	35,973	13.1	−2,898	−1.1
Foreign born	42,175	7,786	18.5	43,056	7,150	16.6	−636	−1.9
Naturalized citizen	19,731	2,347	11.9	20,084	2,255	11.2	−92	−0.7
Not a citizen	22,444	5,439	24.2	22,973	4,895	21.3	−544	−2.9
Region								
Northeast	55,725	7,020	12.6	55,779	6,891	12.4	−129	−0.2
Midwest	67,130	8,714	13.0	67,030	7,849	11.7	−865	−1.3
South	118,193	19,531	16.5	119,955	18,305	15.3	−1,227	−1.3
West	74,756	11,391	15.2	75,690	10,079	13.3	−1,312	−1.9
Residence[c]								
Inside metropolitan statistical areas	265,788	38,416	14.5	274,046	35,718	13.0	N	N
Inside principal cities	99,182	18,708	18.9	103,617	17,368	16.8	N	N
Outside principal cities	166,606	19,708	11.8	170,429	18,350	10.8	N	N
Outside metropolitan statistical areas[d]	50,016	8,241	16.5	44,408	7,405	16.7	N	N
Work experience								
Total, aged 18 to 64	196,254	26,527	13.5	197,260	24,414	12.4	−2,114	−1.1
All workers	147,712	10,155	6.9	150,229	9,457	6.3	−698	−0.6
Worked full-time, year-round	103,379	3,091	3.0	105,695	2,537	2.4	−554	−0.6
Less than full-time, year-round	44,332	7,064	15.9	44,534	6,920	15.5	−144	−0.4
Did not work at least 1 week	48,542	16,372	33.7	47,031	14,957	31.8	−1,415	−1.9
Disability status[e]								
Total, aged 18 to 64	196,254	26,527	13.5	197,260	24,414	12.4	−2,114	−1.1
With a disability	15,429	4,403	28.5	15,276	4,358	28.5	−45	Z
With no disability	179,905	22,055	12.3	181,069	20,000	11.0	−2,056	−1.2

(9.9 million) of African Americans lived in poverty. By 1974 the rate had fallen to 30.3%. It fluctuated between 30% and 35% through the mid-1990s, before falling significantly during the late 1990s and reaching a new low of 22.5% in 2000. The rate rose slightly over the next several years then, with the Great Recession (which officially lasted from December 2007 to June 2009), it returned to levels not seen since the mid-1990s. In

2015, 24.1% (10 million) of all African Americans lived below the poverty line. (See Table 2.1.)

According to Proctor, Semega, and Kollar, the Census Bureau began gathering poverty statistics by Hispanic origin in 1972 and in that year found that 22.8% (2.4 million) of Hispanics lived in poverty. The rate then fluctuated from a low of 21.6% (1978) to a high of 30.7% (1994) over the

TABLE 2.1

People in poverty, by selected characteristics, 2014 and 2015 [CONTINUED]

[Numbers in thousands. People as of March of the following year.]

Characteristic	2014 Total	2014 Below poverty Number	2014 Below poverty Percent	2015 Total	2015 Below poverty Number	2015 Below poverty Percent	Change in poverty (2015 less 2014)[a] Number	Change in poverty (2015 less 2014)[a] Percent
Educational attainment								
Total, aged 25 and older	212,132	25,163	11.9	215,015	22,957	10.7	−2,207	−1.2
No high school diploma	24,582	7,098	28.9	23,453	6,171	26.3	−928	−2.6
High school, no college	62,575	8,898	14.2	62,002	8,016	12.9	−882	−1.3
Some college, no degree	56,031	5,719	10.2	57,660	5,550	9.6	−169	−0.6
Bachelor's degree or higher	68,945	3,449	5.0	71,900	3,221	4.5	−228	−0.5

N Not comparable.
Z Represents or rounds to zero.
[a]Details may not sum to totals because of rounding.
[b]Federal surveys give respondents the option of reporting more than one race. Therefore, two basic ways of defining a race group are possible. A group such as Asian may be defined as those who reported Asian and no other race (the race-alone or single-race concept) or as those who reported Asian regardless of whether they also reported another race (the race-alone-or-in-combination concept). This table shows data using the first approach (race alone). The use of the single-race population does not imply that it is the preferred method of presenting or analyzing data. The Census Bureau uses a variety of approaches. Information on people who reported more than one race, such as White **and** American Indian and Alaska Native or Asian **and** Black or African American, is available from Census 2010 through American FactFinder. About 2.9 percent of people reported more than one race in Census 2010. Data for American Indians and Alaska Natives, Native Hawaiians and Other Pacific Islanders, and those reporting two or more races are not shown separately.
[c]Once a decade, the CPS ASEC transitions to a new sample design and updates all metropolitan statistical area delineations. As a result, the metropolitan/nonmetropolitan estimates for 2014 and 2015 are not comparable. Users may want to use the American Community Survey estimates for metropolitan/nonmetropolitan comparisons.
[d]The "Outside metropolitan statistical areas" category includes both micropolitan statistical areas and territory outside of metropolitan and micropolitan statistical areas.
[e]The sum of those with and without a disability does not equal the total because disability status is not defined for individuals in the Armed Forces.

SOURCE: Adapted from Bernadette D. Proctor, Jessica L. Semega, and Melissa A. Kollar, "Table 3. People in Poverty by Selected Characteristics: 2014 and 2015," in *Income and Poverty in the United States: 2015*, U.S. Census Bureau, September 2016, https://www.census.gov/content/dam/Census/library/publications/2016/demo/p60-256.pdf (accessed August 2, 2017)

following decades, before falling to sustained historic lows between 1999 and 2008, when it remained largely between 20% and 23%. As with other racial and ethnic groups, Hispanics experienced increasing poverty during the Great Recession, with poverty rates rising to a high of 26.5% in 2010. In 2015, 21.4% (12.1 million) of all Hispanics lived in poverty. (See Table 2.1.)

Proctor, Semega, and Kollar indicate that the Census Bureau has been collecting data on poverty for Asian Americans since 2002. (Prior to 2002 the Census Bureau used the category "Asian and Pacific Islander," which yielded slightly different statistical outcomes.) Throughout this period the poverty rate for Asian Americans has more closely resembled that for whites than that for African Americans and Hispanics, fluctuating between 9.8% (2004) and 12.5% (2009). In 2015, 11.4% (2.1 million) of all Asian Americans lived in poverty. (See Table 2.1.)

African American and Hispanic children suffered even more disproportionately from poverty than African American and Hispanic adults and seniors. In 2015, 33.6% of non-Hispanic African Americans under the age of 18 years and 28.9% of Hispanics under the age of 18 years were poor, compared with only 12.1% of non-Hispanic white children in the same age group. (See Table 2.2.) Non-Hispanic African American and Hispanic children who were raised by a single mother were particularly likely to live in poverty in 2015. Nearly half

of children in both groups (46.9% for non-Hispanic African Americans and 48.7% for Hispanics) lived in poverty. However, the difficulty of making ends meet as a single mother was a problem that extended across racial and ethnic boundaries. The poverty rate for non-Hispanic white children who were raised by single mothers was 34.8%—nearly 23 percentage points higher than the rate for non-Hispanic white children in general.

The rates of desperate poverty (having income-to-poverty ratios under 0.5, or half of the poverty threshold) were also much higher for non-Hispanic African American and Hispanic children than for non-Hispanic white children. Only 5.8% of non-Hispanic white children were desperately poor, compared with 11.5% of Hispanic children and 16.2% of non-Hispanic African American children. (See Table 2.2.) Again, single-parenting by females was a strong predictor of the likelihood of living in desperate poverty regardless of racial and ethnic identity. Nearly one out of five (18.1%) non-Hispanic white children who were raised by single mothers lived at half of the poverty line or less, compared with 23.1% of non-Hispanic African American children and 25.9% of Hispanic children in such households.

The median (the middle value—half are higher and half are lower) household income reflects the disparity in poverty levels between different groups. In 2015 Asian Americans had the highest median income among all racial and ethnic groups, at $77,368. (See Table 2.3.)

TABLE 2.2

Percentage of children aged 0–17 living below selected poverty levels, by selected characteristics, selected years 1980–2015

Characteristic	1980	1985	1990	1995	2000	2005	2010	2013	2013[a]	2014	2015
Below 100% poverty											
Total	18.3	20.7	20.6	20.8	16.2	17.6	22.0	19.9	21.5	21.1	19.7
Gender											
Male	18.1	20.3	20.5	20.4	16.0	17.4	22.2	19.8	21.5	21.2	19.5
Female	18.6	21.1	20.8	21.2	16.3	17.8	21.9	20.0	21.5	21.1	19.9
Age											
Ages 0–5	20.7	23.0	23.6	24.1	18.3	20.2	25.8	22.5	24.1	23.9	21.3
Ages 6–17	17.3	19.5	19.0	19.1	15.2	16.3	20.2	18.7	20.3	19.8	19.0
Race and Hispanic origin[b]											
White, non-Hispanic	11.8	12.8	12.3	11.2	9.1	10.0	12.3	10.7	13.4	12.3	12.1
Black, non-Hispanic	42.3	43.3	44.5	41.5	31.0	34.5	39.1	39.1	33.4	37.3	33.6
Hispanic	33.2	40.3	38.4	40.0	28.4	28.3	34.9	30.4	33.0	31.9	28.9
Region[c]											
Northeast	16.3	18.5	18.4	19.0	14.5	15.5	18.5	17.5	18.2	17.8	18.4
South	22.5	22.8	23.8	23.5	18.4	19.7	24.3	22.9	24.2	23.8	22.1
Midwest	16.3	20.7	18.8	16.9	13.1	15.9	20.5	17.0	20.1	18.8	17.2
West	16.1	19.3	19.8	22.1	16.9	17.5	22.2	19.5	20.8	21.2	19.0
Children in married-couple families, total	10.1	11.4	10.3	10.0	8.0	8.5	11.6	9.5	10.1	10.6	9.8
Ages 0–5	11.6	12.9	11.7	11.1	8.7	9.9	13.4	10.3	11.5	11.6	10.1
Ages 6–17	9.4	10.5	9.5	9.4	7.7	7.7	10.7	9.2	9.4	10.2	9.6
White, non-Hispanic	7.5	8.2	6.9	6.0	4.7	4.5	6.4	5.0	6.6	6.4	6.0
Black, non-Hispanic	19.7	17.2	17.8	12.0	8.5	12.4	16.0	16.9	10.3	13.3	11.0
Hispanic	23.0	27.2	26.6	28.4	20.8	20.1	25.1	20.0	19.6	21.2	19.5
Children in female-householder families, no husband present, total	51.4	54.1	54.2	50.7	40.5	43.1	47.1	46.1	47.4	46.4	**42.6**
Ages 0–5	65.4	65.7	65.9	61.9	50.7	52.9	58.7	55.3	55.3	55.1	49.5
Ages 6–17	46.2	49.1	48.4	45.2	36.3	38.9	41.9	42.0	43.8	42.4	39.5
White, non-Hispanic	38.6	39.1	41.4	34.9	29.3	33.8	36.0	34.8	39.6	35.7	34.8
Black, non-Hispanic	64.9	66.7	65.1	61.5	48.9	50.2	52.6	54.6	49.9	52.9	46.9
Hispanic	64.8	73.0	68.9	66.0	50.5	51.0	56.8	52.4	53.2	53.3	48.7

Characteristic	1980	1985	1990	1995	2000	2005	2010	2013[a]	2013[b]	2014	2015
Below 50% poverty											
Total	6.9	8.6	8.8	8.5	6.7	7.7	9.9	8.8	9.9	9.3	8.9
Gender											
Male	6.9	8.6	8.8	8.4	6.6	7.3	10.0	8.6	10.1	9.3	8.8
Female	6.9	8.6	8.8	8.5	6.8	8.1	9.8	9.0	9.7	9.3	9.0
Age											
Ages 0–5	8.3	10.0	10.7	10.8	8.1	9.1	12.0	10.9	12.0	11.2	10.2
Ages 6–17	6.2	7.8	7.8	7.2	6.0	7.0	8.9	7.8	8.9	8.4	8.3
Race and Hispanic origin[b]											
White, non-Hispanic	4.3	5.0	5.0	3.9	3.7	4.1	5.1	4.5	6.3	5.4	5.8
Black, non-Hispanic	17.7	22.1	22.7	20.5	14.9	17.3	20.1	19.1	16.6	18.5	16.2
Hispanic	10.8	14.1	14.2	16.3	10.2	11.5	15.0	12.8	14.6	12.9	11.5
Region[c]											
Northeast	4.7	6.5	7.6	8.6	6.4	7.5	8.9	7.2	7.7	7.7	7.9
South	9.7	10.9	11.3	10.1	7.9	9.0	10.5	10.2	11.0	10.9	10.3
Midwest	6.3	9.5	8.9	6.6	5.5	6.5	9.8	8.1	10.2	7.8	7.6
West	5.1	5.6	6.1	7.8	6.2	7.0	9.8	8.3	9.6	9.0	8.3
Children in married-couple families, total	3.1	3.5	2.7	2.6	2.2	2.4	3.5	2.7	3.1	3.1	3.0
Ages 0–5	3.7	4.0	3.2	2.9	2.2	2.8	4.1	2.9	3.7	3.6	3.1
Ages 6–17	2.8	3.1	2.4	2.5	2.2	2.2	3.2	2.6	2.8	2.9	3.0
White, non-Hispanic	2.5	2.6	2.0	1.5	1.5	1.2	1.8	1.5	2.6	2.1	2.4
Black, non-Hispanic	4.2	5.2	3.9	2.5	2.9	4.5	5.7	5.6	2.1	4.0	4.2
Hispanic	6.2	7.4	6.7	8.6	4.5	5.2	7.5	5.2	4.8	5.4	4.4
Children in female-householder families, no husband present, total	22.3	27.0	28.7	24.4	19.7	22.5	25.3	24.8	25.5	23.9	22.1
Ages 0–5	31.4	35.8	37.7	34.3	28.4	29.4	33.3	32.8	33.7	30.6	29.0
Ages 6–17	18.8	23.2	24.2	19.7	16.1	19.6	21.7	21.1	21.8	20.8	19.0
White, non-Hispanic	15.3	17.5	21.1	14.5	13.4	16.4	18.6	18.1	20.3	18.0	18.1
Black, non-Hispanic	31.0	38.0	37.1	32.6	23.9	26.5	28.2	29.0	26.7	27.5	23.1
Hispanic	24.7	31.1	33.1	33.1	26.0	29.1	31.5	28.7	30.5	28.1	25.9

TABLE 2.2

Percentage of children aged 0–17 living below selected poverty levels, by selected characteristics, selected years 1980–2015 [CONTINUED]

Characteristic	1980	1985	1990	1995	2000	2005	2010	2013[a]	2013[b]	2014	2015
Below 150% poverty											
Total	29.9	32.3	31.4	32.2	26.7	28.2	33.4	32.1	33.2	32.5	31.4
Gender											
Male	29.6	32.2	31.3	31.7	26.6	28.0	33.6	32.2	33.4	32.7	31.0
Female	30.3	32.3	31.6	32.7	26.8	28.3	33.3	32.1	33.1	32.4	31.8
Age											
Ages 0–5	33.2	35.6	34.6	35.5	29.3	31.5	37.1	34.7	35.8	36.3	33.3
Ages 6–17	28.4	30.5	29.7	30.5	25.4	26.5	31.6	30.9	32.0	30.8	30.5
Race and Hispanic origin[b]											
White, non-Hispanic	21.7	22.6	21.4	20.1	16.4	17.2	20.5	19.1	21.9	20.7	20.2
Black, non-Hispanic	57.3	59.5	57.8	56.5	45.4	48.7	54.0	54.2	48.5	50.8	48.5
Hispanic	52.7	57.8	56.0	59.4	47.3	45.9	51.7	48.9	51.5	48.7	46.8
Region[c]											
Northeast	27.0	28.1	26.7	28.8	23.4	24.9	27.5	29.4	27.4	27.5	27.8
South	35.8	36.7	36.0	35.8	29.5	31.2	36.9	35.4	36.4	35.9	34.9
Midwest	26.0	31.0	28.7	26.8	21.8	25.0	31.1	28.0	31.5	29.8	28.2
West	27.9	30.4	31.4	35.0	29.3	28.8	34.2	32.5	33.7	33.0	31.0
Children in married-couple families, total	20.6	22.2	20.1	20.0	16.2	17.0	21.0	19.3	19.9	20.1	18.8
Ages 0–5	23.7	25.7	22.2	21.3	17.8	19.8	23.3	20.7	21.6	22.4	19.7
Ages 6–17	19.1	20.3	18.8	19.2	15.5	15.6	19.8	18.6	19.0	19.0	18.4
White, non-Hispanic	16.5	17.1	14.7	13.4	10.0	10.0	12.9	11.2	13.3	12.7	12.2
Black, non-Hispanic	34.6	37.1	31.6	25.3	20.0	22.9	27.0	29.0	22.4	26.2	21.1
Hispanic	43.4	47.3	46.6	49.8	39.4	38.5	42.3	38.0	39.5	38.3	36.7
Children in female-householder families, no husband present, total	66.7	68.1	67.6	65.7	57.6	58.9	63.2	63.8	62.7	62.1	60.1
Ages 0–5	79.1	77.4	77.1	75.3	67.2	68.8	72.9	71.2	69.1	70.1	67.6
Ages 6–17	62.0	64.1	62.9	61.0	53.7	54.7	58.9	60.4	59.9	58.5	56.7
White, non-Hispanic	53.6	54.4	56.1	50.1	45.1	47.8	50.1	51.2	53.4	52.0	49.8
Black, non-Hispanic	79.9	79.6	77.4	76.2	66.1	66.9	70.4	72.0	66.8	66.8	65.1
Hispanic	80.7	84.8	80.8	81.7	70.3	67.4	72.9	71.0	69.9	70.6	67.8

Characteristic	1980	1985	1990	1995	2000	2005	2010	2013[a]	2013[b]	2014	2015
Below 200% poverty											
Total	42.3	43.5	42.4	43.3	37.5	38.9	43.7	42.6	43.2	42.9	41.8
Gender											
Male	42.3	43.2	42.5	43.1	37.5	38.6	43.7	42.4	43.0	43.3	41.4
Female	42.4	43.7	42.3	43.5	37.6	39.3	43.6	42.8	43.4	42.4	42.1
Age											
Ages 0–5	46.8	47.1	46.0	46.7	41.0	42.4	47.4	45.5	45.9	46.4	44.2
Ages 6–17	40.3	41.6	40.5	41.5	35.9	37.3	41.9	41.2	41.9	41.2	40.6
Race and Hispanic origin[b]											
White, non-Hispanic	33.8	33.6	32.3	30.5	25.5	26.2	29.1	28.5	30.4	29.2	28.9
Black, non-Hispanic	70.1	70.9	68.1	68.0	58.9	61.2	65.1	63.6	60.0	62.4	60.0
Hispanic	67.2	70.3	69.5	72.9	62.6	60.7	64.8	62.5	63.8	62.3	60.8
Region[c]											
Northeast	39.1	37.5	36.3	38.2	33.0	33.9	35.9	37.5	37.5	36.7	36.0
South	47.8	48.6	47.7	48.4	41.6	42.5	47.4	45.8	46.3	46.9	45.0
Midwest	39.1	42.5	39.6	36.9	31.2	35.3	41.2	38.8	40.6	39.3	39.3
West	40.5	41.7	42.7	46.1	40.5	40.5	45.5	44.4	44.6	43.8	42.7
Children in married-couple families, total	33.2	33.9	31.4	31.1	26.4	27.0	30.8	29.3	28.7	29.5	28.3
Ages 0–5	38.1	38.1	34.5	33.2	29.2	30.2	33.4	31.3	31.0	32.2	29.8
Ages 6–17	30.8	31.6	29.6	29.9	25.1	25.4	29.4	28.3	27.6	28.2	27.6
White, non-Hispanic	28.3	27.8	25.4	23.3	18.2	18.1	20.5	19.5	20.1	19.9	20.0
Black, non-Hispanic	50.9	52.5	44.7	38.3	35.3	35.3	40.4	38.9	31.7	37.0	30.8
Hispanic	60.5	62.8	62.1	66.0	55.5	54.1	56.0	53.1	53.5	52.8	51.3
Children in female-householder families, no husband present, total	78.2	77.4	77.6	76.4	69.7	71.2	73.9	74.8	74.5	74.3	72.1
Ages 0–5	87.9	84.5	85.4	84.3	78.6	80.2	82.4	80.6	79.6	80.5	79.1
Ages 6–17	74.5	74.4	73.7	72.5	66.0	67.4	70.1	72.1	72.3	71.5	69.0
White, non-Hispanic	67.8	66.6	68.0	62.6	57.1	60.2	62.0	64.6	66.8	64.8	61.6
Black, non-Hispanic	89.1	87.1	85.7	86.9	78.4	78.8	80.1	80.8	79.4	78.8	77.5
Hispanic	87.3	89.9	89.1	88.6	82.5	80.6	83.5	81.2	79.0	82.2	79.7

The median income for non-Hispanic whites was significantly lower, at $61,394, and the median income for Hispanics was lower still, at $44,782. The median incomes for African Americans ($36,544) and for Native

TABLE 2.2

Percentage of children aged 0–17 living below selected poverty levels, by selected characteristics, selected years 1980–2015 [CONTINUED]

aThe source for the redesigned income in this column is the portion of the 2014 Current Population Survey (CPS) Annual Social and Economic Supplement (ASEC) sample (about 30,000 households) that received the redesigned income questions. The 2014 CPS ASEC included redesigned questions for income that were implemented to a subsample of the 98,000 addresses using a probability split panel design. The redesigned income questions were used for the entire 2015 CPS ASEC sample.
bFrom 1980 to 2002, following the 1977 U.S. Office of Management and Budget standards for collecting and presenting data on race, the CPS asked respondents to choose one race from the following: White, Black, American Indian or Alaskan Native, or Asian or Pacific Islander. An "Other" category was also offered. Beginning in 2003, the CPS allowed respondents to select one or more race categories. All race groups discussed in this table from 2002 onward refer to people who indicated only one racial identity within the categories presented. For this reason, data from 2002 onward are not directly comparable with data from earlier years. People who reported only one race are referred to as the race-alone population. The use of the race-alone population in this table does not imply that it is the preferred method of presenting or analyzing data. Data on race and Hispanic origin are collected separately. Persons of Hispanic origin may be of any race.
cRegions: Northeast includes CT, MA, ME, NH, NJ, NY, PA, RI, and VT. South includes AL, AR, DC, DE, FL, GA, KY, LA, MD, MS, NC, OK, SC, TN, TX, VA, and WV. Midwest includes IA, IL, IN, KS, MI, MN, MO, ND, NE, OH, SD, and WI. West includes AK, AZ, CA, CO, HI, ID, MT, NM, NV, OR, UT, WA, and WY.
Notes: Data for 2010 use the Census 2010-based population controls. The 2004 data have been revised to reflect a correction to the weights in the 2005 ASEC. Data for 1999, 2000, and 2001 use Census 2000 population controls. Data for 2000 onward are from the expanded CPS sample. The poverty level is based on money income and does not include noncash benefits, such as food stamps. Poverty thresholds reflect family size and composition and are adjusted each year using the annual average Consumer Price Index level. In 2015, the poverty threshold for a two parent, two child family was $24,036. The levels shown here are derived from the ratio of the family's income to the family's poverty threshold.

SOURCE: Adapted from "ECON1.A. Child Poverty: Percentage of Children Ages 0–17 Living below Selected Poverty Levels by Selected Characteristics, 1980–2015," in *America's Children in Brief: Key National Indicators of Well-Being, 2017*, Federal Interagency Forum on Child and Family Statistics, July 2017, https://www.childstats.gov/americaschildren/tables/econ1a.asp (accessed August 3, 2017)

TABLE 2.3

Median household income in the past 12 months, by race and Hispanic origin, 2015

	United States	
	Total	Median income (dollars)
Subject	Estimate	Estimate
Households	118,208,250	55,775
One race—		
White	77.0%	59,698
Black or African American	12.3%	36,544
American Indian and Alaska Native	0.7%	38,530
Asian	4.5%	77,368
Native Hawaiian and other Pacific Islander	0.1%	55,607
Some other race	3.4%	42,461
Two or more races	1.9%	51,737
Hispanic or Latino origin (of any race)	12.7%	44,782
White alone, not Hispanic or Latino	68.4%	61,394

Notes: Data are based on a sample and are subject to sampling variability. While the 2015 American Community Survey (ACS) data generally reflect the February 2013 Office of Management and Budget (OMB) definitions of metropolitan and micropolitan statistical areas; in certain instances the names, codes, and boundaries of the principal cities shown in ACS tables may differ from the OMB definitions due to differences in the effective dates of the geographic entities. Estimates of urban and rural population, housing units, and characteristics reflect boundaries of urban areas defined based on Census 2010 data. As a result, data for urban and rural areas from the ACS do not necessarily reflect the results of ongoing urbanization. Although the American Community Survey (ACS) produces population, demographic and housing unit estimates, it is the Census Bureau's Population Estimates Program that produces and disseminates the official estimates of the population for the nation, states, counties, cities and towns and estimates of housing units for states and counties.

SOURCE: Adapted from "S1903. Median Income in the Past 12 Months (in 2015 Inflation-Adjusted Dollars)," in *2015 American Community Survey 1-Year Estimates*, U.S. Census Bureau, American FactFinder, September 15, 2016, d279m997dpfwgl.cloudfront.net/wp/2016/09/ACS_15_1YR_S1903.pdf (accessed August 3, 2017)

Americans and Alaskan Natives ($38,530) were less than half that of Asian Americans.

AGE

Child Poverty

The United States has historically had one of the highest rates of child poverty in the developed world. In

---

Children of the Recession: The Impact of the Economic Crisis on Child Well-Being in Rich Countries (September 2014, https://www.unicef-irc.org/publications/pdf/rc12-eng-web.pdf), the United Nations Children's Fund (UNICEF) provides an overview of government data from 41 of the world's richest countries to create a comparative portrait of child poverty in the developed world in 2008 and 2012. Although the U.S. economy outperformed other developed economies in the years after the Great Recession, UNICEF finds that U.S. children were far more likely to be impoverished than children in comparably wealthy countries. Setting a poverty threshold for the purposes of the study of 60% of the median income in each country (which is consistent with the standards of many international studies that measure poverty), UNICEF finds that 30.1% of U.S. children were impoverished in 2008 and 32.2% were impoverished in 2012. (See Table 2.4.)

These rates were comparable to countries such as Turkey (33% in 2008 and 30.2% in 2012), Romania (32.9% and 30.6%), Israel (35.1% and 35.6%), and Mexico (29.3% and 34.3%). The country with the lowest rate of child poverty in 2012 was Norway, whose rate of 5.3% was more than six times lower than that of the United States. The Organisation for Economic Co-operation and Development (OECD) is an organization consisting of 34 wealthy countries committed to promoting democracy and economic cooperation. In *OECD Better Life Index: Income* (2017, http://www.oecdbetterlifeindex.org/topics/income), the OECD indicates that, as of 2017, the United States had the highest average net household disposable income (income after taxes and living expenses are paid) of any of the world's developed economies, at $41,071 per year. By comparison, Norway had an average net household disposable income of $33,393, and the average disposable incomes of the countries with which the United States' child poverty rate compares were far lower when adjusted for differences in the cost of living. Mexico's average disposable income was $12,806, Turkey's

TABLE 2.4

Child poverty rates in high-income countries, 2008 and 2012

Rank	Country	Change (2008–2012)
1	Chile	−8.67
2	Poland	−7.90
3	Australia	−6.27
4	Slovakia	−5.60
5	Switzerland	−4.80
6	Norway	−4.30
7	Republic of Korea	−3.40
8	Finland	−3.20
9	Turkey	−2.76
10	Japan	−2.70
11	Canada	−2.44
12	Romania	−2.30
13	Belgium	−0.80
14	Sweden	−0.80
15	Austria	−0.70
16	New Zealand	−0.40
17	Czech Republic	−0.40
18	Germany	−0.20
19	Israel	0.55
20	Bulgaria	0.60
21	Malta	0.60
22	Netherlands	1.00
23	Portugal	1.00
24	Denmark	1.10
25	United Kingdom	1.60
26	Slovenia	1.80
27	United States	2.06
28	Cyprus	2.70
29	Hungary	2.90
30	France	3.00
31	Mexico	5.00
32	Estonia	5.10
33	Italy	5.70
34	Luxembourg	6.50
35	Spain	8.10
36	Lithuania	8.30
37	Ireland	10.60
38	Croatia	11.80
39	Latvia	14.60
40	Greece	17.50
41	Iceland	20.40

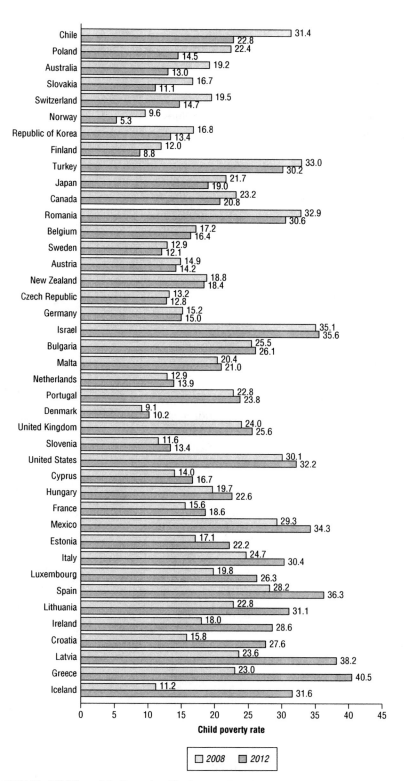

SOURCE: "League Table 1. Change in Child Poverty (Anchored in 2008)," in "Children of the Recession: The Impact of the Economic Crisis on Child Well-Being in Rich Countries," *Innocenti Report Card 12*, UNICEF Office of Research, September 2014, http://www.unicef-irc.org/publications/pdf/rc12-eng-web.pdf (accessed August 3, 2017)

was $13,471, and Israel's was $22,116. (Romania was not an OECD member as of 2017.)

The official poverty line in the United States is not pegged to median income as are most international developed-world statistics, so the Census Bureau's picture of child poverty is considerably less bleak than that indicated by UNICEF. Nevertheless, even when applying the United States' comparatively low poverty threshold, some groups of children experience poverty at extremely high rates. As noted earlier, non-Hispanic African American and Hispanic children are disproportionately likely to live in poverty, as are children of all races who live in households headed by a single mother. What is more, much of the progress in combating poverty in single-mother families was reversed during the first and second decades of the 21st century. According to ChildStats.gov, the poverty rate for children in female-householder families with no husband present fell steadily through the 1990s and the turn of the 21st century, from 54.2% in 1990 to 39.8% in 2002. The poverty rate for such children then rose to 43.1% in 2005, before rising still further in the years after the Great Recession, peaking at 48% in 2011. Child poverty in single-mother families stood at 42.6% in 2015. (See Table 2.2.)

Younger children are more likely to be poor than older children, partly because parents themselves are more likely to be young (and not yet in their peak income-earning years) when children are young. More than one in five (21.3%) of all children aged zero to five years lived in poverty in 2015. (See Table 2.2.) Furthermore, single mothers with young children often cannot obtain or keep jobs because of the constant care that children require before they are old enough to attend school. The child poverty rate for those aged zero to five years in single-mother households was 49.5% in 2015, and nearly three in ten (29%) of such children were desperately poor, or living at 50% of poverty or less. More than two-thirds (67.6%) of children aged zero to five years who were raised by single mothers lived below 150% of poverty, meaning that most young children being raised by a single mother were either poor or at risk of falling into poverty. This shows the difficulty of rising above poverty even when the household head is able to find work.

The poverty rate for children in married-couple households was comparatively stable prior to the Great Recession, and at all times it has been substantially lower than the overall child poverty rate. In 2000 and 2005 the poverty rate for children in married-couple households was around 8%, but in 2010 it rose to 11.6%, a rate not seen since 1985. (See Table 2.2.) In 2015 the rate stood at 9.8%.

Not only are children overrepresented among the poor, they also arguably suffer more from the deprivations of poverty than do adults. Strong evidence suggests that food insecurity and lack of good medical care caused by poverty can limit a child's physical and cognitive development. The higher incidence of poverty among children aged five years and younger is of particular concern to child advocates, given that the preschool years represent the most crucial period for brain development. In "Poverty during Early Childhood May Last a Lifetime" (Discovery.com, February 22, 2010), Jessica Marshall reports on several studies that show that early childhood poverty can cause changes in the brain that lead to problems in adulthood, including lower adult income.

The Children's Defense Fund (CDF) argues in *Portrait of Inequality 2012—Black Children in America* (November 2012, http://www.childrensdefense.org/library/data/portrait-of-inequality-2012.pdf) and in *Portrait of Inequality 2012—Hispanic Children in America* (November 2012, http://www.childrensdefense.org/library/data/a-portrait-of-inequality-2012.pdf) that "poverty destroys childhood and can destroy children." The CDF notes in both reports that children born into poverty are relatively unlikely to receive prenatal care, and that they are disproportionately likely to be born underweight, lack family support systems, experience poor health, lack health insurance coverage, exhibit developmental delays, and fall behind in school at an early age. These children then attend schools that are often poorly funded and inadequate, leaving them ill-prepared for an increasingly competitive job market. All of these disadvantages add up to what the CDF calls the "Cradle to Prison Pipeline." According to E. Ann Carson and Elizabeth Anderson of the Bureau of Justice Statistics, in *Prisoners in 2015* (December 2016, https://www.bjs.gov/content/pub/pdf/p15.pdf), there were nearly 1.5 million men and women serving one year or longer in state and federal prisons as of December 31, 2015. Of that total, 523,000 (35.4%) were African American and 319,400 (21.6%) were Hispanic. Also, as stated earlier, African American and Hispanic children are disproportionately likely to live in poverty, which lends support for the cradle-to-prison scenario.

According to numerous sources, the problem of child poverty is increasingly affecting the U.S. public education system on a large scale. In the research bulletin *A New Majority: Low Income Students Now a Majority in the Nation's Public Schools* (January 2015, http://www.southerneducation.org/getattachment/4ac62e27-5260-47a5-9d02-14896ec3a531/A-New-Majority-2015-Update-Low-Income-Students-Now.aspx), the Southern Education Foundation, a philanthropic organization devoted to educational issues, reports that more than half (51%) of all public school students in 2013 qualified for free or reduced-price meals through the federal school lunch and breakfast programs. Enrollment in these federal programs is considered broadly indicative of student poverty. In 2013 poor children accounted for a majority of the public school population in 21 states, including all states in the South (except Maryland and Virginia) and 7 western states (Arizona, California, Hawaii, Oregon, Nevada, New Mexico, and Utah). The percentage of public school students who were poor was highest in Mississippi (71%), followed by New Mexico (68%) and Louisiana (65%).

In "Poverty and High School Dropouts" (APA.org, May 2013), Russell W. Rumberger of the University of California, Santa Barbara, indicates that the high rate of poverty in U.S. public schools translates into high dropout rates. A 2009 study found that students in the bottom 20% of households by income were five times more likely to drop out of high school than students in the top 20%, and in 2012 an estimated 1.1 million high school seniors failed to earn a diploma. In that year the U.S. high school graduation rate ranked 22nd in the world. High school dropouts are more likely than any other group, by education status, to be unemployed, have incomes below poverty, have numerous poor health outcomes, rely on public assistance programs, and engage in criminal activity.

Poverty among the Elderly

In contrast with children, senior citizens are underrepresented among the poor. Proctor, Semega, and Kollar note that in 2015, 8.8% of adults aged 65 years and older were poor, down from 10% the year before. (See Table 2.1.) Between 1959 and 2015 the number of people aged 65 years and older living in poverty dropped significantly, from a high of about 35% to current levels. (See Figure 1.2 in Chapter 1.) Most observers credit Social Security for the sharp decline in poverty among the elderly. Although it was enacted in 1935, Social Security began paying substantially higher benefits in the era following World War II (1939–1945). Gary V. Engelhardt and Jonathan Gruber of the National Bureau of Economic Research maintain in *Social Security and the Evolution of Elderly Poverty* (May 2004, http://www.nber.org/papers/w10466.pdf) that increases in benefit levels between 1967 and 2000 account for the entirety of the reduction in poverty among the elderly.

Poverty rates among the elderly are the source of some dispute among analysts, however. Because the federal government's official poverty measure does not take into account out-of-pocket medical expenses, which are far higher on average for the elderly than for children and adults under the age of 65 years, many believe that the true poverty rate among the elderly is higher than Census Bureau estimates suggest. The Census Bureau has attempted to account for this issue in its formulation of the Supplemental Poverty Measure (SPM), which adjusts for expenses including out-of-pocket medical costs. In *The Supplemental Poverty Measure: 2015* (September 2016, https://www.census.gov/content/dam/Census/library/publications/2016/demo/p60-258.pdf), Trudi Renwick and Liana Fox of the Census Bureau state that the SPM method found a poverty rate for the elderly of 13.7% in 2015, which is significantly higher than the rate of elderly poverty derived from the official measure (8.8%). Because there are no plans to use the SPM to administer government benefits, it is unclear how or even if the disparity between the two measures of elderly poverty will affect public policy.

LOCATION

According to the official poverty thresholds, people living in cities are more likely to be poor than those living in rural areas, and people living in rural areas are more likely to be poor than those living in suburbs. In 2015, 16.8% of people living in cities (inside metropolitan statistical areas and inside principal cities) and 16.7% of people living in rural areas (outside metropolitan statistical areas) lived below the poverty line. (See Table 2.1.) Poverty in the suburbs (inside metropolitan statistical areas but outside principal cities) stood at a comparatively small 10.8% of the population.

Although urban and rural areas have similar official poverty rates, there is substantial doubt about whether the two populations truly experience the same levels of poverty. Because of sometimes dramatic differences in the cost of living between rural and urban areas, which are not accounted for in the official poverty measure, the equivalence between these two rates has perhaps been overstated. The Census Bureau's SPM, which attempts to account for geographical variation in the cost of living, provides different rates of poverty than the official measure. Renwick and Fox indicate the SPM yields a lower rate of rural poverty (13.2%), a higher rate of urban poverty (17.9%), and a higher rate of suburban poverty (12.5%) than the official measure.

FAMILY STATUS

In 2015 people living in families (11.6%) were much less likely than people living in unrelated subfamilies (41.6%) or in households with unrelated individuals (21.5%) to suffer from poverty. (See Table 2.1.) However, there was a major variation in the poverty rate between different family structures. Whereas 8.6 million families in the United States (10.4% of the total number of families) were living in poverty in 2015, families headed by married couples had a dramatically lower poverty rate (5.4%) than other types of families. (See Table 2.5.) The poverty rate for families with a female householder and no husband present was 28.2% that year. For households headed by a male with no wife present, the rate was 14.9%.

Single-Parent Families

The proportion of single-parent families steadily increased between 1970 and the early 1990s, and the

TABLE 2.5

Families in poverty, by type of family, 2014 and 2015

[Numbers in thousands. Families as of March of the following year.]

	2014			2015			Change in poverty (2015 less 2014)*	
		Below poverty			Below poverty			
Characteristic	Total	Number	Percent	Total	Number	Percent	Number	Percent
Families								
Total	81,730	9,467	11.6	82,199	8,589	10.4	−879	−1.1
Type of family								
Married-couple	60,015	3,735	6.2	60,258	3,245	5.4	−489	−0.8
Female householder, no husband present	15,553	4,764	30.6	15,630	4,404	28.2	−360	−2.5
Male householder, no wife present	6,162	969	15.7	6,311	939	14.9	−29	−0.8

*Details may not sum to totals because of rounding.

SOURCE: Adapted from Bernadette D. Proctor, Jessica L. Semega, and Melissa A. Kollar, "Table 4. Families in Poverty by Type of Family: 2014 and 2015," in *Income and Poverty in the United States: 2015*, U.S. Census Bureau, September 2016, https://www.census.gov/content/dam/Census/library/publications/2016/demo/p60-256.pdf (accessed August 2, 2017)

proportion of married-couple families correspondingly declined. Since then, the structure of U.S. households and families has remained relatively stable. According to the Census Bureau, there were 82.2 million families in the United States in 2015. (See Table 2.6.) Of these, 60.3 million (73.4%) were headed by married couples, 6.3 million (7.7%) were single-parent households headed by men, and 15.6 million (19%) were single-parent households headed by women.

One factor in the rise of single-parent families is the rise in the divorce rate. Jason Fields of the Census Bureau indicates in *America's Families and Living Arrangements: 2003* (November 2004, http://www.census.gov/prod/2004pubs/p20-553.pdf) that in 1970 only 3.5% of men and 5.7% of women were separated or divorced. By 2015, 10.4% of men and 13.5% of women were separated or divorced. (See Table 2.7.) The percentage of divorced women is consistently higher than the percentage of divorced men because divorced men are more likely to remarry, whereas divorced women are more likely to raise the children from the first marriage. As Table 2.8 shows, in 2013 there were an estimated 13.4 million custodial parents, or parents who were raising children in the absence of the second parent. Of these, 11.1 million were female and 2.4 million were male; in other words, 82.5% of custodial parents were mothers.

Another reason for the rise in single-parent families is the rise in people who never marry yet still have children. According to Fields, in 1970 only 28.1% of males aged 15 years and older and 22.1% of females aged 15 years and older had never married. As is shown in Table 2.7, in 2015, 35.3% of males over the age of 15 years had never married, and neither had 29.4% of females over the age of 15 years. The proportion of those who have never married has increased as young adults delay the age at which they marry. As Figure 2.1

shows, the median age at first marriage, after remaining relatively stable between 1890 and 1970, rose dramatically for both men and women between 1970 and 2016. The median age of women at first marriage was 20.8 years in 1970 and 27.9 years in 2016; and the median age of men at first marriage was 23.2 years in 1970 and 29.9 years in 2016. In 2016 there were nearly 8.1 million households headed by opposite-sex unmarried couples; 3 million (37.5%) of these households had at least one biological child under the age of 18 years present. (See Table 2.9.)

Single-parent women were more likely than single-parent men to have never been married. In 2016, 49.3% of single mothers raising their own children and 38.2% of single fathers raising their own children had never been married. (See Table 2.10.)

African American children are far more likely to live with a single parent than are non-Hispanic white or Hispanic children. In 2016, 4.7 million (35.6%) of a total 13.2 million African American children (including only those children who had both African American and other racial characteristics) lived with married parents, and another 645,000 (4.9%) lived with unmarried parents who were both present. (See Table 2.11.) A larger share of African American children lived with a single mother who had either never married (4.3 million, or 32.6%), was divorced (1.1 million, or 8.3%), was separated (698,000, or 5.3%), was widowed (140,000, or 1.1%), or whose married spouse was absent (293,000, or 2.2%). Together, these groups of children parented by single mothers accounted for 6.5 million, or nearly half (49.5%) of all African American children. An additional 510,000 (3.9%) African American children lived with their father only, and 803,000 (6.1%) lived in a household with neither parent present.

Although Hispanic children experienced rates of poverty similar to those of African American children, their

TABLE 2.6

Households by type and selected characteristics, 2016

[Numbers in thousands]

	Total	Family households				Nonfamily households		
		Total	Married couple	Male householder	Female householder	Total	Male householder	Female householder
All households	125,819	82,184	60,251	6,310	15,622	43,635	20,542	23,093
Size of households								
One member	35,388	—	—	—	—	35,388	15,804	19,585
Two members	42,785	36,081	27,374	2,574	6,133	6,704	3,754	2,950
Three members	19,423	18,365	11,604	1,896	4,865	1,058	650	408
Four members	16,267	15,912	12,370	1,005	2,536	355	247	108
Five members	7,548	7,446	5,698	466	1,283	101	67	35
Six members	2,813	2,800	2,077	218	505	13	13	—
Seven or more members	1,596	1,580	1,128	152	300	16	9	7
Number of nonrelatives in household								
No nonrelatives	112,881	77,493	59,500	4,621	13,372	35,388	15,804	19,585
One nonrelative	10,844	4,140	603	1,465	2,072	6,704	3,754	2,950
Two nonrelatives	1,440	382	93	156	133	1,058	650	408
Three or more nonrelatives	655	169	55	68	46	485	335	150
Race of householder								
White alone	99,313	65,261	50,581	4,643	10,037	34,052	16,061	17,990
Black alone	16,539	9,844	4,435	1,022	4,387	6,695	3,052	3,643
Asian alone	6,328	4,697	3,846	348	504	1,631	772	859
All remaining single races and all race combinations	3,638	2,381	1,389	297	695	1,257	657	600
Hispanic origin of householder								
Hispanic[a]	16,667	12,761	8,003	1,473	3,284	3,906	2,163	1,743
White alone, Non-Hispanic	84,445	53,788	43,221	3,351	7,216	30,657	14,203	16,454
Other non-Hispanic	24,707	15,635	9,027	1,486	5,122	9,072	4,176	4,896
White alone or combination householder								
White alone or in combination with one or more other races	100,990	66,287	51,217	4,770	10,300	34,703	16,399	18,303
Other	24,829	15,897	9,035	1,540	5,323	8,932	4,143	4,790
Black alone or combination household								
Black alone or in combination with one or more other races	17,322	10,339	4,670	1,097	4,572	6,983	3,191	3,792
Other	108,496	71,844	55,581	5,213	11,051	36,652	17,351	19,301
Asian alone or combination household								
Asian alone or in combination with one or more other races	6,640	4,879	3,960	377	541	1,761	848	913
Other	119,179	77,305	56,291	5,933	15,081	41,874	19,694	22,180
Marital status of household								
Married, spouse present	60,251	60,251	60,251	—	—	—	—	—
Married, spouse absent[b]	2,192	819	—	229	590	1,373	839	534
Widowed	12,233	2,715	—	578	2,136	9,519	2,324	7,194
Divorced	19,207	6,911	—	1,820	5,091	12,296	5,860	6,436
Separated[c]	3,530	1,910	—	387	1,523	1,621	949	672
Never married	28,404	9,578	—	3,296	6,283	18,826	10,569	8,257
Tenure								
Own/buying	79,903	58,605	48,073	3,462	7,070	21,298	9,268	12,030
Rent	44,265	22,860	11,719	2,764	8,377	21,406	10,775	10,631
No cash rent	1,650	719	459	84	176	931	499	432

Dash ("—") represents or rounds to zero.
[a]Hispanics may be of any race.
[b]In past reports: Married spouse absent—other (excluding separated).
[c]In past reports: Married spouse absent—separated.
Note: This table uses the householder's person weight to describe characteristics of people living in households. As a result, estimates of the number of households do not match estimates of the number of housing units from the Housing Vacancy Survey (HVS). The HVS is weighted to housing units, rather than the population, in order to more accurately estimate the number of occupied and vacant housing units.

SOURCE: "Table H1. Households by Type and Tenure of Householder for Selected Characteristics: 2016," in *America's Families and Living Arrangements: 2016*, U.S. Census Bureau, April 6, 2017, https://www2.census.gov/programs-surveys/demo/tables/families/2016/cps-2016/tabh1-all.xls (accessed August 3, 2017)

living situations were dissimilar. In 2016 there were 18.2 million Hispanic children in the United States. The majority (11 million, or 60.3%) lived with married parents, 1.3 million (6.9%) lived with both of their unmarried parents, 4.6 million (25.3%) lived with their mother only, 700,000 (3.8%) lived with their father only, and 673,000 (3.7%)

TABLE 2.7

Marital status of people aged 15 and over, 2016

[Numbers in thousands, except for percentages]

	Total Number	Married spouse present Number	Married spouse absent Number	Widowed Number	Divorced Number	Separated Number	Never married Number	Total Percent	Married spouse present Percent	Married spouse absent Percent	Widowed Percent	Divorced Percent	Separated Percent	Never married Percent
Both sexes														
Total 15+	257,615	125,256	3,613	14,856	25,539	5,276	83,074	100.0	48.6	1.4	5.8	9.9	2.0	32.2
Male														
Total 15+	124,953	62,628	1,860	3,469	10,708	2,207	44,079	100.0	50.1	1.5	2.8	8.6	1.8	35.3
Female														
Total 15+	132,662	62,628	1,753	11,387	14,831	3,069	38,995	100.0	47.2	1.3	8.6	11.2	2.3	29.4

Note: Prior to 2001, this table included group quarters people.

SOURCE: Adapted from "Table A1. Marital Status of People 15 Years and over, by Age, Sex, and Personal Earnings: 2016," in *America's Families and Living Arrangements: 2016*, U.S. Census Bureau, April 6, 2017, https://www2.census.gov/programs-surveys/demo/tables/families/2016/cps-2016/taba1-all.xls (accessed August 3, 2017)

lived with neither parent. (See Table 2.11.) Non-Hispanic white children were more likely to still live with married parents. In 2016, 28.1 million (75.3%) of a total 38 million non-Hispanic white children lived with married parents, 956,000 (2.5%) lived with both of their unmarried parents, 6 million (15.9%) lived with their mother only, 1.7 million (4.4%) lived with their father only, and 1.2 million (3.2%) lived with neither parent.

CHILD SUPPORT. Child support is often an important source of income for impoverished single parents. In *Custodial Mothers and Fathers and Their Child Support: 2013* (January 2016, https://www.census.gov/content/dam/Census/library/publications/2016/demo/P60-255.pdf), Timothy Grall of the Census Bureau notes that 48.7% of all custodial parents had either legally binding or informal child-support agreements in place in 2013. (See Table 2.8.) Custodial parents with an income below the poverty line were slightly less likely (45%) than other parents to have a child-support agreement in place in 2013. Those who did have child-support agreements in place were due an average of $5,021 that year; however, the average amount that was actually received was $2,918. Only 34.8% of impoverished custodial parents with child-support agreements in 2013 received all payments due to them and 33.6% received no payments at all.

The likelihood that custodial parents will receive a high proportion of the total amount of child support due to them varies strongly in proportion to age, current marital status, and educational attainment, as well as in proportion to the nature of the legal custody agreement and whether the child and the noncustodial parent are in contact with one another. In 2013 the average amount of child support due, as well as the average amount received, was lower for custodial parents below the poverty line than for all custodial parents. (See Table 2.8.) Similarly, the percentage of impoverished custodial parents who received all payments was below average, and the percentage of impoverished custodial parents who received no payments was above average. All these facts suggest another arena in which single parents living in poverty are disadvantaged relative to the population in general.

Studies indicate that a number of factors influence the rates of nonpayment of child support. Many researchers have focused specifically on fathers' willingness and ability to pay child support, given that the overwhelming majority of custodial parents are mothers. According to Lenna Nepomnyaschy and Irwin Garfinkel, in "Child Support Enforcement and Fathers' Contributions to Their Nonmarital Children" (*Social Service Review*, vol. 84, no. 3, September 2010), past studies have noted that a high level of trust between the parents correlates to higher levels of support payments. Additionally, fathers who have lived with the mother and child and fathers who maintain a regular visitation schedule with the child tend to satisfy their child-support obligations more fully than those who have not cohabited and/or do not regularly see their child. Studies also show that child-support payments sometimes decline over time, especially when fathers have new biological children and when mothers move on to new romantic relationships and/or have new biological children.

Child support can be either informal or formal. Informal child-support agreements, wherein the father gives the mother money and in-kind awards without any legal encumbrances, are common during the first 15 months after a child is born. Studies show that informal support tends to decline over time and that formal child-support agreements, which are legally enforceable, become more important sources of income for custodial mothers beginning at 45 months after the child's birth. Enforcement of formal child-support agreements varies by state. Whether

TABLE 2.8

Demographic characteristics of custodial parents by award status and payments received, 2013

[Numbers in thousands, as of spring 2014.]

Characteristics	Total	With child support agreements or awards									
		Total	Percent	Due child support payments in 2013							
				Total	Average due	Average received	Percent received	Received all payments		Did not receive payments	
								Total	Percent	Total	Percent
All custodial parents											
Total	13,418	6,528	48.7	5,697	$5,774	$3,953	68.5	2,595	45.6	1,475	25.9
Standard error	283	200	1.1	187	$124	$138	1.5	127	1.6	96	1.5
Sex											
Male	2,350	739	31.4	648	$6,435	$4,821	74.9	264	40.7	169	26.1
Female	11,069	5,789	52.3	5,049	$5,760	$3,936	68.3	2,331	46.2	1,305	25.8
Age											
Under 30 years	2,971	1,251	42.1	1,072	$4,185	$1,925	46.0	325	30.3	320	29.9
30 to 39 years	4,807	2,579	53.7	2,319	$5,192	$3,437	66.2	922	39.8	648	27.9
40 years and over	5,640	2,698	47.8	2,305	$7,100	$5,414	76.3	1,349	58.5	507	22.0
Race and ethnicity[a]											
White alone	9,173	4,852	52.9	4,202	$6,000	$4,341	72.4	2,050	48.8	963	22.9
White alone, not Hispanic	6,454	3,637	56.4	3,167	$6,166	$4,668	75.7	1,624	51.3	654	20.7
Black alone	3,393	1,268	37.4	1,138	$4,567	$2,320	50.8	383	33.7	405	35.6
Hispanic (any race)	3,103	1,364	44.0	1,164	$5,411	$3,341	61.7	484	41.6	326	28.0
Current marital status[b]											
Married	2,131	1,094	51.3	971	$5,416	$3,896	71.9	457	47.1	241	24.8
Divorced	4,469	2,577	57.7	2,281	$6,772	$5,209	76.9	1,289	56.5	458	20.1
Separated	1,552	634	40.9	530	$6,517	$3,584	55.0	192	36.2	158	29.8
Never married	5,117	2,157	42.2	1,863	$4,486	$2,538	56.6	635	34.1	603	32.4
Educational attainment											
Less than high school diploma	1,799	686	38.1	568	$4,970	$2,373	47.7	172	30.3	218	38.4
High school graduate	4,274	1,965	46.0	1,690	$5,374	$3,232	60.1	588	34.8	501	29.6
Less than 4 years of college	4,706	2,444	51.9	2,132	$5,554	$3,912	70.4	1,021	47.9	509	23.9
Bachelors degree or more	2,640	1,434	54.3	1,306	$7,002	$5,638	80.5	815	62.4	246	18.8
Selected characteristics											
Family income below 2013 poverty level	3,859	1,737	45.0	1,474	$5,021	$2,918	58.1	513	34.8	495	33.6
Worked full-time, year-round	6,660	3,293	49.4	2,922	$5,764	$4,021	69.8	1,414	48.4	680	23.3
Public assistance program participation[c]	5,715	2,687	47.0	2,327	$5,071	$2,858	56.4	801	34.4	777	33.4
With 1 child	7,333	3,062	41.8	2,593	$5,741	$4,050	70.5	1,221	47.1	688	26.5
With 2 or more children	6,086	3,466	57.0	3,104	$5,802	$3,871	66.7	1,374	44.3	786	25.3
Child had contact with other parent in 2013	9,316	4,796	51.5	4,168	$5,937	$4,363	73.5	2,106	50.5	917	22.0
Child had no contact with other parent in 2013	4,102	1,732	42.2	1,529	$5,333	$2,833	53.1	489	32.0	558	36.5
Court ordered physical or legal joint custody	3,503	1,989	56.8	1,771	$6,013	$4,839	80.5	1,037	58.6	312	17.6

[a]Includes those reporting one race alone and not in combination with any other race.
[b]Excludes 150,000 with marital status of widowed.
[c]Received any of the following: Medicaid, food stamps, public housing or rent subsidy, TANF, or general assistance.
Notes: Parents living with own children under 21 years of age whose other parent is not living in the home.

SOURCE: Timothy Grall, "Table 2. Demographic Characteristics of Custodial Parents by Award Status and Payments Received: 2013," in *Custodial Mothers and Fathers and Their Child Support: 2013*, U.S. Census Bureau, January 2016, https://www.census.gov/content/dam/Census/library/publications/2016/demo/P60-255.pdf (accessed August 4, 2017)

or not strong child-support enforcement, as is common in some states, leads to better outcomes for custodial mothers and their children has not been established, in part because strong enforcement is associated with declines in informal support.

Custodial parents are more likely to be poor than other Americans, and custodial mothers are significantly more likely to be poor than custodial fathers. According

to Grall, the poverty rate of families headed by a custodial mother was 31.2% in 2013, compared with 17.4% for families headed by a custodial father. Among custodial-mother families in which the mother did not work and custodial-mother families where there were four or more children, the poverty rate was around 62%. Between 1993 and 2001 the percentage of custodial parents and their children living below the poverty level declined from 33.3% to 23.4%. (See Figure 2.2.) According to

FIGURE 2.1

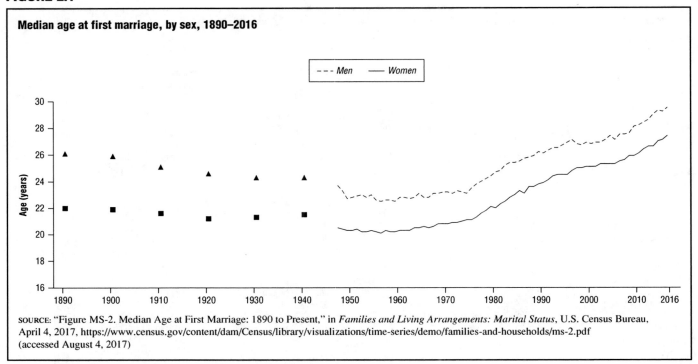

Median age at first marriage, by sex, 1890–2016

- - - Men   —— Women

SOURCE: "Figure MS-2. Median Age at First Marriage: 1890 to Present," in *Families and Living Arrangements: Marital Status*, U.S. Census Bureau, April 4, 2017, https://www.census.gov/content/dam/Census/library/visualizations/time-series/demo/families-and-households/ms-2.pdf (accessed August 4, 2017)

Grall, this percentage did not change significantly between 2001 and 2013. The poverty rate for all custodial families was 28.8% in 2013, nearly double the rate of 14.5% for the total U.S. population.

WORK EXPERIENCE

In strictly economic terms, the probability of a family living in poverty hinges on three primary factors: the size of the family, the number of workers, and the characteristics of the wage earners. As the number of wage earners in a family increases, the probability of poverty declines. The likelihood of a second wage earner is greatest in families that are headed by married couples; this is one of the key reasons that married-couple families consistently outperform single-parent families on measures of economic well-being. Additionally, in the late 20th and early 21st centuries many jobs in sectors that previously paid unskilled workers a middle-class wage, such as manufacturing, have been phased out as corporations move their operations overseas. As a result, many workers without a college education are forced into service jobs (e.g., jobs in food service, cleaning, and retail sales), some of which do not pay enough or offer workers enough hours to allow them to rise above the poverty line. Particularly in cases when a single parent must balance a low-paying job with the time-intensive demands of raising children, the likelihood of working and still failing to escape poverty increases markedly.

In 2015, 65.5% of all Americans aged 16 years and older (165.5 million of 252.8 million) worked at some point during the year. (See Table 2.12.) Approximately 92% (152.2 million) of those who had any labor force activity at all worked more than half of the weeks in the year (27 weeks or more), and among those who worked 27 weeks or more, 94.4% (143.7 million) lived at or above the poverty level. Some people who work less than this amount do so by choice; others do so because they cannot find full-time work or because they experience periods of unemployment.

In any event, employment does not always protect individuals and their families from poverty; 6.6% (11 million) of all those who worked lived in poverty in 2015, along with 21.9% (19.1 million) of the 16-and-older population that did not work. (See Table 2.12.) The poverty rate was higher for those who worked only 26 weeks or less (18.2%) than for those who worked 27 weeks or more (5.6%). The "working-poor rate" (as the U.S. Department of Labor calls the poverty rate of those who work 27 weeks or more per year) grew significantly during the Great Recession, jumping from 5.1% in 2007 to 7.2% in 2010. (See Table 2.13.) It remained at or above 7% through 2013, after which it dropped to 6.3% in 2014 and 5.6% in 2015.

Many poor children live in families in which one or more adults work. In *A Profile of the Working Poor, 2015* (April 2017, https://www.bls.gov/opub/reports/working-poor/2015/pdf/home.pdf), the U.S. Bureau of Labor Statistics (BLS) states that in 2015 there were 3.8 million families with children living below the poverty line despite having at least one family member who worked 27 weeks or

TABLE 2.9

Opposite-sex unmarried couples, by selected characteristics, 2016

[Numbers in thousands, except for percentages]

All opposite sex unmarried couples	Total		Presence of biological children			
			No biological children		At least one biological child under 18, of either partner	
	No.	%	No.	%	No.	%
Total	**8,075**	**100.0**	**5,044**	**100.0**	**3,031**	**100.0**
Age of male partner						
15–24 years	1,050	13.0	704	13.9	347	11.4
25–29 years	1,702	21.1	1,107	21.9	594	19.6
30–34 years	1,340	16.6	694	13.8	647	21.3
35–39 years	858	10.6	317	6.3	541	17.9
40–44 years	696	8.6	309	6.1	387	12.8
45–49 years	659	8.2	395	7.8	264	8.7
50–54 years	570	7.1	433	8.6	137	4.5
55–64 years	759	9.4	657	13.0	102	3.4
65+ years	440	5.4	429	8.5	11	0.4
Age of female partner						
15–24 years	1,569	19.4	1,023	20.3	546	18.0
25–29 years	1,805	22.4	1,121	22.2	684	22.6
30–34 years	1,222	15.1	583	11.6	639	21.1
35–39 years	781	9.7	278	5.5	503	16.6
40–44 years	695	8.6	312	6.2	383	12.6
45–49 years	564	7.0	392	7.8	172	5.7
50–54 years	481	6.0	404	8.0	77	2.5
55–64 years	594	7.4	569	11.3	25	0.8
65+ years	363	4.5	361	7.2	2	0.1
Age difference						
Male 10+ years older than female	930	11.5	551	10.9	379	12.5
Male 6–9 years older than female	915	11.3	543	10.8	372	12.3
Male 4–5 years older than female	844	10.5	518	10.3	326	10.8
Male 2–3 years older than female	1,366	16.9	821	16.3	546	18.0
Male and female within 1 year	2,460	30.5	1,613	32.0	847	27.9
Female 2–3 years older than male	542	6.7	325	6.4	217	7.2
Female 4–5 years older than male	321	4.0	219	4.4	101	3.3
Female 6–9 years older than male	373	4.6	216	4.3	157	5.2
Female 10+ years older than male	324	4.0	238	4.7	86	2.9
Race of male partner						
White alone—non-Hispanic	5,150	63.8	3,641	72.2	1,509	49.8
Black alone—non-Hispanic	984	12.2	516	10.2	467	15.4
Hispanic[a]	1,523	18.9	649	12.9	875	28.9
All remaining single races and all race combinations, non-Hispanic	417	5.2	238	4.7	180	5.9
Race of female partner						
White alone—non-Hispanic	5,175	64.1	3,624	71.8	1,551	51.2
Black alone—non-Hispanic	822	10.2	410	8.1	412	13.6
Hispanic[a]	1,547	19.2	691	13.7	856	28.3
All remaining single races and all race combinations, non-Hispanic	531	6.6	319	6.3	212	7.0
Race difference[b]						
Both white alone—non-Hispanic	4,520	56.0	3,217	63.8	1,304	43.0
Both black alone—non-Hispanic	704	8.7	339	6.7	366	12.1
Both other alone or any combination—non-Hispanic	213	2.6	110	2.2	103	3.4
Both Hispanic	1,150	14.2	446	8.8	704	23.2
Neither Hispanic	717	8.9	485	9.6	232	7.6
One Hispanic, other non-Hispanic	770	9.5	447	8.9	323	10.7
Race of male partner						
White alone	6,476	80.2	4,187	83.0	2,290	75.5
Black alone	1,059	13.1	559	11.1	500	16.5
Asian alone	201	2.5	128	2.5	73	2.4
All remaining single races and all race combinations	338	4.2	170	3.4	168	5.5
Race of female partner						
White alone	6,495	80.4	4,211	83.5	2,284	75.4
Black alone	918	11.4	458	9.1	461	15.2
Asian alone	280	3.5	174	3.4	106	3.5
All remaining single races and all race combinations	381	4.7	202	4.0	180	5.9

TABLE 2.9

Opposite-sex unmarried couples, by selected characteristics, 2016 [CONTINUED]

[Numbers in thousands, except for percentages]

All opposite sex unmarried couples	Total		Presence of biological children			
			No biological children		At least one biological child under 18, of either partner	
	No.	%	No.	%	No.	%
Race difference						
Both white alone	6,076	75.3	3,930	77.9	2,146	70.8
Both black alone	807	10.0	389	7.7	418	13.8
Both Asian alone	147	1.8	81	1.6	66	2.2
Both other alone or any comb.	169	2.1	71	1.4	98	3.2
Partners identify as different races	876	10.8	573	11.4	303	10.0
Origin of male partner						
Hispanic	1,523	18.9	649	12.9	875	28.9
Non-Hispanic	6,551	81.1	4,395	87.1	2,156	71.1
Origin of female partner						
Hispanic	1,547	19.2	691	13.7	856	28.3
Non-Hispanic	6,528	80.8	4,353	86.3	2,174	71.7
Origin difference						
Neither Hispanic	6,154	76.2	4,151	82.3	2,004	66.1
Both Hispanic	1,150	14.2	446	8.8	704	23.2
Male Hispanic, female not	373	4.6	203	4.0	171	5.6
Female Hispanic, male not	397	4.9	245	4.8	152	5.0
Labor force status of male partner						
Not in labor force	1,223	15.1	877	17.4	346	11.4
In labor force	6,852	84.9	4,167	82.6	2,685	88.6
Labor force status of female partner						
Not in labor force	2,152	26.7	1,170	23.2	982	32.4
In labor force	5,922	73.3	3,874	76.8	2,048	67.6
Labor force difference						
Both in labor force	5,331	66.0	3,512	69.6	1,819	60.0
Only male in labor force	1,521	18.8	655	13.0	867	28.6
Only female in labor force	591	7.3	362	7.2	230	7.6
Neither in labor force	631	7.8	515	10.2	116	3.8
Employment of male partner						
Not employed	1,665	20.6	1,095	21.7	570	18.8
Employed	6,409	79.4	3,948	78.3	2,461	81.2
Employment of female partner						
Not employed	2,473	30.6	1,363	27.0	1,110	36.6
Employed	5,602	69.4	3,681	73.0	1,921	63.4
Employment difference						
Both in labor force—both employed	4,775	59.1	3,206	63.6	1,569	51.8
Both in labor force—only male employed	221	2.7	142	2.8	79	2.6
Both in labor force—only female employed	267	3.3	132	2.6	135	4.4
Both in labor force—both unemployed	68	0.8	31	0.6	37	1.2
Male in labor force—male employed	1,414	17.5	600	11.9	814	26.9
Male in labor force—male unemployed	108	1.3	55	1.1	53	1.7
Female in labor force—female employed	560	6.9	342	6.8	217	7.2
Female in labor force—female unemployed	32	0.4	19	0.4	13	0.4
Not in labor force—not employed	631	7.8	515	10.2	116	3.8
Male education						
Not high school graduate	1,077	13.3	501	9.9	576	19.0
High school graduate	2,934	36.3	1,606	31.8	1,328	43.8
Some college	2,296	28.4	1,487	29.5	809	26.7
Bachelor's degree or higher	1,767	21.9	1,450	28.7	317	10.5
Female education						
Not high school graduate	873	10.8	369	7.3	504	16.6
High school graduate	2,440	30.2	1,385	27.5	1,056	34.8
Some college	2,688	33.3	1,610	31.9	1,078	35.6
Bachelor's degree or higher	2,073	25.7	1,680	33.3	393	13.0
Education difference						
Neither has Bachelor's degree	5,404	66.9	2,964	58.8	2,440	80.5
One has Bachelor's degree, other has less	1,501	18.6	1,030	20.4	470	15.5
Both have Bachelor's degree or more	1,170	14.5	1,050	20.8	120	4.0

TABLE 2.9

Opposite-sex unmarried couples, by selected characteristics, 2016 [CONTINUED]

[Numbers in thousands, except for percentages]

| | | | Presence of biological children | | | |
| | Total | | No biological children | | At least one biological child under 18, of either partner | |
All opposite sex unmarried couples	No.	%	No.	%	No.	%
Personal earnings of male partner						
Under $5,000 or loss	213	2.6	120	2.4	93	3.1
Without income	1,221	15.1	838	16.6	383	12.6
$5,000 to $9,999	280	3.5	162	3.2	119	3.9
$10,000 to $14,999	404	5.0	212	4.2	192	6.3
$15,000 to $19,999	496	6.1	273	5.4	223	7.3
$20,000 to $24,999	628	7.8	339	6.7	289	9.5
$25,000 to $29,999	709	8.8	365	7.2	344	11.3
$30,000 to $39,999	1,083	13.4	681	13.5	402	13.3
$40,000 to $49,999	902	11.2	578	11.5	324	10.7
$50,000 to $74,999	1,213	15.0	829	16.4	384	12.7
$75,000 to $99,999	420	5.2	277	5.5	143	4.7
$100,000 and over	505	6.3	370	7.3	135	4.5
Personal earnings of female partner						
Under $5,000 or loss	426	5.3	198	3.9	228	7.5
Without income	1,961	24.3	1,102	21.8	859	28.3
$5,000 to $9,999	422	5.2	240	4.8	182	6.0
$10,000 to $14,999	578	7.2	323	6.4	256	8.4
$15,000 to $19,999	609	7.5	364	7.2	245	8.1
$20,000 to $24,999	596	7.4	331	6.6	264	8.7
$25,000 to $29,999	580	7.2	371	7.4	209	6.9
$30,000 to $39,999	1,011	12.5	710	14.1	301	9.9
$40,000 to $49,999	693	8.6	466	9.2	227	7.5
$50,000 to $74,999	766	9.5	593	11.8	173	5.7
$75,000 to $99,999	218	2.7	173	3.4	44	1.5
$100,000 and over	215	2.7	173	3.4	42	1.4
Personal earnings difference						
Male earns $50,000+ more	913	11.3	565	11.2	348	11.5
Male earns $30,000–$49,999 more	980	12.1	593	11.8	387	12.8
Male earns $10,000–$29,999 more	1,857	23.0	986	19.6	871	28.7
Male earns $5,000–$9,999 more	546	6.8	326	6.5	220	7.3
Male earns within $4,999 of female	1,692	21.0	1,180	23.4	512	16.9
Female earns $5,000–$9,999 more	404	5.0	272	5.4	132	4.4
Female earns $10,000–$29,999 more	983	12.2	605	12.0	378	12.5
Female earns $30,000–$49,999 more	441	5.5	312	6.2	129	4.3
Female earns $50,000+ more	259	3.2	205	4.1	54	1.8

[a]Hispanics may be of any race.
[b]"White" refers to Non-Hispanic white alone, "black" to Non-Hispanic black alone, and "other" to Non-Hispanic other alone or in combination.

SOURCE: "Table UC3. Opposite Sex Unmarried Couples by Presence of Biological Children under 18, and Age, Earnings, Education, and Race and Hispanic Origin of Both Partners: 2016," in *America's Families and Living Arrangements: 2016*, U.S. Census Bureau, April 6, 2017, https://www2.census.gov/programs-surveys/demo/tables/families/2016/cps-2016/tabuc3-all.xls (accessed August 4, 2017)

more that year. (See Table 2.14.) Families with children that were headed by single women (24.8%) were more likely than those headed by single men (15.3%) or married couples (6.2%) to be living below the poverty level despite having a family member in the workforce for most of 2015.

In 2015, 4.5 million working women and 4.1 million working men had incomes below the poverty level. (See Table 2.15.) Working women had a higher poverty rate (6.3%) than working men (5%). Approximately 5.7 million (67.1%) of the working poor were white, 2.5 million (29.4%) were Hispanic, 2.1 million (24.2%) were African American, and 364,000 (4.3%) were Asian American. Although whites constituted the bulk of the working poor, African Americans and Hispanics experienced poverty while employed at much higher rates than whites. In 2015, 11.2% of African Americans in the labor force were below the poverty line, as were 10.1% of Hispanics, compared with 4.8% of whites and 4.1% of Asian Americans.

Workers between the ages of 16 and 24 years were much more likely to be in poverty than older workers in 2015. Approximately 10.8% of workers aged 16 to 19 years and 12.2% of workers aged 20 to 24 years did not make enough money to rise above the poverty line, compared with 6.6% of workers aged 25 to 34 years and even lower rates for older cohorts. (See Table 2.14.) Much of the reason for this is that many younger workers are still in school and/or work at part-time or entry-level jobs that often do not pay well. In general, as age increases, the likelihood of being both in the labor force and poor decreases.

TABLE 2.10

Single-parent family groups with own children under 18, by marital status and demographic characteristics, 2016

[Numbers in thousands, except for percentages]

	One-parent unmarried family groups		Maintained by father										Maintained by mother									
			Total		Never married		Divorced		Separated[b]		Widowed		Total		Never married		Divorced		Separated[b]		Widowed	
	N	%	N	%	N	%	N	%	N	%	N	%	N	%	N	%	N	%	N	%	N	%
All family groups	11,814	100.0	2,034	100.0	778	38.2	809	39.8	330	16.2	117	5.7	9,781	100.0	4,822	49.3	2,945	30.1	1,668	17.0	346	3.5
Region																						
Northeast	1,935	16.4	292	100.0	128	43.8	86	29.3	59	20.3	19	6.6	1,643	100.0	850	51.8	430	26.2	291	17.7	72	4.4
Midwest	2,472	20.9	482	100.0	188	39.0	202	41.9	60	12.5	32	6.6	1,991	100.0	1,038	52.1	642	32.2	247	12.4	64	3.2
South	4,995	42.3	768	100.0	278	36.1	337	43.9	117	15.3	36	4.6	4,228	100.0	2,070	49.0	1,221	28.9	809	19.1	128	3.0
West	2,413	20.4	491	100.0	184	37.5	184	37.5	93	18.9	30	6.1	1,922	100.0	865	45.0	653	34.0	322	16.7	82	4.3
Size of family group																						
Two members	5,276	44.7	1,157	100.0	502	43.4	453	39.1	150	13.0	52	4.5	4,119	100.0	2,330	56.6	1,153	28.0	515	12.5	121	2.9
Three members	3,743	31.7	581	100.0	169	29.2	254	43.8	111	19.0	47	8.0	3,162	100.0	1,390	44.0	1,068	33.8	582	18.4	122	3.9
Four members	1,729	14.6	197	100.0	65	33.1	74	37.5	45	22.8	13	6.6	1,531	100.0	636	41.5	494	32.2	334	21.8	67	4.4
Five members	706	6.0	70	100.0	21	30.6	25	35.3	21	30.2	3	3.9	636	100.0	320	50.4	152	23.9	145	22.7	19	3.0
Six or more members	360	3.0	29	100.0	20	67.5	4	12.7	3	11.7	2	8.1	331	100.0	145	43.9	78	23.5	92	27.7	16	4.9
Age of reference person																						
Under 20 years	169	1.4	13	100.0	13	100.0	—	—	—	—	—	—	157	100.0	144	92.2	3	1.6	10	6.2	—	—
20–24 years	1,081	9.1	99	100.0	99	90.0	4	3.6	7	6.4	—	—	970	100.0	849	87.5	50	5.2	69	7.1	2	0.2
25–29 years	1,779	15.1	230	100.0	161	70.2	43	18.7	26	11.1	—	—	1,549	100.0	1,128	72.8	166	10.7	238	15.4	17	1.1
30–34 years	2,057	17.4	306	100.0	172	56.3	74	24.1	57	18.5	3	1.1	1,751	100.0	1,025	58.6	379	21.6	319	18.2	28	1.6
35–39 years	2,196	18.6	368	100.0	145	39.4	141	38.4	70	18.9	12	3.3	1,827	100.0	811	44.4	601	32.9	358	19.6	57	3.1
40–44 years	1,917	16.2	350	100.0	73	20.9	185	52.9	75	21.3	17	4.9	1,566	100.0	464	29.6	706	45.1	322	20.5	74	4.7
45–54 years	2,111	17.9	489	100.0	89	18.2	272	55.6	74	15.2	54	11.0	1,621	100.0	309	19.1	868	53.5	320	19.7	124	7.7
55+ years	505	4.3	166	100.0	25	14.8	89	53.7	22	13.4	30	18.2	338	100.0	91	26.9	172	50.9	32	9.4	43	12.8
Family income																						
Family income under $10,000	1,684	14.3	173	100.0	85	48.7	50	29.0	29	17.0	9	5.3	1,510	100.0	935	61.9	272	18.0	283	18.8	20	1.3
$10,000 to $14,999	903	7.6	90	100.0	39	43.5	26	28.7	19	20.7	6	7.2	813	100.0	411	50.6	214	26.3	157	19.3	31	3.8
$15,000 to $19,999	879	7.4	117	100.0	47	40.5	47	40.2	17	14.1	6	5.1	763	100.0	428	56.2	170	22.2	145	19.0	20	2.6
$20,000 to $24,999	1,029	8.7	116	100.0	54	46.3	41	35.1	10	8.9	11	9.7	913	100.0	489	53.5	248	27.2	148	16.2	28	3.1
$25,000 to $29,999	892	7.6	126	100.0	67	53.1	43	33.9	9	7.4	7	5.5	766	100.0	381	49.7	214	28.0	143	18.7	28	3.6
$30,000 to $39,999	1,440	12.2	255	100.0	99	38.9	95	37.1	49	19.1	12	4.8	1,185	100.0	578	48.8	387	32.7	177	15.0	43	3.6
$40,000 to $49,999	1,094	9.3	228	100.0	92	40.4	90	39.7	33	14.4	13	5.6	867	100.0	387	44.7	313	36.1	140	16.1	27	3.1
$50,000 to $74,999	1,775	15.0	343	100.0	113	32.9	148	43.1	68	19.9	14	4.1	1,430	100.0	577	40.3	536	37.5	258	18.0	59	4.1
$75,000 to $99,999	854	7.2	217	100.0	72	33.1	95	43.9	35	16.0	15	6.9	638	100.0	254	39.9	266	41.7	80	12.5	38	5.9
$100,000 and over	1,263	10.7	368	100.0	110	29.9	174	47.3	61	16.6	23	6.2	896	100.0	381	42.5	325	36.3	137	15.3	53	5.9
Poverty status																						
Below poverty level	3,675	31.1	385	100.0	187	48.4	114	29.7	60	15.6	24	6.2	3,290	100.0	1,879	57.1	689	20.9	647	19.7	75	2.3
At or above poverty level	8,140	68.9	1,648	100.0	591	35.9	694	42.1	270	16.4	93	5.6	6,492	100.0	2,944	45.3	2,256	34.8	1,021	15.7	271	4.2
Number of own children[a] under 18																						
One own child under 18	6,613	56.0	1,357	100.0	563	41.5	541	39.9	186	13.7	67	4.9	5,256	100.0	2,806	53.4	1,584	30.1	680	12.9	186	3.5
Two own children under 18	3,455	29.2	496	100.0	143	28.8	206	41.5	106	21.3	41	8.3	2,960	100.0	1,313	44.4	938	31.7	594	20.1	115	3.9
Three own children under 18	1,240	10.5	145	100.0	56	38.8	52	36.1	30	20.4	7	4.7	1,095	100.0	472	43.1	317	29.0	278	25.4	28	2.5
Four or more own children under 18	506	4.3	36	100.0	15	42.2	10	27.4	9	25.0	2	5.4	470	100.0	232	49.3	106	22.5	115	24.5	17	3.7

TABLE 2.10

Single-parent family groups with own children under 18, by marital status and demographic characteristics, 2016 [CONTINUED]

[Numbers in thousands, except for percentages]

Characteristic	One-parent unmarried family groups N	%	Maintained by father — Total N	%	Never married N	%	Divorced N	%	Separated[b] N	%	Widowed N	%	Maintained by mother — Total N	%	Never married N	%	Divorced N	%	Separated[b] N	%	Widowed N	%
Own children 6–17 years																						
Without own children 6–17	2,723	23.1	448	100.0	302	67.4	83	18.5	58	12.9	5	1.2	2,275	100.0	1,737	76.3	264	11.6	254	11.2	20	0.9
One own child 6–17	5,533	46.8	1,086	100.0	343	31.5	499	45.9	180	16.6	64	5.9	4,447	100.0	1,927	43.3	1,603	36.0	724	16.3	193	4.3
Two own children 6–17	2,563	21.7	392	100.0	102	26.1	180	45.9	69	17.6	41	10.5	2,171	100.0	820	37.8	790	36.4	462	21.3	99	4.6
Three own children 6–17	778	6.6	83	100.0	23	27.2	38	45.7	18	22.0	4	5.1	695	100.0	277	39.8	227	32.7	167	24.0	24	3.5
Four or more own children 6–17	218	1.8	25	100.0	9	34.5	9	37.8	5	20.1	2	7.6	192	100.0	61	31.9	61	31.7	61	31.5	9	4.9
Own children 12–17 years																						
Without own children 12–17	6,233	52.8	1,021	100.0	527	51.6	284	27.8	184	18.0	26	2.6	5,212	100.0	3,299	63.3	1,061	20.4	757	14.5	95	1.8
One own child 12–17	4,227	35.8	808	100.0	203	25.1	421	52.0	113	14.0	71	8.8	3,418	100.0	1,180	34.5	1,415	41.4	642	18.8	181	5.3
Two own children 12–17	1,147	9.7	179	100.0	44	24.7	89	49.6	28	15.4	18	10.3	968	100.0	274	28.3	410	42.3	226	23.4	58	6.0
Three or more own children 12–17	207	1.8	24	100.0	3	12.0	15	63.4	5	21.3	1	3.3	183	100.0	69	37.8	60	32.5	42	23.0	12	6.7
Own children 6–11 years																						
Without own children 6–11	6,615	56.0	1,224	100.0	484	39.6	510	41.7	158	12.9	72	5.9	5,391	100.0	2,745	50.9	1,642	30.5	795	14.7	209	3.9
One own child 6–11	3,889	32.9	655	100.0	246	37.5	236	36.1	137	21.0	36	5.5	3,233	100.0	1,548	47.9	949	29.3	627	19.4	109	3.4
Two own children 6–11	1,100	9.3	137	100.0	40	29.1	58	42.2	32	23.5	7	5.3	963	100.0	438	45.5	310	32.2	191	19.8	24	2.5
Three or more own children 6–11	211	1.8	17	100.0	8	46.8	4	26.3	3	15.7	2	11.2	194	100.0	91	46.7	44	22.9	55	28.4	4	2.0
Own children under 6 years																						
Without own children under 6	7,367	62.4	1,428	100.0	408	28.6	693	48.5	221	15.5	106	7.4	5,939	100.0	2,264	38.1	2,324	39.1	1,058	17.8	293	4.9
One own child under 6	3,511	29.7	506	100.0	310	61.2	96	19.0	89	17.6	11	2.1	3,005	100.0	2,014	67.0	511	17.0	442	14.7	38	1.3
Two own children under 6	823	7.0	91	100.0	53	58.3	18	20.1	20	21.6	—	—	732	100.0	479	65.5	94	12.8	147	20.1	12	1.6
Three or more own children under 6	114	1.0	8	100.0	6	72.7	2	22.6	—	—	—	—	104	100.0	65	62.4	16	15.4	21	19.8	2	2.3
Own children under 3 years																						
Without own children under 3	9,525	80.6	1,743	100.0	567	32.5	777	44.6	286	16.4	113	6.5	7,782	100.0	3,380	43.4	2,720	35.0	1,363	17.5	319	4.1
One own child under 3	2,097	17.7	267	100.0	192	71.8	30	11.2	42	15.7	3	1.3	1,829	100.0	1,320	72.2	206	11.2	276	15.1	27	1.5
Two or more own children under 3	193	1.6	22	100.0	18	82.8	2	8.2	2	8.9	—	—	171	100.0	123	72.1	20	11.6	28	16.4	—	—
Age of own children																						
With own children under 18 years	11,814	100.0	2,034	100.0	778	38.2	809	39.8	330	16.2	117	5.7	9,781	100.0	4,822	49.3	2,945	30.1	1,668	17.0	346	3.5
Without own children under 12 years	3,591	30.4	761	100.0	177	23.2	425	56.0	94	12.3	65	8.5	2,831	100.0	863	30.5	1,296	45.8	491	17.3	181	6.4
With own children under 12 years	8,223	69.6	1,272	100.0	601	47.2	383	30.1	236	18.6	52	4.1	6,950	100.0	3,959	57.0	1,649	23.7	1,177	16.9	165	2.4
Without own children under 6 years	7,367	62.4	1,428	100.0	408	28.6	693	48.5	221	15.5	106	7.4	5,939	100.0	2,264	38.1	2,324	39.1	1,058	17.8	293	4.9
With own children under 6 years	4,447	37.6	605	100.0	369	61.0	116	19.2	109	18.0	11	1.8	3,842	100.0	2,558	66.6	621	16.2	610	15.9	53	1.4
Without own children under 5 years	8,010	67.8	1,510	100.0	445	29.4	718	47.6	240	15.9	107	7.1	6,500	100.0	2,571	39.6	2,486	38.2	1,140	17.5	303	4.7
With own children under 5 years	3,804	32.2	523	100.0	333	63.6	91	17.4	89	17.1	10	1.9	3,280	100.0	2,251	68.6	459	14.0	527	16.1	43	1.3
Without own children under 3 years	9,525	80.6	1,743	100.0	567	32.5	777	44.6	286	16.4	113	6.5	7,782	100.0	3,380	43.4	2,720	35.0	1,363	17.5	319	4.1
With own children under 3 years	2,290	19.4	290	100.0	211	72.7	32	11.0	44	15.2	3	1.2	1,999	100.0	1,443	72.1	225	11.3	304	15.2	27	1.4
Without own children under 1 year	11,136	94.3	1,943	100.0	704	36.2	804	41.4	320	16.5	115	5.9	9,193	100.0	4,358	47.4	2,898	31.5	1,594	17.3	343	3.7
With own children under 1 year	678	5.7	91	100.0	74	81.8	5	5.1	10	11.2	2	1.9	587	100.0	464	79.0	47	8.0	73	12.5	3	0.5
Without own children 3–5 years	9,109	77.1	1,676	100.0	589	35.2	717	42.8	260	15.5	110	6.5	7,432	100.0	3,377	45.4	2,487	33.5	1,259	16.9	309	4.2
With own children 3–5 years	2,705	22.9	356	100.0	188	52.8	91	25.6	70	19.5	7	2.1	2,350	100.0	1,446	61.5	458	19.5	409	17.4	37	1.6
Without own children 6–11 years	6,615	56.0	1,224	100.0	484	39.6	510	41.7	158	12.9	72	5.9	5,391	100.0	2,745	50.9	1,642	30.5	795	14.7	209	3.9
With own children 6–11 years	5,200	44.0	810	100.0	294	36.3	299	36.9	172	21.3	45	5.6	4,391	100.0	2,077	47.3	1,304	29.7	873	19.9	137	3.1
Without own children 12–17 years	6,233	52.8	1,021	100.0	527	51.6	284	27.8	184	18.0	26	2.6	5,212	100.0	3,299	63.3	1,061	20.4	757	14.5	95	1.8
With own children 12–17 years	5,582	47.2	1,011	100.0	250	24.7	525	51.9	146	14.4	90	8.9	4,570	100.0	1,523	33.3	1,885	41.2	911	19.9	251	5.5
Without own children 6–17 years	2,723	23.1	448	100.0	302	67.4	83	18.5	58	12.9	5	1.2	2,275	100.0	1,737	76.3	264	11.6	254	11.2	20	0.9
With own children 6–17 years	9,091	76.9	1,585	100.0	476	30.0	726	45.8	272	17.2	111	7.0	7,505	100.0	3,085	41.1	2,681	35.7	1,413	18.8	326	4.3

TABLE 2.10

Single-parent family groups with own children under 18, by marital status and demographic characteristics, 2016 [CONTINUED]

[Numbers in thousands, except for percentages]

| | Maintained by father | | | | | | | | | | | | Maintained by mother | | | | | | | | | |
| | One-parent unmarried family groups | | Total | | Never married | | Divorced | | Separated[b] | | Widowed | | Total | | Never married | | Divorced | | Separated[b] | | Widowed | |
	N	%	N	%	N	%	N	%	N	%	N	%	N	%	N	%	N	%	N	%	N	%
Own children by age groups																						
Children in two or more age groups	4,401	37.2	512	100.0	147	28.7	206	40.3	117	22.8	42	8.3	3,888	100.0	1,669	42.9	1,210	31.1	857	22.1	152	3.9
Families with children 12–17 only	2,805	23.7	662	100.0	174	26.3	364	55.0	72	10.9	52	7.8	2,144	100.0	664	31.0	993	46.3	353	16.5	134	6.2
Families with children 6–11 only	2,262	19.1	448	100.0	181	40.4	163	36.3	87	19.4	17	3.9	1,815	100.0	969	53.4	526	29.0	275	15.2	45	2.5
Families with children 3–5 only	1,123	9.5	220	100.0	126	57.4	62	28.2	28	12.7	4	1.7	903	100.0	678	75.1	137	15.2	79	8.7	9	1.0
Families with children under 3 only	1,224	10.4	192	100.0	150	78.2	14	7.2	26	13.7	2	0.9	1,032	100.0	843	81.6	80	7.8	103	10.0	6	0.6
Under 6 only	2,723	23.1	448	100.0	302	67.4	83	18.5	58	12.9	5	1.2	2,275	100.0	1,737	76.3	264	11.6	254	11.2	20	0.9
Some under 6, some 6–17	1,724	14.6	158	100.0	68	42.7	33	21.2	52	32.8	5	3.3	1,567	100.0	821	52.4	357	22.8	356	22.7	33	2.1
6–17 only	7,367	62.4	1,428	100.0	408	28.6	693	48.5	221	15.5	106	7.4	5,939	100.0	2,264	38.1	2,324	39.1	1,058	17.8	293	4.9

N = numbers.
— = represents or rounds to zero.

[a]"Own children" excludes ever-married children under 18 years.

[b]Includes "married spouse absent."

SOURCE: "Table FG6. One-Parent Unmarried Family Groups with Own Children under 18, by Marital Status of the Reference Person: 2016," in *America's Families and Living Arrangements: 2016*, U.S. Census Bureau, April 6, 2017, https://www2.census.gov/programs-surveys/demo/tables/families/2016/cps-2016/tabfg6-all_one.xls (accessed August 4, 2017)

TABLE 2.11

Living arrangements of children and marital status of parents, by selected characteristics, 2016

[Numbers in thousands]

	Total	Living with both parents		Living with mother only					Living with father only					Living with neither parent
		Married to each other	Not married to each other	Married spouse absent	Widowed	Divorced	Separated	Never married	Married spouse absent	Widowed	Divorced	Separated	Never married	No parent present
All children	**73,745**	**47,724**	**2,955**	**878**	**606**	**5,131**	**2,389**	**8,219**	**160**	**174**	**1,164**	**366**	**1,142**	**2,836**
Male	37,569	24,597	1,447	446	282	2,559	1,169	4,081	85	88	645	174	591	1,406
Female	36,176	23,127	1,508	433	324	2,571	1,221	4,137	75	87	520	192	551	1,430
Both sexes														
Total	**73,745**	**47,724**	**2,955**	**878**	**606**	**5,131**	**2,389**	**8,219**	**160**	**174**	**1,164**	**366**	**1,142**	**2,836**
Age of child														
Under 1 year	3,877	2,520	441	20	▲	61	72	546	1	2	6	11	92	101
1–2 years	8,067	5,222	605	93	26	212	202	1,205	11	2	30	28	168	263
3–5 years	11,887	7,708	612	120	42	528	359	1,644	22	8	106	64	216	457
6–8 years	12,410	7,947	517	162	64	783	425	1,569	29	24	158	85	193	455
9–11 years	12,401	8,123	353	151	102	1,015	436	1,260	28	30	212	64	174	453
12–14 years	12,322	8,173	226	151	129	1,099	458	1,075	32	43	251	67	166	452
15–17 years	12,780	8,031	202	180	239	1,432	437	919	37	65	401	47	133	656
Race														
White alone	53,628	37,819	2,035	494	424	3,766	1,546	3,501	114	140	959	285	776	1,769
Black alone	11,101	3,785	509	269	115	907	637	3,794	25	15	121	43	235	648
Asian alone	3,758	3,248	83	52	34	84	38	71	14	13	12	5	23	81
All remaining single races and all race combinations	5,258	2,872	328	64	33	374	168	854	8	7	72	34	109	338
Race														
Hispanic*	18,231	10,990	1,262	269	114	993	961	2,269	57	40	189	90	324	673
White alone, non-Hispanic	37,951	28,063	956	275	334	2,945	704	1,783	58	102	825	198	501	1,207
All remaining single races and all race combinations, non-hispanic	17,563	8,672	737	334	158	1,193	725	4,167	45	32	150	77	317	956
Race														
White alone or in combination with one or more other races	57,070	39,778	2,264	535	454	4,004	1,663	4,008	119	143	1,022	303	831	1,945
Other	16,675	7,946	691	343	152	1,127	726	4,211	41	31	142	63	311	891
Race														
Black alone or in combination with one or more other races	13,150	4,684	645	293	140	1,095	698	4,282	26	18	146	53	267	803
Other	60,595	43,040	2,310	585	466	4,036	1,691	3,936	134	156	1,019	313	875	2,034
Race														
Asian alone or in combination with one or more other races	4,702	3,964	136	58	36	123	67	106	15	13	25	21	35	102
Other	69,044	43,760	2,819	820	570	5,008	2,323	8,113	145	161	1,139	344	1,106	2,735

TABLE 2.11

Living arrangements of children and marital status of parents, by selected characteristics, 2016 [CONTINUED]

[Numbers in thousands]

	Total	Living with both parents		Living with mother only					Living with father only					Living with neither parent
		Married to each other	Not married to each other	Married spouse absent	Widowed	Divorced	Separated	Never married	Married spouse absent	Widowed	Divorced	Separated	Never married	No parent present
Presence of siblings														
None	15,324	7,278	719	146	126	1,206	355	2,482	41	47	448	93	528	1,856
One sibling	28,415	19,689	1,019	321	232	2,023	854	2,759	52	78	451	156	311	470
Two siblings	18,137	12,703	661	221	137	1,244	699	1,643	43	32	203	86	193	273
Three siblings	7,500	5,092	308	106	62	404	321	901	17	12	54	30	58	134
Four siblings	2,734	1,806	149	45	22	187	110	327	2	5	2	1	41	37
Five or more siblings	1,636	1,156	99	39	27	68	50	108	5	—	6	—	12	66
Presence of parent's unmarried partner														
Child's parent does not have opposite sex partner	68,566	47,724	207	860	532	4,430	2,273	7,456	144	158	940	305	701	2,836
Child's parent has opposite sex partner	5,179	X	2,748	18	74	701	117	763	16	17	224	61	441	X
Partner is also other parent	2,748	X	2,748	X	X	X	X	X	X	X	X	X	X	X
Partner is not other parent	2,431	X	X	18	74	701	117	763	16	17	224	61	441	X
Highest education of either parent														
No parents present	2,836	X	X	X	X	X	X	X	X	X	X	X	X	2,836
Less than 9th grade	2,314	1,379	170	69	26	123	163	288	7	9	24	11	43	X
9th to 12th grade, no diploma	4,470	1,861	236	86	40	269	347	1,306	40	12	70	35	167	X
High school graduate	14,894	7,468	997	255	190	1,156	689	3,063	51	59	363	142	461	X
Some college or AA degree	19,852	11,776	1,092	265	209	2,017	844	2,766	25	37	368	107	346	X
Bachelor's degree	16,068	13,280	316	127	88	1,053	227	552	20	41	217	44	103	X
Prof. or graduate degree	13,311	11,960	144	77	52	513	119	243	17	15	121	28	22	X
Parents labor force status														
Father in labor force, mother not present	2,574	X	X	X	X	X	X	X	120	132	1,020	313	989	X
Father not in labor force, mother not present	432	X	X	X	X	X	X	X	40	43	144	53	152	X
Mother in labor force, father not present	12,961	X	X	612	366	4,231	1,800	5,952	X	X	X	X	X	X
Mother not in labor force, father not present	4,262	X	X	266	240	899	589	2,267	X	X	X	X	X	X
Mother and father in labor force	30,588	29,046	1,542	X	X	X	X	X	X	X	X	X	X	X
Father in labor force, mother not in labor force	15,831	14,794	1,037	X	X	X	X	X	X	X	X	X	X	X
Mother in labor force, father not in labor force	2,518	2,284	235	X	X	X	X	X	X	X	X	X	X	X
Father not in labor force, mother not in labor force	1,741	1,600	141	X	X	X	X	X	X	X	X	X	X	X
No parents present	2,836	X	X	X	X	X	X	X	X	X	X	X	X	2,836
Family income														
Under $2,500	2,684	341	435	75	18	176	200	649	14	5	37	19	55	659
$2,500 to $4,999	717	104	48	30	7	82	81	302	—	—	7	6	19	31
$5,000 to $7,499	1,052	217	84	38	9	123	49	417	—	4	10	7	38	55
$7,500 to $9,999	1,144	151	100	28	7	125	86	491	1	3	12	3	54	85
$10,000 to $12,499	1,513	283	154	21	33	217	195	421	10	6	27	3	31	113
$12,500 to $14,999	1,035	230	60	21	22	170	116	322	4	—	17	7	23	44
$15,000 to $19,999	3,194	1,068	250	122	42	367	226	809	8	8	59	21	60	155
$20,000 to $24,999	3,462	1,238	254	110	41	468	185	849	4	17	62	15	95	124
$25,000 to $29,999	3,233	1,291	294	78	59	353	216	662	6	13	57	8	90	106

TABLE 2.11

Living arrangements of children and marital status of parents, by selected characteristics, 2016 [CONTINUED]

[Numbers in thousands]

	Total	Living with both parents		Living with mother only					Living with father only					Living with neither parent
		Married to each other	Not married to each other	Married spouse absent	Widowed	Divorced	Separated	Never married	Married spouse absent	Widowed	Divorced	Separated	Never married	No parent present
$30,000 to $39,999	6,333	3,314	341	62	72	657	280	958	37	20	148	63	150	232
$40,000 to $49,999	5,473	3,274	255	87	50	535	157	620	3	18	133	45	137	161
$50,000 to $74,999	11,833	8,300	338	101	102	897	331	842	25	19	239	77	170	393
$75,000 to $99,999	8,857	7,238	138	52	63	424	85	345	24	24	118	24	78	243
$100,00 and over	23,216	20,677	204	54	81	538	185	531	23	37	238	69	143	436
Health insurance coverage														
Covered by health insurance	69,941	45,559	2,713	800	571	4,912	2,244	7,783	146	154	1,090	334	1,069	2,564
Not covered by health insurance	3,804	2,166	242	78	35	219	145	436	14	20	74	32	72	272
Poverty status														
Below 100% of poverty	14,799	4,652	1,300	437	158	1,448	1,072	3,836	37	36	179	67	332	1,245
100% to 199% of poverty	16,152	8,804	842	227	172	1,489	722	2,531	56	44	282	100	316	566
200% of poverty and above	42,793	34,269	813	214	276	2,193	595	1,851	67	95	703	199	493	1,025
Household food stamp receipt														
No	58,509	42,784	1,929	514	436	3,562	1,237	3,747	111	145	972	300	808	1,962
Yes	15,236	4,940	1,026	364	170	1,569	1,152	4,472	49	29	192	66	334	875
Household public asst receipt														
No	71,266	47,121	2,857	836	590	4,911	2,178	7,306	158	170	1,152	352	1,104	2,531
Yes	2,479	603	98	43	16	219	211	913	2	5	12	14	38	305
100 percent of poverty														
Below 100% of poverty	14,799	4,652	1,300	437	158	1,448	1,072	3,836	37	36	179	67	332	1,245
100% of poverty and above	58,946	43,073	1,655	441	448	3,682	1,318	4,383	123	138	985	299	809	1,592
125 percent of poverty														
Below 125% of poverty	18,995	6,673	1,538	516	200	1,843	1,309	4,628	66	46	240	84	414	1,436
125% of poverty and above	54,750	41,051	1,417	362	406	3,287	1,081	3,591	94	128	924	282	728	1,400
Household tenure														
Own/buying	44,492	34,191	995	361	353	2,336	757	2,210	77	115	732	174	491	1,701
Rent	28,556	13,159	1,931	505	245	2,743	1,585	5,904	77	49	417	187	643	1,110
No cash rent	697	375	29	13	7	53	47	105	6	10	15	5	8	25

X Not applicable.
Dash ("—") represents or rounds to zero.
*Hispanics may be of any race.
Notes: Excludes children in group quarters, and those who are a family reference person or spouse.

SOURCE: Adapted from "Table C3. Living Arrangements of Children under 18 Years and Marital Status of Parents, by Age, Sex, Race, and Hispanic Origin and Selected Characteristics of the Child for All Children: 2016," in *America's Families and Living Arrangements: 2016*, U.S. Census Bureau, April 6, 2017, https://www2.census.gov/programs-surveys/demo/tables/families/2016/cps-2016/tabc3-all.xls (accessed August 4, 2017)

FIGURE 2.2

Poverty status of custodial parents, 1993–2013

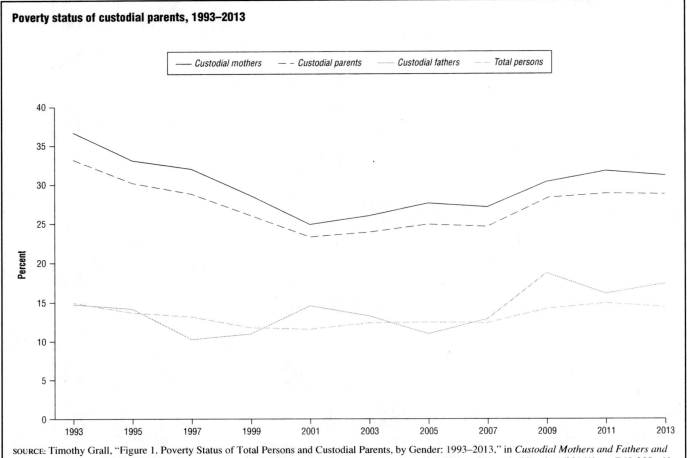

SOURCE: Timothy Grall, "Figure 1. Poverty Status of Total Persons and Custodial Parents, by Gender: 1993–2013," in *Custodial Mothers and Fathers and Their Child Support: 2013*, U.S. Census Bureau, January 2016, https://www.census.gov/content/dam/Census/library/publications/2016/demo/P60-255.pdf (accessed August 4, 2017)

Educational levels typically correlate directly with the risk of poverty among workers. Among workers in the labor force for at least 27 weeks in 2015, 16.2% of those with less than a high school diploma fell below the poverty level, compared with 7.6% of high school graduates with no college experience, 5.6% of workers with some college or an associate's degree, and 1.7% of workers with a bachelor's degree or higher. (See Table 2.16.) African American and Hispanic workers at all education levels had higher poverty rates than white workers. Working women tended to have higher poverty rates than did working men, but there were exceptions among Asian Americans, African Americans with less than a high school degree, and workers with bachelor's degrees or higher. The highest poverty rate for any group was for African American women workers with one to three years of high school (34.2%), followed by Hispanic women workers with one to three years of high school (25.8%).

Finally, labor market conditions play a major role in whether a working family lives in poverty. Three primary labor market problems contributed to poverty among workers in 2015: low earnings, unemployment, and involuntary part-time employment (a situation where an individual wants to work full time but lacks an opportunity to do so). Most full-time workers (84%) did not experience any of these three problems in 2015, and very few workers who experienced none of these problems (0.7%) were poor. (See Table 2.17.) By contrast, 21.6% of workers who had low earnings (and neither of the other two problems) lived in poverty. Unemployment alone accounted for the poverty of 7% of workers and involuntary part-time work for 2.3%. However, it was the combination of two or more factors that had the most devastating effect on families. Workers who experienced both unemployment and low earnings had a poverty rate of 41.4%, as did 40.3% of those who experienced all three labor market problems.

EDUCATION

Income and poverty levels correlate strongly with an individual's level of education. The BLS publishes quarterly statistics about the earnings of workers by various characteristics, including education. For example, in the press release "Usual Weekly Earnings of Wage and

TABLE 2.12

Poverty status and work experience of people in families and unrelated individuals, 2015

[Numbers in thousands]

Poverty status and work experience	Total people	In married-couple families[a]				In families maintained by women[b]			In families maintained by men[b]			Unrelated individuals
		Husbands	Wives	Related children under 18 years	Other relatives	Householder	Related children under 18 years	Other relatives	Householder	Related children under 18 years	Other relatives	
Total												
All people	252,766	59,618	60,205	5,484	21,742	15,595	2,288	14,416	6,265	711	6,873	59,568
With labor force activity	165,495	45,164	37,268	1,368	13,651	10,897	534	8,744	4,807	153	4,447	38,462
1 to 26 weeks	13,265	1,640	2,791	776	2,646	751	297	1,070	253	68	464	2,509
27 weeks or more	152,230	43,523	34,477	592	11,005	10,145	237	7,674	4,554	85	3,984	35,953
With no labor force activity	87,271	14,454	22,937	4,116	8,091	4,698	1,754	5,672	1,458	558	2,426	21,106
At or above poverty level												
All people	222,699	56,411	56,960	5,052	20,754	11,196	1,539	11,957	5,339	571	6,227	46,693
With labor force activity	154,515	43,537	36,479	1,337	13,342	8,579	410	7,887	4,317	145	4,254	34,228
1 to 26 weeks	10,846	1,511	2,584	758	2,554	314	208	827	181	63	434	1,412
27 weeks or more	143,670	42,027	33,895	579	10,788	8,265	201	7,060	4,136	82	3,821	32,817
With no labor force activity	68,183	12,874	20,481	3,715	7,412	2,617	1,130	4,070	1,022	426	1,972	12,464
Below poverty level												
All people	30,067	3,207	3,245	432	987	4,399	749	2,460	926	140	647	12,876
With labor force activity	10,980	1,626	789	32	309	2,317	125	858	490	8	193	4,234
1 to 26 weeks	2,420	130	208	19	91	437	89	243	72	5	30	1,097
27 weeks or more	8,560	1,497	581	13	218	1,880	35	615	418	4	163	3,137
With no labor force activity	19,087	1,581	2,456	401	679	2,082	624	1,602	435	132	454	8,642
Rate[c]												
All people	11.9	5.4	5.4	7.9	4.5	28.2	32.7	17.1	14.8	19.7	9.4	21.6
With labor force activity	6.6	3.6	2.1	2.3	2.3	21.3	23.3	9.8	10.2	5.4	4.3	11.0
1 to 26 weeks	18.2	7.9	7.4	2.4	3.4	58.2	30.0	22.7	28.5	—	6.5	43.7
27 weeks or more	5.6	3.4	1.7	2.2	2.0	18.5	15.0	8.0	9.2	4.3	4.1	8.7
With no labor force activity	21.9	10.9	10.7	9.7	8.4	44.3	35.6	28.2	29.9	23.6	18.7	40.9

[a]Refers to opposite-sex married-couple families only.

[b]No opposite-sex spouse present.

[c]Number below the poverty level as a percentage of the total.

Note: Dash represents zero, rounds to zero, or indicates that base is less than 80,000.

SOURCE: "Table 6. People in Families and Unrelated Individuals: Poverty Status and Work Experience, 2015," in *A Profile of the Working Poor, 2015*, U.S. Department of Labor, Bureau of Labor Statistics, April 2017, https://www.bls.gov/opub/reports/working-poor/2015/pdf/home.pdf (accessed August 4, 2017)

TABLE 2.13

Poverty status of people and primary families in the labor force for 27 or more weeks, 2007–15

[Numbers in thousands]

Characteristic	2007	2008	2009	2010	2011	2012	2013	2014	2015
Total in the labor force[a]	**146,567**	**147,838**	**147,902**	**146,859**	**147,475**	**148,735**	**149,483**	**150,319**	**152,230**
In poverty	7,521	8,883	10,391	10,512	10,382	10,612	10,450	9,487	8,560
Working-poor rate	5.1	6.0	7.0	7.2	7.0	7.1	7.0	6.3	5.6
Unrelated individuals	**33,226**	**32,785**	**33,798**	**34,099**	**33,731**	**34,810**	**35,061**	**35,018**	**35,953**
In poverty	2,558	3,275	3,947	3,947	3,621	3,851	4,141	3,395	3,137
Working-poor rate	7.7	10.0	11.7	11.6	10.7	11.1	11.8	9.7	8.7
Primary families[b]	**65,158**	**65,907**	**65,467**	**64,931**	**66,225**	**66,541**	**66,462**	**66,732**	**67,193**
In poverty	4,169	4,538	5,193	5,269	5,469	5,478	5,137	5,108	4,607
Working-poor rate	6.4	6.9	7.9	8.1	8.3	8.2	7.7	7.7	6.9

[a]Includes individuals in families, not shown separately.
[b]Primary families with at least one member in the labor force for more than half the year.

SOURCE: "Table A. Poverty Status of People and Primary Families in the Labor Force for 27 Weeks or More, 2007–2015," in *A Profile of the Working Poor, 2015*, U.S. Department of Labor, Bureau of Labor Statistics, April 2017, https://www.bls.gov/opub/reports/working-poor/2015/pdf/home.pdf (accessed August 4, 2017)

TABLE 2.14

Poverty status and selected characteristics of families with one member in the labor force for 27 weeks or more, 2015

[Numbers in thousands]

Characteristic	Total families	At or above poverty level	Below poverty level	Rate[a]
Total primary families	**67,193**	**62,586**	**4,607**	**6.9**
With related children under 18 years	34,948	31,052	3,896	11.1
Without children	32,245	31,534	711	2.2
With one member in the labor force	29,232	25,247	3,985	13.6
With two or more members in the labor force	37,960	37,339	621	1.6
With two members	31,654	31,095	560	1.8
With three or more members	6,306	6,244	62	1.0
Married-couple families[b]	49,515	47,668	1,847	3.7
With related children under 18 years	24,230	22,729	1,500	6.2
Without children	25,285	24,939	347	1.4
With one member in the labor force	17,345	15,877	1,468	8.5
Husband	12,240	11,106	1,135	9.3
Wife	4,299	4,023	276	6.4
Relative	806	749	57	7.1
With two or more members in the labor force	32,170	31,791	379	1.2
With two members	27,234	26,889	345	1.3
With three or more members	4,936	4,901	35	0.7
Families maintained by women[c]	12,287	10,042	2,245	18.3
With related children under 18 years	7,988	6,011	1,978	24.8
Without children	4,299	4,032	267	6.2
With one member in the labor force	8,602	6,544	2,058	23.9
Householder	6,932	5,205	1,727	24.9
Relative	1,670	1,339	331	19.8
With two or more members in the labor force	3,686	3,498	187	5.1
Families maintained by men[c]	5,390	4,875	515	9.6
With related children under 18 years	2,730	2,312	418	15.3
Without children	2,660	2,563	97	3.6
With one member in the labor force	3,285	2,826	460	14.0
Householder	2,650	2,286	365	13.8
Relative	635	540	95	15.0
With two or more members in the labor force	2,105	2,050	55	2.6

[a]Number below the poverty level as a percentage of the total in the labor force for 27 weeks or more who worked during the year.
[b]Refers to opposite-sex married-couple families only.
[c]No opposite-sex spouse present.
Note: Data relate to primary families with at least one member in the labor force for 27 weeks or more.

SOURCE: "Table 5. Primary Families: Poverty Status, Presence of Related Children, and Work Experience of Family Members in the Labor Force for 27 Weeks or More, 2015," in *A Profile of the Working Poor, 2015*, U.S. Department of Labor, Bureau of Labor Statistics, April 2017, https://www.bls.gov/opub/reports/working-poor/2015/pdf/home.pdf (accessed August 4, 2017)

TABLE 2.15

Poverty status of people in the labor force for 27 weeks or more, by age, sex, race, and Hispanic origin, 2015

[Numbers in thousands]

Age and gender	Total					Below poverty level					Rate*				
	Total	White	Black or African American	Asian	Hispanic or Latino	Total	White	Black or African American	Asian	Hispanic or Latino	Total	White	Black or African American	Asian	Hispanic or Latino
Total, 16 years and older	152,230	119,878	18,502	8,965	25,019	8,560	5,746	2,073	364	2,520	5.6	4.8	11.2	4.1	10.1
16 to 19 years	3,436	2,638	458	104	668	372	241	90	12	96	10.8	9.1	19.6	12.0	14.4
20 to 24 years	13,187	9,990	1,948	561	2,913	1,609	1,043	421	58	358	12.2	10.4	21.6	10.4	12.3
25 to 34 years	34,008	25,788	4,628	2,197	6,712	2,251	1,443	636	77	667	6.6	5.6	13.7	3.5	9.9
35 to 44 years	31,909	24,315	4,163	2,354	6,281	2,031	1,372	472	86	784	6.4	5.6	11.3	3.7	12.5
45 to 54 years	33,364	26,654	3,959	1,917	4,978	1,242	865	250	86	403	3.7	3.2	6.3	4.5	8.1
55 to 64 years	26,832	22,333	2,574	1,405	2,740	904	671	178	33	171	3.4	3.0	6.9	2.4	6.2
65 years and older	9,495	8,159	772	426	727	153	112	26	12	41	1.6	1.4	3.4	2.9	5.6
Men, 16 years and older	81,218	65,149	8,751	4,810	14,388	4,053	2,882	772	209	1,374	5.0	4.4	8.8	4.3	9.5
16 to 19 years	1,704	1,330	226	51	336	147	85	38	8	34	8.6	6.4	16.7	—	10.1
20 to 24 years	6,829	5,206	985	272	1,594	717	470	161	37	172	10.5	9.0	16.4	13.7	10.8
25 to 34 years	18,408	14,230	2,216	1,243	3,988	1,013	725	216	37	364	5.5	5.1	9.7	3.0	9.1
35 to 44 years	17,276	13,577	1,893	1,261	3,710	1,005	746	160	48	469	5.8	5.5	8.5	3.8	12.6
45 to 54 years	17,677	14,399	1,875	984	2,822	650	469	104	53	227	3.7	3.3	5.6	5.3	8.1
55 to 64 years	14,025	11,791	1,218	734	1,520	439	328	76	21	86	3.1	2.8	6.3	2.8	5.7
65 years and older	5,297	4,616	337	265	419	82	60	16	6	21	1.5	1.3	4.8	2.3	5.0
Women, 16 years an older	71,013	54,729	9,751	4,154	10,631	4,508	2,864	1,301	156	1,146	6.3	5.2	13.3	3.7	10.8
16 to 19 years	1,731	1,308	231	53	332	225	155	52	5	62	13.0	11.9	22.4	—	18.7
20 to 24 years	6,358	4,784	963	289	1,319	891	574	260	21	186	14.0	12.0	27.0	7.2	14.1
25 to 34 years	15,599	11,558	2,411	954	2,724	1,238	719	420	40	304	7.9	6.2	17.4	4.2	11.1
35 to 44 years	14,633	10,738	2,271	1,092	2,571	1,026	626	311	38	314	7.0	5.8	13.7	3.5	12.2
45 to 54 years	15,687	12,255	2,084	933	2,156	592	395	146	33	176	3.8	3.2	7.0	3.6	8.1
55 to 64 years	12,807	10,542	1,356	671	1,220	465	342	102	12	84	3.6	3.2	7.5	1.9	6.9
65 years and older	4,197	3,543	435	161	308	71	52	10	6	20	1.7	1.5	2.3	4.0	6.4

*Number below the poverty level as a percent of the total in the labor force for 27 weeks or more.

Note: Estimates for the race groups shown (White, Black or African American, and Asian) do not sum to totals because data are not presented for all races. People whose ethnicity is identified as Hispanic or Latino may be of any race. Dash represents zero, rounds to zero, or indicates that base is less than 80,000.

SOURCE: "Table 2. People in the Labor Force for 27 Weeks or More: Poverty Status by Age, Gender, Race, and Hispanic or Latino Ethnicity, 2015," in *A Profile of the Working Poor, 2015*, U.S. Department of Labor, Bureau of Labor Statistics, April 2017, https://www.bls.gov/opub/reports/working-poor/2015/pdf/home.pdf (accessed August 4, 2017)

TABLE 2.16

Poverty status of people in the labor force for 27 weeks or more, by educational attainment, race, Hispanic origin, and sex, 2015

[Numbers in thousands]

Educational attainment, race, and Hispanic or Latino ethnicity	Total	Men	Women	Below poverty level Total	Below poverty level Men	Below poverty level Women	Rate[a] Total	Rate[a] Men	Rate[a] Women
Total, 16 years and older	**152,230**	**81,218**	**71,013**	**8,560**	**4,053**	**4,508**	**5.6**	**5.0**	**6.3**
Less than a high school diploma	12,900	8,071	4,829	2,096	1,141	955	16.2	14.1	19.8
Less than 1 year of high school	4,280	2,805	1,475	710	453	257	16.6	16.2	17.4
1–3 years of high school	6,773	4,107	2,666	1,094	526	568	16.1	12.8	21.3
4 years of high school, no diploma	1,847	1,159	687	292	162	130	15.8	14.0	19.0
High school graduates, no college[b]	40,385	23,715	16,670	3,064	1,464	1,600	7.6	6.2	9.6
Some college or associate's degree	44,115	21,741	22,374	2,469	951	1,519	5.6	4.4	6.8
Some college, no degree	27,985	14,219	13,766	1,854	737	1,117	6.6	5.2	8.1
Associate's degree	16,129	7,522	8,608	615	214	401	3.8	2.8	4.7
Bachelor's degree and higher[c]	54,830	27,690	27,140	931	497	434	1.7	1.8	1.6
White, 16 years and older	**119,878**	**65,149**	**54,729**	**5,746**	**2,882**	**2,864**	**4.8**	**4.4**	**5.2**
Less than a high school diploma	10,198	6,630	3,568	1,580	905	675	15.5	13.6	18.9
Less than 1 year of high school	3,602	2,408	1,194	615	404	211	17.1	16.8	17.7
1–3 years of high school	5,303	3,368	1,935	783	402	381	14.8	11.9	19.7
4 years of high school, no diploma	1,293	854	439	182	99	83	14.1	11.6	18.9
High school graduates, no college[b]	31,638	19,014	12,624	1,963	1,008	955	6.2	5.3	7.6
Some college or associate's degree	34,485	17,335	17,149	1,580	652	928	4.6	3.8	5.4
Some college, no degree	21,414	11,084	10,330	1,158	493	664	5.4	4.5	6.4
Associate's degree	13,071	6,251	6,819	422	159	264	3.2	2.5	3.9
Bachelor's degree and higher[c]	43,557	22,170	21,387	623	317	306	1.4	1.4	1.4
Black or African American, 16 years and older	**18,502**	**8,751**	**9,751**	**2,073**	**772**	**1,301**	**11.2**	**8.8**	**13.3**
Less than a high school diploma	1,569	810	758	391	173	218	24.9	21.4	28.8
Less than 1 year of high school	290	159	130	58	32	26	20.0	20.1	19.8
1–3 years of high school	924	456	468	248	88	160	26.9	19.4	34.2
4 years of high school, no diploma	355	196	159	85	53	32	23.9	27.0	20.1
High school graduates, no college[b]	5,867	3,108	2,759	876	309	566	14.9	10.0	20.5
Some college or associate's degree	6,262	2,733	3,529	638	184	454	10.2	6.7	12.9
Some college, no degree	4,351	2,002	2,349	502	151	351	11.5	7.6	14.9
Associate's degree	1,911	731	1,180	136	33	103	7.1	4.5	8.7
Bachelor's degree and higher[c]	4,804	2,100	2,705	168	105	62	3.5	5.0	2.3
Asian, 16 years and older	**8,965**	**4,810**	**4,154**	**364**	**209**	**156**	**4.1**	**4.3**	**3.7**
Less than a high school diploma	555	287	269	62	33	29	11.2	11.6	10.8
Less than 1 year of high school	229	120	109	21	10	11	9.2	8.7	9.8
1–3 years of high school	206	103	103	22	14	8	10.9	14.0	7.7
4 years of high school, no diploma	121	64	57	19	8	10	15.6	—	—
High school graduates, no college[b]	1,470	780	690	86	57	29	5.8	7.3	4.2
Some college or associate's degree	1,670	828	842	105	60	46	6.3	7.2	5.4
Some college, no degree	1,011	536	475	81	46	35	8.0	8.5	7.4
Associate's degree	659	292	367	25	14	11	3.7	4.8	2.9
Bachelor's degree and higher[c]	5,269	2,915	2,354	111	59	52	2.1	2.0	2.2
Hispanic or Latino ethnicity, 16 years and older	**25,019**	**14,388**	**10,631**	**2,520**	**1,374**	**1,146**	**10.1**	**9.5**	**10.8**
Less than a high school diploma	6,389	4,216	2,173	1,190	714	475	18.6	16.9	21.9
Less than 1 year of high school	3,213	2,163	1,050	567	369	198	17.7	17.1	18.9
1–3 years of high school	2,524	1,626	898	503	271	232	19.9	16.7	25.8
4 years of high school, no diploma	652	428	225	119	74	45	18.3	17.3	20.1
High school graduates, no college[b]	7,895	4,824	3,071	766	415	351	9.7	8.6	11.4
Some college or associate's degree	6,401	3,175	3,227	417	174	242	6.5	5.5	7.5
Some college, no degree	4,377	2,219	2,158	309	137	171	7.1	6.2	7.9
Associate's degree	2,024	955	1,069	108	37	71	5.3	3.9	6.7
Bachelor's degree and higher[c]	4,334	2,174	2,160	147	70	77	3.4	3.2	3.6

[a]Number below the poverty level as a percentage of the total in the labor force for 27 weeks or more.
[b]Includes people with a high school diploma or equivalent.
[c]Includes people with bachelor's, master's, professional, and doctoral degrees.
Note: Estimates for the race groups shown (White, Black or African American, and Asian) do not sum to totals because data are not presented for all races. People whose ethnicity is identified as Hispanic or Latino may be of any race. Dash represents zero, rounds to zero, or indicates that base is less than 80,000.

SOURCE: "Table 3. People in the Labor Force for 27 or More Weeks: Poverty Status, by Educational Attainment, Race, Hispanic or Latino Ethnicity, and Gender, 2015," in *A Profile of the Working Poor, 2015*, U.S. Department of Labor, Bureau of Labor Statistics, April 2017, https://www.bls.gov/opub/reports/working-poor/2015/pdf/home.pdf (accessed August 4, 2017)

Salary Workers, Second Quarter 2017" (July 19, 2017, https://www.bls.gov/news.release/pdf/wkyeng.pdf), the BLS notes that during the second quarter of 2017 the 113.4 million full-time wage and salary workers in the United States had median weekly earnings of $859. Full-time workers aged 25 years and older without a high school diploma had median weekly earnings ($515) that were well below the overall median earnings level. Those with

TABLE 2.17

Poverty status and labor market problems of full-time wage and salary workers, 2015

[Numbers in thousands]

Labor market problems	Total	At or above poverty level	Below poverty level	Rate[a]
Total, full-time wage and salary workers	118,203	114,450	3,753	3.2
No unemployment, involuntary part-time employment, or low earnings[b]	99,264	98,579	685	0.7
Workers experiencing one labor market problem				
Unemployment only	5,259	4,891	368	7.0
Involuntary part-time employment only	2,538	2,478	60	2.3
Low earnings only	7,697	6,037	1,660	21.6
Workers experiencing multiple labor market problems				
Unemployment and involuntary part-time employment	993	911	82	8.2
Unemployment and low earnings	1,357	795	561	41.4
Involuntary part-time employment and low earnings	728	539	189	26.0
Unemployment, involuntary part-time employment, and low earnings	368	220	148	40.3
Workers experiencing each labor market problem				
Unemployment (alone or with other problems)	7,976	6,817	1,159	14.5
Involuntary part-time employment (alone or with other problems)	4,626	4,147	479	10.3
Low earnings (alone or with other problems)	10,149	7,591	2,558	25.2

[a]Number below the poverty level as a percentage of the total in the labor force for 27 weeks or more.
[b]The low-earnings threshold in 2015 was $348.85 per week.

SOURCE: "Table 8. People in the Labor Force for 27 Weeks or More: Poverty Status and Labor Market Problems of Full-Time Wage and Salary Workers, 2015," in *A Profile of the Working Poor, 2015*, U.S. Department of Labor, Bureau of Labor Statistics, April 2017, https://www.bls.gov/opub/reports/working-poor/2015/pdf/home.pdf (accessed August 4, 2017)

a high school education but no college diploma had median weekly earnings ($718) significantly below the overall level as well. By contrast, full-time workers over the age of 25 years with college degrees had median weekly earnings of $1,290.

Poverty, however, is not exclusive to the less educated. In *Basic Facts about Low-Income Children: Children under 18 Years, 2015* (January 2017, http://www.nccp.org/publications/pdf/text_1170.pdf), Yang Jiang, Maribel R. Granja, and Heather Koball of the National Center for Children in Poverty at Columbia University indicate that although a majority of children who lived in poor families in 2015 had parents without any college education, approximately 41% of poor families were headed by parents with at least some college education. Thus, although lack of parental education was closely linked to the likelihood that a family will live in poverty, education was by no means a guarantee of prosperity in the early 21st century.

CHRONIC AND EPISODIC POVERTY

For most poor Americans poverty is not a static condition. Some people near the poverty level improve their economic status within two years or less, whereas others at near-poverty levels become poor through economic catastrophes, such as an illness or job loss. Most data collected by the Census Bureau reflect a single point in time; in other words, they show how many people are in poverty or participating in a means-tested government program in a certain month or at a certain point in time each year. These snapshot surveys, while valuable, do not reflect the dynamic nature of poverty for individual people and families.

The Census Bureau collects longitudinal information (measurements over time for specific individuals or families) about poverty and government program participation rates in its Survey of Income and Program Participation (SIPP). The SIPP consists of interviews with a representative sample of U.S. households every four months, and it includes information about demographic characteristics, labor force status, participation in government programs, and a wide range of income data. Collecting such information over time from the same sample of people allows the Census Bureau to track the movement of individuals and families into and out of poverty (entry and exit rates), the duration of poverty spells (the number of months in poverty for those who were not poor during the first interview month, but who became poor at some point during the study), and the length of time individuals and families use government programs. Accordingly, SIPP data supplement the more commonly cited monthly and annual statistics by providing a detailed view of the experience of poverty.

Edwards uses data from the 2008 SIPP panel to examine poverty in the period from January 2009 to December 2011. Figure 2.3 shows Edwards's comparative analysis of data from the 2004 SIPP panel (covering January 2005 to December 2007) and the 2008 SIPP panel (covering January 2009 to December 2011). The first period covers a time of economic expansion, while the second period covers the peak of the Great Recession, its official end, and its aftermath. Accordingly, the 2008 SIPP data reflect

FIGURE 2.3

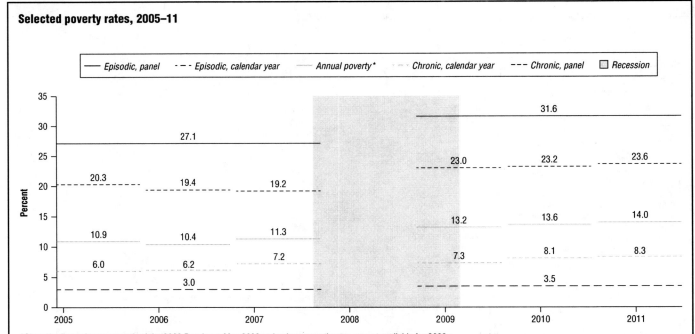

Selected poverty rates, 2005–11

Legend: ——— Episodic, panel　- - - Episodic, calendar year　⋯⋯⋯ Annual poverty*　⋯⋯ Chronic, calendar year　– – – Chronic, panel　☐ Recession

*Since the first reference month of the 2008 Panel was May 2008, calendar year estimates are not available for 2008.
Note: Panel and yearly estimates are based on different samples. The 3-year panel estimates include only respondents in the panel for 36 months whereas calendar year estimates include respondents in sample for 12 months. The numbers of respondents in each sample are as follows: 25,371 in the 2004 3-year panel, 48,937 in the 2008 3-year panel, 76,953 in 2005, 34,372 in 2006, 34,489 in 2007, 73,695 in 2009, 67,452 in 2010, and 62,841 in 2011. Calendar months October, November, and December of 2007 are missing for some rotation groups in the 2004 Panel. For longitudinal estimates covering these calendar months, a carry forward imputation method was applied.

SOURCE: Ashley N. Edwards, "Figure 1. Selected Poverty Rates: 2005 to 2011," in *Dynamics of Economic Well-Being: Poverty, 2009–2011*, U.S. Census Bureau, January 2014, http://www.census.gov/prod/2014pubs/p70-137.pdf (accessed August 4, 2017)

increased poverty levels no matter the form of measurement. The rate of episodic poverty (the percentage of survey respondents who lived below the poverty line for at least two months) over the entire three-year period of 2009–11 was 31.6%; and the episodic poverty rates for each individual calendar year were 23% (2009), 23.2% (2010), and 23.6% (2011). Likewise, the annual poverty rate (the percentage in poverty for a calendar year, determined by averaging monthly income) rose during this period, from 13.2% in 2009 to 14% in 2011. The chronic poverty rate for each calendar year (the percentage in poverty each month of the year) also rose, from 7.3% in 2009 to 8.3% in 2011. The rate of chronic poverty over the course of the entire panel period (the percentage of people who remained in poverty each month of the three-year period) was 3.5%. Although this level was comparatively small, as with all of the poverty measurements, it was noticeably higher than in the 2004 SIPP panel.

Figure 2.4 plots the degrees of both chronic and episodic poverty by selected demographic characteristics. Among different racial and ethnic groups, African Americans had the highest rate of chronic poverty, whereas Hispanics had the highest rate of episodic poverty. Adults aged 18 to 64 years and those 65 years and older both experienced below-average rates of chronic poverty. Working-age adults experienced average levels of episodic poverty,

while elderly adults experienced rates of episodic poverty far below the average. Meanwhile, children experienced above-average rates of both chronic and episodic poverty. Among all demographic subgroups, female-householder families had the highest rates of both types of poverty, once again suggesting that single motherhood is a major predictor of the likelihood that someone will live in poverty.

Edwards also provides data for poverty entry rates (the percentage of survey respondents not in poverty in 2009 who had entered poverty by the end of the survey period in 2011) by demographic characteristics. Across all groups, the poverty entry rate was 5.4%. Hispanics had the highest poverty entry rate, at 10.7%, or nearly double that of the rate for all people in the survey; and African Americans had the next highest entry rate, at 8.9%. The poverty entry rate for children (7.1%) was higher than the rates for either working-age adults (5.3%) or the elderly (3.1%). Female-householder families entered poverty at a rate (10%) more than double that of married-couple families (4%), but male-householder families also entered poverty at an elevated rate (8.6%).

According to Edwards, the poverty exit rate (the percentage of people who were in poverty in 2009 and no longer in poverty in 2011) was 35.4% for all survey

FIGURE 2.4

Chronic and episodic poverty, by selected characteristics, 2009–11

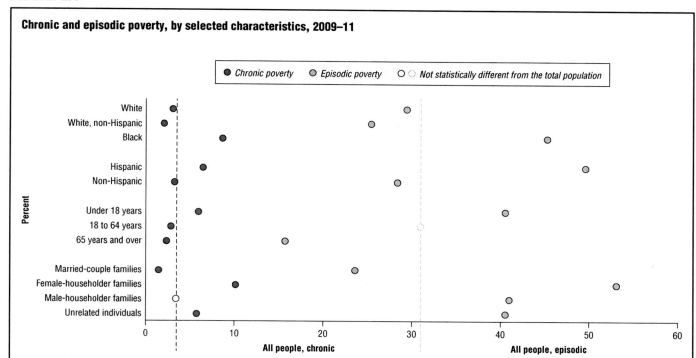

Note: Federal surveys, including the SIPP (Survey of Income and Program Participation) 2008 Panel, give respondents the option of reporting more than one race. These data can be shown in two ways: (1) as mutually exclusive from other race groups, which may be denoted by "alone" or (2) not mutually exclusive with other race groups, denoted by "alone or in combination with other race groups." This figure shows race using the first method. Because Hispanics may be of any race, data for Hispanics are not mutually exclusive with race. Female householders refer to female householders, no husband present; male householders refer to male householders, no wife present.

SOURCE: Ashley N. Edwards, "Figure 3. Chronic and Episodic Poverty by Selected Characteristics: 2009 to 2011," in *Dynamics of Economic Well-Being: Poverty, 2009–2011*, U.S. Census Bureau, January 2014, http://www.census.gov/prod/2014pubs/p70-137.pdf (accessed August 4, 2017)

respondents. African Americans were far less likely (22.7%) to have exited poverty over the three years of the survey than either whites (39.1%) or Hispanics (35.8%). Children (29.6%) and the elderly (31.5%) were less likely than working-age adults (39.7%) to have exited poverty over the three years of the survey. Female-householder families (25.2%) were far less likely than married-couple families (44.3%) to have exited poverty and significantly less likely than male-householder families (37.6%) to have exited poverty.

CHAPTER 3
PUBLIC PROGRAMS TO FIGHT POVERTY

The federal government and individual states use many methods and administer a variety of assistance programs to combat poverty, by helping those whose incomes are below the poverty line as well as those who are at risk of poverty. These programs are often collectively referred to as welfare. Some, such as Temporary Assistance for Needy Families (TANF), which offers cash assistance to the poor, are designed to help people improve their situation and escape poverty. A number of programs, including the Supplemental Nutrition Assistance Program (SNAP; previously called the Food Stamp Program), are designed to help those in poverty meet their basic needs. Meanwhile, the Supplemental Security Income (SSI) program provides assistance to people who have disabilities or conditions that make it difficult for them to earn a living. Besides welfare programs, the government has established policies such as the minimum wage and unemployment compensation that are intended to help people avoid poverty in the first place.

The first comprehensive welfare programs were established during the 1930s, and the overall welfare system was supplemented substantially during the 1960s. The most important change to the welfare system enacted since that time is the Personal Responsibility and Work Opportunity Reconciliation Act (PRWORA). First enacted in 1996 and renewed since, the PRWORA replaced a welfare system that was based primarily on the Aid to Families with Dependent Children (AFDC) program with one centered on TANF. Critics of the AFDC asserted that the system produced welfare dependency rather than temporary assistance to help recipients move into a job and off welfare. TANF was specifically designed to limit the amount of time individuals could receive benefits and to require them to work. The intention of the law was to reduce the number of people receiving welfare by bringing them into the workforce and out of poverty. The PRWORA also changed some

other welfare programs to place greater emphasis on these priorities. In *Policy Basics: An Introduction to TANF* (June 15, 2015, http://www.cbpp.org/files/7-22-10tanf2.pdf), the Center on Budget and Policy Priorities (CBPP) notes that additional work requirements for TANF recipients put in place by the Deficit Reduction Act of 2005 further reduced the TANF caseload.

Far fewer families receive TANF cash assistance than received AFDC cash assistance. As Figure 3.1 shows, in 1996, 68 out of 100 families with children in poverty received cash assistance under the AFDC, but by 2014 that number stood at 23 out of 100. This decline in the distribution of cash assistance was not a result of decreasing poverty but of TANF's intentionally limited ability to serve the poor population.

In 2015 only 16.9% of all people below the poverty line lived with someone who received any form of means-tested cash assistance (TANF is the main source of means-tested cash assistance). (See Table 3.1.) As is noted in Chapter 2, the poverty rate for children in female-householder families was 42.6% in 2015, the poverty rate for children aged zero to five years in such households was 49.5%, and the rate of desperate poverty (the percentage of such children in households earning less than 50% of poverty) was 29%. Nevertheless, in 2015 among people who lived below the poverty line in households headed by single women and including children, only 23% lived in households where any member received means-tested cash assistance. (See Table 3.1.) Among people who lived below the poverty line in households headed by single women and including children younger than six years, only 22.7% lived in households where any member received means-tested cash assistance.

Other government assistance programs were more responsive to overall levels of poverty. As Table 3.1 shows, three-quarters (75.2%) of all people below the poverty level lived in a household where at least one

FIGURE 3.1

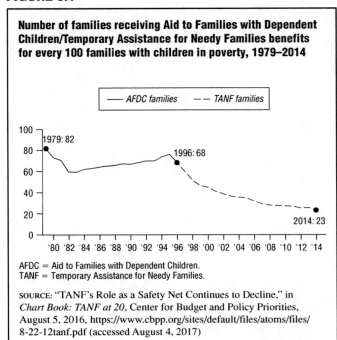

Number of families receiving Aid to Families with Dependent Children/Temporary Assistance for Needy Families benefits for every 100 families with children in poverty, 1979–2014

AFDC = Aid to Families with Dependent Children.
TANF = Temporary Assistance for Needy Families.

SOURCE: "TANF's Role as a Safety Net Continues to Decline," in *Chart Book: TANF at 20*, Center for Budget and Policy Priorities, August 5, 2016, https://www.cbpp.org/sites/default/files/atoms/files/8-22-12tanf.pdf (accessed August 4, 2017)

person received some form of means-tested aid, including free or reduced-price school lunches, cash assistance, SNAP benefits (food stamps), Medicaid (a state and federal health insurance program for low-income people), or public or subsidized housing. Nearly half (48.8%) of people in poverty and 62.9% of children in poverty lived in households where someone received SNAP benefits, and 63.1% of people in poverty and 80.1% of children in poverty lived in households where someone was covered by Medicaid.

THE PERSONAL RESPONSIBILITY AND WORK OPPORTUNITY RECONCILIATION ACT

The following pages discuss the specific provisions of the PRWORA.

Title I: Block Grants

Under the PRWORA, each state receives a single block grant (a lump sum of money). States have considerable control over how they implement the programs that are covered by the block grant, but the act requires that:

- Families on welfare for five cumulative years no longer receive further cash assistance. States can set shorter time limits and can exempt up to 20% of their caseload from the time limits.

- To count toward meeting the work requirement, a state must require individuals to participate in employment (public or private), on-the-job training, community service, work experience, vocational training (up to 12 months), or child care for other

workers for at least 20 hours per week. State and local communities are responsible for the development of work, whether by creating community service jobs or by providing income subsidies or hiring incentives for potential employers.

- Unmarried parents under the age of 18 years must live with an adult or have adult supervision and must participate in educational or job training to receive benefits. In addition, the law encourages second-chance homes (group homes or apartment clusters with adult supervision) to provide teen parents with the skills and support they need.

None of the block grant funds can be used for adults who have been on welfare for more than five years or who do not work after receiving benefits for two years. However, states are given some flexibility in how they spend their TANF funds.

Title II: Supplemental Security Income

The PRWORA redefined the term *disability* for children who receive SSI. A child is considered disabled if he or she has a medically determinable physical or mental impairment that results in marked and severe functional limitations that have lasted or can be expected to last at least 12 months or that can be expected to cause death. The PRWORA removed "maladaptive behavior" (behavior that impedes an individual's ability to make healthy life decisions) as a medical criterion from the listing of impairments used for evaluating mental disabilities in children.

Title III: Child Support

To be eligible for federal funds, each state must operate a Child Support Enforcement program that meets federal guidelines. The state must establish centralized registries of child support orders and centers for the collection and disbursement of child support payments, and parents must sign their child support rights over to the state to be eligible for TANF benefits. The state must also establish enforcement methods, such as revoking the driver's and professional licenses of delinquent parents. The Administration for Children and Families' Office of Child Support Enforcement notes in "OCSE Fact Sheet" (August 7, 2017, https://www.acf.hhs.gov/sites/default/files/assets/2017factsheets_ocse.pdf) that in fiscal year (FY) 2016 the program served 15.6 million children at a cost of $4 billion.

To receive full benefits, a mother must cooperate with state efforts to establish paternity. She may be denied assistance if she refuses to disclose the father.

Title IV: Restricting Welfare and Public Benefits for Noncitizens

The PRWORA originally severely limited or banned benefits to most legal immigrants who entered the country on or after August 22, 1996, when the bill became law.

TABLE 3.1

Program participation status of households for people below poverty level, 2015

[Numbers in thousands. People who lived with someone (a nonrelative or a relative) who received aid. Not every person tallied here received the aid themselves.]

All races below poverty levels	Total	In household that received means-tested assistance		In household that received means-tested assistance excluding school lunch		In household that received means-tested cash assistance		In household that received food stamps		In household in which one or more persons were covered by Medicaid		Lived in public or authorized housing	
		Number	Percent	Number	Percent	Number	Percent	Number	Percent	Number	Percent	Number	Percent
Both sexes													
Total[a]	**43,123**	**32,443**	**75.2**	**31,108**	**72.1**	**7,294**	**16.9**	**21,063**	**48.8**	**27,218**	**63.1**	**6,363**	**14.8**
Under 18 years	14,509	13,283	91.6	12,609	86.9	2,531	17.4	9,128	62.9	11,619	80.1	2,400	16.5
18 to 24 years	5,658	3,486	61.6	3,379	59.7	644	11.4	2,008	35.5	2,905	51.3	711	12.6
25 to 34 years	5,666	4,174	73.7	4,045	71.4	773	13.6	2,669	47.1	3,570	63.0	759	13.4
35 to 44 years	4,801	3,943	82.1	3,699	77.0	854	17.8	2,479	51.6	3,319	69.1	634	13.2
45 to 54 years	4,045	2,919	72.2	2,799	69.2	813	20.1	1,829	45.2	2,350	58.1	565	14.0
55 to 59 years	2,162	1,427	66.0	1,399	64.7	564	26.1	954	44.1	1,135	52.5	337	15.6
60 to 64 years	2,081	1,182	56.8	1,166	56.0	409	19.7	740	35.6	921	44.2	311	14.9
65 years and over	4,201	2,029	48.3	2,011	47.9	707	16.8	1,256	29.9	1,399	33.3	646	15.4
65 to 74 years	2,233	1,122	50.3	1,111	49.7	374	16.7	686	30.7	817	36.6	329	14.7
75 years and over	1,968	907	46.1	901	45.8	333	16.9	569	28.9	582	29.6	317	16.1
Male													
Total[a]	**19,037**	**14,085**	**74.0**	**13,468**	**70.7**	**3,055**	**16.0**	**8,906**	**46.8**	**11,724**	**61.6**	**2,400**	**12.6**
Under 18 years	7,327	6,666	91.0	6,330	86.4	1,256	17.1	4,585	62.6	5,807	79.3	1,121	15.3
18 to 24 years	2,474	1,416	57.2	1,365	55.2	282	11.4	779	31.5	1,164	47.0	266	10.8
25 to 34 years	2,163	1,441	66.6	1,393	64.4	276	12.8	819	37.9	1,189	54.9	192	8.9
35 to 44 years	1,939	1,521	78.4	1,415	73.0	308	15.9	888	45.8	1,231	63.5	180	9.3
45 to 54 years	1,756	1,225	69.8	1,177	67.0	311	17.7	718	40.9	976	55.6	210	11.9
55 to 59 years	958	610	63.7	596	62.2	240	25.0	403	42.0	477	49.8	119	12.4
60 to 64 years	932	492	52.8	484	51.9	133	14.3	307	32.9	366	39.3	105	11.3
65 years and over	1,487	713	48.0	709	47.7	249	16.8	408	27.4	514	34.6	206	13.9
65 to 74 years	884	423	47.9	420	47.5	147	16.6	240	27.2	329	37.2	113	12.8
75 years and over	603	290	48.1	289	47.9	102	16.9	168	27.8	185	30.7	93	15.4
Female													
Total[a]	**24,086**	**18,358**	**76.2**	**17,640**	**73.2**	**4,239**	**17.6**	**12,157**	**50.5**	**15,494**	**64.3**	**3,963**	**16.5**
Under 18 years	7,182	6,617	92.1	6,279	87.4	1,274	17.7	4,543	63.3	5,812	80.9	1,279	17.8
18 to 24 years	3,184	2,070	65.0	2,015	63.3	362	11.4	1,230	38.6	1,741	54.7	445	14.0
25 to 34 years	3,503	2,733	78.0	2,652	75.7	497	14.2	1,851	52.8	2,381	68.0	567	16.2
35 to 44 years	2,862	2,422	84.6	2,284	79.8	546	19.1	1,591	55.6	2,088	73.0	454	15.9
45 to 54 years	2,288	1,694	74.0	1,622	70.9	502	22.0	1,111	48.5	1,374	60.0	355	15.5
55 to 59 years	1,204	817	67.8	803	66.7	324	26.9	551	45.7	658	54.6	217	18.0
60 to 64 years	1,149	690	60.0	683	59.4	276	24.0	434	37.7	554	48.3	206	17.9
65 years and over	2,714	1,316	48.5	1,303	48.0	458	16.9	848	31.2	885	32.6	440	16.2
65 to 74 years	1,349	699	51.8	691	51.2	227	16.8	446	33.0	488	36.1	216	16.0
75 years and over	1,365	617	45.2	612	44.8	231	16.9	402	29.4	397	29.1	224	16.4

TABLE 3.1

Program participation status of households for people below poverty level, 2015 [CONTINUED]

[Numbers in thousands. People who lived with someone (a nonrelative or a relative) who received aid. Not every person tallied here received the aid themselves.]

All races below poverty levels / Household relationship	Total	In household that received means-tested assistance		In household that received means-tested assistance excluding school lunch		In household that received means-tested cash assistance		In household that received food stamps		In household in which one or more persons were covered by Medicaid		Lived in public or authorized housing	
		Number	Percent	Number	Percent	Number	Percent	Number	Percent	Number	Percent	Number	Percent
Household relationship													
Total[a]	43,123	32,443	75.2	31,108	72.1	7,294	16.9	21,063	48.8	27,218	63.1	6,363	14.8
65 years and over	4,201	2,029	48.3	2,011	47.9	707	16.8	1,256	29.9	1,399	33.3	646	15.4
In families[b]	29,893	25,253	84.5	24,018	80.3	5,046	16.9	16,889	56.5	21,850	73.1	4,558	15.2
Householder	8,589	6,856	79.8	6,543	76.2	1,415	16.5	4,542	52.9	5,885	68.5	1,363	15.9
Under 65 years	7,650	6,407	83.7	6,106	79.8	1,303	17.0	4,273	55.9	5,547	72.5	1,291	16.9
65 years and over	939	449	47.8	436	46.5	112	12.0	269	28.7	338	36.0	72	7.7
Related children under 18 years[e]	13,962	12,841	92.0	12,196	87.3	2,484	17.8	8,912	63.8	11,235	80.5	2,376	17.0
Under 6 years	4,923	4,450	90.4	4,338	88.1	834	16.9	3,136	63.7	4,025	81.8	904	18.4
6 to 17 years	9,039	8,391	92.8	7,858	86.9	1,650	18.3	5,776	63.9	7,210	79.8	1,472	16.3
Own children 18 years and over[d]	2,539	2,159	85.0	2,077	81.8	590	23.3	1,429	56.3	1,876	73.9	442	17.4
In married-couple families[f]	12,270	9,331	76.0	8,753	71.3	1,315	10.7	5,438	44.3	7,956	64.8	884	7.2
Husbands[f]	3,245	2,145	66.1	2,021	62.3	355	10.9	1,209	37.3	1,808	55.7	226	7.0
Under 65 years	2,610	1,917	73.5	1,796	68.8	292	11.2	1,093	41.9	1,633	62.6	187	7.2
65 years and over	635	228	35.9	225	35.4	63	9.9	116	18.3	175	27.5	39	6.1
Wives[f]	3,245	2,145	66.1	2,021	62.3	355	10.9	1,209	37.3	1,808	55.7	226	7.0
Under 65 years	2,774	1,985	71.5	1,864	67.2	307	11.1	1,127	40.6	1,684	60.7	198	7.1
65 years and over	471	160	34.0	157	33.4	48	10.2	82	17.4	124	26.3	28	5.9
Related children under 18 years[e]	4,792	4,227	88.2	3,944	82.3	491	10.2	2,552	53.2	3,651	76.2	360	7.5
Under 6 years	1,633	1,393	85.3	1,311	80.3	140	8.6	845	51.8	1,221	74.8	121	7.4
6 to 17 years	3,160	2,834	89.7	2,634	83.3	351	11.1	1,707	54.0	2,431	76.9	238	7.5
Own children 18 years and over[d]	728	591	81.2	558	76.6	81	11.2	324	44.5	506	69.4	55	7.6
In families with male householder, no spouse present	2,904	2,370	81.6	2,240	77.2	344	11.8	1,365	47.0	1,994	68.7	255	8.8
Householder	939	752	80.1	711	75.7	118	12.6	433	46.1	637	67.8	83	8.9
Under 65 years	880	714	81.2	673	76.5	109	12.4	414	47.0	604	68.7	77	8.8
65 years and over	59	38	63.5	38	63.3	9	15.4	20	33.4	33	55.2	6	10.1
Related children under 18 years[e]	1,316	1,195	90.8	1,137	86.4	156	11.9	718	54.5	1,006	76.4	114	8.7
Under 6 years	463	425	91.8	420	90.8	51	11.0	238	51.5	389	84.1	38	8.3
6 to 17 years	853	770	90.3	717	84.0	106	12.4	479	56.2	617	72.3	76	8.9
Own children 18 years and over[d]	189	125	66.1	116	61.3	35	18.5	56	29.4	104	55.2	20	10.8
In families with female householder, no spouse present	14,719	13,552	92.1	13,024	88.5	3,388	23.0	10,086	68.5	11,899	80.8	3,419	23.2
Householder	4,404	3,958	89.9	3,811	86.5	943	21.4	2,900	65.8	3,440	78.1	1,054	23.9
Under 65 years	4,092	3,744	91.5	3,605	88.1	893	21.8	2,751	67.2	3,283	80.2	1,023	25.0
65 years and over	312	214	68.7	206	65.8	49	15.8	149	47.8	156	50.0	31	9.9
Related children under 18 years[e]	7,854	7,419	94.5	7,115	90.6	1,837	23.4	5,643	71.9	6,578	83.8	1,902	24.2
Under 6 years	2,828	2,633	93.1	2,607	92.2	643	22.7	2,053	72.6	2,415	85.4	745	26.3
6 to 17 years	5,026	4,787	95.2	4,508	89.7	1,194	23.8	3,590	71.4	4,162	82.8	1,157	23.0
Own children 18 years and over[d]	1,622	1,444	89.0	1,404	86.6	474	29.2	1,050	64.7	1,267	78.1	366	22.6

TABLE 3.1

Program participation status of households for people below poverty level, 2015 [CONTINUED]

[Numbers in thousands. People who lived with someone (a nonrelative or a relative) who received aid. Not every person tallied here received the aid themselves.]

All races below poverty levels	Total	In household that received means-tested assistance		In household that received means-tested assistance excluding school lunch		In household that received means-tested cash assistance		In household that received food stamps		In household in which one or more persons were covered by Medicaid		Lived in public or authorized housing	
		Number	Percent	Number	Percent	Number	Percent	Number	Percent	Number	Percent	Number	Percent
In unrelated subfamilies[c]	559	486	87.0	470	84.2	60	10.7	279	50.0	435	77.8	30	5.4
Under 18 years	321	284	88.4	274	85.3	30	9.4	163	50.6	255	79.2	17	5.2
Under 6 years	100	84	83.9	84	83.9	4	3.7	50	50.5	80	79.8	5	4.6
6 to 17 years	222	200	90.3	191	86.0	27	12.0	112	50.6	175	78.9	12	5.5
18 years and over	237	202	85.2	196	82.6	30	12.5	117	49.1	180	76.0	14	5.7
Unrelated individuals[d]	12,671	6,704	52.9	6,620	52.2	2,188	17.3	3,895	30.7	4,933	38.9	1,774	14.0
Male	5,513	2,860	51.9	2,812	51.0	895	16.2	1,601	29.0	2,075	37.6	710	12.9
Under 65 years	4,818	2,488	51.6	2,442	50.7	742	15.4	1,373	28.5	1,839	38.2	553	11.5
Living alone	2,117	1,117	52.7	1,116	52.7	417	19.7	711	33.6	754	35.6	398	18.8
65 years and over	695	372	53.5	371	53.3	153	22.0	228	32.8	237	34.1	157	22.6
Living alone	548	280	51.1	280	51.1	105	19.1	182	33.2	165	30.2	150	27.4
Female	7,159	3,844	53.7	3,807	53.2	1,292	18.1	2,294	32.0	2,858	39.9	1,064	14.9
Under 65 years	5,411	3,043	56.2	3,006	55.6	968	17.9	1,775	32.8	2,378	43.9	709	13.1
Living alone	2,328	1,418	60.9	1,412	60.6	652	28.0	985	42.3	1,038	44.6	560	24.1
65 years and over	1,747	801	45.8	801	45.8	324	18.5	519	29.7	480	27.5	356	20.4
Living alone	1,563	722	46.2	722	46.2	300	19.2	476	30.5	425	27.2	342	21.9

[a]Universe: All people except unrelated individuals under age 15 (such as foster children). Since the Current Population Survey asks income questions only to people age 15 and over, if a child under age 15 is not part of a family by birth, marriage, or adoption, we do not know their income and cannot determine whether or not they are poor. Those people are excluded from the totals so as not to affect the percentages.

[b]People in families: People who are related to the householder by birth, marriage, or adoption. People who are related to each other but not to the householder are counted elsewhere (usually as unrelated subfamilies).

[c]People in unrelated subfamilies: People who are not related to the householder, but who are related to each other, either as a married couple or as a parent-child relationship with an unmarried child under 18.

[d]Unrelated individuals: People who are not in primary families (the householder's family) or unrelated subfamilies.

[e]People in families with related children: People living in a family where at least one member is a related child–a person under 18 who is related to the householder or spouse.

[f]In married-couple families the householder may be either the husband or the wife.

[g]Own children: Sons and daughters, including stepchildren and adopted children, of the householder.

SOURCE: "POV26. Program Participation Status of Household—Poverty Status of People: 2015—All Races—Below Poverty Levels," in *Current Population Survey (CPS) 2015 Annual Social and Economic Supplement*, U.S. Census Bureau, September 12, 2016, https://www.2.census.gov/programs-surveys/cps/tables/pov-26/2016/pov26_2_1.xls (accessed August 4, 2017)

Ineligibility continued for a five-year period or until the legal immigrants attained citizenship. In addition, states had the option of withholding eligibility for Medicaid, TANF, and other social services from legal immigrants already residing in the United States.

Immigrants who were not authorized to be in the country no longer had any entitlement to benefit programs, such as TANF or Medicaid. However, they could receive emergency medical care, short-term disaster relief, immunizations, and treatment for communicable diseases (in the interest of public health). They could also use community services such as soup kitchens and shelters, some housing programs, and school lunches/breakfasts if their children were eligible for free public education. States have established programs to verify the legal residence of immigrants before paying benefits and may elect to deny Special Supplemental Nutrition Program for Women, Infants, and Children benefits and other child nutrition programs to unauthorized immigrants.

Title V: Child Protection

The PRWORA gave states the authority to use current federal funds to pay for foster care for children in child care institutions. It also extended the enhanced federal match for statewide automated child welfare information systems.

Title VI: Child Care

The law required that states maintain spending for child care for low-income families at the level of FY 1994 or FY 1995, whichever was greater, to be eligible for federally matched funds. Mandatory funding was set at $13.9 billion through June 30, 2004, with states receiving an estimated $1.2 billion per year before matching began. The remainder of the funds was available for state matching at the Medicaid rate.

Liz Schott and Ife Finch of the CBPP explain in *How States Use Funds under the TANF Block Grant* (January 5, 2017, https://www.cbpp.org/sites/default/files/atoms/files/1-5-17tanf.pdf) that the child care portion of TANF was one of the program's bright spots in the early years after welfare reform. Federal and state spending on child care rose from $1.1 billion in 1997 to $5.9 billion in 2000. Spending remained stagnant over the following 11 years, however, fluctuating between $5 billion and $6 billion. When taking inflation into account, the 2015 spending total of $5.4 billion represented a 35% decline from the 2000 figure of $5.9 billion.

Title VII: Child Nutrition Programs

The PRWORA continued existing child nutrition programs, such as the National School Lunch Program and the School Breakfast Program. However, maximum reimbursement was reduced for the Summer Food Service Program and for some institutional food programs. States were allowed to decide whether to include or exclude legal immigrants from these programs.

Title VIII: Supplemental Nutrition Assistance Program

The PRWORA reduced maximum benefits for the Food Stamp Program, which became known as SNAP in 2008. The act set SNAP benefits at the level of the Thrifty Food Plan, an index set by the U.S. Department of Agriculture (USDA) that reflects the amount of money needed to purchase food to meet minimal nutrition requirements. Benefits were indexed to the rate of inflation so that they increase as inflation rises.

The law also restructured the way certain expenses and earnings were counted in establishing eligibility for food stamps. Under the PRWORA, when recipients' benefits are calculated, their countable monthly income is reduced by several deductions, including a standard deduction, a deduction for excessively high shelter expenses, a dependent care deduction, and medical expenses for the elderly and disabled. These deductions raised food stamp allotments.

In response to the Great Recession (which officially lasted from December 2007 to June 2009), President Barack Obama (1961–) signed the American Recovery and Reinvestment Act (ARRA) in February 2009. The USDA reports in "ARRA" (October 11, 2016, https://www.ers.usda.gov/topics/food-nutrition-assistance/supplemental-nutrition-assistance-program-snap/arra/) that the act increased SNAP benefits by 13.6% over the June value of the Thrifty Food Plan. The maximum benefits for a family of four in the continental United States increased by $80 a month, and the maximum monthly allotment for a family of three increased to $63. The ARRA increases in SNAP monthly benefits expired in October 2013. In *SNAP Benefits Will Be Cut for Nearly All Participants in November 2013* (August 2, 2013, https://www.cbpp.org/sites/default/files/atoms/files/2-8-13fa.pdf), Stacy Dean and Dottie Rosenbaum of the CBPP note that without the additional funding provided by the ARRA, the average amount of SNAP benefits fell below $1.40 per person per meal.

By law, all SNAP recipients who are 18 to 50 years old and without children (known as able-bodied adults without dependents [ABAWD]) must work at least part time or be limited to three months of assistance during a 36-month period. Recipients who were in a workfare program (a welfare program that usually requires recipients to perform public service duties) for 30 days but lost their placement may qualify for an additional three months of food assistance. (This provision was revised to allow states to exempt 15% of ABAWD recipients from this restriction.)

Reauthorization of the PRWORA

The PRWORA was reauthorized through 2010, when President George W. Bush (1946–) signed the Deficit Reduction Act in February 2006. The CBPP explains in *Implementing the TANF Changes in the Deficit Reduction Act: "Win-Win" Solutions for Families and States* (February 2007, http://www.cbpp.org/files/2-9-07tanf.pdf) that this bill did not increase funding for TANF programs; however, it did make the eligibility requirements stricter. The basic TANF block grant did not increase with inflation but remained capped at $16 billion. Thus, actual TANF funding has measurably decreased since that time. The reauthorization bill required 50% of TANF recipients to work in 2006, increasing by 5% each year to 70% in 2010. Funding for child care was set at $2 billion for each year between 2006 and 2010. Child support enforcement funding was reduced. Drug testing became required for every TANF applicant and recipient. Finally, the bill allowed TANF funds to be used to promote the value of marriage through public advertising and high school and adult classes and mentoring programs.

Although the law was scheduled for full-scale reauthorization in 2010, which would have entailed opportunities to enhance or alter its components, Congress instead passed short-term funding extensions in the years that followed. Tazra Mitchell of the CBPP reports in "President Trump's Budget Cuts TANF Despite Stated Goal to Reduce Poverty, Boost Work" (May 24, 2017, https://www.cbpp.org/blog/president-trumps-budget-cuts-tanf-despite-stated-goal-to-reduce-poverty-boost-work) that in his 2018 federal budget, President Donald Trump (1946–) proposed reducing TANF funding by 10%, from $16.5 billion to $14.9 billion. As of October 2017, the 2018 federal budget had yet to be approved by Congress.

ELIGIBILITY FOR TANF AND BENEFIT PAYMENTS

Under TANF, states decide how much to aid a needy family. No federal guidelines exist for determining eligibility, and no requirement mandates that states aid all needy families. TANF does not require states to have a need standard or a gross income limit, as the AFDC did, but many states base their TANF programs in part on their earlier practices.

The maximum benefit is the amount paid to a family with no countable income. (Federal law specifies what income counts toward figuring benefits and what income, such as child support, is to be disregarded by the state.) The maximum benefit is to be paid only to those families that comply with TANF's work requirements or other program requirements established by the state, such as parental and personal responsibility rules.

Most states vary benefits according to family size, such as by eliminating or restricting benefit increases due to the birth of a new child to a recipient already receiving benefits. In 16 states benefits depend on family size at the time of enrollment. Idaho pays a flat monthly grant that is the same regardless of family size. Wisconsin pays benefits based on work activity of the recipient and not on family size. Five states provide an increase in benefits to TANF families following the birth of an additional child. The CBPP points out in *Chart Book: TANF at 20* (August 5, 2016, https://www.cbpp.org/sites/default/files/atoms/files/8-22-12tanf_0.pdf) that in 2016 the median benefit level for a family of three was $429 per month (or $5,148 per year, an amount equal to 25.2% of poverty for a family of three that year), and in 14 states a family of three received less than $300 per month. In 2016 TANF benefit levels for a family of three were below 50% of poverty in all 50 states, and in 16 states they were below 20% of poverty. (See Figure 3.2.)

As Table 3.2 shows, most states have not changed their maximum benefit levels appreciably since 1996, despite the major changes brought about by the PRWORA, and despite the fact that inflation means that these steady amounts represent yearly reductions in benefits. The mean (average) maximum TANF benefit for a family of three was $393 in 1996 and $437 in 2015. According to the U.S. Bureau of Labor Statistics (BLS), in "CPI Inflation Calculator" https://data.bls.gov/cgi-bin/cpicalc.pl), had benefit levels kept pace with inflation, the mean maximum TANF award would have been $595 in 2015. The value of the mean maximum TANF benefit in 2015 was thus only 73.4% of the mean maximum TANF benefit in 1996.

Many families receiving TANF benefits are also eligible for SNAP. A single benefit determination is made for both cash and food assistance. Whereas TANF eligibility and benefit amounts are determined by the states, SNAP eligibility and benefit amounts are determined by federal law and are consistent in all states. Because SNAP benefits are determined in relation to income and are not contingent on a recipient's employment status, the program is generally regarded as much more responsive to the changing financial status of households during periods such as the Great Recession.

SNAP benefit levels vary less from state to state than do TANF benefit levels. In FY 2015 the average monthly SNAP benefit nationally was $257.73 per household, and the average monthly benefits ranged from a low of $214.49 (New Hampshire) to a high of $440.86 (Hawaii). (See Table 3.3.) The U.S. territory of Guam ($584.50) had an even higher average monthly benefit than Hawaii, due not only to high levels of poverty there but also to differences in the administration of the social welfare system relative to the 50 states.

THE WELFARE-TO-WORK CONCEPT

TANF recipients are expected to participate in work activities while receiving benefits. After 24 months of assistance, states must require recipients to work at least

FIGURE 3.2

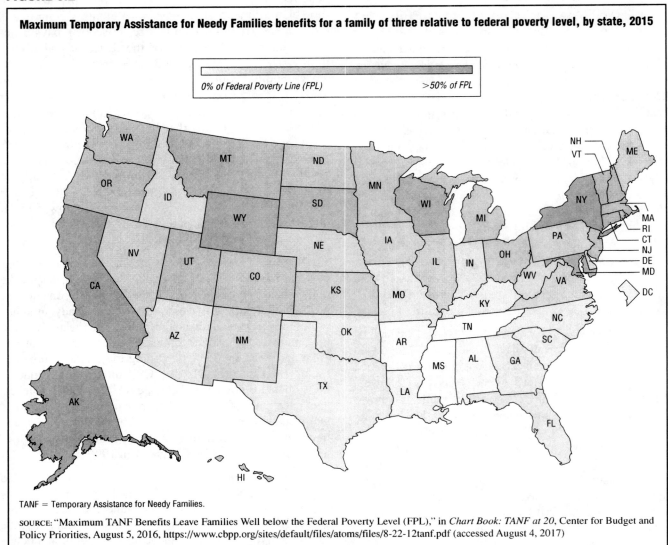

Maximum Temporary Assistance for Needy Families benefits for a family of three relative to federal poverty level, by state, 2015

0% of Federal Poverty Line (FPL)   >50% of FPL

TANF = Temporary Assistance for Needy Families.

SOURCE: "Maximum TANF Benefits Leave Families Well below the Federal Poverty Level (FPL)," in *Chart Book: TANF at 20*, Center for Budget and Policy Priorities, August 5, 2016, https://www.cbpp.org/sites/default/files/atoms/files/8-22-12tanf.pdf (accessed August 4, 2017)

part time to continue to receive cash benefits. States are permitted to exempt certain groups of people from the work-activity requirements, including parents of very young children (up to one year) and disabled adults. TANF defines the work activities that count when determining a state's work participation rate.

As part of their plans, states must require parents to work after two years of receiving benefits. In 2000 states were required to have 40% of all parents and at least one adult in 90% of all two-parent families engaged in a work activity for a minimum of 20 hours per week for single parents and 35 hours per week for at least one adult in two-parent families. This work requirement became stricter with the 2006 reauthorization of the PRWORA, which required 50% of all single-parent TANF recipients to work.

TANF recipients required to work must spend a minimum number of hours per week engaged in one of the following activities:

- An unsubsidized job (no government help)
- A subsidized private job
- A subsidized public job
- Work experience
- On-the-job training
- Job search and job readiness (a usual maximum of six weeks total)
- Community service
- Vocational educational training (a 12-month maximum)
- Job skills training
- Education related to employment
- High school or a general equivalency diploma completion
- Providing child care for a community service participant

TABLE 3.2

Maximum Temporary Assistance for Needy Families benefits for a family of three with no income, by state, selected years 1996–2015

State	1996	2002	2009	2015
Alabama	$164	$164	**$215**	$215
Alaska	$923	$923	$923	$923
Arizona	$347	$347	**$277**	$277
Arkansas	$204	$204	$204	$204
California[a]	n.a.	n.a.	n.a.	n.a.
Nonexempt	$594	**$679**	**$694**	**$704**
Exempt	$663	**$758**	**$776**	**$788**
Colorado	$356	$356	**$462**	$462
Connecticut[a]	$543	$543	**$560**	**$597**
Delaware	$338	$338	$338	$338
D.C.	$415	**$379**	**$428**	**$434**
Florida	$303	$303	$303	$303
Georgia	$280	$280	$280	$280
Hawaii	$712	**$570**[b]	636[c]	**$610**[d]
Idaho	$317	**$309**	$309	$309
Illinois[a]	$377	**$396**	**$432**	$432
Indiana	$288	$288	$288	$288
Iowa	$426	$426	$426	$426
Kansas[a]	$429	$429	$429	$429
Kentucky	$262	$262	$262	$262
Louisiana	$190[a]	**$240**	$240	$240
Maine	$418	**$485**	$485	$485
Maryland	$373	**$472**	$574	**$636**
Massachusetts				
Nonexempt	$565	**$618**	$618	$618
Exempt	$579	**$633**	$633	$633
Michigan	$459[a]	$459[a]	**$492**	$492
Minnesota	$532	$532	$532	$532
Mississippi	$120	**$170**	$170	$170
Missouri	$292	$292	$292	$292
Montana	$425	**$507**	**$504**	**$586**
Nebraska	$364	$364	$364	$364
Nevada	$348	$348	**$383**	$383
New Hampshire	$550	**$625**	**$675**	$675
New Jersey	$424	$424	$424	$424
New Mexico	$389	$389	**$447**	**$380**
New York[a]	$577	$577	**$691**	**$789**
North Carolina	$272	$272	$272	$272
North Dakota	$431	**$477**	**$527**	**$486**
Ohio	$341	**$373**	**$434**	**$473**
Oklahoma	$307	**$292**	$292	$292
Oregon	$460	**$503**	**$514**	**$506**
Pennsylvania[a]	$403	$403	$403	$403
Rhode Island	$554	$554	$554	$554
South Carolina	$200	**$204**	**$271**	**$277**
South Dakota	$430	**$483**	**$539**	**$599**
Tennessee	$185	**$185**[e]	$185[e]	$185[e]
Texas	$188	**$208**	**$249**	**$281**
Utah	$426	**$474**	**$498**	$498
Vermont[a]	$597[f]	**$638**[g]	**$640**[g]	$640[g]
Virginia[a]	$291	**$320**	$320	**$389**
Washington	$546	$546	$562	**$521**
West Virginia	$253	**$453**	**$340**	$340
Wisconsin	$518[a]			
W-2 Transition	n.a.	**$628**	$628	**$608**
Community Service Jobs	n.a.	**$673**	$673	**$653**
Unsubsidized Employment	n.a.	**n.a.**[h]	n.a.[h]	n.a.[h]
Wyoming	$360	**$340**	**$546**	**$652**
Mean[i]	$393	**$413**	**$434**	**$437**
Median[i]	$377	**$396**	**$429**	**$428**

Additional provisions apply to young parents who are under the age of 20 years and are either household heads or married and who lack a high school diploma. They are considered "engaged in work" if they either maintain satisfactory attendance in high school (no hours specified) or participate in education directly related to work (20 hours per week).

TABLE 3.2

Maximum Temporary Assistance for Needy Families benefits for a family of three with no income, by state, selected years 1996–2015 [CONTINUED]

n.a. = not available.

[a]Dollar amount used to calculate benefit varies within the state, either by county or by region of the state. Calculations are based on the dollar amount that applies to the majority of the state.

[b]The benefit amount applies to units that have received assistance for two or more months in a lifetime. For units applying for their first or second months of benefits, the maximum monthly benefit for a family of three is $712.

[c]The benefit amount applies to units that have received assistance for two or more months in a lifetime. For units applying for their first or second month of benefits, the maximum monthly benefit for a family of three is $795.

[d]The benefit amount applies to units that have received assistance for two or more months in a lifetime. For units applying for their first or second months of benefits, the maximum monthly benefit for a family of three is $763.

[e]For units where the caretaker is over age 65, disabled, caring full-time for a disabled family member, or excluded from the assistance unit, the maximum monthly benefit for a family of three is $232.

[f]In addition to the maximum benefit, a family of three with no income outside of Chittenden county may receive a housing allowance of $371. A family of three with no income within Chittenden county may receive a housing allowance of $450 in addition to the maximum benefit.

[g]In addition to the maximum benefit, a family of three with no income outside of Chittenden county may receive a housing allowance of $400. A family of three with no income within Chittenden county may receive a housing allowance of $450 in addition to the maximum benefit.

[h]The benefits in these components are based on the wages earned by individual recipients.

[i]The calculations only include one value per state (the policy affecting the most populous area).

Note: Bolded text indicates a change from the previous year shown. Maximum benefits are calculated assuming that the unit contains one adult and two children who are not subject to a family cap, has no special needs, pays for shelter, and lives in the most populated area of the state. Only earned income disregards are described in the table. Child care disregards and other special disregards, such as deductions for units subject to a time limit or a family cap, are not included. The table describes benefit computation disregards for recipients. If the disregards differ for applicants, it is footnoted. Data shown in the table for the year 1996 reflect states' AFDC policies; data shown in the table for all subsequent years reflect states' TANF policies.

SOURCE: Elissa Cohen et al., "Table L5. Maximum Monthly Benefit for a Family of Three with No Income, 1996–2015 (July)," in *Welfare Rules Databook: State TANF Policies as of July 2015*, U.S. Department of Health and Human Services, Administration for Children and Families, Office of Planning, Research, and Evaluation, September 2016, https://www.acf.hhs.gov/sites/default/files/opre/2015_welfare_rules_databook_final_09_26_16_b508.pdf (accessed August 4, 2017)

The PRWORA imposed strict limits on the number of TANF recipients who may get work credit through participation in education and training. No more than 30% of TANF families who are counted as engaged in work may consist of people who are participating in vocational educational training. Vocational educational training is the only creditable work activity not explicitly confined to high school dropouts.

In 2012 the states of Utah and Nevada appealed to the federal government, requesting that certain TANF work requirements be waived because the rigidity of the rules was making it increasingly difficult for them to fulfill the spirit of the law, which was to help people find permanent jobs. For example, the rules relating to job training, educational programs, and work in government-subsidized jobs made it difficult for states to help TANF recipients simultaneously meet the PRWORA work requirements and prepare themselves for the forms of long-term employment that would lift them out of poverty for good. In July 2012 the U.S. Department of Health

TABLE 3.3

Supplemental Nutrition Assistance Program average monthly benefit per household, by state/territory, fiscal year 2015

State	Average monthly benefit per person	Average monthly benefit per household
Connecticut	$134.82	$240.17
Maine	$116.01	$223.66
Massachusetts	$127.51	$222.91
New Hampshire	$103.87	$214.49
New York	$138.38	$252.47
Rhode Island	$134.64	$233.43
Vermont	$121.98	$230.64
Delaware	$127.20	$265.63
District of Columbia	$131.66	$233.42
Maryland	$122.66	$236.73
New Jersey	$118.82	$237.39
Pennsylvania	$123.16	$244.86
Virgin Islands	$171.35	$373.17
Virginia	$119.21	$253.66
West Virginia	$112.63	$227.74
Alabama	$125.73	$267.56
Florida	$129.66	$235.90
Georgia	$129.76	$278.40
Kentucky	$120.56	$251.49
Mississippi	$120.03	$257.96
North Carolina	$121.27	$248.45
South Carolina	$125.18	$265.05
Tennessee	$127.75	$256.71
Illinois	$134.78	$259.53
Indiana	$124.66	$272.90
Michigan	$125.65	$239.32
Minnesota	$105.43	$217.53
Ohio	$125.72	$257.40
Wisconsin	$108.74	$215.35
Arkansas	$115.30	$252.57
Louisiana	$125.86	$277.79
New Mexico	$126.01	$277.81
Oklahoma	$120.48	$265.91
Texas	$117.80	$281.53
Colorado	$129.92	$275.96
Iowa	$110.04	$232.90
Kansas	$113.89	$255.78
Missouri	$124.18	$263.07
Montana	$119.96	$254.57
Nebraska	$115.88	$259.46
North Dakota	$122.16	$262.11
South Dakota	$125.88	$287.32
Utah	$115.92	$296.63
Wyoming	$118.71	$279.12
Alaska	$172.64	$409.64
Arizona	$121.71	$276.86
California	$142.00	$299.16
Guam	$192.78	$584.50
Hawaii	$222.99	$440.86
Idaho	$115.88	$272.01
Nevada	$120.04	$240.56
Oregon	$123.22	$217.33
Washington	$118.88	$222.47
US	$127.57	$257.73

SOURCE: "Table 2. Supplemental Nutrition Assistance Program Average Monthly Benefit—FY 2015," in *Supplemental Nutrition Assistance Program State Activity Report: Fiscal Year 2015*, U.S. Department of Agriculture, Food and Nutrition Service, August 2016, https://fns-prod.azureedge.net/sites/default/files/snap/FY15-State-Activity-Report.pdf (accessed August 4, 2017)

and Human Services granted the states waivers provided they devised better solutions for helping TANF benefit recipients find permanent jobs. This established a path for other states to address deficiencies in the work requirements and propose alternative plans.

Finding and Creating Jobs for TANF Recipients

Job availability is one of the most difficult challenges that states face when moving recipients from welfare to work. Welfare recipients, who often lack job skills and work experience, are at a pronounced disadvantage in the labor pool. In *TANF Recipients with Barriers to Employment* (July 2011, http://www.urban.org/UploadedPDF/412567-TANF-Recipients-with-Barriers-to-Employment.pdf), Dan Bloom, Pamela J. Loprest, and Sheila R. Zedlewski of the Urban Institute note that numerous surveys estimate that approximately 40% of TANF recipients lack a high school diploma and that many lack current work experience. The labor-market disadvantages of welfare recipients increase during recessionary periods, when unemployment is high and even well-qualified workers find themselves out of work. Even when the national unemployment rate is low, unemployment in some areas of the country might be much higher, or available jobs might not match the skills of those welfare recipients who are looking for work. TANF work requirements, which are designed to keep people from becoming dependent on welfare, can thus burden states unduly. States can lose funding even though benefits administrators and welfare recipients alike are doing everything possible to obtain jobs.

If suitable jobs cannot be found, states must create work-activity placements and may use TANF block grant funds to do so. Welfare agencies have had to change their focus and train staff to function more as job developers and counselors than as caseworkers. They make an initial assessment of recipients' skills as required by TANF. They may then develop personal responsibility plans for recipients, identifying what is needed (e.g., training, job-placement services, and support services) to move them into the workforce.

Addressing Other Barriers to Work

Low-income adults and public assistance recipients face multiple barriers to working that put them at a disadvantage relative to other participants in the labor market. Beyond the lack of education and job experience described earlier, a number of other barriers to work are common among welfare recipients. These include mental and physical health issues, child care, and transportation. In many cases, federal funding can be used to address these problems, but states are granted a wide degree of latitude. Some states employ specialized strategies to help beneficiaries overcome barriers, whereas others do little to address such problems.

HEALTH OF RECIPIENTS AND THEIR CHILDREN. Bloom, Loprest, and Zedlewski note that numerous estimates place the proportion of TANF recipients with work-limiting health conditions at between 25% and 30%. Additionally, one study has estimated the proportion of the

TANF recipient population with poor mental/emotional health at 13.8%, and another has estimated it at 24.4%. Still other TANF families (between 3.2% and 7.6%, depending on the study) have children on SSI (i.e., children with severe disabilities or other conditions that entitle them to federal benefits); these children often require round-the-clock parental care long after infancy.

No obvious or widely validated solutions to increasing the work participation of such welfare recipients exist. However, Bloom, Loprest, and Zedlewski indicate that some states use federal TANF funds to promote intensive case management approaches that connect recipients with mental health professionals, substance abuse treatment, and domestic violence counseling, among other services. According to Bloom, Loprest, and Zedlewski, these states "struggle with integrating services while maintaining a work focus and operating with limited resources."

State welfare caseworkers also sometimes facilitate referrals to the SSI program for those TANF recipients whose health problems rise to the level of a qualifying disability. The process for applying to receive SSI benefits is intricate, requiring a large amount of documentation and legal hearings. Welfare agencies can connect TANF recipients to nonprofit and other agencies that can help them with this time-consuming process, and recipients are generally exempt from the TANF work requirements while their SSI applications are being processed.

CHILD CARE. Access to affordable child care is one critical element in encouraging low-income parents to seek and keep jobs. In *Child Care in America: 2016 State Fact Sheets* (July 2016, https://usa.childcareaware.org/wp-content/uploads/2016/07/Full-Report_final.pdf), Child Care Aware of America, a leading nonprofit devoted to extending access to affordable child care, noted that in 2015 the average yearly cost for full-time infant care in a child care center ranged from $4,822 in Mississippi to $17,062 in Massachusetts. The full-time costs for a four-year-old ranged from $3,997 in Mississippi to $12,781 in Massachusetts. Full-time four-year-old care in an accredited home-based business ranged from $3,675 in Mississippi to $10,030 in Alaska. These costs put full-time child care out of reach not only for families living in poverty but also for families well above poverty. For example, a Massachusetts single mother of one infant with an income of twice the 2015 poverty level ($31,860) would have to spend more than half ($17,062, or 53.6%) of her income to enroll her child in full-time center-based care.

The 1996 welfare reform law created a block grant to states for child care. The amount of the block grant was equivalent to what states received under the AFDC. However, states that maintain the amount that they spent for child care under the AFDC are eligible for additional matching funds. The block grant and the supplemental matching funds are referred to as the Child Care Development Fund. In addition, states were given the option of transferring some of their TANF funds to the Child Care Development Fund or spending them directly on child care services.

Because states can use TANF funds for child care, they have more flexibility to design child care programs, not only for welfare recipients but also for working-poor families that may need child care support to continue working and stay off welfare. States determine who is eligible for child care support, how much those parents will pay (often using a sliding fee scale), and the amount the state will reimburse providers of subsidized care. Children under the age of 13 years are eligible for child care subsidies; depending on the state, families with incomes up to 85% of the state's median income for a family of that size are eligible, although few states guarantee payments to all eligible families.

The Administration for Children and Families' Office of Child Care reports in "Characteristics of Families Served by the Child Care and Development Fund (CCDF) Based on Preliminary FY 2015 Data" (October 22, 2015, https://www.acf.hhs.gov/occ/resource/characteristics-of-families-served-by-child-care-and-development-fund-ccdf) that in FY 2015 states provided child care subsidies to roughly 1.4 million low-income children in 847,400 families. Of the families served by the program, 49% were below the poverty level, 27% had incomes between 100% and 150% of poverty, and 13% had incomes above 150% of poverty. Of the children served, 35% were aged six years and older, 10% were aged five years, 26% were aged three to four years, and 28% were aged three years and younger. Furthermore, 73% were cared for in a child care center, 23% in home-based care, and 3% in the child's own home. Approximately 78% of families were responsible for a copayment in addition to the subsidized amount, and these copayments averaged 6% of the family income. Almost all (92%) families stated they needed care because of parental employment, education, or training; the remainder sought out care because of the need for protective services.

TRANSPORTATION. Transportation is another critical factor facing welfare recipients moving into a job. Recipients without a car must depend on public transportation. However, when available jobs are in suburban areas outside the range of public transportation, when job locations are accessible to public transportation but day care centers and schools are not, or when jobs require work at times when public transportation schedules are limited, welfare recipients may find a lack of transportation options to be a significant barrier to employment. Even for those recipients with cars, the expense of gas and repairs can deplete earnings. For low-income rural families, many of these problems are exacerbated by a lack of any public transportation options.

Most states enforce asset limits on welfare recipients (restrictions regarding how much personal wealth, in the form of savings and possessions, an individual or household may have while still qualifying for benefits). To promote employment, TANF's vehicle asset limits are broader than they were under the AFDC. Each state has the flexibility to determine its own vehicle asset level, but all states have chosen to increase the limit for the value of the primary automobile in the family beyond that set under the AFDC. Some states offer transportation-specific assistance to individuals transitioning off TANF and into the job market. As with many aspects of TANF, the wide latitude granted to states means that no one-size-fits-all approach exists.

GOVERNMENT PROGRAMS TO COMBAT HUNGER

Supplemental Nutrition Assistance Program

SNAP, which is administered by the USDA, is the largest food assistance program in the United States. SNAP is designed to help low-income families purchase a nutritionally adequate, low-cost diet. Generally, SNAP may only be used to buy food to be prepared at home. It cannot be used for alcohol, tobacco, or hot foods that are intended to be consumed immediately, such as restaurant or delicatessen food. Because TANF benefits have declined and fewer families receive cash assistance, SNAP has increasingly become (with Medicaid) the centerpiece of the U.S. welfare system.

SNAP calculates 30% of each recipient family's earnings and then issues enough food credits to make up the difference between that amount and the amount that is needed to buy an adequate diet. These monthly allotments are usually provided electronically through an electronic benefit transfer, a debit card that is similar to a bank card. The cash value of these benefits is based on the size of the household and how much the family earns. Households without an elderly or disabled member generally must have a monthly total (gross) cash income at or below 130% of the poverty level and may not have liquid assets (cash, savings, or other assets that can be easily sold) of more than $2,000. (If the household has a member aged 60 years or older, the asset limit is $3,000.) The net monthly income limit (gross income minus any approved deductions for child care, some housing costs, and other expenses) must be 100% or less of the poverty level, or $2,025 per month for a family of four between October 2016 and September 2017. (See Table 3.4.)

With some exceptions, SNAP is automatically available to SSI and TANF recipients. SNAP benefits are higher in states with lower TANF benefits because those benefits are considered a part of a family's countable income. To receive SNAP, certain household members must register for work, accept suitable job offers, or fulfill work or training requirements (such as looking or training for a job).

TABLE 3.4

Supplemental Nutrition Assistance Program eligibility income thresholds, by household size, 2016–17

[Oct. 1, 2016 through Sept. 30, 2017]

Household size	Gross monthly income (130 percent of poverty)	Net monthly income (100 percent of poverty)
1	$1,287	$990
2	1,736	1,335
3	2,184	1,680
4	2,633	2,025
5	3,081	2,370
6	3,530	2,715
7	3,980	3,061
8	4,430	3,408
Each additional member	+451	+347

SOURCE: "Income," in *Supplemental Nutrition Assistance Program (SNAP): Eligibility*, U.S. Department of Agriculture, Food and Nutrition Service, October 2016, https://www.fns.usda.gov/snap/eligibility#Income (accessed August 4, 2017)

Although the federal government sets guidelines and provides funding, SNAP is administered by the states. State agencies certify eligibility as well as calculate and issue benefit allotments. Most often, the welfare agency and staff that administer the TANF and Medicaid programs also run SNAP. The program operates in all 50 states, the District of Columbia, Guam, and the Virgin Islands. (Puerto Rico is covered under a separate nutrition assistance program.)

Except for some small differences in Alaska, Hawaii, and the U.S. territories, the program is run the same way throughout the United States. The states pay 50% of the administrative costs, and the federal government pays 100% of SNAP benefits and the other 50% of the administrative costs.

Unlike TANF, SNAP is responsive to fluctuations in unemployment and the poverty level, with participation increasing in times of economic distress and decreasing as unemployment and poverty rates fall. In FY 2000, at a time of economic expansion and low unemployment, the federal government paid $15 billion in SNAP benefits. (See Table 3.5.) In FY 2016, as the U.S. economy continued to suffer the aftereffects of the Great Recession and many unemployed people had given up looking for work, the federal government spent $66.5 billion on SNAP benefits, or an estimated average monthly benefit of $125.40 per recipient. The ARRA supplemented SNAP's structural responsiveness to the recession by providing an additional $500 million to support participation in the program and by increasing benefit levels to 113.6% of the value of the Thrifty Food Plan. This supplemental funding expired in October 2013.

National School Lunch and School Breakfast Programs

The National School Lunch Program (NSLP) and the School Breakfast Program provide federal cash and

TABLE 3.5

Supplemental Nutrition Assistance Program participation and costs, fiscal years 1969–2016

Fiscal year	Average participation Thousands	Average benefit per person[a] Dollars	Total benefits Millions of dollars	All other costs[b] Millions of dollars	Total costs Millions of dollars
1969	2,878	6.63	228.80	21.70	250.50
1970	4,340	10.55	549.70	27.20	576.90
1971	9,368	13.55	1,522.70	53.20	1,575.90
1972	11,109	13.48	1,797.30	69.40	1,866.70
1973	12,166	14.60	2,131.40	76.00	2,207.40
1974	12,862	17.61	2,718.30	119.20	2,837.50
1975	17,064	21.40	4,385.50	233.20	4,618.70
1976	18,549	23.93	5,326.50	359.00	5,685.50
1977	17,077	24.71	5,067.00	394.00	5,461.00
1978	16,001	26.77	5,139.20	380.50	5,519.70
1979	17,653	30.59	6,480.20	459.60	6,939.80
1980	21,082	34.47	8,720.90	485.60	9,206.50
1981	22,430	39.49	10,629.90	595.40	11,225.20
1982[c]	21,717	39.17	10,208.30	628.40	10,836.70
1983	21,625	42.98	11,152.30	694.80	11,847.10
1984	20,854	42.74	10,696.10	882.60	11,578.80
1985	19,899	44.99	10,743.60	959.60	11,703.20
1986	19,429	45.49	10,605.20	1,033.20	11,638.40
1987	19,113	45.78	10,500.30	1,103.90	11,604.20
1988	18,645	49.83	11,149.10	1,167.70	12,316.80
1989	18,806	51.71	11,669.78	1,231.81	12,901.59
1990	20,049	58.78	14,142.79	1,304.47	15,447.26
1991	22,625	63.78	17,315.77	1,431.50	18,747.27
1992	25,407	68.57	20,905.68	1,556.66	22,462.34
1993	26,987	67.95	22,006.03	1,646.94	23,652.97
1994	27,474	69.00	22,748.58	1,744.87	24,493.45
1995	26,619	71.27	22,764.07	1,856.30	24,620.37
1996	25,543	73.21	22,440.11	1,890.88	24,330.99
1997	22,858	71.27	19,548.86	1,958.68	21,507.55
1998	19,791	71.12	16,890.49	2,097.84	18,988.32
1999	18,183	72.27	15,769.40	2,051.52	17,820.92
2000	17,194	72.62	14,983.32	2,070.70	17,054.02
2001	17,318	74.81	15,547.39	2,242.00	17,789.39
2002	19,096	79.67	18,256.20	2,380.82	20,637.02
2003	21,250	83.94	21,404.28	2,412.01	23,816.28
2004	23,811	86.16	24,618.89	2,480.14	27,099.03
2005	25,628	92.89	28,567.88	2,504.13	31,072.01
2006	26,549	94.75	30,187.35	2,715.72	32,903.06
2007	26,316	96.18	30,373.27	2,800.25	33,173.52
2008	28,223	102.19	34,608.40	3,031.25	37,639.64
2009	33,490	125.31	50,359.92	3,260.00	53,619.92
2010	40,302	133.79	64,702.16	3,581.30	68,283.47
2011	44,709	133.85	71,810.92	3,875.62	75,686.54
2012	46,609	133.41	74,619.34	3,791.75	78,411.10
2013	47,636	133.07	76,066.32	3,792.75	79,859.07
2014	46,664	125.01	69,998.84	4,059.63	74,058.46
2015	45,767	126.81	69,645.14	4,315.68	73,960.82
2016	44,219	125.40	66,539.35	4,384.18	70,923.53

[a]Represents average monthly benefits per person.
[b]Includes the federal share of state administrative expenses, nutrition education, and employment and training programs. Also includes federal costs (e.g., Benefit and Retailer Redemption and Monitoring, Payment Accuracy, EBT Systems, Program Evaluation and Modernization, Program Access, Health and Nutrition Pilot Projects).
[c]Puerto Rico initiated food stamp operations during fiscal year 1975 and participated through June of fiscal year 1982. A separate nutrition assistance grant began in July 1982.
Note: All data are subject to revision.

SOURCE: "Supplemental Nutrition Assistance Program Participation and Costs," in *Supplemental Nutrition Assistance Program (SNAP)*, U.S. Department of Agriculture, Food and Nutrition Service, August 2017, https://www.fns.usda.gov/sites/default/files/pd/SNAPsummary.pdf (accessed August 4, 2017)

commodity support to participating public and private schools and to nonprofit residential institutions that serve meals to children. Children from households with incomes at or below 130% of the poverty line receive free meals. Children from households with incomes between 130% and 185% of the poverty level receive meals at a reduced price (no more than $0.40). Table 3.6 shows the income eligibility guidelines, based on the poverty guidelines, effective from July 1, 2017, to June 30, 2018. The levels were higher in Alaska and Hawaii

than in the 48 contiguous states, the District of Columbia, Guam, and other U.S. territories. Children in TANF families are automatically eligible to receive free breakfasts and lunches. Almost 90% of federal funding for the NSLP is used to subsidize free and reduced-price lunches for low-income children.

The NSLP, which was created in 1946 under the National School Lunch Act, supplies subsidized lunches to children in almost all schools and in 6,000 residential

TABLE 3.6

Income eligibility guidelines for free and reduced-price school meals, 2017–18

Household size	Federal poverty guidelines Annual	Reduced price meals—185%					Free meals—130%				
		Annual	Monthly	Twice per month	Every two weeks	Weekly	Annual	Monthly	Twice per month	Every two weeks	Weekly
48 contiguous states, District of Columbia, Guam, and territories											
1	12,060	22,311	1,860	930	859	430	15,678	1,307	654	603	302
2	16,240	30,044	2,504	1,252	1,156	578	21,112	1,760	880	812	406
3	20,420	37,777	3,149	1,575	1,453	727	26,546	2,213	1,107	1,021	511
4	24,600	45,510	3,793	1,897	1,751	876	31,980	2,665	1,333	1,230	615
5	28,780	53,243	4,437	2,219	2,048	1,024	37,414	3,118	1,559	1,439	720
6	32,960	60,976	5,082	2,541	2,346	1,173	42,848	3,571	1,786	1,648	824
7	37,140	68,709	5,726	2,863	2,643	1,322	48,282	4,024	2,012	1,857	929
8	41,320	76,442	6,371	3,186	2,941	1,471	53,716	4,477	2,239	2,066	1,033
For each add'l family member, add	4,180	7,733	645	323	298	149	5,434	453	227	209	105
Alaska											
1	15,060	27,861	2,322	1,161	1,072	536	19,578	1,632	816	753	377
2	20,290	37,537	3,129	1,565	1,444	722	26,377	2,199	1,100	1,015	508
3	25,520	47,212	3,935	1,968	1,816	908	33,176	2,765	1,383	1,276	638
4	30,750	56,888	4,741	2,371	2,188	1,094	39,975	3,332	1,666	1,538	769
5	35,980	66,563	5,547	2,774	2,561	1,281	46,774	3,898	1,949	1,799	900
6	41,210	76,239	6,354	3,177	2,933	1,467	53,573	4,465	2,233	2,061	1,031
7	46,440	85,914	7,160	3,580	3,305	1,653	60,372	5,031	2,516	2,322	1,161
8	51,670	95,590	7,966	3,983	3,677	1,839	67,171	5,598	2,799	2,584	1,292
For each add'l family member, add	5,230	9,676	807	404	373	187	6,799	567	284	262	131
Hawaii											
1	13,860	25,641	2,137	1,069	987	494	18,018	1,502	751	693	347
2	18,670	34,540	2,879	1,440	1,329	665	24,271	2,023	1,012	934	467
3	23,480	43,438	3,620	1,810	1,671	836	30,524	2,544	1,272	1,174	587
4	28,290	52,337	4,362	2,181	2,013	1,007	36,777	3,065	1,533	1,415	708
5	33,100	61,235	5,103	2,552	2,356	1,178	43,030	3,586	1,793	1,655	828
6	37,910	70,134	5,845	2,923	2,698	1,349	49,283	4,107	2,054	1,896	948
7	42,720	79,032	6,586	3,293	3,040	1,520	55,536	4,628	2,314	2,136	1,068
8	47,530	87,931	7,328	3,664	3,382	1,691	61,789	5,150	2,575	2,377	1,189
For each add'l family member, add	4,810	8,899	742	371	343	172	6,253	522	261	241	121

SOURCE: "Income Eligibility Guidelines," in "Child Nutrition Programs: Income Eligibility Guidelines," *Federal Register*, vol. 82, no. 67, April 10, 2017, https://www.gpo.gov/fdsys/pkg/FR-2017-04-10/pdf/2017-07043.pdf (accessed August 4, 2017)

and day care institutions. During the 1996–97 school year the USDA changed certain policies so that school meals would meet the recommendations of the Dietary Guidelines for America, the federal standards for what constitutes a healthy diet. The program has grown steadily since its introduction. In FY 2016 the program served free lunches to 20.1 million children and reduced-price lunches to another 2 million. (See Table 3.7.)

The School Breakfast Program, which was created under the Child Nutrition Act of 1966, serves far fewer students than does the NSLP. The School Breakfast Program also differs from the NSLP in that most schools offering the program are in low-income areas, and the children who participate in the program are mainly from low- and moderate-income families. In FY 2016 the program served free breakfasts to 11.5 million children and reduced-price breakfasts to another 900,000. (See Table 3.8.)

In December 2010 President Obama signed the Healthy, Hunger-Free Kids Act into law. This act upgraded

nutritional standards for school meal programs and required schools to make information on the nutritional quality of meals available to parents. The act provided several ways to certify additional children for the free and reduced-price meal programs, such as using Medicaid data to directly certify children rather than relying on paper applications or using census data in high-poverty communities to certify schoolwide income eligibility. In addition, the act expanded the school meal program to after-school meals through the existing Child and Adult Care Food Program providers across the nation.

Special Supplemental Nutrition Program for Women, Infants, and Children

The Special Supplemental Nutrition Program for Women, Infants, and Children (WIC) provides food assistance as well as nutrition counseling and health services to low-income pregnant women, to women who have just given birth and their babies, and to low-income children up to five years old. Participants in the program must have incomes at or below 185% of the

TABLE 3.7

National school lunch program participation and lunches served, fiscal years 1969–2016

| Fiscal year | Average participation | | | | Total lunches served | Percent free/ reduced price of total |
| | Free | Reduced price | Full price | Total | | |
	Millions	Millions	Millions	Millions	Millions	%
1969	2.9	*	16.5	19.4	3,368.2	15.1
1970	4.6	*	17.8	22.4	3,565.1	20.7
1971	5.8	0.5	17.8	24.1	3,848.3	26.1
1972	7.3	0.5	16.6	24.4	3,972.1	32.4
1973	8.1	0.5	16.1	24.7	4,008.8	35.0
1974	8.6	0.5	15.5	24.6	3,981.6	37.1
1975	9.4	0.6	14.9	24.9	4,063.0	40.3
1976	10.2	0.8	14.6	25.6	4,147.9	43.1
1977	10.5	1.3	14.5	26.2	4,250.0	44.8
1978	10.3	1.5	14.9	26.7	4,294.1	44.4
1979	10.0	1.7	15.3	27.0	4,357.4	43.6
1980	10.0	1.9	14.7	26.6	4,387.0	45.1
1981	10.6	1.9	13.3	25.8	4,210.6	48.6
1982	9.8	1.6	11.5	22.9	3,755.0	50.2
1983	10.3	1.5	11.2	23.0	3,803.3	51.7
1984	10.3	1.5	11.5	23.4	3,826.2	51.0
1985	9.9	1.6	12.1	23.6	3,890.1	49.1
1986	10.0	1.6	12.2	23.7	3,942.5	49.1
1987	10.0	1.6	12.4	23.9	3,939.9	48.6
1988	9.8	1.6	12.8	24.2	4,032.9	47.4
1989	9.7	1.6	12.9	24.2	4,004.9	47.2
1990	9.8	1.7	12.6	24.1	4,009.0	48.3
1991	10.3	1.8	12.2	24.2	4,050.7	50.4
1992	11.2	1.7	11.7	24.6	4,101.4	53.1
1993	11.7	1.7	11.4	24.9	4,137.7	54.8
1994	12.2	1.8	11.3	25.3	4,201.6	55.9
1995	12.4	1.9	11.4	25.7	4,253.3	56.4
1996	12.6	2.0	11.3	25.9	4,313.2	56.9
1997	12.9	2.1	11.3	26.3	4,409.0	57.6
1998	13.0	2.2	11.4	26.6	4,425.0	57.8
1999	13.0	2.4	11.6	27.0	4,513.6	57.6
2000	13.0	2.5	11.9	27.3	4,575.0	57.1
2001	12.9	2.6	12.0	27.5	4,585.2	56.8
2002	13.3	2.6	12.0	28.0	4,716.6	57.6
2003	13.7	2.7	11.9	28.4	4,762.9	58.5
2004	14.1	2.8	12.0	29.0	4,842.4	59.1
2005	14.6	2.9	12.2	29.6	4,976.4	59.4
2006	14.8	2.9	12.4	30.1	5,027.9	59.3
2007	15.0	3.1	12.6	30.6	5,071.3	59.3
2008	15.4	3.1	12.5	31.0	5,208.5	60.1
2009	16.3	3.2	11.9	31.3	5,186.0	62.6
2010	17.6	3.0	11.1	31.8	5,278.4	65.3
2011	18.4	2.7	10.8	31.8	5,274.5	66.6
2012	18.7	2.7	10.2	31.7	5,214.8	68.2
2013	18.9	2.6	9.2	30.7	5,097.6	70.5
2014	19.2	2.5	8.8	30.5	5,020.4	71.6
2015	19.8	2.2	8.5	30.5	5,005.5	72.6
2016	20.1	2.0	8.2	30.4	5,052.3	73.3

*Included with free meals.

Notes: Fiscal year 2016 data are preliminary; all data are subject to revision. Participation data are 9-month averages (summer months are excluded).

SOURCE: "National School Lunch Program: Participation and Lunches Served," in *Child Nutrition Tables*, U.S. Department of Agriculture, Food and Nutrition Service, August 2017, https://www.fns.usda.gov/sites/default/files/pd/slsummar.pdf (accessed August 4, 2017)

poverty level (all but five states use this cutoff level) and must be nutritionally at risk.

As explained by the Child Nutrition Act of 1966, nutritional risk includes abnormal nutritional conditions, medical conditions related to nutrition, health-impairing dietary deficiencies, or conditions that might predispose a person to these conditions. Pregnant women may receive benefits throughout their pregnancies and for up to six months after childbirth or up to one year for nursing mothers.

Those receiving WIC benefits get supplemental food each month in the form of actual food items or, more commonly, vouchers (coupons) for the purchase of specific items at the store. Permitted foods contain high amounts of protein, iron, calcium, vitamin A, and vitamin C. Items that may be purchased include milk, cheese, eggs, infant formula, cereals, and fruit or vegetable juices. Mothers participating in WIC are encouraged to breast-feed their infants if possible, but state WIC agencies will provide formula for mothers who choose to use it.

TABLE 3.8

National school breakfast program participation and meals served, fiscal years 1969–2016

| Fiscal years | Total participation[a] | | | | Meals served | Free/reduced price of total meals |
| | Free | Reduced price | Paid | Total | | |
	Millions	Millions	Millions	Millions	Millions	%
1969	—	—	—	0.22	39.70	71.0
1970	—	—	—	0.45	71.80	71.5
1971	0.60	[b]	0.20	0.80	125.50	76.3
1972	0.81	[b]	0.23	1.04	169.30	78.5
1973	0.99	[b]	0.20	1.19	194.10	83.4
1974	1.14	[b]	0.24	1.37	226.70	82.8
1975	1.45	0.04	0.33	1.82	294.70	82.1
1976	1.76	0.06	0.37	2.20	353.60	84.2
1977	2.02	0.11	0.36	2.49	434.30	85.7
1978	2.23	0.16	0.42	2.80	478.80	85.3
1979	2.56	0.21	0.54	3.32	565.60	84.1
1980	2.79	0.25	0.56	3.60	619.90	85.2
1981	3.05	0.25	0.51	3.81	644.20	86.9
1982	2.80	0.16	0.36	3.32	567.40	89.3
1983	2.87	0.15	0.34	3.36	580.70	90.3
1984	2.91	0.15	0.37	3.43	589.20	89.7
1985	2.88	0.16	0.40	3.44	594.90	88.6
1986	2.93	0.16	0.41	3.50	610.60	88.7
1987	3.01	0.17	0.43	3.61	621.50	88.4
1988	3.03	0.18	0.47	3.68	642.50	87.5
1989	3.11	0.19	0.51	3.81	658.45	86.8
1990	3.30	0.22	0.55	4.07	707.49	86.7
1991	3.61	0.25	0.58	4.44	771.86	87.3
1992	4.05	0.26	0.61	4.92	852.43	88.0
1993	4.41	0.28	0.66	5.36	923.56	87.9
1994	4.76	0.32	0.75	5.83	1,001.52	87.4
1995	5.10	0.37	0.85	6.32	1,078.92	86.8
1996	5.27	0.41	0.90	6.58	1,125.74	86.5
1997	5.52	0.45	0.95	6.92	1,191.21	86.5
1998	5.64	0.50	1.01	7.14	1,220.90	86.1
1999	5.72	0.56	1.09	7.37	1,267.62	85.4
2000	5.73	0.61	1.21	7.55	1,303.35	84.2
2001	5.80	0.67	1.32	7.79	1,334.51	83.2
2002	6.03	0.70	1.41	8.15	1,404.76	82.9
2003	6.22	0.74	1.47	8.43	1,447.90	82.8
2004	6.52	0.80	1.58	8.90	1,524.91	82.4
2005	6.80	0.86	1.70	9.36	1,603.88	82.1
2006	6.99	0.92	1.86	9.76	1,663.07	81.2
2007	7.15	0.98	1.99	10.12	1,713.96	80.6
2008	7.48	1.04	2.08	10.61	1,812.41	80.6
2009	7.99	1.07	2.01	11.08	1,866.65	82.1
2010	8.68	1.05	1.94	11.67	1,968.01	83.5
2011	9.20	0.98	2.00	12.17	2,048.09	83.7
2012	9.77	1.04	2.05	12.87	2,145.04	84.2
2013	10.16	1.02	2.02	13.20	2,223.00	84.8
2014	10.54	1.01	2.08	13.64	2,273.59	84.9
2015	11.05	0.90	2.10	14.04	2,334.19	85.2
2016	11.53	0.86	2.18	14.57	2,448.36	85.1

[a]Nine month average: October-May plus September.
[b]Included with free participation.
Notes: Fiscal year 2016 data are preliminary; all data are subject to revision.

SOURCE: "School Breakfast Program Participation and Meals Served," in *Child Nutrition Tables*, U.S. Department of Agriculture, Food and Nutrition Service, August 2017, https://www.fns.usda.gov/sites/default/files/pd/sbsummar.pdf (accessed August 4, 2017)

The USDA estimates that the national average monthly cost of a WIC food package in FY 2016 was $42.76 per participant. (See Table 3.9.) The federal government spent just under $6 billion to operate WIC in FY 2016, which was down significantly from previous years, and program participation had fallen from a high of 9.2 million women, infants, and children in FY 2010 to 7.7 million in FY 2016. WIC works in conjunction with the Farmers' Market Nutrition Program, which was established in 1992 to provide WIC recipients with increased access, in the form of vouchers, to fresh fruits and vegetables.

OTHER PUBLIC PROGRAMS TO FIGHT POVERTY

Unemployment Insurance

The federal government and the states combine to offer a system of unemployment insurance, often called unemployment compensation, that provides a temporary

TABLE 3.9

Special Supplemental Nutrition Program for Women, Infants, and Children program participation and costs, fiscal years 1974–2016

| Fiscal year | Total participation[a] (Thousands) | Program costs | | | Average monthly food cost per person (Dollars) |
		Food (Millions of dollars)	NSA (Millions of dollars)	Total[b] (Millions of dollars)	
1974	88	8.2	2.2	10.4	15.68
1975	344	76.7	12.6	89.3	18.58
1976	520	122.3	20.3	142.6	19.60
1977	848	211.7	44.2	255.9	20.80
1978	1,181	311.5	68.1	379.6	21.99
1979	1,483	428.6	96.8	525.4	24.09
1980	1,914	584.1	140.5	727.7	25.43
1981	2,119	708.0	160.6	871.6	27.84
1982	2,189	757.6	190.5	948.8	28.83
1983	2,537	901.8	221.3	1,126.0	29.62
1984	3,045	1,117.3	268.8	1,388.1	30.58
1985	3,138	1,193.2	294.4	1,489.3	31.69
1986	3,312	1,264.4	316.4	1,582.9	31.82
1987	3,429	1,344.7	333.1	1,679.6	32.68
1988	3,593	1,434.8	360.6	1,797.5	33.28
1989	4,119	1,489.4	416.5	1,910.9	30.13
1990	4,517	1,636.8	478.7	2,122.4	30.20
1991	4,893	1,751.9	544.0	2,301.0	29.84
1992	5,403	1,960.5	632.7	2,600.6	30.24
1993	5,921	2,115.1	705.6	2,828.6	29.77
1994	6,477	2,325.2	834.4	3,169.3	29.92
1995	6,894	2,511.6	904.6	3,436.2	30.36
1996	7,186	2,689.9	985.1	3,695.4	31.19
1997	7,407	2,815.5	1,008.2	3,843.8	31.68
1998	7,367	2,808.1	1,061.4	3,890.4	31.76
1999	7,311	2,851.6	1,063.9	3,938.1	32.50
2000	7,192	2,853.1	1,102.6	3,982.1	33.06
2001	7,306	3,007.9	1,110.6	4,149.4	34.31
2002	7,491	3,129.7	1,182.3	4,339.8	34.82
2003	7,631	3,230.3	1,260.0	4,524.4	35.28
2004	7,904	3,562.0	1,272.4	4,887.3	37.55
2005	8,023	3,602.8	1,335.5	4,992.6	37.42
2006	8,088	3,597.5	1,402.6	5,072.0	37.07
2007	8,285	3,881.1	1,479.0	5,409.6	39.04
2008	8,705	4,534.0	1,607.6	6,188.8	43.40
2009	9,122	4,640.9	1,788.0	6,471.6	42.40
2010	9,175	4,561.9	1,907.9	6,689.9	41.43
2011	8,961	5,020.8	1,961.3	7,180.7	46.69
2012	8,908	4,810.5	1,877.8	6,801.3	45.00
2013	8,663	4,497.2	1,881.6	6,500.1	43.26
2014	8,258	4,324.3	1,903.4	6,350.8	43.64
2015	8,024	4,175.9	1,922.1	6,214.8	43.37
2016	7,696	3,949.4	1,946.0	5,965.9	42.76

NSA = Nutrition Services and Administrative costs. Nutrition Services includes nutrition education, preventative and coordination services (such as health care), and promotion of breastfeeding and immunization.

[a]Participation data are annual averages (6 months in fiscal year 1974; 12 months all subsequent years).

[b]In addition to food and NSA costs, total expenditures includes funds for program evaluation, Farmers' Market Nutrition Program (FY 1989 onward), special projects and infrastructure.

Note: Fiscal year 2016 data are preliminary; all data are subject to revision.

SOURCE: "WIC Program Participation and Costs," in *WIC Program*, U.S. Department of Agriculture, Food and Nutrition Service, August 2017, https://www.fns .usda.gov/sites/default/files/pd/wisummary.pdf (accessed August 4, 2017)

source of income to those who have lost their jobs. Besides giving workers support as they seek new jobs, unemployment compensation is intended to exert a stabilizing influence on the economy. When workers lose their jobs, unemployment benefits allow them to continue satisfying their consumer needs, which keeps demand for goods and services from dropping precipitately in times of economic crisis or stagnation.

The unemployment insurance system was designed in 1935 during the administration of President Franklin D. Roosevelt (1882–1945) with the intent of giving states wide latitude in operating their own programs. For the basic system, states set their own eligibility criteria and benefit levels with minimal intervention so long as they operate within broad federal guidelines. The federal government pays for administrative costs, but the states manage their own funds for actual payments to those who have lost their jobs. Both state and federal spending on unemployment compensation is generated via taxes on employers, but economists note that this money ultimately comes from the workers themselves because employers reduce the wages they pay in proportion to the taxes they are required to contribute to unemployment insurance funds. Most states offer up to 26 weeks of unemployment insurance benefits, although the duration of benefits is often shorter because of irregularities in an individual's employment history. Qualifying workers typically receive approximately half of the amount of money they made on the job.

The general criteria for unemployment compensation eligibility are consistent across the states. A qualifying worker must have met certain thresholds for the amount of time on the job and the income generated during that time, and he or she must have lost the job through no fault of his or her own. Additionally, the person must be ready and willing to work, and he or she must be actively seeking a new job. Unemployment insurance is not intended to cover numerous classes of workers, including self-employed workers, temporary workers, and those who voluntarily leave their jobs.

Different states, however, interpret these general criteria very differently. In some states it is more difficult for employees to prove that they were fired through no fault of their own than in other, more pro-worker states. The period of employment used to calculate eligibility and benefits varies by state, compensation levels vary by state, and the degree to which part-time workers are covered varies by state. According to Chad Stone and William Chen of the CBPP, in *Introduction to Unemployment Insurance* (July 30, 2014, http://www.cbpp.org/files/12-19-02ui.pdf), since the 1950s basic unemployment compensation has provided support for fewer than half of unemployed workers. The researchers note that a "growing percentage of unemployed workers who meet the basic criteria ... yet fail to satisfy their *state's* eligibility criteria—often established decades ago (in a very different labor market)—has made it harder for [the unemployment insurance system] to fulfill its mission."

Besides the basic unemployment insurance system, there is a permanent Extended Benefits program that covers workers for an additional period in states whose job markets are poor. The length of the extension of benefits varies based on the state's unemployment rate and the laws governing its unemployment insurance program. Historically, Extended Benefits is funded by both the federal government and the states, and the program operates even when the overall national economy is strong. However, with the Great Recession and the passage of the ARRA in 2009, the federal government began fully funding the Extended Benefits program. This measure was kept in place through 2013.

Additionally, the federal government has created numerous other temporary programs meant to supplement the basic state programs during periods of high unemployment nationwide. In 2008 Congress created the Emergency Unemployment Compensation program to respond to the massive job losses during the Great Recession. Because of lingering unemployment even after the recession officially ended in June 2009, the Emergency Unemployment Compensation program was repeatedly reauthorized, and it remained in operation through 2013. In states with particularly high unemployment during the recession and its aftermath, some workers were able to collect benefits for as long as 99 weeks. As the unemployment rate climbed from below 5% in 2007 to a peak of 10% in 2009, the average duration of a worker's unemployment compensation rose from 15 weeks to almost 20 weeks, according to statistics available at the website of the U.S. Department of Labor's Employment and Training Administration (https://oui.doleta.gov/unemploy/chartbook.asp).

Federal Minimum Wage

The federal minimum wage dates back to the passage of the Fair Labor Standards Act of 1938, which established basic national standards for minimum wages, overtime pay, and the employment of child workers. (The minimum wage is a cash wage only and does not include any fringe benefits. Consequently, the total compensation for minimum-wage workers is even lower than the total compensation for higher-paid workers, who generally receive some kind of benefits besides wages. Most minimum-wage workers do not receive any benefits.) The provisions of the act have been extended to cover many other areas of employment since 1938.

The first minimum wage instituted in 1938 was $0.25 per hour. (See Table 3.10.) It gradually increased over the years, reaching $4.25 in 1991. In July 1996 Congress passed legislation that raised the minimum wage to $5.15 in 1997 by means of two $0.45 increases. In July 2007 the minimum wage was raised to $5.85, in July 2008 it was raised to $6.55, and in July 2009 it was raised to $7.25. As of 2017, a person working 40 hours per week for 50 weeks per year at minimum wage ($7.25 per hour) would gross $290 per week, or $14,500 per year, an income below the poverty level for a family of two ($16,240 in 2017) and substantially below the poverty level for a family of three ($20,420). (See Table 1.1 in Chapter 1.)

WHO WORKS FOR MINIMUM WAGE? Although workers must receive at least the minimum wage for most jobs, there are some exceptions in which a person may be paid less than the minimum wage. Full-time students working on a part-time basis in the service and retail industries or at the students' academic institution, certain disabled people, and workers who are "customarily and regularly" tipped may receive less than the minimum wage. According to the BLS, in *Characteristics of Minimum Wage Workers, 2016* (April 2017, https://www.bls.gov/opub/reports/minimum-wage/2016/pdf/home.pdf), 701,000 workers earned exactly the federal minimum wage in 2016 and 1.5 million earned below the minimum. The percentage of workers earning at or below the minimum wage was substantially higher than in the prerecession years. In 2006 only 2.2% of all salary

TABLE 3.10

Federal minimum wage rates under the Fair Labor Standards Act, 1938–2017

Effective date	1938 act[a]	1961 amendments[b]	1966 & subsequent amendments[c]	
			Nonfarm	Farm
Oct. 24, 1938	$0.25			
Oct. 24, 1939	$0.30			
Oct. 24, 1945	$0.40			
Jan. 25, 1950	$0.75			
Mar. 1, 1956	$1.00			
Sept. 3, 1961	$1.15	$1.00		
Sept. 3, 1963	$1.25			
Sept. 3, 1964		$1.15		
Sept. 3, 1965		$1.25		
Feb. 1, 1967	$1.40	$1.40	$1.00	$1.00
Feb. 1, 1968	$1.60	$1.60	$1.15	$1.15
Feb. 1, 1969			$1.30	$1.30
Feb. 1, 1970			$1.45	
Feb. 1, 1971			$1.60	
May 1, 1974	$2.00	$2.00	$1.90	$1.60
Jan. 1, 1975	$2.10	$2.10	$2.00	$1.80
Jan. 1, 1976	$2.30	$2.30	$2.20	$2.00
Jan. 1, 1977			$2.30	$2.20
Jan. 1, 1978	$2.65 for all covered, nonexempt workers			
Jan. 1, 1979	$2.90 for all covered, nonexempt workers			
Jan. 1, 1980	$3.10 for all covered, nonexempt workers			
Jan. 1, 1981	$3.35 for all covered, nonexempt workers			
Apr. 1, 1990[d]	$3.80 for all covered, nonexempt workers			
Apr. 1, 1991	$4.25 for all covered, nonexempt workers			
Oct. 1, 1996[e]	$4.75 for all covered, nonexempt workers			
Sept. 1, 1997	$5.15 for all covered, nonexempt workers			
Jul. 24, 2007	$5.85 for all covered, nonexempt workers			
Jul. 24, 2008	$6.55 for all covered, nonexempt workers			
Jul. 24, 2009	$7.25 for all covered, nonexempt workers			

[a]The 1938 Act was applicable generally to employees engaged in interstate commerce or in the production of goods for interstate commerce.

[b]The 1961 Amendments extended coverage primarily to employees in large retail and service enterprises as well as to local transit, construction, and gasoline service station employees.

[c]The 1966 Amendments extended coverage to State and local government employees of hospitals, nursing homes, and schools, and to laundries, dry cleaners, and large hotels, motels, restaurants, and farms. Subsequent amendments extended coverage to the remaining Federal, State and local government employees who were not protected in 1966, to certain workers in retail and service trades previously exempted, and to certain domestic workers in private household employment.

[d]Grandfather Clause: Employees who do not meet the tests for individual coverage, and whose employers were covered by the FLSA, on March 31, 1990, and fail to meet the increased annual dollar volume (ADV) test for enterprise coverage, must continue to receive at least $3.35 an hour.

[e]A subminimum wage—$4.25 an hour—is established for employees under 20 years of age during their first 90 consecutive calendar days of employment with an employer.

SOURCE: "Federal Minimum Wage Rates under the Fair Labor Standards Act," U.S. Department of Labor, Wage, and Hour Division, http://www.dol.gov/whd/minwage/chart.pdf (accessed August 4, 2017)

and wage workers made at or below minimum wage; this percentage rose to 6% in 2010, the highest level since the late 1990s, before falling to 2.7% in 2016.

The BLS notes that in 2016, two-thirds (66.5%) of all U.S. workers who made the minimum wage or less were in the service occupations and that a majority of those service workers were in food preparation and serving jobs. The industry with the highest percentage of hourly workers making at or below minimum wage was leisure and hospitality, at 12.6%. Many of these workers receive tips in addition to their base pay of minimum wage or less.

Earnings at or below the minimum wage were more common among part-time hourly workers (6.2% of whom were paid at or below the minimum wage) than full-time workers (1.5%). (See Table 3.11.) Young workers hold minimum-wage jobs at rates that are disproportionate with their numbers as a share of the overall labor force. Two-fifths (40.9%) of the total number of workers making the minimum wage or less in 2016 were under the age of 25 years, even though this age group represented only 19.8% (15.9 million) of the 79.9 million U.S. workers who were paid by the hour. The pool of workers making the minimum wage or less was disproportionately female: 1.4 million such workers were women and 769,000 were men. White workers accounted for 1.6 million (74.2%) of the 2.2 million total workers making at or below the minimum wage, which was consistent with the percentage of white hourly workers among all hourly workers (61.1 million of 79.9 million, or 76.5%). African American workers accounted for 390,000 (18.1%) of all those who earned at or below minimum wage, Hispanic workers for 366,000 (17%), and Asian American workers for 96,000 (4.5%).

THE INSUFFICIENCY OF MINIMUM WAGE TO MEET EXPENSES. Minimum wage is insufficient to meet the living expenses in almost all locations of the United States, and even full-time minimum-wage workers are eligible for public assistance programs. For example, in *Fast Food, Poverty Wages: The Public Cost of Low-Wage Jobs in the Fast-Food Industry* (October 15, 2013, http://laborcenter.berkeley.edu/pdf/2013/fast_food_poverty_wages.pdf), Sylvia Allegretto et al. find that 52% of people in the families of fast-food workers (one of the industries with the largest number of minimum-wage workers) are enrolled in at least one government assistance program. The researchers also find that 20% of these families live below poverty and 43% have incomes below 200% of poverty. Some of the workers in these families did not work full time; however, even among those who did work 40 or more hours per week, more than half were enrolled in government assistance programs.

As a result of such facts, a nationwide movement of fast-food workers emerged during the second decade of the 21st century. Steven Greenhouse reports in "Strong Voice in 'Fight for 15' Fast-Food Wage Campaign" (NYTimes.com, December 4, 2014) that in 2012, 200 fast-food workers in New York City walked off the job to protest their low pay, and such walkouts spread across the country. In the following years the organizers of these protests combined forces, creating the Fight for 15 movement (https://fightfor15.org), which united fast-food workers in 150 cities, 33 countries, and six continents. One of the movement's key leaders and spokespersons was Terrance Wise, a Kansas City, Missouri, father of three who worked 16 hours a day at two fast-food jobs. In spite of spending all of his waking hours at work, Wise did not make enough money to pay for housing, and when his fiancée was injured and could no

TABLE 3.11

Workers paid hourly rates at or below minimum wage, by selected characteristics, 2016

Characteristic	Number of workers (in thousands)				Percent distribution				Percentage of workers paid		
		At or below the minimum wage				At or below the minimum wage			At or below the minimum wage		
	Total paid hourly rates	Total	At minimum wage	Below minimum wage	Total paid hourly rates	Total	At minimum wage	Below minimum wage	Total	At minimum wage	Below minimum wage
Age and gender											
Total, 16 years and older	79,883	2,153	701	1,451	100.0	100.0	100.0	100.0	2.7	0.9	1.8
16 to 24 years	15,856	976	383	594	19.8	45.4	54.5	40.9	6.2	2.4	3.7
16 to 19 years	4,592	443	214	229	5.7	20.6	30.5	15.8	9.7	4.7	5.0
25 years and older	64,026	1,176	319	857	80.2	54.6	45.5	59.1	1.8	0.5	1.3
Men, 16 years and older	39,568	769	270	499	49.5	35.7	38.4	34.4	1.9	0.7	1.3
16 to 24 years	7,967	357	147	210	10.0	16.6	21.0	14.5	4.5	1.8	2.6
16 to 19 years	2,278	183	87	96	2.9	8.5	12.3	6.6	8.0	3.8	4.2
25 years and older	30,601	412	122	289	39.6	19.1	17.5	19.9	1.3	0.4	0.9
Women, 16 years and older	40,315	1,384	432	952	50.5	64.3	61.6	65.6	3.4	1.1	2.4
16 to 24 years	7,890	619	235	384	9.9	28.8	33.6	26.5	7.8	3.0	4.9
16 to 19 years	2,314	260	127	133	2.9	12.1	18.1	9.2	11.3	5.5	5.8
25 years and older	32,425	764	196	568	40.6	35.5	28.0	39.1	2.4	0.6	1.8
Race and Hispanic or Latino ethnicity											
White[a]	61,080	1,597	469	1,127	76.5	74.2	66.9	77.7	2.6	0.8	1.8
Men	30,823	554	190	364	38.6	25.7	27.1	25.1	1.8	0.6	1.2
Women	30,256	1,043	280	763	37.9	48.5	39.9	52.6	3.4	0.9	2.5
Black or African American[a]	11,681	390	193	197	14.6	18.1	27.5	13.5	3.3	1.7	1.7
Men	5,297	156	62	93	6.6	7.2	8.9	6.4	2.9	1.2	1.8
Women	6,385	234	131	103	8.0	10.9	18.7	7.1	3.7	2.1	1.6
Asian[a]	3,692	96	21	75	5.0	4.5	3.0	5.2	2.4	0.5	1.9
Men	1,841	35	10	25	2.3	1.6	1.4	1.7	1.9	0.5	1.4
Women	2,121	61	11	50	2.7	2.8	1.6	3.4	2.9	0.5	2.3
Hispanic or Latino	16,241	366	103	264	20.3	17.0	14.6	18.2	2.3	0.6	1.6
Men	9,044	137	44	93	11.3	6.4	6.3	6.4	1.5	0.5	1.0
Women	7,197	229	59	171	9.0	10.6	8.4	11.8	3.2	0.8	2.4
Full-and part-time status											
Full-time workers[b]	59,198	884	183	702	74.1	41.1	26.0	48.4	1.5	0.3	1.2
Men	32,418	334	66	268	40.6	15.5	9.5	18.5	1.0	0.2	0.8
Women	26,780	550	116	434	33.5	25.6	16.6	29.9	2.1	0.4	1.6
Part-time workers[b]	20,582	1,267	519	748	25.8	58.9	74.0	51.6	6.2	2.5	3.6
Men	7,108	434	203	231	8.9	20.2	29.0	15.9	6.1	2.9	3.3
Women	13,474	833	316	517	16.9	38.7	45.0	35.6	6.2	2.3	3.8

[a]Estimates for the above race groups—White, Black or African American, and Asian—do not sum to totals because data are not presented for all races. Persons whose ethnicity is identified as Hispanic or Latino may be of any race.

[b]The distinction between full- and part-time workers is based on hours usually worked. These data will not sum to totals because full- or part-time status on the principal job is not identifiable for a small number of multiple jobholders. Full time is 35 hours or more per week; part time is less than 35 hours.

Note: Data exclude all self-employed workers, whether or not their businesses are incorporated.

SOURCE: "Table 1. Wage and Salary Workers Paid Hourly Rates with Earnings at or below the Prevailing Federal Minimum Wage, by Selected Characteristics, 2016 Annual Averages," in *Characteristics of Minimum Wage Workers, 2016*, U.S. Department of Labor, Bureau of Labor Statistics, April 2017, https://www.bls.gov/opub/reports/minimum-wage/2016/pdf/home.pdf (accessed August 4, 2017)

longer work, the family was evicted from their apartment and spent three months homeless.

Supplemental Security Income

SSI is a means-tested income assistance program authorized in 1972 by Title XVI of the Social Security Act. The SSI program replaced the combined federal-state programs of Old Age Assistance, Aid to the Blind, and Aid to the Permanently and Totally Disabled in the 50 states and the District of Columbia. These programs, however, still exist in the U.S. territories of Guam, Puerto Rico, and the Virgin Islands. Since the first payments in 1974, SSI has provided monthly cash payments to needy aged, blind, and disabled individuals who meet the eligibility requirements. States may supplement the basic federal SSI payment.

A number of requirements must be met to receive financial benefits from SSI. Applicants must be U.S. residents, although citizenship is not always necessary; some noncitizens who are lawfully residing in the United States are eligible. The applicant must meet the program criteria for age, blindness, or disability. The aged, or elderly, are people aged 65 years and older. To be considered legally blind, a person must have vision of 20/200 or less in the better eye with the use of corrective lenses, have tunnel vision of 20 degrees or less (can only see a small area straight ahead), or have met state qualifications for the earlier Aid to the Blind program. A person is disabled if he or she cannot earn money at a job because of a physical or mental illness or injury that may cause his or her death, or if the condition lasts for 12 months or longer. Those who met earlier state Aid to the Permanently and Totally Disabled requirements may also qualify for assistance.

Unmarried children under the age of 18 years (or age 22 if a full-time student) may qualify for SSI if they have a medically determinable physical or mental impairment that substantially reduces their ability to function independently or to engage in age-appropriate activities. This impairment must be expected to last for a continuous period of more than 12 months or to result in death.

Because SSI is a means-tested benefit, a person's income and property must be counted before he or she can receive benefits. The income thresholds for SSI eligibility vary by state. Income included in the determination of benefits includes any money earned, any Social Security or private pension benefits, and the value of the applicant's shelter and food, if the applicant gets those things from someone else. The applicant must not own assets (excluding the house one lives in and, in most cases, one's car) worth more than $2,000. A couple applying for SSI must not have assets exceeding $3,000. When applying for SSI, applicants must also apply for other forms of government assistance, including SNAP and Medicaid.

Although the income and property eligibility thresholds vary by state, the baseline monthly SSI payment is the same nationwide. According to the Social Security Administration, in "You May Be Able to Get Supplemental Security Income (SSI)" (2017, https://www.ssa.gov/pubs/EN-05-11069.pdf), the basic payment for one person in 2017 was $735 per month, and the basic payment per couple was $1,103 per month. The actual amount an applicant may receive often varies from this basic level. Most states pay a supplement to the federal SSI benefit, increasing the overall disability benefit that eligible applicants receive. Other applicants receive less than the nationwide basic payment because they or their family members have other sources of income or because of other factors related to location and household characteristics.

Tax Relief for the Poor

Both conservatives and liberals hailed the Tax Reform Act of 1986 as a major step toward relieving the tax burden of low-income families, one group of Americans whose wages and benefits have been eroding since 1979. The law enlarged and inflation-proofed the Earned Income Tax Credit (EITC), which provides a refundable tax credit that both offsets taxes and often operates as a wage supplement. Only those who work can qualify, and household earnings must fall below a certain threshold, which varies depending on whether the taxpayer is a single head of household or married and

filing jointly, as well as on the number of children in the household. Children must be under age 19 or under age 24 and enrolled full time in college.

The Internal Revenue Service provides information about income thresholds and the corresponding size of tax credit amounts in "Income Limits and Range of EITC" (August 16, 2017, https://www.eitc.irs.gov/eitc-central/about-eitc/income-limits-and-range-of-eitc/income-limits-and-range-of-eitc). An individual with one child and an income of less than $39,296, or a couple with one child and an income of less than $44,846, was eligible for a credit of $9 to $3,373. An individual with two children and an income of less than $44,648, or a couple with two children and an income of less than $50,198, was eligible for a credit of $10 to $5,572. An individual with three or more children and an income of less than $47,955, or a couple with three or more children and an income of less than $53,505, was eligible for a credit of $11 to $6,269.

Although income must be below these thresholds, families with incomes below the poverty line do not necessarily receive the most generous EITC amounts because they may receive other forms of public assistance. The largest EITC benefits go to working families that are not eligible for most forms of means-tested benefits, and the EITC is considered an effective tool at helping former welfare recipients transition away from government assistance. The gradual phase-out and availability of the EITC at above-poverty income levels helps stabilize a parent's employment by providing additional money to cover expenses that are associated with working, such as child care and transportation. Research finds that the EITC has been an effective work incentive and has significantly increased work participation among single mothers.

Those who do not owe income tax, or who owe an amount smaller than the credit, receive a check directly from the Internal Revenue Service for the credit due them. Most recipients claim the credit when they file an income tax form. In "Statistics for Tax Returns with EITC" (August 2017, https://www.eitc.irs.gov/EITC-Central/eitcstats), the Internal Revenue Service indicates that for tax year 2016 more than 27 million U.S. taxpayers filed EITC claims for an average credit amount of $2,455. The average credit amount per tax return varied by state from $1,957 (Vermont) to $2,917 (Mississippi). (See Table 3.12.)

Although the Tax Reform Act of 1986 has helped ease the burden of federal taxes, most of the poor still pay a substantial share of their income in state and local taxes. To address the needs of such low-income families, 29 states and the District of Columbia have enacted a state EITC to supplement the federal credit, as the CBPP reports in "Policy Basics: State Earned Income Tax Credits" (August 21, 2017, https://www.cbpp.org/sites/default/files/atoms/files/policybasics-seitc.pdf).

TABLE 3.12

Earned Income Tax Credit claims and dollar values, by state, 2016

State*	Number of EITC claims*	Total EITC amount*	Average EITC amount*
Alabama	498 K	$1.4 B	$2,825
Alaska	45 K	$94.6 M	$2,106
Arizona	572 K	$1.5 B	$2,612
Arkansas	295 K	$785 M	$2,660
California	3 M	$7.3 B	$2,409
Colorado	351 K	$777 M	$2,213
Connecticut	219 K	$484 M	$2,212
Delaware	73 K	$176 M	$2,394
District of Columbia	53 K	$124 M	$2,337
Florida	2.1 M	$5.2 B	$2,534
Georgia	1.1 M	$3.0 B	$2,800
Hawaii	104 K	$230 M	$2,210
Idaho	130 K	$304 M	$2,341
Illinois	994 K	$2.5 B	$2,520
Indiana	544 K	$1.3 B	$2,429
Iowa	206 K	$470 M	$2,279
Kansas	207 K	$496 M	$2,394
Kentucky	397 K	$968 M	$2,436
Louisiana	506 K	$1.4 B	$2,862
Maine	99 K	$209 M	$2,108
Maryland	412 K	$973 M	$2,366
Massachusetts	398 K	$838 M	$2,107
Michigan	788 K	$2.0 B	$2,488
Minnesota	334 K	$737 M	$2,210
Mississippi	378 K	$1.1 B	$2,917
Missouri	500 K	$1.2 B	$2,459
Montana	76 K	$166 M	$2,168
Nebraska	132 K	$313 M	$2,361
Nevada	249 K	$616 M	$2,476
New Hampshire	75 K	$150 M	$1,992
New Jersey	593 K	$1.4 B	$2,349
New Mexico	210 K	$522 M	$2,485
New York	1.7 M	$4.1 B	$2,366
North Carolina	921 K	$2.3 B	$2,523
North Dakota	42 K	$90 M	$2,136
Ohio	939 K	$2.3 B	$2,449
Oklahoma	331 K	$844 M	$2,548
Oregon	274 K	$586 M	$2,136
Pennsylvania	919 K	$2.1 B	$2,271
Rhode Island	82 K	$190 M	$2,305
South Carolina	485 K	$1.3 B	$2,592
South Dakota	61 K	$137 M	$2,249
Tennessee	640 K	$1.6 B	$2,573
Texas	2.6 M	$7.1 B	$2,749
Utah	188 K	$444 M	$2,357
Vermont	43 K	$85 M	$1,957
Virginia	606 K	$1.4 B	$2,352
Washington	436 K	$956 M	$2,190
West Virginia	155 K	$357 M	$2,305
Wisconsin	376 K	$849 M	$2,256
Wyoming	36 K	$77 M	$2,150
International	20 K	$43 M	$2,208

*Calendar Half Year Report. Historically, half year data represents over 95 percent of EITC returns.
EITC = Earned Income Tax Credit

SOURCE: "Statistics for Tax Returns with EITC," in *EITC Central*, Internal Revenue Service, August 2017, https://www.eitc.irs.gov/eitc-central/statistics-for-tax-returns-with-eitc/statistics-for-tax-returns-with-eitc (accessed August 4, 2017)

CHAPTER 4
WHO RECEIVES GOVERNMENT BENEFITS?

A variety of government programs exist to assist low-income and impoverished families as well as those unable to work either permanently, due to disability, or temporarily, due to job loss. Means-tested assistance programs (programs that are only available to individuals or households whose incomes are below certain thresholds), such as Temporary Assistance for Needy Families (TANF) and the Supplemental Nutrition Assistance Program (SNAP; previously called the Food Stamp Program), provide the most assistance to the largest proportion of impoverished families, and they are particularly important sources of support for children. Meanwhile, Supplemental Security Income (SSI) provides assistance to disabled Americans of all ages. Other forms of government assistance, such as unemployment compensation and tax credits, are aimed specifically at working Americans. Collectively, these programs represent an important safety net for a wide variety of the country's citizens.

A substantial portion of the American population benefits from government assistance programs. As Rich Morin, Paul Taylor, and Eileen Patten of the Pew Research Center report in *A Bipartisan Nation of Beneficiaries* (December 18, 2012, http://assets.pewresearch.org/wp-content/uploads/sites/3/2012/12/Benefits_FINAL_12-20.pdf), a majority (55%) of adults surveyed in 2012 had received benefits from at least one major government assistance program at some point during their lives. The amount of time an individual receives government benefits varies. In *Dynamics of Economic Well-Being: Participation in Government Programs, 2009–2012: Who Gets Assistance?* (May 2015, https://www.census.gov/content/dam/Census/library/publications/2015/demo/p70-141.pdf), Shelly K. Irving and Tracy A. Loveless of the U.S. Census Bureau note that 43% of all people who benefited from the major federal means-tested assistance programs between 2009 and 2012 received assistance for a total of somewhere between 37 and 48 months. Slightly less than

one-third (31.2%) participated in assistance programs for 1 to 12 months. Another 13.9% received benefits for 13 to 24 months, while 11.9% received benefits for 25 to 36 months. Nearly half (49.4%) of people who received housing benefits between 2009 and 2012 were enrolled in that program for between 37 and 48 months. By comparison, 62.9% of people receiving TANF or general state assistance participated between 1 and 12 months.

Assistance programs are among the most controversial of the federal government's operations, in large part due to conservative opposition to the notion of redistribution—the transfer of money from one group of people to another. In the case of means-tested public assistance programs, middle-class and wealthy households pay money via taxes that are used to fund the government programs that aid the poor. In spite of the fact that U.S. antipoverty programs are modest by international standards, and in spite of the cutbacks in assistance that have come in the wake of welfare reform, a growing population of poor people has translated into steady growth in federal spending on most programs. Romina Boccia, Alison Acosta Fraser, and Emily Goff of the Heritage Foundation, a conservative advocacy group, note in *Federal Spending by the Numbers, 2013: Government Spending Trends in Graphics, Tables, and Key Points* (August 20, 2013, http://thf_media.s3.amazonaws.com/2013/pdf/SR140.pdf) that between 2003 and 2013 SNAP spending rose 160%, spending on the Children's Health Insurance Program (discussed at greater length in Chapter 8) rose 84%, and spending on the U.S. Department of Agriculture's (USDA) child nutrition programs rose 54%. In all, the federal government spent $566.7 billion on its 10 major antipoverty programs in 2013. The largest of these by spending was Medicaid, which cost $266.6 billion; the second-largest program by spending, SNAP, was much smaller at $82.6 billion.

However, spending on the 10 major antipoverty programs was far lower than spending on the other programs that represented the federal government's largest outlays. In *Federal Spending by the Numbers, 2014: Government Spending Trends in Graphics, Tables, and Key Points (Including 51 Examples of Government Waste)* (December 8, 2014, http://thf_media.s3.amazonaws.com/2014/pdf/SR162.pdf), Boccia indicates that Social Security represented the largest single outlay among all government programs in 2013, at $813.6 billion, followed by national defense, at $633.4 billion. Spending on these programs had risen since 2003 at rates comparable to those by which antipoverty spending had risen.

Although assumptions about aid recipients' unwillingness to work are common, a sizable proportion of even the poorest welfare beneficiaries typically derive some amount of their income through work. In fact, Arloc Sherman, Robert Greenstein, and Kathy Ruffing of the Center on Budget and Policy Priorities (CBPP) report in *Contrary to "Entitlement Society" Rhetoric, over Nine-Tenths of Entitlement Benefits Go to Elderly, Disabled, or Working Households* (February 10, 2012, http://www.cbpp.org/files/2-10-12pov.pdf) that 91% of the recipients of government aid in 2010 were either elderly, disabled, or employed. According to the researchers, "people who are neither elderly nor disabled—and do not live in a working household—received only 9 percent of the benefits" from entitlement programs in 2010.

Conservative opposition to spending on antipoverty programs also focuses on notions of these programs' inability to solve the problems they address. In contrast, supporters of safety-net programs point to statistics showing that the programs are indeed effective and that their limitations typically reflect the low levels of spending on aid relative to the size of the poor population and the depth of poverty. For example, Danilo Trisi of the CBPP demonstrates the effectiveness of two key antipoverty programs in "SNAP and Unemployment Insurance Kept Millions out of Poverty Last Year, Census Supplemental Poverty Measure Shows" (Offthechartsblog.org, November 6, 2013). Using the U.S. Census Bureau's Supplemental Poverty Measure, which includes public benefits in its calculations of household income, SNAP kept 4.9 million people (including 2.2 million children) above the poverty line in 2012, and unemployment insurance kept 2.5 million people (including 600,000 children) out of poverty in 2012.

Other programs that function as antipoverty programs even though they are available to people living above the poverty level are also effective at lifting people above poverty. Social Security is widely credited with drastic reductions in poverty among the elderly between 1967 and 2000, as is noted in Chapter 2. Additionally, the Earned Income Tax Credit (EITC), which benefited more than 27 million people in 2016 (see Table 3.12 in Chapter 3), is widely believed to have multiple and long-term impacts on poverty. According to Chuck Marr, Chye-Ching Huang,

and Arloc Sherman of the CBPP, in *Earned Income Tax Credit Promotes Work, Encourages Children's Success at School, Research Finds* (October 1, 2015, http://www.cbpp.org/files/6-26-12tax.pdf), studies show that the EITC has done as much to increase the labor-force participation of single mothers since the 1990s as the welfare-to-work requirements of the Personal Responsibility and Work Opportunity Reconciliation Act (PRWORA). Women benefiting from the EITC saw higher wage growth than similar low-income women who did not. This wage growth translates into higher Social Security payments in old age, because Social Security benefit amounts are calculated according to a worker's career earnings.

This chapter focuses on the populations that benefit from the most prominent antipoverty programs in the U.S. social welfare system: TANF, SNAP, unemployment compensation, and SSI. Beneficiaries of other prominent antipoverty programs that focus on health are discussed in Chapter 8.

TEMPORARY ASSISTANCE FOR NEEDY FAMILIES

Who Receives TANF Benefits?

In *Temporary Assistance for Needy Families Program (TANF): Eleventh Report to Congress* (April 7, 2016, https://www.acf.hhs.gov/sites/default/files/ofa/eleventh_report_to_congress.pdf), the U.S. Department of Health and Human Services' Office of Family Assistance (OFA) describes the TANF caseload as of the end of fiscal year (FY) 2013. Over the course of the full fiscal year, an average of 1.8 million families with 4.1 million individual members received cash assistance payments every month. OFA notes that this was only 31.2% of all TANF spending that year, as many program participants receive non-cash benefits, such as child care, that the agency is not authorized to track. Out of the 4.1 million recipients, 24.7% (1 million) were adults and 75.3% (3.1 million) were children. (See Table 4.1.) With an average of 1.4 million recipients a month, California had the largest TANF caseload during FY 2013. New York was second, with an average of 396,974 recipients per month, and Pennsylvania was third, with an average of 178,607 recipients per month. Whites accounted for 33.4% of the TANF adult caseload in FY 2013; African Americans, 33.1%; and Hispanics, 27.7%. Among child recipients of TANF in FY 2013, whites accounted for 25.5%, African Americans for 30.5%, and Hispanics for 38.6%.

There are three basic types of TANF cases: single-parent cases, two-parent cases, and child-only cases (cases in which no adult in the household is a recipient of TANF benefits). Pamela J. Loprest of the Urban Institute explains in *How Has the TANF Caseload Changed over Time?* (March 2012, https://www.acf.hhs.gov/sites/default/files/opre/change_time_1.pdf) that the proportion

TABLE 4.1

Number of adults and number of children receiving Temporary Assistance for Needy Families and Separate State Programs benefits, by state, fiscal year 2013

	Total recipients	Adults	Children	Percentage adults	Percentage children
U.S. totals	**4,101,621**	**1,011,273**	**3,090,348**	**24.7%**	**75.3%**
Alabama	47,676	12,309	35,366	25.8%	74.2%
Alaska	9,646	3,118	6,528	32.3%	67.7%
Arizona	37,217	10,728	26,489	28.8%	71.2%
Arkansas	15,715	4,493	11,222	28.6%	71.4%
California	1,355,305	278,824	1,076,481	20.6%	79.4%
Colorado	39,502	11,311	28,191	28.6%	71.4%
Connecticut	29,180	8,638	20,542	29.6%	70.4%
Delaware	14,072	5,451	8,621	38.7%	61.3%
Dist. of Col.	17,446	4,108	13,339	23.5%	76.5%
Florida	94,587	16,733	77,855	17.7%	82.3%
Georgia	35,038	4,332	30,706	12.4%	87.6%
Guam	3,204	786	2,418	24.5%	75.5%
Hawaii	27,081	9,179	17,902	33.9%	66.1%
Idaho	2,810	178	2,632	6.3%	93.7%
Illinois	46,185	8,032	38,153	17.4%	82.6%
Indiana	26,767	3,379	23,389	12.6%	87.4%
Iowa	45,039	13,647	31,392	30.3%	69.7%
Kansas	20,467	5,784	14,683	28.3%	71.7%
Kentucky	61,812	12,793	49,020	20.7%	79.3%
Louisiana	16,980	2,334	14,645	13.7%	86.3%
Maine	59,679	26,451	33,228	44.3%	55.7%
Maryland	53,033	14,255	38,778	26.9%	73.1%
Massachusetts	150,433	49,551	100,882	32.9%	67.1%
Michigan	81,392	20,620	60,772	25.3%	74.7%
Minnesota	51,776	12,392	39,384	23.9%	76.1%
Mississippi	21,172	5,677	15,495	26.8%	73.2%
Missouri	85,394	27,327	58,067	32.0%	68.0%
Montana	7,488	2,023	5,465	27.0%	73.0%
Nebraska	16,139	3,034	13,105	18.8%	81.2%
Nevada	26,929	6,939	19,991	25.8%	74.2%
New Hampshire	15,356	5,016	10,340	32.7%	67.3%
New Jersey	75,727	21,469	54,258	28.4%	71.6%
New Mexico	37,434	9,759	27,676	26.1%	73.9%
New York	396,974	112,651	284,323	28.4%	71.6%
North Carolina	38,955	6,150	32,805	15.8%	84.2%
North Dakota	3,636	784	2,852	21.6%	78.4%
Ohio	137,108	26,010	111,098	19.0%	81.0%
Oklahoma	17,213	2,827	14,386	16.4%	83.6%
Oregon	112,496	37,696	74,800	33.5%	66.5%
Pennsylvania	178,607	50,380	128,227	28.2%	71.8%
Puerto Rico	38,080	14,080	24,000	37.0%	63.0%
Rhode Island	14,670	4,621	10,048	31.5%	68.5%
South Carolina	28,971	6,490	22,481	22.4%	77.6%
South Dakota	6,407	868	5,539	13.5%	86.5%
Tennessee	126,443	34,513	91,931	27.3%	72.7%
Texas	91,281	11,739	79,542	12.9%	87.1%
Utah	10,762	2,884	7,878	26.8%	73.2%
Vermont	8,918	2,804	6,115	31.4%	68.6%
Virgin Islands	1,252	355	897	28.3%	71.7%
Virginia	68,824	18,985	49,839	27.6%	72.4%
Washington	109,780	35,300	74,480	32.2%	67.8%
West Virginia	19,686	5,163	14,523	26.2%	73.8%
Wisconsin	63,148	16,161	46,988	25.6%	74.4%
Wyoming	728	145	583	20.0%	80.0%

SOURCE: "Figure 2-D. TANF and SSP Average Monthly Number of Adults and Children, FY 2013," in *Temporary Assistance for Needy Families Program (TANF): Eleventh Report to Congress*, U.S. Department of Health and Human Services, Administration for Children and Families, Office of Family Assistance, April 7, 2016, https://www.acf.hhs.gov/sites/default/files/ofa/eleventh_report_to_congress.pdf (accessed August 4, 2017)

of each case type in the overall caseload has changed substantially in the years since the 1996 passage of the PRWORA, which replaced Aid to Families with Dependent Children (AFDC) with TANF. In 1997 single-parent families accounted for 72% of the caseload, child-only cases for 20%, and two-parent families for 7%. By 2009 single-parent households represented 47% of the national caseload, child-only cases represented 48%, and two-parent families represented 5%.

These changes in the caseload composition do not correspond to increases in the child-only caseload, however, but to massive declines in the overall caseload. As Figure 4.1 shows, the AFDC caseload peaked in FY 1994 at a monthly

FIGURE 4.1

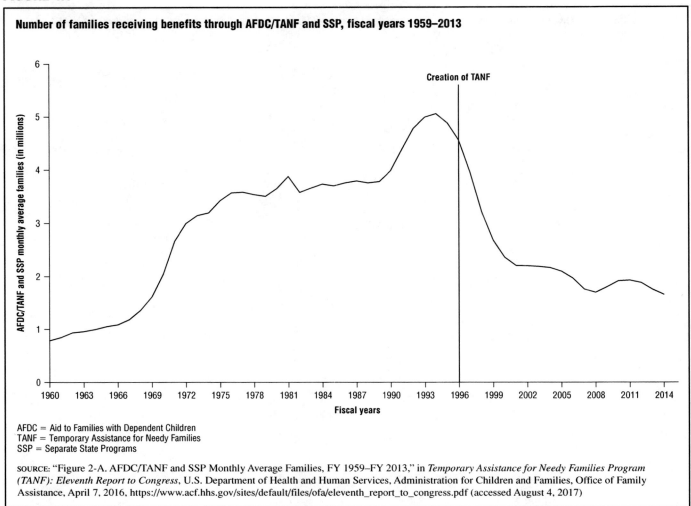

Number of families receiving benefits through AFDC/TANF and SSP, fiscal years 1959–2013

AFDC = Aid to Families with Dependent Children
TANF = Temporary Assistance for Needy Families
SSP = Separate State Programs

SOURCE: "Figure 2-A. AFDC/TANF and SSP Monthly Average Families, FY 1959–FY 2013," in *Temporary Assistance for Needy Families Program (TANF): Eleventh Report to Congress*, U.S. Department of Health and Human Services, Administration for Children and Families, Office of Family Assistance, April 7, 2016, https://www.acf.hhs.gov/sites/default/files/ofa/eleventh_report_to_congress.pdf (accessed August 4, 2017)

average of 5.1 million families and then fell precipitously in the years after welfare reform, to 2.4 million TANF families in 2000. According to the OFA, a significant portion of this decline in the caseload was attributable to a sharp increase in the number of single mothers leaving the TANF rolls. The caseload continued to decline in the years that followed, although it rose slightly between 2008 and 2010 as a result of the Great Recession (which officially lasted from December 2007 to June 2009). After reaching a recession-era peak of 2 million families in December 2010, the TANF caseload began falling again. Between October 2015 and December 2016 the average monthly caseload stood at 1.2 million families and demonstrated a downward trend from late 2015 through all of 2016. (See Table 4.2.) The trend toward declining caseloads was evident across most of the states.

Amid this overall trend toward declining caseloads between 1994 and 2016, the percentage of child-only cases among the total caseload grew steadily. Numerous adults became ineligible for TANF during this time due to rising incomes, work requirements, benefit time limits,

and other factors related both to changes in the economy and to welfare reform. Many of the households that received child-only benefits likely included an adult TANF recipient whose eligibility expired, who no longer qualified for benefits, or who had chosen not to enroll due to the eligibility restrictions. Child-only cases are subject to fewer eligibility restrictions and time limits than adult cases, so much of the changing composition of the TANF caseload reflects the fact that the need for assistance has remained relatively constant even though many adults have been removed from the welfare rolls.

Between FYs 2000 and 2011 the distribution of adult TANF recipients by age shifted noticeably toward younger adults. Adults aged 20 to 29 years accounted for 42.5% of all beneficiaries in FY 2000 and for 51.8% in FY 2011, whereas the proportion of teenaged recipients remained flat and the proportions of adults aged 30 to 39 years and adults over the age of 39 years declined. (See Table 4.3.) Over this same period, the proportion of the caseload accounted for by adult white recipients increased marginally, from 33% to 33.4%; the proportion

TABLE 4.2

Families receiving Temporary Assistance for Needy Families benefits, by state, October 2015–December 2016

State	Oct-15	Nov-15	Dec-15	Jan-16	Feb-16	Mar-16	Apr-16	May-16	Jun-16
U.S. Totals	1,281,791	1,268,461	1,262,247	1,245,498	1,222,527	1,205,511	1,187,510	1,178,830	1,169,128
Alabama	12,567	12,356	12,212	11,806	11,465	11,124	10,820	10,556	10,399
Alaska	2,955	2,861	2,946	2,974	2,986	2,989	3,048	3,083	3,088
Arizona	11,124	10,784	10,453	10,235	10,076	9,731	9,898	9,771	9,767
Arkansas	4,311	4,229	4,261	4,042	3,989	3,834	3,652	3,567	3,532
California	425,157	419,743	419,475	417,773	411,750	408,867	400,576	395,753	389,596
Colorado	16,586	16,402	16,478	16,410	16,333	16,375	16,057	16,360	16,288
Connecticut	12,426	12,268	12,041	11,868	11,537	11,276	11,059	11,045	10,938
Delaware	4,422	4,359	4,223	4,224	4,278	4,304	4,246	4,199	4,180
District of Columbia	6,121	6,317	6,169	5,764	5,724	5,577	5,481	5,268	5,371
Florida	48,580	49,652	49,602	48,616	47,482	47,566	46,513	46,172	46,763
Georgia	13,261	13,209	13,350	13,105	12,964	12,829	12,583	12,408	12,464
Guam	1,020	979	970	925	911	885	909	904	879
Hawaii	6,961	6,891	6,895	6,795	6,612	6,460	6,245	6,180	6,074
Idaho	1,884	1,875	1,878	1,907	1,927	1,938	1,920	1,924	1,941
Illinois	17,084	16,635	16,521	16,862	16,409	15,825	15,654	15,326	14,809
Indiana	8,619	8,565	8,429	8,280	8,264	8,071	7,834	7,655	7,560
Iowa	11,178	11,081	11,128	10,983	10,814	10,668	10,542	10,398	10,206
Kansas	5,803	5,610	5,500	5,372	5,162	4,941	4,918	5,040	5,186
Kentucky	23,728	23,406	23,228	22,864	22,571	21,532	21,922	23,331	22,936
Louisiana	5,623	5,698	5,794	5,726	5,714	5,560	5,485	5,595	5,630
Maine	4,362	4,391	4,277	4,257	4,221	4,137	4,049	3,846	3,798
Maryland	22,893	22,340	22,295	21,456	21,066	20,828	20,831	20,726	20,676
Massachusetts	34,451	33,966	33,867	32,779	31,763	31,388	31,463	31,436	30,945
Michigan	18,427	18,380	18,062	17,883	17,620	17,037	16,522	16,104	16,064
Minnesota	19,655	19,697	19,473	19,480	19,246	19,169	19,082	18,996	19,160
Mississippi	6,596	6,471	6,294	6,075	5,928	5,727	5,712	5,612	5,631
Missouri	22,667	22,093	22,009	20,852	16,252	15,111	14,230	13,730	13,336
Montana	3,044	3,041	3,117	3,086	3,044	3,035	2,999	3,018	3,091
Nebraska	4,572	4,577	4,640	4,648	4,588	4,532	4,441	4,450	4,484
Nevada	10,402	10,285	10,371	10,106	10,010	9,869	9,590	9,473	9,313
New Hampshire	2,615	2,576	2,536	2,523	2,498	2,446	2,425	2,413	2,414
New Jersey	21,155	20,599	20,265	19,374	18,689	18,208	17,726	17,163	16,735
New Mexico	11,874	11,907	11,811	11,611	11,462	11,190	11,071	11,281	11,408
New York	110,688	109,482	109,312	107,731	107,517	107,045	105,636	105,064	104,336
North Carolina	18,240	18,556	18,319	17,687	17,431	16,950	16,846	16,809	16,742
North Dakota	1,152	1,159	1,120	1,127	1,101	1,090	1,088	1,069	1,069
Ohio	59,186	58,920	58,871	58,146	57,884	57,409	56,870	56,831	56,834
Oklahoma	7,337	7,328	7,438	7,354	7,276	7,152	6,983	6,930	7,002
Oregon	18,359	17,881	17,908	17,716	17,662	17,481	17,011	16,668	16,777
Pennsylvania	62,845	61,385	60,795	59,745	58,028	57,263	56,884	56,518	57,283
Puerto Rico	9,419	10,047	9,960	9,433	9,119	8,325	8,730	8,309	8,229
Rhode Island	4,497	4,390	4,247	4,208	4,036	3,918	3,939	3,886	3,891
South Carolina	10,036	10,046	9,937	9,605	9,659	9,495	9,223	9,236	9,369
South Dakota	3,025	3,093	3,103	3,043	3,048	2,999	2,974	2,994	3,037
Tennessee	33,351	32,803	31,725	31,095	31,017	30,415	30,309	30,366	29,698
Texas	31,658	31,568	30,574	30,085	29,515	28,454	28,124	28,343	28,087
Utah	3,642	3,451	3,500	3,495	3,499	3,506	3,682	3,665	3,741
Vermont	2,674	2,642	2,723	2,614	2,584	2,556	2,660	2,678	2,730
Virgin Islands	333	322	313	297	281	264	271	266	254
Virginia	23,128	22,793	22,505	22,112	21,616	21,293	21,151	20,974	21,016
Washington	31,720	31,559	31,962	32,254	30,974	30,492	29,970	29,530	29,263
West Virginia	7,416	7,339	7,330	7,269	7,257	7,172	7,082	7,104	7,147
Wisconsin	20,599	20,104	19,650	19,427	19,267	18,757	18,116	18,365	17,488
Wyoming	363	350	385	394	401	446	458	442	473

accounted for by Hispanic recipients increased by almost four percentage points (from 23.9% to 27.7%), and the proportion accounted for by African American recipients declined by five percentage points (from 38.1% in FY 2000 to 33.1% in FY 2013). (See Table 4.4.)

Children who receive TANF benefits, either as part of the family of an adult TANF recipient or under a child-only designation, are overwhelmingly young. In FY 2013, 75.2% of TANF children were aged 11 years or younger, 16.4% were aged between 12 and 15 years, and 8.4% were aged between 16 and 18 years. (See Table 4.5.) Children under the age of two years represented 14.3% of the child caseload, and children between the ages of two and five years represented 28.7% of the caseload. The proportion of the child caseload has shifted slightly toward the younger end of the age spectrum. In FY 2000 children aged five years and younger accounted for 38.7% of the total child caseload. In FY 2013 they accounted for 43%. The proportion of the caseload consisting of children aged six to 11 years fell from 36.3% to 32.2%, and that for children aged

TABLE 4.2

Families receiving Temporary Assistance for Needy Families benefits, by state, October 2015–December 2016 [CONTINUED]

State	Jul-16	Aug-16	Sep-16	Oct-16	Nov-16	Dec-16	Average FY 2016	Average CY 2016
U.S. Totals	1,154,967	1,156,562	1,151,141	1,151,690	1,138,294	1,131,992	1,207,014	1,174,471
Alabama	10,449	10,545	10,564	10,532	10,505	10,455	11,239	10,768
Alaska	3,042	3,041	3,097	3,073	3,085	3,131	3,009	3,053
Arizona	9,030	9,091	9,107	9,309	9,150	9,044	9,922	9,517
Arkansas	3,471	3,533	3,478	3,414	3,375	3,367	3,825	3,605
California	383,001	381,328	377,680	373,492	369,987	369,128	402,558	389,911
Colorado	16,540	16,885	16,814	16,983	16,693	16,822	16,461	16,547
Connecticut	10,817	10,853	10,683	10,521	9,841	9,644	11,401	10,840
Delaware	4,187	4,204	4,216	4,184	4,159	4,097	4,254	4,207
District of Columbia	4,966	4,470	4,432	4,999	3,599	3,632	5,472	4,940
Florida	46,251	46,870	47,034	46,732	47,204	47,352	47,592	47,046
Georgia	12,369	12,565	12,570	12,511	12,485	12,373	12,806	12,602
Guam	817	789	764	738	722	720	896	830
Hawaii	5,992	5,934	5,901	5,882	5,818	5,762	6,412	6,138
Idaho	1,923	1,952	1,957	1,968	1,962	1,938	1,919	1,938
Illinois	14,622	14,324	14,205	14,213	14,303	14,138	15,690	15,058
Indiana	7,661	7,656	7,680	7,804	7,850	7,710	8,023	7,835
Iowa	10,243	10,334	10,440	10,461	10,321	10,193	10,668	10,467
Kansas	5,234	5,320	5,262	5,231	5,069	5,004	5,279	5,145
Kentucky	20,947	23,387	23,242	23,330	22,850	22,539	22,758	22,621
Louisiana	5,607	5,681	5,772	5,957	5,933	5,881	5,657	5,712
Maine	3,765	3,608	3,540	3,547	3,463	3,440	4,021	3,806
Maryland	20,660	20,528	20,586	20,582	20,202	20,097	21,240	20,687
Massachusetts	30,202	30,171	30,290	30,444	30,256	30,036	31,893	30,931
Michigan	15,497	16,290	15,417	15,404	15,319	15,121	16,942	16,190
Minnesota	19,091	19,247	19,256	19,316	19,205	19,064	19,296	19,193
Mississippi	5,599	5,686	5,759	5,731	5,661	5,635	5,924	5,730
Missouri	13,001	13,079	12,847	12,745	12,366	12,164	16,601	14,143
Montana	3,175	3,285	3,388	3,456	3,490	3,523	3,110	3,216
Nebraska	4,471	4,580	4,610	4,573	4,566	4,618	4,549	4,547
Nevada	9,375	9,549	9,525	9,589	9,522	9,556	9,822	9,623
New Hampshire	2,376	2,373	2,396	2,386	2,378	2,412	2,466	2,420
New Jersey	16,403	16,262	15,941	15,750	15,433	15,164	18,210	16,904
New Mexico	11,723	11,872	11,821	11,779	11,649	11,562	11,586	11,536
New York	103,824	103,859	103,720	103,862	102,797	102,591	106,518	104,832
North Carolina	16,478	16,556	16,859	16,777	16,764	16,507	17,289	16,867
North Dakota	1,080	1,086	1,124	1,167	1,140	1,108	1,105	1,104
Ohio	56,543	57,050	57,184	57,103	56,990	56,675	57,644	57,127
Oklahoma	6,938	7,036	7,147	7,199	7,195	7,153	7,160	7,114
Oregon	16,519	16,633	16,615	16,325	16,115	16,211	17,269	16,811
Pennsylvania	56,856	53,484	53,678	56,356	55,283	54,708	57,897	56,341
Puerto Rico	8,229	8,160	8,051	8,177	8,199	8,108	8,834	8,422
Rhode Island	3,873	3,881	3,794	5,963	6,266	6,439	4,047	4,508
South Carolina	9,043	9,392	9,396	9,186	9,302	9,211	9,536	9,343
South Dakota	3,044	3,068	3,100	3,075	3,112	3,114	3,044	3,051
Tennessee	29,588	29,739	29,123	29,146	28,399	28,053	30,769	29,746
Texas	28,800	29,516	30,074	30,663	30,020	29,426	29,567	29,259
Utah	3,752	3,776	3,785	3,812	3,844	3,836	3,625	3,699
Vermont	2,742	2,675	2,669	2,713	2,631	2,666	2,662	2,660
Virgin Islands	255	253	251	253	238	232	280	260
Virginia	21,026	20,946	20,881	19,661	18,359	17,293	21,620	20,527
Washington	28,795	28,712	28,392	28,500	28,533	28,856	30,302	29,523
West Virginia	7,158	7,360	7,362	7,370	7,350	7,284	7,250	7,243
Wisconsin	17,469	17,603	17,177	17,291	16,801	16,676	18,669	17,870
Wyoming	448	485	485	455	535	523	428	462

FY = fiscal year. CY = calendar year.

Notes: Calendar year average is based on data Jan. 2016 through December 2016. Fiscal year average is based on data Oct. 2015 through Sep. 2016.

SOURCE: "TANF: Total Number of Families," in *TANF Caseload Data 2016*, U.S. Department of Health and Human Services, Office of the Administration for Children and Families, Office of Family Assistance, January 12, 2017, https://www.acf.hhs.gov/sites/default/files/ofa/2016_family_tan.pdf (accessed August 4, 2017)

12 to 15 years fell from 17.4% to 16.4%. The share of older children rose from 7.6% (for children aged 16 to 19 years) to 8.4% (for children aged 16 to 18 years).

In FY 2013 white children accounted for 25.5% of the child TANF caseload, African American children for 30.5%, and Hispanic children for 38.6%. (See Table 4.6.) Between FYs 2000 and 2013, the proportion of child recipients who were Hispanic rose by 11.4 percentage points, while the proportion of African American child recipients fell by 10.1 percentage points and the proportion of white child recipients fell by 1.7 percentage points.

According to the OFA, roughly 1 out of 5 (22.6%) TANF adults were employed in FY 2013; this was a dramatic increase over the AFDC employment rate of

TABLE 4.3

Trend in adult Temporary Assistance for Needy Families recipients, by age, fiscal years 2000–11

	Under 20	20–29	30–39	Over 39
2000	7.1%	42.5%	32.1%	18.3%
2001	7.4%	42.4%	31.2%	19.0%
2002	7.5%	44.9%	29.9%	17.7%
2003	7.7%	46.8%	28.7%	16.8%
2004	7.4%	47.6%	28.2%	16.8%
2005	7.3%	47.1%	28.1%	17.4%
2006	7.2%	48.5%	26.8%	17.5%
2007	7.3%	48.7%	27.0%	17.0%
2008	7.3%	50.1%	26.4%	16.1%
2009	8.0%	50.0%	26.0%	16.0%
2010	7.9%	51.3%	25.4%	15.4%
2011	6.9%	51.8%	26.6%	14.7%

SOURCE: "Figure 10-E. Trend in TANF Adult Recipients by Age Group, FY 2000–FY 2011," in *Temporary Assistance for Needy Families Program (TANF): Tenth Report to Congress*, U.S. Department of Health and Human Services, Administration for Children and Families, Office of Family Assistance, December 12, 2013, http://www.acf.hhs.gov/sites/default/files/ofa/10th_tanf_report_congress.pdf (accessed August 4, 2017)

TABLE 4.4

Trend in adult Temporary Assistance for Needy Families recipients, by race and Hispanic origin, fiscal years 1997–2013

Year	White	Black	AIAN[a]	Asian	NHOPI[a]	Multi[a]	Hispanic[a]
1997	36.4	35.9	1.4	4.1	—	0.7[b]	21.5
1998	35.8	37.3	1.6	4.6	—	0.6[b]	20.1
1999	32.7	36.6	1.7	5	—	0.7[b]	23.3
2000	33.0	38.1	1.8	2.6	0.5	0.1	23.9
2001	32.4	39.3	1.3	2.5	0.6	0.2	23.7
2002	34.4	39.3	1.6	2.2	0.5	0.3	21.7
2003	35.5	39.2	1.7	2.0	0.6	0.3	20.7
2004	37.2	39.3	1.7	1.5	0.6	0.3	19.4
2005	36.6	38.9	1.6	1.9	0.5	0.5	20.0
2006	38.3	37.5	1.5	1.7	0.5	0.4	20.1
2007	36.2	36.7	1.4	2.0	0.5	0.4	22.8
2008	35.6	35.3	1.5	2.6	0.7	0.8	23.5
2009	35.9	34.4	1.4	2.3	0.7	0.9	24.4
2010	37.2	33.4	1.2	2.4	0.9	0.9	24.0
2011	34.8	35.3	1.2	2.4	1.0	0.9	24.4
2012	34.5	33.9	1.2	2.4	1.0	1.0	26.0
2013	33.4	33.1	1.1	2.3	1.1	1.3	27.7

[a]Hispanic may be of any race; AIAN = American Indian or Alaska Native. NHOPI = Native Hawaiian or Other Pacific Islander. Multi = mutiracial.
[b]Categorized as "other."

SOURCE: "Figure 10-F. Percentage of TANF Adults by Race/Ethnicity, FY 1997–FY 2013," in *Temporary Assistance for Needy Families Program (TANF): Eleventh Report to Congress*, U.S. Department of Health and Human Services, Administration for Children and Families, Office of Family Assistance, April 7, 2016, https://www.acf.hhs.gov/sites/default/files/ofa/eleventh_report_to_congress.pdf (accessed August 4, 2017)

TABLE 4.5

Trend in child Temporary Assistance for Needy Families recipients, by age, fiscal years 1997–2013

Fiscal year	Under 2	2–5	6–11	12–15	16–19
1997	13.8	29.9	33.9	15.9	6.5
1998	12.4	27.8	35.7	16.5	7.5
1999	12.4	26.4	36.3	17.0	7.9
2000	13.1	25.6	36.3	17.4	7.6
2001	13.4	24.9	35.8	18.4	7.5
2002	14.6	25.1	34.4	18.3	7.6
2003	14.6	25.4	33.5	18.8	7.7
2004	14.7	25.7	32.2	19.4	8.0
2005	14.5	25.0	31.8	19.9	8.8
2006	14.5	25.5	31.1	19.7	9.2
2007	15.4	25.3	30.6	19.2	9.5
2008	16.0	25.5	30.5	18.5	9.5
2009	16.1	26.9	29.9	17.9	9.2
2010	16.0	28.0	30.1	16.7	9.2
2011	15.7	28.9	30.3	16.6	8.5
2012	15.1	28.8	30.9	16.8	8.4
2013	14.3	28.7	32.2	16.4	8.4*

*Ages 16–18.

SOURCE: "Figure 10-I. Percentage of TANF Child Recipients by Age Group: FY 1997–FY 2013," in *Temporary Assistance for Needy Families Program (TANF): Eleventh Report to Congress*, U.S. Department of Health and Human Services, Administration for Children and Families, Office of Family Assistance, April 7, 2016, https://www.acf.hhs.gov/sites/default/files/ofa/eleventh_report_to_congress.pdf (accessed August 4, 2017)

TABLE 4.6

Trend in child Temporary Assistance for Needy Families recipients, by race and Hispanic origin, fiscal years 1997–2013

Fiscal year	White	Black	AIAN*	Asian	NHOPI*	Multi*	Hispanic*
1997	29.9	40.9	1.6	3.4	—	—	24.2
1998	29.0	41.2	1.5	4.3	—	—	24.0
1999	26.4	40.6	1.7	4.7	—	—	26.6
2000	27.2	40.6	1.6	2.8	0.6	0.0	27.2
2001	26.0	41.4	1.2	2.7	0.5	0.0	28.2
2002	27.2	40.4	1.4	2.7	0.5	0.0	27.8
2003	27.5	40.0	1.4	2.5	0.6	0.0	28.0
2004	28.5	39.6	1.4	2.2	0.5	0.0	27.8
2005	28.2	38.3	1.3	2.5	0.5	0.0	29.2
2006	29.3	37.1	1.3	2.1	0.5	0.0	29.7
2007	28.2	37.0	1.2	2.3	0.6	0.0	30.7
2008	26.9	35.1	1.2	2.7	0.7	0.0	33.4
2009	26.9	34.2	1.2	2.6	0.7	0.0	34.4
2010	28.0	32.4	1.0	2.1	0.7	0.0	35.8
2011	26.0	32.9	1.0	2.0	0.8	1.5	35.8
2012	25.8	31.6	1.1	2.1	0.8	1.5	37.1
2013	25.5	30.5	1.0	1.8	0.7	1.9	38.6

*Hispanic may be of any race; AIAN = American Indian or Alaska Native. NHOPI = Native Hawaiian or Other Pacific Islander. Multi = Multiracial.
Note: Unknown redistributed.

SOURCE: "Figure 10-J. Percentage Distribution of TANF Child Recipients by Race/Ethnicity, FY 1997–FY 2013," in *Temporary Assistance for Needy Families Program (TANF): Eleventh Report to Congress*, U.S. Department of Health and Human Services, Administration for Children and Families, Office of Family Assistance, April 7, 2016, https://www.acf.hhs.gov/sites/default/files/ofa/eleventh_report_to_congress.pdf (accessed August 4, 2017)

6.6% in FY 1992 but a decrease from the peak TANF employment rate of 27.6% in FY 1999. (See Figure 4.2.)

Duration of TANF Benefits

According to Loprest, the majority of adult TANF recipients collect benefits for short periods. Setting aside child-only cases, which generally are not subject to time limits, 41% of TANF recipients in FY 2009 had been collecting benefits for less than one year and 23% of beneficiaries had been collecting benefits for less

FIGURE 4.2

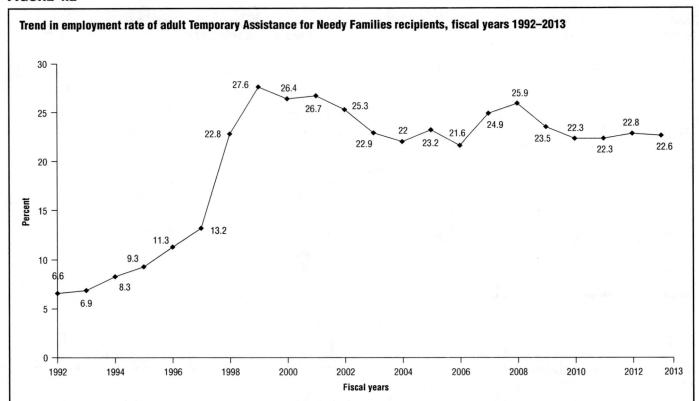

Trend in employment rate of adult Temporary Assistance for Needy Families recipients, fiscal years 1992–2013

SOURCE: "Figure 10-G. Employment Rate of AFDC/TANF Adult Recipients, 1992–2013," in *Temporary Assistance for Needy Families Program (TANF): Eleventh Report to Congress*, U.S. Department of Health and Human Services, Administration for Children and Families, Office of Family Assistance, April 7, 2016, https://www.acf.hhs.gov/sites/default/files/ofa/eleventh_report_to_congress.pdf (accessed August 4, 2017)

than two years; 12% of the overall caseload consisted of adults who had been receiving benefits for more than four years.

The PRWORA limited the duration that a family can collect TANF benefits to a lifetime maximum of 60 months, and states have the freedom to set shorter maximum time limits. In *Many States Cutting TANF Benefits Harshly Despite High Unemployment and Unprecedented Need* (October 3, 2011, http://www.cbpp.org/files/5-19-11tanf.pdf), Liz Schott and LaDonna Pavetti of the CBPP explain that fiscal pressures at the state level during the Great Recession led to numerous cuts in TANF benefits, including reductions in the program time limits. For example, in 2010 Arizona cut its TANF time limit from the federally established 60 months to 36 months, before further shortening the lifetime maximum period to 24 months in 2011. California, which is home to approximately one-third of the entire TANF caseload, also shortened its time limit from 60 to 48 months in 2011. Schott and Pavetti suggest that "the TANF block grant has been in place long enough for us to know that families who reach time limits are among the most vulnerable families. They are far more likely than other TANF recipients to face employment barriers such as physical and mental health problems and to have lower levels of education that significantly reduce their chances of finding jobs."

SUPPLEMENTAL NUTRITION ASSISTANCE PROGRAM

In the years since the passage of the PRWORA in 1996, SNAP has increasingly functioned as a central part of the U.S. welfare system. The AFDC/TANF, formerly the centerpiece of the national safety net, contracted following welfare reform and then proved relatively unresponsive to increasing levels of poverty during the Great Recession. Unlike TANF, SNAP is not tied to work requirements, which can be especially hard to meet during times of recession and high unemployment. SNAP is also available to a wider proportion of the impoverished population than other social welfare programs, including nonelderly adults, nondisabled adults, and childless adults.

Many conservatives criticize the SNAP program as being wasteful or ineffective. For example, in *SNAP Failure: The Food Stamp Program Needs Reform* (October 16, 2013, https://object.cato.org/sites/cato.org/files/pubs/pdf/pa738_web.pdf), Michael Tanner of the Cato Institute asserts that the lack of strong work requirements associated with SNAP "increasingly breeds greater dependence on government" among its beneficiaries. Tanner also argues that SNAP is susceptible to a high rate of abuse, citing a USDA report indicating that the program lost $858 million to direct fraud in 2012. Tanner further asserts that another $2.2 billion in SNAP benefits were lost due to erroneous payments to ineligible recipients. As Tanner notes, taken together this sum accounted for roughly 3.9% of total SNAP expenditures in 2012.

Advocates for SNAP contend that the rates of error and fraud in SNAP are relatively low, and are far outweighed by the benefits recipients derive from the program. In "Pros and Cons of Restricting SNAP Purchases" (February 16, 2017, https://www.brookings.edu/testimonies/pros-and-cons-of-restricting-snap-purchases), Diane Whitmore Schanzenbach of the left-leaning Brookings Institution reports that SNAP helped lift roughly five million people out of poverty in 2014. Schanzenbach also notes that SNAP had been proven to play a major role in helping children eat healthier food, attain higher educational achievement, and ultimately enjoy higher rates of economic self-sufficiency as adults. Sheila Zedlewski, Elaine Waxman, and Craig Gundersen of the Urban Institute observe in *SNAP's Role in the Great Recession and Beyond* (July 2012, https://www.urban.org/sites/default/files/publication/25626/412613-SNAP-s-Role-in-the-Great-Recession-and-Beyond.PDF) that "SNAP does more than combat hunger. It is an anti-poverty program, a work support, a promoter of health and nutrition, and an automatic stabilizer in recessions—filling in the gaps that other safety net programs leave behind."

SNAP is overseen by the USDA's Food and Nutrition Service (FNS) and is the largest of 15 food and nutrition assistance programs in the United States. SNAP issues an electronic debit card that may be used at participating U.S. grocery stores, farmers' markets, homeless meal providers, treatment centers, group homes, and other authorized outlets. According to the FNS, in *Fiscal Year 2016 at a Glance* (December 15, 2016, https://fns-prod.azureedge.net/sites/default/files/snap/2016-SNAP-Retailer-Management-Year-End-Summary.pdf), approximately $66.4 billion in SNAP benefits were redeemed in FY 2016 at the 260,115 retailers and other outlets that were authorized to participate in the program. The value of an individual household's benefits varies according to family size and income: maximum amounts between October 2016 and September 2017 ranged from $194 per month for one person to $1,169 for a family of eight. (See Table 4.7.)

In *Characteristics of Supplemental Nutrition Assistance Program Households: Fiscal Year 2015* (November 2016, https://fns-prod.azureedge.net/sites/default/files/ops/Characteristics2015.pdf), Kelsey Farson Gray, Sarah Fisher, and Sarah Lauffer of the FNS provide detailed information about SNAP recipients. They report that SNAP has grown significantly since the 1980s, broadly tracking changes in the larger economy, in particular the number of individuals whose gross incomes are at or below 130% of poverty (the level at which one may become eligible for SNAP, depending on other eligibility variables). (See Figure 4.3.) The

TABLE 4.7

Supplemental Nutrition Assistance Program maximum benefits, 2016–17

[October 1, 2016 through September 30, 2017]

People in household	Maximum monthly allotment
1	$194
2	$357
3	$511
4	$649
5	$771
6	$925
7	$1,022
8	$1,169
Each additional person	$146

SOURCE: "Benefits," in *Supplemental Nutrition Assistance Program (SNAP): Eligibility*, U.S. Department of Agriculture, Food and Nutrition Service, August 2017, http://www.fns.usda.gov/snap/eligibility (accessed August 4, 2017)

number of SNAP beneficiaries declined slightly between 1985 and 1989, grew rapidly during the early 1990s before peaking in 1994, and then declined again through 2000. The number of beneficiaries subsequently experienced a steady increase, rising from 17.1 million individuals in 2000 to 47.5 million individuals in 2013, before falling to 45.5 million in 2015.

Measuring Levels of Food Insecurity

SNAP is without a doubt the most important program to that portion of the population that experiences food insecurity. This group includes most people living below the poverty line as well as many whose incomes are marginally higher than the poverty line.

Since 1995 the FNS and the Census Bureau have conducted annual surveys of food security, low food security (or food insecurity), and very low food security (previously called hunger). Alisha Coleman-Jensen et al. of the USDA's Economic Research Service indicate in *Household Food Security in the United States in 2016* (September 2017, https://www.ers.usda.gov/webdocs/publications/84973/err-237.pdf?v=42979) that the agency uses 18 questions to assess a family's level of food security (questions 11 to 18 are asked only if the household includes children aged 17 years and younger):

1. "We worried whether our food would run out before we got money to buy more." Was that often, sometimes, or never true for you in the last 12 months?

2. "The food that we bought just didn't last and we didn't have money to get more." Was that often, sometimes, or never true for you in the last 12 months?

3. "We couldn't afford to eat balanced meals." Was that often, sometimes, or never true for you in the last 12 months?

FIGURE 4.3

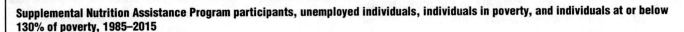

Supplemental Nutrition Assistance Program participants, unemployed individuals, individuals in poverty, and individuals at or below 130% of poverty, 1985–2015

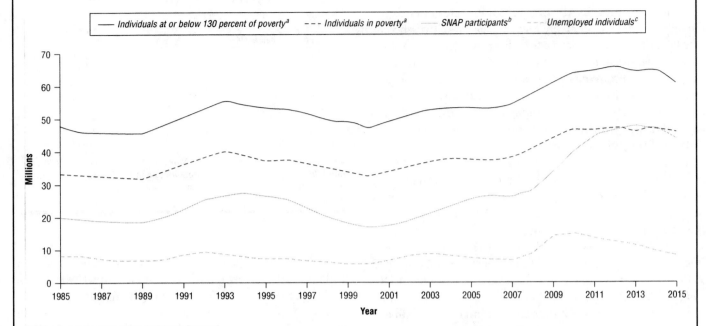

SNAP = Supplemental Nutrition Assistance Program.
[a]Annual values. Source: Special tabulations of the Current Population Survey Annual Social and Economic Supplement (CPS ASEC) by Decision Demographics, Arlington, VA.
[b]Average monthly values, Food and Nutrition Service Fiscal Year Program Operations data.
[c]Average monthly values, Department of Labor, Bureau of Labor Statistics.

SOURCE: Kelsey Farson Gray, Sarah Fisher, and Sara Lauffer, "Figure 2.1. SNAP Participants, Unemployed Individuals, Individuals in Poverty, and Individuals at or below 130 Percent of Poverty, Calendar Years 1985–2015," in *Characteristics of Supplemental Nutrition Assistance Program Households: Fiscal Year 2015*, U.S. Department of Agriculture, Food and Nutrition Service, November 2016, https://fns-prod.azureedge.net/sites/default/files/ops/Characteristics2015.pdf (accessed August 4, 2017)

4. In the last 12 months, did you or other adults in the household ever cut the size of your meals or skip meals because there wasn't enough money for food? (Yes/No)

5. (If yes to question 4) How often did this happen—almost every month, some months but not every month, or in only 1 or 2 months?

6. In the last 12 months, did you ever eat less than you felt you should because there wasn't enough money for food? (Yes/No)

7. In the last 12 months, were you ever hungry, but didn't eat because there wasn't enough money for food? (Yes/No)

8. In the last 12 months, did you lose weight because there wasn't enough money for food? (Yes/No)

9. In the last 12 months, did you or other adults in your household ever not eat for a whole day because there wasn't enough money for food? (Yes/No)

10. (If yes to question 9) How often did this happen—almost every month, some months but not every month, or in only 1 or 2 months?

11. "We relied on only a few kinds of low-cost food to feed our children because we were running out of money to buy food." Was that often, sometimes, or never true for you in the last 12 months?

12. "We couldn't feed our children a balanced meal, because we couldn't afford that." Was that often, sometimes, or never true for you in the last 12 months?

13. "The children were not eating enough because we just couldn't afford enough food." Was that often, sometimes, or never true for you in the last 12 months?

14. In the last 12 months, did you ever cut the size of any of the children's meals because there wasn't enough money for food? (Yes/No)

15. In the last 12 months, were the children ever hungry but you just couldn't afford more food? (Yes/No)

16. In the last 12 months, did any of the children ever skip a meal because there wasn't enough money for food? (Yes/No)

17. (If yes to question 16) How often did this happen—almost every month, some months but not every month, or in only 1 or 2 months?

18. In the last 12 months did any of the children ever not eat for a whole day because there wasn't enough money for food? (Yes/No)

Food-secure households are those that have access at all times to enough food for an active, healthy life. Low-food-security households are uncertain of having, or are unable to acquire, enough food to meet basic needs at all times during the year. Households with very low food security often worry that their food will run out, report that their food does run out before they have money to buy more, cannot afford to eat balanced meals, often have adults who skip meals because there is not enough money for food, and report that they eat less than they should because of a lack of money.

In 2015, 12.7% of U.S. households reported some level of food insecurity during the year, with 7.7% of U.S. households reporting low food security and 5% reporting very low food security. (See Figure 4.4.) The prevalence of food insecurity in 2015 was high by historical standards, as it had been since the onset of the Great Recession in late 2007. Figure 4.5 shows that the levels of food insecurity steadily rose from 1999 to 2004, but dropped in 2005 before rising again. Then food insecurity rose precipitously between 2007 and 2008, as the effects of the Great Recession began to be felt, and remained

relatively high through 2015. The prevalence rate of very low food security followed a similar pattern, although the recession-era increase was less pronounced.

Poor and low-income households were more likely to experience food insecurity and very low food security

FIGURE 4.4

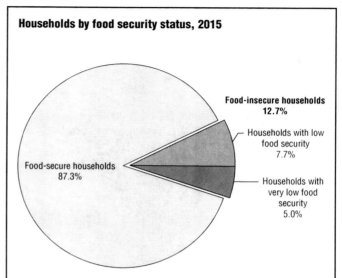

Households by food security status, 2015

Food-insecure households
12.7%

Households with low food security
7.7%

Food-secure households
87.3%

Households with very low food security
5.0%

SOURCE: Alisha Coleman-Jensen et al., "Figure 1. U.S. Households by Food Security Status, 2015," in *Household Food Security in the United States in 2015*, U.S. Department of Agriculture, Economic Research Service, September 2016, http://www.ers.usda.gov/webdocs/publications/79761/err-215.pdf?v=42636 (accessed August 4, 2017)

FIGURE 4.5

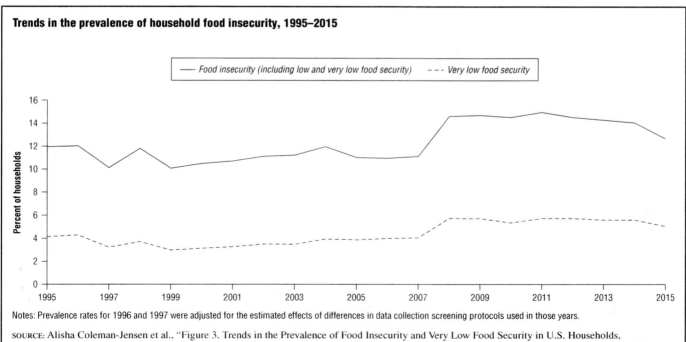

Trends in the prevalence of household food insecurity, 1995–2015

—— Food insecurity (including low and very low food security)   - - - Very low food security

Notes: Prevalence rates for 1996 and 1997 were adjusted for the estimated effects of differences in data collection screening protocols used in those years.

SOURCE: Alisha Coleman-Jensen et al., "Figure 3. Trends in the Prevalence of Food Insecurity and Very Low Food Security in U.S. Households, 1995–2015," in *Household Food Security in the United States in 2015*, U.S. Department of Agriculture, Economic Research Service, September 2016, http://www.ers.usda.gov/webdocs/publications/79761/err-215.pdf?v=42636 (accessed August 4, 2017)

during the year than were households with higher incomes. In 2015, 21.4% of households with an income below the poverty line reported low food security and 16.9% reported very low food security. (See Table 4.8.) Moreover, food insecurity did not decrease substantially until households reached income levels well above the poverty line. Among households under 130% of the poverty line, 21% experienced low food security and 15.8% experienced very low food security. Among households under 185% of poverty, 19.2% experienced low food security and 13.6% experienced very low food security.

Who Receives SNAP Benefits?

Although not all food-insecure households participate in SNAP, the two population sets overlap considerably. In FY 2015, 22.3 million households received SNAP benefits. (See Table 4.9.) A little over one-fifth (22.2%, or 4.9 million) of these households had zero gross income, whereas nearly one-third (31.8%, or 7.1 million) had earned income of some kind. About one-fifth (20.5%, or 4.6 million) of SNAP recipients also received SSI benefits, and one-quarter (24.7%, or 5.5 million) received Social Security benefits. Much smaller percentages of SNAP recipients received assistance

TABLE 4.8

Households by food security status and selected characteristics, 2015

Category	Total[a] 1,000	Food secure 1,000	Food secure Percent	Food insecure All 1,000	Food insecure All Percent	With low food security 1,000	With low food security Percent	With very low food security 1,000	With very low food security Percent
All households	125,164	109,315	87.3	15,849	12.7	9,540	7.7	6,309	5.0
Household composition:									
With children < 18 years	38,978	32,519	83.4	6,459	16.6	4,557	11.7	1,902	4.9
With children < 6 years	16,995	14,129	83.1	2,866	16.9	2,146	12.7	720	4.2
Married-couple families	25,232	22,670	89.8	2,562	10.2	1,923	7.7	639	2.5
Female head, no spouse	10,117	7,052	69.7	3,065	30.3	2,109	20.9	956	9.4
Male head, no spouse	3,133	2,432	77.6	701	22.4	443	14.2	258	8.2
Other household with child[b]	496	366	73.8	130	26.2	82	16.5	48	9.7
With no children < 18 years	86,187	76,796	89.1	9,391	10.9	4,983	5.8	4,408	5.1
More than one adult	51,357	46,976	91.5	4,381	8.5	2,504	4.8	1,877	3.7
Women living alone	18,954	16,169	85.3	2,785	14.7	1,413	7.5	1,372	7.2
Men living alone	15,876	13,652	86.0	2,224	14.0	1,065	6.7	1,159	7.3
With elderly	35,265	32,340	91.7	2,925	8.3	1,789	5.1	1,136	3.2
Elderly living alone	13,137	11,932	90.8	1,205	9.2	657	5.0	548	4.2
Race/ethnicity of households:									
White, non-Hispanic	83,931	75,563	90.0	8,368	10.0	4,759	5.7	3,609	4.3
Black, non-Hispanic	15,734	12,357	78.5	3,377	21.5	2,127	13.6	1,250	7.9
Hispanic[c]	16,803	13,592	80.9	3,211	19.1	2,132	12.7	1,079	6.4
Other, non-Hispanic	8,695	7,803	89.7	892	10.3	521	6.0	371	4.3
Household income-to-poverty ratio:									
Under 1.00	14,070	8,687	61.7	5,383	38.3	3,006	21.4	2,377	16.9
Under 1.30	18,917	11,954	63.2	6,963	36.8	3,966	21.0	2,997	15.8
Under 1.85	28,994	19,479	67.2	9,515	32.8	5,572	19.2	3,943	13.6
1.85 and over	65,319	61,552	94.2	3,767	5.8	2,376	3.7	1,391	2.1
Income unknown	30,851	28,282	91.7	2,569	8.3	1,593	5.1	976	3.2
Area of residence:[d]									
Inside metropolitan area	106,990	93,947	87.8	13,043	12.2	7,843	7.3	5,200	4.9
In principal cities[e]	36,809	31,606	85.9	5,203	14.1	3,240	8.8	1,963	5.3
Not in principal cities	53,585	48,023	89.6	5,562	10.4	3,304	6.2	2,258	4.2
Outside metropolitan area	18,175	15,369	84.6	2,806	15.4	1,697	9.3	1,109	6.1
Census geographic region:									
Northeast	22,300	19,640	88.1	2,660	11.9	1,616	7.2	1,044	4.7
Midwest	27,199	23,727	87.2	3,472	12.8	2,069	7.6	1,403	5.2
South	47,389	41,101	86.7	6,288	13.3	3,750	7.9	2,538	5.4
West	28,277	24,848	87.9	3,429	12.1	2,105	7.4	1,324	4.7

[a]Totals exclude households for which food security status is unknown because household respondents did not give a valid response to any of the questions in the food security scale. In 2015, these exclusions represented 381,000 households (0.3 percent of all households).
[b]Households with children in complex living arrangements, e.g., children of other relatives or unrelated roommate or boarder.
[c]Hispanics may be of any race.
[d]Metropolitan area residence is based on 2013 Office of Management and Budget delineation. Prevalence rates by area of residence are comparable with those for 2014 but are not precisely comparable with those of earlier years.
[e]Households within incorporated areas of the largest cities in each metropolitan area. Residence inside or outside of principal cities is not identified for about 16 percent of households in metropolitan statistical areas.

SOURCE: Alisha Coleman-Jensen et al., "Table 2. Households by Food Security Status and Selected Household Characteristics, 2015," in *Household Food Security in the United States in 2015*, U.S. Department of Agriculture, Economic Research Service, September 2016, https://www.ers.usda.gov/webdocs/publications/79761/err-215.pdf?v=42636 (accessed August 4, 2017)

TABLE 4.9

Characteristics of Supplemental Nutrition Assistance Program recipient households, fiscal year 2015

Household composition	All households Number (000)	All households Column percent	Earned income Number (000)	Earned income Column percent	Social Security Number (000)	Social Security Column percent	Households with countable: Social Security Income Number (000)	Social Security Income Column percent	Zero gross income Number (000)	Zero gross income Column percent	TANF Number (000)	TANF Column percent	GA Number (000)	GA Column percent
Total[a]	22,293	100.0	7,081	100.0	5,451	100.0	4,559	100.0	4,943	100.0	1,293	100.0	694	100.0
Children	9,510	42.7	5,219	73.7	850	15.6	1,128	24.7	1,267	25.6	1,231	95.2	138	19.9
Single-adult household	5,587	25.1	2,519	35.6	565	10.4	692	15.2	926	18.7	829	64.1	91	13.1
Multiple-adult household	2,629	11.8	1,790	25.3	267	4.9	380	8.3	239	4.8	211	16.3	36	5.2
Married head	1,610	7.2	1,175	16.6	138	2.5	180	4.0	141	2.9	102	7.9	16	2.4
Other multiple-adult	1,019	4.6	614	8.7	129	2.4	200	4.4	98	2.0	108	8.4	20	2.8
Children only	1,294	5.8	910	12.9	18	0.3	56	1.2	102	2.1	191	14.8	11	1.6
Elderly individuals	4,361	19.6	321	4.5	3,005	55.1	1,550	34.0	304	6.2	39	3.0	157	22.7
Living alone	3,495	15.7	157	2.2	2,435	44.7	1,264	27.7	275	5.6	5	0.4	132	19.0
Not living alone	866	3.9	164	2.3	570	10.5	286	6.3	29	0.6	33	2.6	25	3.6
Non-elderly individuals with disabilities	4,498	20.2	483	6.8	2,249	41.3	3,075	67.4	—	—	243	18.8	141	20.3
Living alone	2,761	12.4	111	1.6	1,533	28.1	1,750	38.4	—	—	3	0.2	86	12.4
Not living alone	1,737	7.8	372	5.3	716	13.1	1,325	29.1	—	—	240	18.6	55	7.9
Other households[b]	5,554	24.9	1,455	20.5	12	0.2	1	0.0	3,375	68.3	47	3.6	311	44.9
Single-person	5,101	22.9	1,201	17.0	2	0.0	0	0.0	3,242	65.6	39	3.0	301	43.3
Multiperson	453	2.0	254	3.6	10	0.2	0	0.0	133	2.7	8	0.6	11	1.5
Adults age 18 to 49 without disabilities in childless households[c]	4,265	19.1	1,124	15.9	160	2.9	123	2.7	2,475	50.1	41	3.2	207	29.8
Living alone	3,614	16.2	860	12.1	1	0.0	0	0.0	2,355	47.6	32	2.5	192	27.7
Not living alone	650	2.9	265	3.7	159	2.9	122	2.7	120	2.4	9	0.7	14	2.1
Single-person households	11,711	52.5	1,690	23.9	3,979	73.0	3,016	66.2	3,555	71.9	108	8.4	520	74.9

— = No sample households are in this category. TANF = Temporary Assistance for Needy Families. GA = State general assistance benefits.
[a]The sums of the household types do not match the numbers in the total row because a household may have more than one of the characteristics.
[b]Households not containing children, elderly individuals, or non-elderly individuals with disabilities.
[c]With some exceptions, these participants are subject to work requirements and time limits.

SOURCE: Kelsey Farson Gray, Sarah Fisher, and Sara Lauffer, "Table 3.2. Household Receipt of Countable Income Types by Household Composition," in *Characteristics of Supplemental Nutrition Assistance Program Households: Fiscal Year 2015*, U.S. Department of Agriculture, Food and Nutrition Service, November 2016, https://fns-prod.azureedge.net/sites/default/files/ops/Characteristics 2015.pdf (accessed August 4, 2017)

through TANF (5.8%, or 1.3 million) or general state assistance programs (3.1%, 694,000). Most households receiving SNAP benefits in FY 2015 included one or more children (42.7%, or 9.6 million), elderly individuals (19.6%, or 4.4 million), or individuals with disabilities (20.2%, 4.5 million), but roughly one quarter of beneficiary households (24.9%, or 5.6 million) contained only nondisabled, non-elderly adults.

As Table 4.10 shows, the composition of SNAP participant households has changed along with the absolute number of households. In FY 1989, 7.1% of SNAP households had zero gross income and 18.3% had zero net income. Meanwhile, 41.9% of SNAP households received cash assistance through the AFDC/TANF. The dramatic increase in the percentage of SNAP households in FY 2015 with zero gross income (22.3%) and zero net income (39.6%) corresponds with a dramatic decline in the percentage of SNAP households receiving cash assistance through TANF (5.8%). Other notable changes in the composition of the SNAP caseload include an increase in the percentage of households with earned income, from 19.6% in FY 1989 to 31.8% in FY 2015; an increase in the proportion of non-elderly disabled individuals, from 9.1% to 20.2%; and a decline in the proportion of households with children, from 60.4% to 42.7%.

TABLE 4.10

Characteristics of Supplemental Nutrition Assistance Program recipient households, fiscal years 1989–2015

| Time period | Total households (000) | Percentage of households with: | | | | | | | | | |
		Zero gross income	Zero net income[a]	Minimum benefit	Elderly individuals	Children	Non–elderly individuals withs disabilities[b]	AFDC[c]/ TANF	Earnings	Social Security income	Any noncitizen
Fiscal year 1989	7,217	7.1	18.3	7.5	19.3	60.4	9.1	41.9	19.6	20.6	9.8
Fiscal year 1990	7,811	7.4	19.3	5.0	18.1	60.3	8.9	42.0	19.0	19.6	10.3
Fiscal year 1991	8,863	8.3	20.5	4.1	16.5	60.4	9.0	40.5	19.8	18.6	11.8
Fiscal year 1992	10,059	9.6	21.9	3.6	15.4	62.2	9.5	39.5	20.2	18.4	10.4
Fiscal year 1993	10,791	9.7	23.7	4.0	15.5	62.1	10.7	39.4	20.6	19.4	11.6
Fiscal year 1994	11,091	10.2	23.8	4.5	15.8	61.1	12.5	38.1	21.4	21.4	10.7
Fiscal year 1995	10,883	9.7	25.0	4.3	16.0	59.7	18.9	38.3	21.4	22.6	10.7
Fiscal year 1996	10,552	10.2	24.9	4.5	16.2	59.5	20.2	36.6	22.5	24.1	10.5
Fiscal year 1997	9,452	9.2	22.7	6.6	17.6	58.3	22.3	34.6	24.2	26.5	8.4
Fiscal year 1998	8,246	8.8	20.8	8.3	18.2	58.3	24.4	31.4	26.3	28.1	4.3
Fiscal year 1999	7,670	8.5	20.6	9.7	20.1	55.7	26.4	27.3	26.8	30.2	6.0
Fiscal year 2000	7,335	8.4	20.1	10.9	21.0	53.9	27.5	25.8	27.2	31.7	6.4
Fiscal year 2001	7,450	9.4	22.2	11.2	20.4	53.6	27.7	23.1	27.0	31.8	5.4
Fiscal year 2002	8,201	10.5	24.3	10.7	18.7	54.1	27.0	20.9	28.0	29.5	5.2
Fiscal year 2003	8,971	12.7	27.7	7.0	17.1	55.1	22.1	17.2	27.5	26.3	5.4
Fiscal year 2004	10,069	13.1	29.7	5.9	17.3	54.3	22.7	16.2	28.5	26.8	6.2
Fiscal year 2005	10,852	13.7	30.0	5.2	17.1	53.7	23.0	14.5	29.1	26.4	6.2
Fiscal year 2006	11,313	14.1	31.0	6.2	17.9	52.0	23.1	13.0	29.5	26.8	6.1
Fiscal year 2007	11,561	14.7	31.4	6.6	17.8	51.0	23.8	12.1	29.6	27.7	5.7
Fiscal year 2008	12,464	16.2	33.6	6.7	18.5	50.6	22.6	10.6	28.9	26.2	5.6
Fiscal year 2009	14,981	17.6	36.0	4.1	16.6	49.9	21.2	9.7	29.4	23.6	5.9
Fiscal year 2010	18,369	19.7	38.3	3.8	15.5	48.7	19.8	8.0	29.9	20.9	5.9
Fiscal year 2011	20,803	20.0	39.4	4.2	16.5	47.1	20.2	7.6	30.5	20.2	5.8
Fiscal year 2012	22,046	20.5	38.4	4.8	17.2	45.3	20.0	7.1	31.3	20.2	5.7
Fiscal year 2013	22,802	21.5	39.4	5.2	17.4	44.8	20.3	6.5	31.2	19.9	5.8
Fiscal year 2014	22,445	21.9	40.6	6.4	19.0	43.6	20.4	6.1	31.3	20.4	6.1
Fiscal year 2015	22,293	22.2	39.6	7.2	19.6	42.7	20.2	5.8	31.8	20.5	6.0

TANF = Temporary Assistance for Needy Families.
SNAP = Supplemental Nutrition Assitance Program.
[a]Beginning in 2004, net income is not calculated for MFIP households or SSI-CAP households in States that use standardized SSI-CAP benefits.
[b]The substantial increase in 1995 and decrease in 2003 are in part a result of changes in the definition of a household with an individual with a disability. Prior to 1995, these households were defined as those with SSI and no members over age 59. In 1995, that definition changed to households with at least one member under age 65 who received SSI, or at least one member age 18 to 61 who received Social Security income, veterans' benefits, or other government benefits as a result of a disability. Due to changes in the SNAP QC data in 2003, the definition changed again, to households with individuals under the age of 60 with SSI income, a medical expense deduction and without an elderly person, or with a non-elderly adult who worked fewer than 30 hours a week and received Social Security income, veterans' benefits, or workers' compensation. In 2015, the definition of individuals with disabilities was expanded to also include non-elderly adults in single-person SNAP households who received Social Security income.
[c]Aid to Families with Dependent Children.
Note: Fiscal year analysis files were not developed for the years before 1989. The fiscal year 2003 through fiscal year 2015 estimates differ methodologically from estimates for earlier years and, in some cases, from estimates presented in reports prior to 2009. Under the current methodology, the weighting of the SNAP QC data reflects adjustments to FNS' Program Operations counts of households to account for receipt of benefits in error or for disaster assistance. In addition, the weighted SNAP QC data match adjusted Program Operations counts of households, individuals, and benefit amounts. Beginning with the fiscal year 2009 report, we also incorporated corrected SNAP Program Operations data from Missouri for every fiscal year from 2003 to 2008. FNS = Food and Nutrition Service. SNAP QC = SNAP Quality Control. SSI-CAP = Supplemental Security Income-Combined Application Project. MFIP = Minnesota Family Investment Program.

SOURCE: Kelsey Farson Gray, Sarah Fisher, and Sara Lauffer, "Table A.26. Comparison of Participating Households with Key SNAP Household Characteristics for Fiscal Years 1989 to 2015," in *Characteristics of Supplemental Nutrition Assistance Program Households: Fiscal Year 2015*, U.S. Department of Agriculture, Food and Nutrition Service, November 2016, https://fns-prod.azureedge.net/sites/default/files/ops/Characteristics2015.pdf (accessed August 4, 2017)

In FY 2015, 16.6 million (36.7%) of SNAP's nearly 45.2 million individual recipients were non-Hispanic white, 11.8 million (26.1%) were African American, and 7.7 million (17.1%) were Hispanic. (See Table 4.11.) There were also 1.3 million (2.9%) non-Hispanic Asian American individual recipients and 560,000 (1.2%) non-Hispanic Native American individual recipients. Children under the age of 18 years accounted for 19.9 million (44%) of SNAP's individual recipients in FY 2015. Non-elderly adults accounted for 20.5 million (45.4%) individual recipients; they were split almost equally between people aged 18 to 35 years (22.5%, 10.2 million) and people aged 36 to 59 years (22.9%, 10.3 million). Those aged 60 years and older accounted for 4.8 million (10.6%) of the SNAP individual recipient population. Except among children, where there were no statistically significant disparities by sex, females were substantially more likely to receive SNAP benefits than males. A little over 6.6 million women aged 18 to 35 years received SNAP benefits, compared with 3.6 million men; 6.1 million women aged 36 to 59 years received benefits, compared with 4.2 million men; and 3.1 million women aged 60 years and older received benefits, compared with 1.7 million men.

TABLE 4.11

Individual Supplemental Nutrition Assistance Program recipients, by selected demographic characteristic, fiscal year 2015

Participant characteristic	Total participants		Female participants		Male participants		Prorated benefits[b]	
	Number (000)	Percent[a]	Number (000)	Percent[a]	Number (000)	Percent[a]	Dollars (000)	Percent
Total	**45,184**	**100.0**	**25,637**	**56.7**	**19,547**	**43.3**	**5,667,680**	**100.0**
Age								
Child	19,891	44.0	9,858	21.8	10,034	22.2	2,439,391	43.0
Preschool-age (4 or younger)	6,119	13.5	3,014	6.7	3,105	6.9	778,638	13.7
School-age (5 to 17)	13,772	30.5	6,843	15.1	6,928	15.3	1,660,753	29.3
Non-elderly adult	20,494	45.4	12,728	28.2	7,766	17.2	2,736,440	48.3
18 to 35	10,159	22.5	6,608	14.6	3,551	7.9	1,365,106	24.1
36 to 59	10,335	22.9	6,120	13.5	4,214	9.3	1,371,334	24.2
Elderly individual (60 or older)	4,799	10.6	3,052	6.8	1,748	3.9	491,849	8.7
Citizenship								
U.S.-born citizen	41,542	91.9	23,462	51.9	18,080	40.0	5,191,519	91.6
Naturalized citizen	1,786	4.0	1,156	2.6	631	1.4	228,982	4.0
Refugee	361	0.8	186	0.4	175	0.4	48,920	0.9
Other noncitizen	1,495	3.3	833	1.8	662	1.5	198,259	3.5
Citizen children living with noncitizen adults[c]	3,921	8.7	1,934	4.3	1,988	4.4	505,721	8.9
Non-elderly individuals with disabilities	5,283	11.7	2,926	6.5	2,356	5.2	547,033	9.7
Children with disabilities	971	2.2	391	0.9	581	1.3	91,428	1.6
Non-elderly adults with disabilities	4,311	9.5	2,536	5.6	1,776	3.9	455,605	8.0
Adults age 18 to 49 without disabilities in childless households[d]	4,600	10.2	2,022	4.5	2,578	5.7	774,726	13.7
Race and Hispanic status[e]								
White, not Hispanic	16,574	36.7	9,405	20.8	7,170	15.9	2,020,624	35.7
African American, not Hispanic	11,772	26.1	6,846	15.2	4,926	10.9	1,513,410	26.7
Hispanic, any race	7,730	17.1	4,336	9.6	3,394	7.5	1,004,995	17.7
Asian, not Hispanic	1,301	2.9	716	1.6	585	1.3	177,058	3.1
Native American, not Hispanic	560	1.2	302	0.7	258	0.6	69,815	1.2
Multiple races reported, not Hispanic	431	1.0	257	0.6	175	0.4	58,175	1.0
Race unknown	6,816	15.1	3,776	8.4	3,039	6.7	823,602	14.5

SNAP = Supplemental Nutrition Assistance Program
[a]Percent of all participants.
[b]Prorated benefits equal the benefits paid to households multiplied by the ratio of participants with selected characteristic to total household size.
[c]Noncitizens may be inside or outside the SNAP unit.
[d]With some exceptions, these participants are subject to work requirements and a time limit.
[e]Codes to allow reporting of multiple races were implemented beginning in April 2007. We have grouped the codes together to form general race and ethnicity categories. "White, not Hispanic" includes "white, not Hispanic or Latino"; "African American, not Hispanic" includes "black or African American, not Hispanic or Latino" and "(black or African American) and white"; "Hispanic, any race" includes "Hispanic" and "(Hispanic or Latino) with any race or race combination"; "Asian, not Hispanic" includes "Asian," "Native Hawaiian or other Pacific Islander," and "Asian and white"; "Native American, not Hispanic" includes "American Indian or Alaska Native," "(American Indian or Alaska Native) and white," and "(American Indian or Alaska Native) and (black or African American)"; "Multiple races reported, not Hispanic" includes individuals who reported more than one race and who do not fit into any previously mentioned value; and "Race unknown" includes "Racial/ethnic data not available" and "Racial/ethnic data not recorded." Reporting of race and ethnicity is now voluntary and was missing for 15 percent of participants in fiscal year 2015. As a result, fiscal year 2015 race and ethnicity distributions are not comparable to distributions for years prior to fiscal year 2007.

SOURCE: Kelsey Farson Gray, Sarah Fisher, and Sara Lauffer, "Table A.23. Gender and SNAP Benefits of Participants by Selected Demographic Characteristic," in *Characteristics of Supplemental Nutrition Assistance Program Households: Fiscal Year 2015*, U.S. Department of Agriculture, Food and Nutrition Service, November 2016, https://fns-prod.azureedge.net/sites/default/files/ops/Characteristics2015.pdf (accessed August 4, 2017)

According to Zedlewski, Waxman, and Gunderson, between 2000 and 2009 SNAP was responsible for an average annual decrease in the poverty rate of 4.4% and an average annual decrease in the child poverty rate of 5.6%. More pronounced than its effects on moving individuals out of poverty, however, was SNAP's ability to ameliorate the depth and severity of poverty. Most families do not exit poverty as a result of food assistance, but studies show that those families whose incomes are far below the poverty line see significant increases in well-being due to SNAP.

UNEMPLOYMENT COMPENSATION

The U.S. Department of Labor's Bureau of Labor Statistics (BLS), which collects data on the labor force (the total number of employed and unemployed people), defines an unemployed person as someone who is jobless, looking for a job, and available for work. Those who are jobless but not looking for work are not considered unemployed; they are classified as not being part of the labor force. The unemployment rate, as it is publicized each month in the media, is often mistakenly assumed to represent the number of jobless workers who have filed for unemployment compensation. Many workers who are jobless, actively looking for work, and available for work, however, have either come to the end of their unemployment benefits, are not eligible for benefits, or fail to apply for benefits. The BLS's official unemployment rate, then, is derived not from unemployment compensation records but from the monthly Current Population Surveys that are conducted in partnership with the Census Bureau. A separate agency of the Department of Labor, the Employment and Training Administration, maintains and publishes data on those who file claims for unemployment insurance.

Table 4.12 shows the differences, on a state-by-state basis, between total unemployment and insured unemployment. As the data indicate, the insured unemployed made up only a fraction of the total unemployed in most states during the first quarter of 2017. In California, for example, the state with the largest civilian labor force in the United States, the unemployment rate was 5.3%, but the insured unemployment rate (the unemployment rate among those qualifying for unemployment compensation) was only 2.6%. Larger gaps were in evidence in some states experiencing above-average unemployment, such as New Mexico (6.8% total unemployed and 1.6% insured unemployed), Alabama (6.1% and 1%), Louisiana (5.6% and 0.8%), Kentucky (5.6% and 1.1%), North Carolina (5.1% and 0.6%), Georgia (5.2% and 0.8%), Mississippi (5.1% and 0.9%), and Ohio (5.7% and 1.5%). Although the unemployment insurance program provides a key form of support for covered workers, a large number among the total labor force do not qualify for benefits.

Who Receives Unemployment Insurance Benefits?

In 2010 the Employment and Training Administration released a wide range of reports resulting from a landmark five-year study of the unemployment compensation program. Conducted by the research firm IMPAQ International, the study assessed many aspects of the program, including the characteristics of those receiving unemployment insurance (UI) benefits, between the 1950s and 2007. In *UI Benefits Study: Recent Changes in the Characteristics of Unemployed Workers* (August 2009, https://wdr.doleta.gov/research/FullText_Documents/UI%20Benefits%20Study%20-%20Recent%20Change%20in%20Characteristics%20of%20Unemployed%20Workers.pdf), Marios Michaelides of IMPAQ International provides an overview of gender, racial, and ethnic disparities in unemployment and the collection of unemployment compensation over that period. Michaelides finds that, after controlling for industry and occupation differences:

1. women have higher unemployment rates than men but are equally likely to receive UI benefits;

2. the racial unemployment rate gap is smaller than in earlier years but remains substantial, yet nonwhites are only marginally more likely to receive UI benefits than whites; and

3. there is a dramatic convergence in the unemployment rates between Hispanics and non-Hispanics, although Hispanics remain less likely to receive UI benefits.

Michaelides points out that although there was a sizable gap in the unemployment rate for men and women between 1953 and 1957, that gap closed by the mid-1980s, and in the period 1993 to 2007 the unemployment rate for women was slightly less than that for men. The gap in the unemployment rate for white and nonwhite workers remained wide over the course of those same 54 years, however. Between 1953 and 1967 the rate averaged 4.1% for white workers and 8.6% for nonwhite workers. By the first decade of the 21st century the gap had closed only marginally, with 4.6% of white workers and 8.2% of nonwhite workers experiencing unemployment between 2003 and 2007. Moreover, the gap had widened in the interim, peaking during the mid-1980s, when 6.5% of white workers were unemployed, compared with 14.1% of nonwhite workers. The gap between non-Hispanic workers and Hispanic workers closed more significantly: from a difference of 3.3 percentage points during the mid-1970s to a separation of 1.4 percentage points between 2003 and 2007.

The explanations for these phenomena are complex. Uneven distribution in different industries and occupations likely explains some portion of the changing dynamic between unemployment for men and unemployment for women. Some of the industries and occupations subject to the highest levels of unemployment over time,

TABLE 4.12

Unemployment compensation recipiency rates, by state, first quarter 2017

[In thousands]

State	IUR (%)	TUR (%)	Covered Employment[a]	Civilian labor force	Total unemployment	Insured unemployment	
						Regular programs[b]	All programs[c]
Alabama	1.0	6.1	1,863	2,179	131.9	19.4	19.4
Alaska	4.4	7.3	324	360	26.2	13.7	13.7
Arizona	0.9	4.9	2,589	3,307	162.3	22.8	22.8
Arkansas	1.3	4.0	1,158	1,332	53.3	15.0	15.0
California	2.6	5.3	16,504	19,125	1,009.2	422.3	422.3
Colorado	1.2	3.1	2,526	2,920	89.2	30.5	30.5
Connecticut	3.0	5.4	1,643	1,898	101.6	49.3	49.3
Delaware	1.7	4.8	437	472	22.8	7.4	7.4
District of Columbia	1.7	5.9	557	398	23.5	9.2	9.2
Florida	0.4	4.7	8,096	10,036	476.7	36.2	36.2
Georgia	0.8	5.2	4,172	5,002	259.2	33.0	33.0
Hawaii	1.4	2.8	610	696	19.2	8.6	8.6
Idaho	2.0	4.2	689	818	34.2	13.2	13.2
Illinois	2.5	5.6	5,833	6,475	361.7	146.6	146.6
Indiana	1.1	4.4	2,963	3,305	144.7	32.4	32.4
Iowa	2.3	3.7	1,529	1,684	62.1	35.2	35.2
Kansas	1.1	4.0	1,336	1,476	59.4	15.2	15.2
Kentucky	1.1	5.6	1,810	2,046	114.8	19.9	19.9
Louisiana	0.8	5.6	1,866	2,093	118.0	15.4	15.4
Maine	1.7	3.8	606	690	26.5	10.3	10.3
Maryland	1.5	4.4	2,480	3,196	142.0	37.4	37.4
Massachusetts	2.6	4.0	3,468	3,634	146.3	90.2	90.2
Michigan	2.1	5.4	4,217	4,872	262.1	89.2	89.2
Minnesota	2.5	4.7	2,806	3,001	140.8	69.7	69.7
Mississippi	0.9	5.1	1,096	1,288	66.0	9.7	9.7
Missouri	1.2	4.5	2,689	3,068	138.9	32.0	32.0
Montana	2.9	4.5	445	521	23.7	12.9	12.9
Nebraska	0.9	3.4	957	1,004	33.7	8.1	8.1
Nevada	1.8	5.0	1,271	1,434	71.1	22.9	22.9
New Hampshire	0.7	3.2	643	749	24.3	4.7	4.7
New Jersey	3.2	4.7	3,877	4,503	209.8	123.9	123.9
New Mexico	1.6	6.8	775	932	63.7	12.4	12.4
New York	2.1	4.8	8,995	9,558	457.3	188.6	188.6
North Carolina	0.6	5.1	4,187	4,919	249.2	25.3	25.3
North Dakota	2.6	3.6	409	417	14.8	10.7	10.7
Ohio	1.5	5.7	5,273	5,706	326.9	80.5	80.5
Oklahoma	1.2	4.5	1,508	1,828	81.4	18.0	18.0
Oregon	1.9	4.2	1,815	2,058	86.2	35.0	35.0
Pennsylvania	2.8	5.2	5,653	6,399	335.6	156.2	156.2
Puerto Rico	2.3	11.3	863	1,133	128.2	20.2	20.2
Rhode Island	2.8	5.1	466	550	28.0	13.0	13.0
South Carolina	0.8	4.5	1,968	2,314	104.4	16.0	16.0
South Dakota	0.9	3.3	415	453	15.0	3.6	3.6
Tennessee	0.5	5.1	2,841	3,170	161.5	14.4	14.4
Texas	1.3	5.0	11,590	13,447	676.7	155.9	155.9
Utah	1.0	3.4	1,361	1,546	52.0	13.7	13.7
Vermont	2.2	3.4	302	346	11.9	6.7	6.7
Virgin Islands	1.4		37			0.5	0.5
Virginia	0.8	4.0	3,614	4,268	169.7	30.3	30.3
Washington	2.0	5.3	3,203	3,682	194.2	60.9	60.9
West Virginia	2.5	5.9	649	772	45.6	16.4	16.4
Wisconsin	2.0	4.1	2,819	3,109	129.0	55.7	55.7
Wyoming	2.3	5.2	268	301	15.5	6.1	6.1
United States	**1.7**	**4.9**	**140,072**	**159,357**	**7,773.0**	**2,396.2**	**2,396.3**

IUR = Insured unemployment rate

TUR = Total unemployment rate

[a]Wages and Covered Employment lag the rest of the Data Summary information by 6 months.

[b]Includes State Unemployment insurance, Unemployment Compensation for Federal Employees, Unemployment Compensation for ex-servicemembers.

[c]Includes Emergency Unemployment Compensation 2008 + Federal Extended State Benefit.

Note: Blank cells appearing in any section of this report indicates that information is unavailable.

SOURCE: "Labor Force Information by State (Levels in Thousands) for CYQ 2017.1," in *Unemployment Insurance Data Summary*, U.S. Department of Labor, Employment and Training Administration, 2017, https://workforcesecurity.doleta.gov/unemploy/content/data_stats/datasum17/DataSum_2017_1.pdf (accessed August 5, 2017)

such as the construction industry, are heavily dominated by men. By contrast, women are far more likely to work in white-collar jobs than men. Thus, although women may face lingering disadvantages due to workplace bias, their overall unemployment rate has converged with that of men.

Michaelides notes that between 1992 and 2007 whites and nonwhites were approximately equally likely to work in both blue-collar and white-collar jobs, but nonwhites were far more likely to be unemployed in all occupation categories. Thus, the gap in the employment rate cannot be attributed to the differing concentrations of whites and nonwhites in various industries. Instead, social factors, such as access to educational opportunities and workplace discrimination, are likely to play a role in the disparity.

Nonwhite workers, in spite of their significantly higher rates of unemployment in almost all occupations between 1992 and 2007, were not substantially more likely than white workers to receive unemployment compensation. Michaelides states, "Since UI is only available to the experienced labor force, we might expect higher unemployment among experienced nonwhites to lead to greater levels of UI receipt. On the other hand, however, even in the same industries and occupations nonwhites suffer greater employment instability and lower earnings, making them less likely to meet states' minimum earnings or employment requirements. They may also be more likely to separate from jobs under circumstances that make them ineligible for benefits."

Hispanics were also overrepresented among the unemployed in the years surveyed by Michaelides and the Department of Labor. The trend of Hispanic unemployment relative to the group's presence in the overall labor force had begun to resemble that of the trend between women and men, however, in the later years considered in the study. During the 1980s and 1990s the proportion of Hispanics among the unemployed grew more rapidly than the proportion of Hispanics in the labor force, but by 2000 the proportion of Hispanics among the unemployed had stopped increasing, even though the proportion of Hispanics in the labor force continued to grow.

Hispanics' likelihood of receiving unemployment compensation has changed over time. During the early 1990s Hispanics were more likely to receive unemployment benefits than non-Hispanics, in keeping with the fact that they experienced unemployment at a higher rate than non-Hispanics. After 2000, however, non-Hispanic workers became marginally more likely to receive unemployment compensation than Hispanics, even though Hispanics were more likely to be unemployed. Michaelides hypothesizes that this gap, which is not explained by differing distributions across industries, may be attributable to unfamiliarity, on the part of some Hispanic workers, with U.S. laws regarding their eligibility for unemployment benefits.

In the years following the period studied by Michaelides and the Department of Labor, unemployment rose dramatically as a result of the Great Recession, and many of the same trends described by Michaelides persisted. Nonwhites and Hispanics continued to be overrepresented among the unemployed. As Table 4.13 shows, the 2016 unemployment rate for white male workers aged 16 years and older was 4.4% and for Asian American male workers of the same age it was 3.5%, compared with 9.1% for African American male workers and 5.4% for Hispanic male workers. Overall, women were slightly less likely to be unemployed than men in 2016, and white (4.2%) and Asian American (3.9%) women were less likely than African American (7.8%) and Hispanic (6.3%) women to be unemployed. Across all categories, single people were generally more likely to be unemployed than married people, with the never-married proportion of each demographic group experiencing higher rates of unemployment than any other subset.

SUPPLEMENTAL SECURITY INCOME

SSI is a means-tested income assistance program that was created in 1972 to provide monthly cash assistance to senior citizens, blind people, and disabled individuals. A number of requirements must be met before an applicant can receive financial benefits from SSI. First, a person must meet the program criteria for age, blindness, or disability. In addition, because SSI is a means-tested program, only those who meet the income eligibility requirements receive payments. Total SSI payments to all recipients grew steadily from $5.1 billion in 1974 to just under $55 billion in 2015. (See Table 4.14.) During that period, the number of SSI recipients grew from 3.2 million to 8.3 million. (See Table 4.15.) According to the CBPP, in *Introduction to the Supplemental Security Income (SSI) Program* (February 27, 2014, https://www.cbpp.org/sites/default/files/atoms/files/1-10-11socsec.pdf), this growth has come as a result of the program's shifting emphasis. SSI's main function during its early years was to supplement the incomes of elderly beneficiaries of the primary Social Security program, whose official name is Old Age, Survivors, and Disability Insurance (OASDI). Since that time, SSI has become a broader antipoverty program, serving as a primary resource for children and adults who are both poor and disabled.

Who Receives Supplemental Security Income Benefits?

Of the 8.3 million recipients in December 2015, approximately 7.1 million (85.5%) were disabled and 1.2 million (14.5%) were aged; less than 1% (67,851) were blind. (See Table 4.16.) Among these three eligibility categories, the disabled and the blind received the highest average monthly payments from SSI in December 2015, at $559.63 and $558.02, respectively. Aged beneficiaries (most of whom were also entitled to OASDI benefits) received an average monthly payment of $428.10. Approximately 4.9 million (59%) of the total number of SSI beneficiaries were between the ages of 18 and 64 years, 1.3 million (15.7%) were aged 17 years and

TABLE 4.13

Unemployed persons, by selected demographic characteristics, 2015 and 2016

[Numbers in thousands]

Marital status, race, Hispanic or Latino ethnicity, and age	Men				Women			
	Unemployed		Unemployment rates		Unemployed		Unemployment rates	
	2015	2016	2015	2016	2015	2016	2015	2016
Total, 16 years and over	**4,490**	**4,187**	**5.4**	**4.9**	**3,807**	**3,564**	**5.2**	**4.8**
Married, spouse present[a]	1,310	1,259	2.8	2.7	1,138	1,093	3.1	3.0
Widowed, divorced, or separated[b]	643	600	6.1	5.6	812	757	5.5	5.1
Never married	2,537	2,328	9.5	8.5	1,857	1,715	8.2	7.4
White, 16 years and over	3,126	2,952	4.7	4.4	2,537	2,393	4.5	4.2
Married, spouse present[a]	986	961	2.6	2.5	885	834	3.0	2.8
Widowed, divorced, or separated[b]	461	455	5.4	5.4	577	541	5.1	4.8
Never married	1,679	1,536	8.3	7.5	1,074	1,018	6.9	6.4
Black or African American, 16 years and over	935	845	10.3	9.1	911	810	8.9	7.8
Married, spouse present[a]	179	171	5.0	4.7	127	125	4.4	4.4
Widowed, divorced, or separated[b]	133	104	9.7	7.4	175	153	7.4	6.5
Never married	623	570	15.1	13.4	608	532	12.3	10.4
Asian, 16 years and over	191	176	4.0	3.5	156	172	3.7	3.9
Married, spouse present[a]	89	64	2.9	2.0	78	91	3.1	3.4
Widowed, divorced, or separated[b]	16	17	4.7	4.3	21	28	3.7	4.4
Never married	86	95	6.2	6.4	57	53	5.1	4.5
Hispanic or Latino ethnicity, 16 years and over	943	833	6.3	5.4	783	715	7.1	6.3
Married, spouse present[a]	298	270	3.9	3.4	248	238	5.2	4.9
Widowed, divorced, or separated[b]	111	99	6.1	5.5	144	144	6.3	6.1
Never married	533	465	9.7	8.2	390	333	9.9	8.0
Total, 25 years and over	3,094	2,934	4.3	4.0	2,735	2,607	4.3	4.1
Married, spouse present[a]	1,270	1,228	2.8	2.7	1,070	1,041	3.0	2.9
Widowed, divorced, or separated[b]	618	576	6.0	5.5	773	725	5.4	5.0
Never married	1,206	1,129	7.2	6.5	892	841	6.5	5.9
White, 25 years and over	2,170	2,110	3.7	3.6	1,860	1,753	3.8	3.5
Married, spouse present[a]	957	937	2.5	2.5	834	790	2.9	2.7
Widowed, divorced, or separated[b]	443	436	5.3	5.2	550	519	5.0	4.7
Never married	771	738	6.2	5.7	475	444	5.4	4.9
Black or African American, 25 years and over	626	551	8.2	7.0	637	581	7.4	6.6
Married, spouse present[a]	173	166	4.9	4.6	117	120	4.1	4.3
Widowed, divorced, or separated[b]	129	101	9.5	7.4	168	149	7.3	6.5
Never married	324	285	11.9	9.8	352	312	10.1	8.5
Asian, 25 years and over	147	137	3.4	3.0	118	143	3.1	3.5
Married, spouse present[a]	88	64	2.9	2.0	76	90	3.0	3.4
Widowed, divorced, or separated[b]	16	16	4.6	4.3	21	27	3.7	4.4
Never married	43	56	4.4	5.4	21	26	3.0	3.3
Hispanic or Latino ethnicity, 25 years and over	623	549	5.0	4.2	544	500	6.0	5.4
Married, spouse present[a]	288	260	3.8	3.4	230	218	5.0	4.6
Widowed, divorced, or separated[b]	104	95	5.9	5.5	135	132	6.1	5.8
Never married	231	193	7.0	5.6	179	150	8.1	6.4

[a]Refers to persons in opposite-sex married couples only.
[b]Separated includes persons who are married, spouse absent.
Note: Estimates for the above race groups (white, black or African American, and Asian) do not sum to totals because data are not presented for all races. Persons whose ethnicity is identified as Hispanic or Latino may be of any race. Updated population controls are introduced annually with the release of January data.

SOURCE: "24. Unemployed Persons by Marital Status, Race, Hispanic or Latino Ethnicity, Age, and Sex," in *Labor Force Statistics from the Current Population Survey*, U.S. Department of Labor, Bureau of Labor Statistics, 2017, http://www.bls.gov/cps/cpsaat24.pdf (accessed August 5, 2017)

younger, and 2.2 million (26.5%) were aged 65 years and older. Among the different age groups, children received the highest average monthly payment from SSI, due largely to an absence of other income sources.

Although SSI benefits are often not enough to lift recipients out of poverty, the CBPP and others credit the program with a high level of effectiveness in lifting recipients out of extreme poverty (above 50% of the poverty line).

TABLE 4.14

Total Supplemental Security Income payments, by eligibility category, selected years 1974–2015

[In thousand of dollars]

Year	Total	Federal SSI	Federally administered state supplementation
All recipients			
1974	5,096,813	3,833,161	1,263,652
1975	5,716,072	4,313,538	1,402,534
1980	7,714,640	5,866,354	1,848,286
1985	10,749,938	8,777,341	1,972,597
1990	16,132,959	12,893,805	3,239,154
1995	27,037,280	23,919,430	3,117,850
1996	28,252,474	25,264,878	2,987,596
1997	28,370,568	25,457,387	2,913,181
1998	29,408,208	26,404,793	3,003,415
1999	30,106,132	26,805,156	3,300,976
2000	30,671,699	27,290,248	3,381,451
2001	32,165,856	28,705,503	3,460,353
2002	33,718,999	29,898,765	3,820,234
2003	34,693,278	30,688,029	4,005,249
2004	36,065,358	31,886,509	4,178,849
2005	37,235,843	33,058,056	4,177,787
2006	38,888,961	34,736,088	4,152,873
2007	41,204,645	36,884,066	4,320,579
2008	43,040,481	38,655,780	4,384,701
2009	46,592,308	42,628,709	3,963,606
2010	48,194,514	44,605,122	3,589,392
2011	49,520,299	45,999,647	3,520,652
2012	52,074,525	48,769,579	3,304,947
2013	53,899,898	50,624,771	3,275,127
2014	54,693,013	51,574,587	3,118,426
2015	54,966,168	52,335,253	2,630,915

SSI = Supplemental Security Income

SOURCE: Adapted from "Table 7.A4. Total Federally Administered Payments, by Eligibility Category, Selected Years 1974–2015," in *Annual Statistical Supplement to the Social Security Bulletin, 2016*, U.S. Social Security Administration, Office of Retirement and Disability Policy, May 2017, https://www.ssa.gov/policy/docs/statcomps/supplement/2016/supplement16.pdf (accessed August 5, 2017)

TABLE 4.15

Number of recipients of Supplemental Security Income payments, by eligibility category, selected years 1974–2015

Month and year	Total	Federal SSI	Federally administered state supplementation	State supplementation only
All recipients				
January 1974	3,215,632	2,955,959	1,480,309	259,673
December				
1975	4,314,275	3,893,419	1,684,018	420,856
1980	4,142,017	3,682,411	1,684,765	459,606
1985	4,138,021	3,799,092	1,660,847	338,929
1990	4,817,127	4,412,131	2,058,273	404,996
1995	6,514,134	6,194,493	2,517,805	319,641
2000	6,601,686	6,319,907	2,480,637	281,779
2001	6,688,489	6,410,138	2,520,005	278,351
2002	6,787,857	6,505,227	2,461,652	282,630
2003	6,902,364	6,614,465	2,467,116	287,899
2004	6,987,845	6,694,577	2,497,589	293,268
2005	7,113,879	6,818,944	2,242,112	294,935
2006	7,235,583	6,938,690	2,268,579	296,893
2007	7,359,525	7,061,234	2,302,130	298,291
2008	7,520,501	7,219,012	2,343,599	301,489
2009	7,676,686	7,422,879	2,339,346	253,807
2010	7,912,266	7,655,667	2,385,933	256,599
2011	8,112,773	7,866,390	2,389,113	246,383
2012	8,262,877	8,039,984	2,215,840	222,893
2013	8,363,477	8,143,829	2,228,380	219,648
2014	8,335,704	8,161,835	1,549,447	173,869
2015	8,309,564	8,142,177	1,530,785	167,387

SSI = Supplemental Security Income

SOURCE: Adapted from "Table 7.A3. Number of Recipients of Federally Administered Payments, by Eligibility Category, January 1974 and December 1975–2015, Selected Years," in *Annual Statistical Supplement to the Social Security Bulletin, 2016*, U.S. Social Security Administration, Office of Retirement and Disability Policy, May 2017, https://www.ssa.gov/policy/docs/statcomps/supplement/2016/supplement16.pdf (accessed August 5, 2017)

TABLE 4.16

Number of Supplemental Security Income recipients, total payments, and average monthly payment, by eligibility category, December 2015

Source of payment	All recipients	Category			Age		
		Aged	Blind	Disabled	Under 18	18–64	65 or older[a]
				Number of recipients			
Total	8,309,564	1,157,492	67,851	7,084,221	1,267,160	4,888,555	2,153,849
Federal payment only	6,778,779	744,541	47,289	5,986,949	1,125,191	4,152,106	1,501,482
Federal payment and state supplementation	1,363,398	356,523	17,702	989,173	141,028	658,263	564,107
State supplementation only	167,387	56,428	2,860	108,099	941	78,186	88,260
Total with—							
Federal payment	8,142,177	1,101,064	64,991	6,976,122	1,266,219	4,810,369	2,065,589
State supplementation	1,530,785	412,951	20,562	1,097,272	141,969	736,449	652,367
				Total payments[b] (thousands of dollars)			
Total	4,721,982	495,852	38,705	4,187,426	849,963	2,932,904	939,115
Federal payments	4,496,482	434,464	34,728	4,027,289	840,735	2,814,929	840,818
State supplementation	225,501	61,388	3,977	160,136	9,228	117,975	98,297
				Average monthly payment[c] (dollars)			
Total	541.28	428.10	558.02	559.63	643.06	561.60	435.47
Federal payments	525.72	394.48	522.59	546.49	636.61	547.74	406.71
State supplementation	141.80	147.55	189.36	138.74	61.81	150.35	149.51

SSI = Supplemental Security Income
[a]Includes blind persons and disabled persons aged 65 or older.
[b]Includes retroactive payments.
[c]Excludes retroactive payments.
Note: Totals do not necessarily equal the sum of rounded components.

SOURCE: "Table 7.A1. Number of Recipients of Federally Administered Payments, Total Payments, and Average Monthly Payment, by Source of Payment, Eligibility Category, and Age, December 2015," in *Annual Statistical Supplement to the Social Security Bulletin, 2016*, U.S. Social Security Administration, Office of Retirement and Disability Policy, May 2017, https://www.ssa.gov/policy/docs/statcomps/supplement/2016/supplement16.pdf (accessed August 5, 2017)

CHAPTER 5

CHARACTERISTICS OF THE HOMELESS

ESTIMATING THE SIZE OF THE HOMELESS POPULATION

Lacking fixed residences and regular means of contact, the homeless population is uniquely resistant to comprehensive data collection and research. As is discussed in Chapter 1, the U.S. Census Bureau's efforts to count the homeless population have been fraught with methodological problems, in large part because its decennial counts have historically failed to count unsheltered homeless people and thus underestimated the overall scope of homelessness. The Census Bureau no longer attempts to count the entire homeless population, explicitly limiting its decennial count to the occupants of emergency and transitional shelters.

The U.S. Department of Housing and Urban Development (HUD) attempts to arrive at a more complete picture of homelessness through its annual point-in-time (PIT) counts, which estimate the size of both the sheltered and unsheltered homeless populations across the country on a single night. These efforts combine actual counting of the homeless with statistical sampling, and they supply much of the data in the annual reports on homelessness that HUD has delivered to Congress since 2001. Called the *Annual Homeless Assessment Report* (*AHAR*), each annual report also includes data on shelter availability and occupancy levels. Part 1 of each *AHAR* presents PIT count and shelter availability data and is typically released before the end of the year in which the count takes place. Part 2 adds a range of longitudinal data collected in the Homeless Management Information Systems (HMIS), an electronic system that collects nationally representative information about homeless people who use shelters and subsidized housing programs over the course of a given year.

Although HUD's PIT counts are widely considered to be the most authoritative sources of up-to-date information on the U.S. homeless population, these counts are best viewed not as comprehensive resources but as estimated snapshots of homelessness on one particular day each year. In fact, some advocacy groups maintain that even highly accurate PIT counts drastically underestimate the scope of homelessness. Defining the homeless as those who are without a home on any given night results in a much smaller number than would a definition that encompasses a larger time horizon, such as a year. Individuals are continuously joining the population of those who are homeless on any given night, and others are continuously leaving this population. If all people who are homeless during a given year were counted, the official homeless population would be much higher. For example, in "Message from Our Executive Director" (2017, https://www.nlchp.org/message), the National Law Center on Homelessness and Poverty estimates that 3.5 million people experience homelessness in the United States each year and another 7 million are at "imminent risk" of becoming homeless.

Meghan Henry et al. note in *The 2016 Annual Homeless Assessment Report (AHAR) to Congress—Part 1: Point-in-Time Estimates of Homelessness* (November 2016, https://www.hudexchange.info/resources/documents/2016-AHAR-Part-1.pdf) that between 2007 and 2014 the homeless population on any given night ranged from a high of 647,258 (2007) to a low of 549,928 (2016). In the fact sheet "How Many People Experience Homelessness?" (July 2009, http://www.nationalhomeless.org/factsheets/How_Many.html), the National Coalition for the Homeless (NCH) indicates that estimates conducted during the late 1990s, at which point PIT counts ranged from 440,000 to 842,000, suggested that the population of those who experienced homelessness during a given year was between 2.3 million and 3.5 million. Because HUD's 2007 to 2016 PIT counts fall within the range of the PIT counts cited by the NCH, it is reasonable to assume that comparable numbers of people continue to experience homelessness in the course of a year.

These figures are also consistent with HUD's HMIS data as presented in *The 2015 Annual Homeless Assessment Report (AHAR) to Congress—Part 2: Estimates of Homelessness in the United States* (October 2016, https://www.hudexchange.info/onecpd/assets/File/2015-AHAR-Part-2.pdf) by Claudia D. Solari et al. This installment of the *AHAR* suggests that during 2015 approximately 1.5 million people were homeless in shelters. The HMIS does not count unsheltered homeless people, but HUD's PIT count for 2015 set the percentage of the sheltered population at 69.3% (391,440) of the total homeless population (564,708) on one night in January of that year. (See Figure 1.6 in Chapter 1.) If this percentage is roughly accurate for 2015 as a whole, it can be estimated that approximately 2.2 million people experienced homelessness over the course of that year, according to the best available HUD data.

As is discussed in Chapter 1, however, some homeless advocates dispute estimates of homelessness not simply on methodological grounds but on the grounds that the definition of homelessness is too narrow, leading HUD to forgo counting many people who experience homelessness by most commonsense definitions. The current official definition of homelessness, which specifies the homeless as those without a proper shelter of their own on any given night, leaves out many people who may consider themselves without a home and who do not have a home in the sense that the term is conventionally understood. Such people include prostitutes who spend their nights in different hotel rooms, children in foster care, people who have shelter that lacks essential services such as plumbing or heating, people living temporarily with relatives, and people living "doubled-up" (the Census Bureau defines doubled-up households as those including one or more person over the age of 18 years who is not enrolled in school and is not the householder, spouse, or cohabiting partner of the householder).

One source of reliable data employing a broadened definition of homelessness is the National Center for Homeless Education (NCHE), a nonprofit organization that acts as the U.S. Department of Education's technical assistance and information center on matters concerning the education of homeless youth. The NCHE collects data on homeless children in public schools rather than in the places where the homeless spend their nights, and the resulting publications count students who are living doubled-up as well as students who are living temporarily in hotels and motels. The NCHE statistics also estimate student homelessness over the course of an entire school year. Accordingly, the NCHE's yearly data releases identify a drastically larger population of homeless children than do HUD statistics, even though the NCHE does not account for infants and many preschool-aged children who are homeless (because the information is collected in schools). Because of the expanded definition of homelessness the NCHE uses, the group's data are considered superior to HUD data by many advocates for homeless children.

Several other organizations periodically collect and publish data on the homeless population. The National Alliance to End Homelessness (NAEH) collects information and analyzes HUD data in ways that enable a broader understanding of homelessness in the United States. In 2016 the NAEH released the sixth in its ongoing series of reports, *The State of Homelessness in America*, each of which makes use of and supplements HUD PIT count data, with the goal of promoting efforts to eradicate homelessness. Although the NAEH and HUD both attempt to estimate the size and characteristics of the homeless population and in many cases use the same data, the two organizations sometimes arrive at different figures and conclusions. The Association of Gospel Rescue Missions (AGRM), an association of more than 300 Christian-oriented missions that offer emergency shelter and services to the homeless, regularly undertakes its own surveys of those whom it serves. AGRM missions, however, do not serve the homeless exclusively, and the portion of the homeless population that makes use of shelters with a religious orientation may differ from the homeless population at large. Thus, like the NAEH reports, the AGRM annual surveys supplement rather than rival HUD data.

AN OVERVIEW OF THE HOMELESS POPULATION

Common conceptions of the homeless usually involve images of people, including children, who live on the street permanently and sleep under bridges and in cardboard boxes. There are, of course, people in this category, but they are the minority among the homeless. HUD, the NAEH, and other experts call such people the chronically homeless. Most of the homeless are not chronically homeless but are temporarily without a residence. After some period of homelessness, during which they often occupy emergency or transitional shelters, they often find a more permanent home of their own or move in with relatives.

Henry et al. note that an estimated 549,928 people were homeless nationwide on the single night in January 2016 when that year's PIT count took place. (See Figure 1.6 in Chapter 1.) The number of homeless people had declined considerably since 2007, when 647,258 were counted on one night in January of that year. The level of decline was minimal between 2007 and 2010, when the effects of the Great Recession (which officially lasted from December 2007 to June 2009) were being felt most severely. The rate of decline then accelerated between 2010 and 2016.

Much of the decrease in homeless numbers since 2010 is likely a result of two factors: improving economic conditions and a concerted federal effort to reduce levels of chronic homelessness and homelessness among military veterans (who are disproportionately likely to be chronically homeless). In May 2009 Congress enacted the Homeless Emergency Assistance and Rapid Transition to Housing Act to combat homelessness, charging the U.S. Interagency Council on Homelessness (USICH), a consortium of 19 federal agencies and their state and local partners, to produce a national strategic plan for ending homelessness. In June 2010 the USICH released *Opening Doors: Federal Strategic Plan to Prevent and End Homelessness* (https://www.usich .gov/resources/uploads/asset_library/USICH_OpeningDoors _Amendment2015_FINAL.pdf), which set leadership and collaboration goals among agencies; called for increased investment in employment and health services for the homeless, as well as investment in affordable housing and permanent supportive housing (PSH; long-term housing with support services for disabled, previously homeless people); and attempted to reconfigure the ways that agencies respond to homelessness. This national strategic plan enhanced efforts already under way to combat chronic and veteran homelessness. The plan was amended in 2012 to include a focus on educational outcomes for homeless children, and amended again in 2015 to emphasize the role of Medicaid and other social services in battling homelessness.

The new strategic direction in homeless policy involved a pronounced shift away from transitional housing (TH; temporary housing for formerly homeless people, usually including support services and available for up to two years) and toward PSH. As its name suggests, PSH represents a permanent intervention in the lives of homeless individuals and families, allowing even those with debilitating conditions to live on their own and stay off the streets on a long-term basis. As Figure 5.1 shows, in 2007 there were 188,636 PSH beds and 211,205 TH beds nationally. By 2016 there were 340,906 PSH beds (an increase of 152,270, or 80.7%) and 144,749 TH beds (a decrease of 66,456, or 31.5%). Meanwhile, the number of emergency shelter beds (beds available to homeless people on a nightly or short-term basis) increased from 211,451 in 2007 to 264,629 in 2016, a gain of 25.1%.

This shift to an emphasis on PSH represents a corresponding evolution in the thinking of homelessness experts. Robert Samuels describes this evolution in "This Group Thinks It's Found a Way to End Chronic Homelessness. It's Working" (WashingtonPost.com, June 11, 2014), which profiles Community Solutions, a nonprofit organization that has pioneered the shift to PSH in partnership with local governments (and drawing on federal funding from HUD and the U.S. Department of Veterans Affairs [VA], among other agencies). According to Samuels, groups such as Community Solutions locate the chronically homeless on the streets and place them in permanent housing immediately. Whereas TH focuses on readying the homeless to become permanently housed (often by connecting them with mental health providers, caseworkers, and employment or training opportunities), PSH focuses on housing people first and then finding case managers and counselors who can help them manage the problems that may have caused them to become homeless. Samuels explains, "The homeless person never has to leave the apartment, so long as they keep the place clean or follow whatever plan has been decided by the case manager. Government pays the rent. The group charts the success of keeping the formerly homeless off the streets at about 80 percent."

The PSH inventory targeted to chronically homeless people increased by 194.6% between 2007 and 2016, from 37,807 beds to 111,390 beds. (See Figure 5.2.) During this same period the chronically homeless population declined by 35.3%, from 119,813 to 77,486. (See Figure 5.3.)

These successes in combating chronic homelessness have not been duplicated among the majority of the homeless population, whose fate is more often tied to trends in the broader economy than to disabilities and mental health or substance abuse issues, as is often the case with the chronically homeless. Although improving economic conditions between 2010 and 2016 likely drove some portion of the overall reductions in homelessness, unemployment declined only gradually through 2016, while the poverty rate experienced only a slight drop during these years. (See Table 1.5 [unemployment rates] and Figure 1.1 [poverty rates] in Chapter 1.) At the same time, rising housing prices also made it difficult for low-income Americans to find shelter. In *The State of Homelessness in America 2016* (2016, http://endhomelessness .org/wp-content/uploads/2016/10/2016-soh.pdf), the NAEH states, "Housing is difficult to access and maintain for a large swath of the American public due to a lack of affordable housing stock combined with insufficient and stagnant incomes. This was the case prior to the recession, worsened during the recession, and has not improved substantially since the end of the recession. In fact, it appears that lower-income populations may not be experiencing the same benefits of the improving economy as those in higher income levels despite decreases in unemployment. And, the recovery of the housing market is making housing even more difficult to afford than earlier in the recovery when rents remained lower."

The AGRM makes a similar point in "AGRM's Snapshot Survey: Homeless Statistical Comparison" (November 2016, http://www.agrm.org/images/agrm/Documents/Snapshot/2016/2016%20yearly%20comparison%20 .pdf), noting that in a November 2016 survey of nearly

FIGURE 5.1

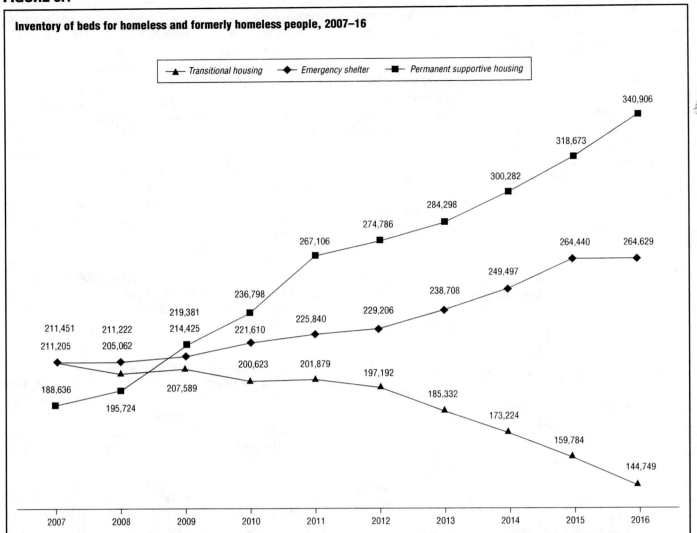

Inventory of beds for homeless and formerly homeless people, 2007–16

Legend:
- Transitional housing
- Emergency shelter
- Permanent supportive housing

Transitional housing: 211,205 (2007), 205,062 (2008), 207,589 (2009), 200,623 (2010), 201,879 (2011), 197,192 (2012), 185,332 (2013), 173,224 (2014), 159,784 (2015), 144,749 (2016)

Emergency shelter: 211,451 (2007), 211,222 (2008), 214,425 (2009), 221,610 (2010), 225,840 (2011), 229,206 (2012), 238,708 (2013), 249,497 (2014), 264,440 (2015), 264,629 (2016)

Permanent supportive housing: 188,636 (2007), 195,724 (2008), 219,381 (2009), 236,798 (2010), 267,106 (2011), 274,786 (2012), 284,298 (2013), 300,282 (2014), 318,673 (2015), 340,906 (2016)

SOURCE: Meghan Henry et al., "Exhibit 7.1. Inventory of Beds for Homeless and Formerly Homeless People, 2007–2016," in *The 2016 Annual Homeless Assessment Report (AHAR) to Congress—Part 1: Point-in-Time Estimates of Homelessness,* U.S. Department of Housing and Urban Development, Office of Community Planning and Development, November 2016, https://www.hudexchange.info/resources/documents/2016-AHAR-Part-1.pdf (accessed August 2, 2017)

16,000 people being served at 85 North American rescue missions, 37% of respondents reported that they had never been homeless before. (See Table 5.1.) People who find themselves homeless for the first time are typically members of low-income households (often families) that experience phenomena such as job loss, illness, and increased housing costs. In times of low unemployment, adequate wages, and affordable housing costs, such people can more easily avoid homelessness. The percentage of those experiencing homelessness for the first time in 2016 was up 7 percentage points from the previous year, but this marked a return to the level of first-time homelessness reported in 2013 and 2014.

Individuals and Families

A majority of the homeless people counted on one night in January 2016 were living alone as homeless individuals rather than as part of a family. Such individuals accounted for 355,212 (64.6%) of the total homeless population of 549,928. (See Figure 5.4.) Homeless individuals were more likely to be sheltered than unsheltered (198,008, or 55.7%, occupied shelters at the time of HUD's PIT count), but individuals constituted most of the total unsheltered homeless population. As Figure 1.6 in Chapter 1 shows, there were 176,357 unsheltered homeless people in 2016, so the 157,204 unsheltered individuals that year accounted for 89.1% of all of the unsheltered homeless. Between 2007 and 2016 there was a 57,488 (13.9%) decrease in the number of homeless individuals. This was driven primarily by a decline in the number of unsheltered homeless individuals, from 199,627 to 157,204. Between 2014 and 2016, however, the number of unsheltered homeless individuals rose slightly, while the number of sheltered homeless individuals declined.

FIGURE 5.2

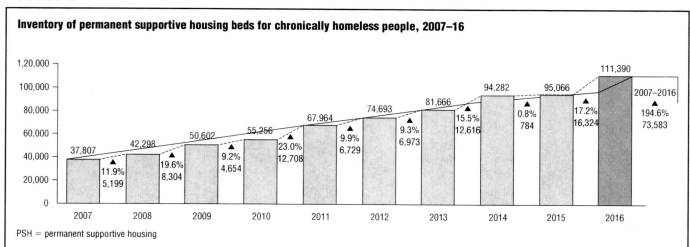

Inventory of permanent supportive housing beds for chronically homeless people, 2007–16

PSH = permanent supportive housing

SOURCE: Meghan Henry et al., "Exhibit 7.5. Inventory of PSH Beds for Chronically Homeless People, 2007–2016," in *The 2016 Annual Homeless Assessment Report (AHAR) to Congress—Part 1: Point-in-Time Estimates of Homelessness*, U.S. Department of Housing and Urban Development, Office of Community Planning and Development, November 2016, https://www.hudexchange.info/resources/documents/2016-AHAR-Part-1.pdf (accessed August 2, 2017)

FIGURE 5.3

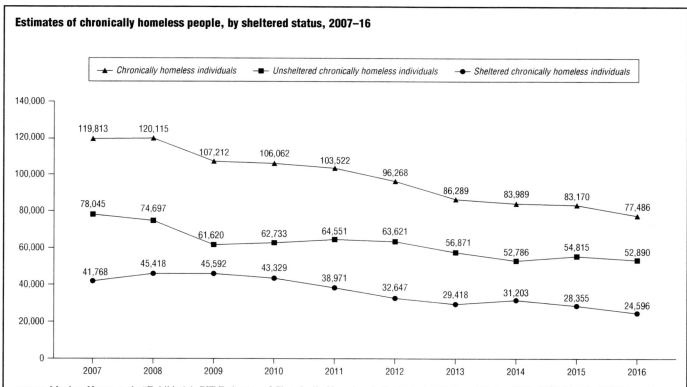

Estimates of chronically homeless people, by sheltered status, 2007–16

SOURCE: Meghan Henry et al., "Exhibit 6.1. PIT Estimates of Chronically Homeless Individuals, by Sheltered Status, 2007–2016," in *The 2016 Annual Homeless Assessment Report (AHAR) to Congress—Part 1: Point-in-Time Estimates of Homelessness*, U.S. Department of Housing and Urban Development, Office of Community Planning and Development, November 2016, https://www.hudexchange.info/resources/documents/2016-AHAR-Part-1.pdf (accessed August 2, 2017)

As Figure 5.5 shows, an estimated 194,716 (35.4%) of the total homeless population on one night in January 2016 consisted of people living in families. Homeless families were much more likely to be sheltered than were homeless individuals: 175,563 (90.2%) were sheltered and only 19,153 (9.8%) were unsheltered. Homeless families are also only rarely among the chronically homeless. According to Henry et al., 8,646 homeless people in

TABLE 5.1

Demographic overview of the homeless population served by the Association of Gospel Rescue Missions, 2012–2016

	2016	2015	2014	2013	2012
Gender (of total mission population)					
Male	72%	71%	73%	72%	72%
Female	28%	29%	27%	28%	28%
Age groups (of total mission population)					
Under 18	6%	5%	6%	6%	7%
18–25	8%	9%	9%	9%	9%
26–35	18%	19%	18%	18%	18%
36–45	22%	22%	22%	22%	23%
46–65	41%	38%	42%	41%	39%
65+	4%	6%	4%	4%	3%
Race/ethnic groups (of total mission population)					
White/Caucasian	48%	50%	49%	49%	50%
Black or African American	33%	33%	34%	32%	34%
Hispanic, Latin, or Spanish origin	10%	9%	9%	11%	10%
Asian	1%	1%	1%	1%	1%
American Indian or Alaskan Native	3%	3%	3%	3%	2%
Native Hawaiian or other Pacific Islander	1%	0%	1%	0%	0%
Other or 2+ races	3%	3%	2%	4%	3%
Single individuals (of total mission population)	86%	84%	86%	82%	81%
Women/children/families (of family units identified)					
Couples	20%	23%	20%	19%	23%
Women with children	58%	58%	54%	52%	51%
Men with children	8%	9%	11%	12%	11%
Intact families	15%	10%	15%	17%	16%
Veteran status (of total mission population)					
Veterans (male)	10%	11%	11%	11%	13%
Veterans (female)	1%	1%	2%	1%	2%
Homeless status (of total mission population)					
Not currently homeless	14%	15%	16%	19%	17%
Currently homeless	86%	85%	84%	81%	83%
Of currently homeless:					
Less than 3 months	32%	30%	31%	30%	30%
3 to 6 months	19%	21%	20%	21%	24%
6 months to 1 year	19%	20%	20%	19%	20%
More than 1 year	31%	30%	29%	30%	27%
Never before homeless	37%	30%	37%	37%	34%
Homeless once previously	23%	27%	24%	24%	26%
Homeless twice previously	16%	18%	16%	16%	17%
Homeless three-plus times previously	24%	25%	23%	23%	22%
Other information (of total mission population)					
Struggles with mental illness	33%	37%	32%	31%	30%
Victim of physical violence in last 12 months	21%	22%	20%	19%	24%
Prefer spiritual emphasis in services	79%	82%	81%	79%	81%
Comes daily to the mission	86%	81%	84%	81%	84%

SOURCE: "AGRM's 2016 Snapshot Survey: Homeless Statistical Comparison," Association of Gospel and Rescue Missions, November 2016, http://www.agrm.org/images/agrm/Documents/Snapshot/2016/2016%20yearly%20comparison%20.pdf (accessed August 5, 2017)

families, or 4.4% of all homeless people in families, were chronically homeless, and 5,512 (63.8%) of these people lived in shelters. Children accounted for 59.9% of all homeless people in families, 60.6% of sheltered homeless people in families, and 53.8% of unsheltered homeless people in families. (See Figure 5.6.)

Between 2007 and 2016 the number of homeless people living in families fell less dramatically than the number of homeless individuals. From a population of 234,558 in 2007, the number of people in homeless families fell to 194,716 by 2016, a decline of 17%. (See Figure 5.5.) Moreover, this decline was almost entirely attributable to a decline in the unsheltered portion of the

homeless family population, which fell from 56,230 to 19,153, while the sheltered homeless family population dropped only slightly, from 178,328 to 175,563. The movement of families from unsheltered to sheltered status was something of a mixed achievement. Sheltered families typically enjoy better living conditions than unsheltered ones, but persistently high levels of overall family homelessness were cause for continuing concern.

DEMOGRAPHIC CHARACTERISTICS OF THE HOMELESS

HUD's yearly PIT counts provide only limited insight into the demographic characteristics of the homeless

FIGURE 5.4

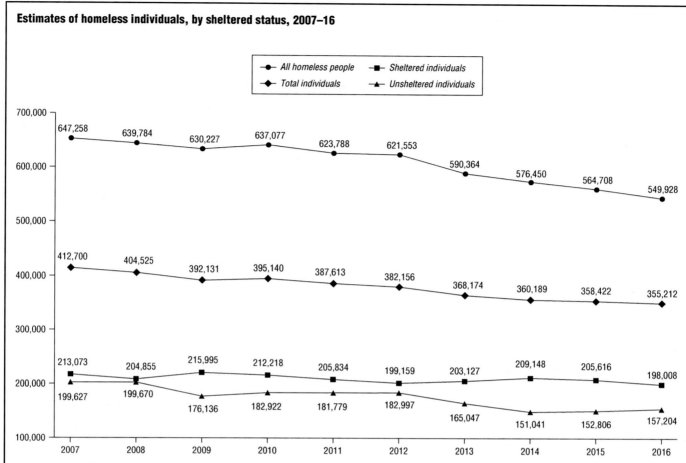

Estimates of homeless individuals, by sheltered status, 2007–16

Legend:
- All homeless people
- Total individuals
- Sheltered individuals
- Unsheltered individuals

All homeless people: 647,258 (2007), 639,784 (2008), 630,227 (2009), 637,077 (2010), 623,788 (2011), 621,553 (2012), 590,364 (2013), 576,450 (2014), 564,708 (2015), 549,928 (2016)

Total individuals: 412,700 (2007), 404,525 (2008), 392,131 (2009), 395,140 (2010), 387,613 (2011), 382,156 (2012), 368,174 (2013), 360,189 (2014), 358,422 (2015), 355,212 (2016)

Sheltered individuals: 213,073 (2007), 204,855 (2008), 215,995 (2009), 212,218 (2010), 205,834 (2011), 199,159 (2012), 203,127 (2013), 209,148 (2014), 205,616 (2015), 198,008 (2016)

Unsheltered individuals: 199,627 (2007), 199,670 (2008), 176,136 (2009), 182,922 (2010), 181,779 (2011), 182,997 (2012), 165,047 (2013), 151,041 (2014), 152,806 (2015), 157,204 (2016)

SOURCE: Meghan Henry et al., "Exhibit 2.1. PIT Estimates of Homeless Individuals, by Sheltered Status, 2007–2016," in *The 2016 Annual Homeless Assessment Report (AHAR) to Congress—Part 1: Point-in-Time Estimates of Homelessness*, U.S. Department of Housing and Urban Development, Office of Community Planning and Development, November 2016, https://www.hudexchange.info/resources/documents/2016-AHAR-Part-1.pdf (accessed August 2, 2017)

population. The agency's HMIS data, which are presented in part 2 of each year's *AHAR*, offer the most reliable demographic information about the homeless population. As noted earlier, however, this information is at any given moment less up-to-date than PIT count data, and it pertains only to the sheltered homeless population.

Gender

As Table 5.2 shows, 60.2% of the overall homeless adult population was male in 2016. The general U.S. adult population was 49.2% male that same year. This gender imbalance is particularly striking when considered in the context of the population that experiences poverty in a typical year. For example, Bernadette D. Proctor, Jessica L. Semega, and Melissa A. Kollar of the U.S. Census Bureau report in *Income and Poverty in the United States: 2015* (September 2016, https://www.census.gov/content/dam/Census/library/publications/2016/demo/p60-256.pdf) that the population living below the poverty line in 2015 was 55.9% female.

The gender breakdown among the sheltered homeless varied dramatically among the homeless individual and family subpopulations, with men much more likely to be living as homeless individuals in 2015 and women much more likely to be living in homeless families with children. According to Solari et al., 73.2% of homeless adults being sheltered as individuals that year were male, whereas 82% of homeless adults being sheltered as part of a family with children were female.

Age

Solari et al. report that in 2015 more than one-third (33.8%) of sheltered homeless people were aged 31 to 50 years, 22.4% were aged 18 to 30 years, and 22.3% were under the age of 18 years. People aged 51 to 61 years accounted for 17.2% of the sheltered homeless population, while those aged 62 years and older accounted for a very small proportion of the sheltered homeless population, at 4.2%. Elderly adults' access to Social Security, Medicare, and other benefits was likely a key factor in the relative improbability of experiencing homelessness

FIGURE 5.5

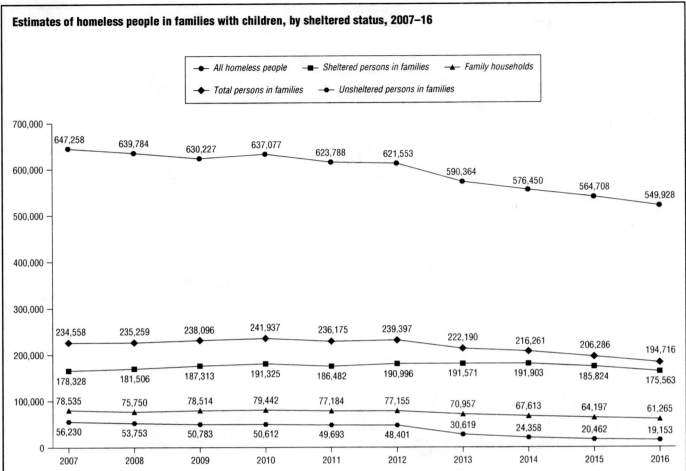

Estimates of homeless people in families with children, by sheltered status, 2007–16

Legend:
- All homeless people
- Sheltered persons in families
- Family households
- Total persons in families
- Unsheltered persons in families

All homeless people: 647,258 (2007), 639,784 (2008), 630,227 (2009), 637,077 (2010), 623,788 (2011), 621,553 (2012), 590,364 (2013), 576,450 (2014), 564,708 (2015), 549,928 (2016)

Total persons in families: 234,558 (2007), 235,259 (2008), 238,096 (2009), 241,937 (2010), 236,175 (2011), 239,397 (2012), 222,190 (2013), 216,261 (2014), 206,286 (2015), 194,716 (2016)

Sheltered persons in families: 178,328 (2007), 181,506 (2008), 187,313 (2009), 191,325 (2010), 186,482 (2011), 190,996 (2012), 191,571 (2013), 191,903 (2014), 185,824 (2015), 175,563 (2016)

Family households: 78,535 (2007), 75,750 (2008), 78,514 (2009), 79,442 (2010), 77,184 (2011), 77,155 (2012), 70,957 (2013), 67,613 (2014), 64,197 (2015), 61,265 (2016)

Unsheltered persons in families: 56,230 (2007), 53,753 (2008), 50,783 (2009), 50,612 (2010), 49,693 (2011), 48,401 (2012), 30,619 (2013), 24,358 (2014), 20,462 (2015), 19,153 (2016)

SOURCE: Meghan Henry et al., "PIT Exhibit 3.1. Estimates of Homeless People in Families with Children, by Sheltered Status, 2007–2016," in *The 2016 Annual Homeless Assessment Report (AHAR) to Congress—Part 1: Point-in-Time Estimates of Homelessness*, U.S. Department of Housing and Urban Development, Office of Community Planning and Development, November 2016, https://www.hudexchange.info/resources/documents/2016-AHAR-Part-1.pdf (accessed August 2, 2017)

past the age of 62. Still, Solari et al. note that the proportion of sheltered homeless people who were elderly rose steadily in the years following the Great Recession, from 2.9% in 2007 to 3.8% in 2014 to 4.2% in 2015.

These proportions, however, varied dramatically by subpopulation. Solari et al. state that adults aged 31 to 50 years (42.5%) constituted the largest group of the sheltered individual population in 2015, followed by adults aged 51 to 61 years (25.4%) and young adults aged 18 to 30 years (23.6%). Children accounted for only 2.2% of the sheltered individual population. By contrast, in 2015 children constituted 60.9% of the sheltered family population, adults aged 18 to 30 years made up 20.3% of the sheltered family population, and adults aged 31 to 50 years constituted 17.2% of the sheltered family population. Only 1.6% of those living in sheltered families were over the age of 50 years.

Race and Ethnicity

In 2016 the sheltered homeless population was disproportionately African American. As Table 5.2 shows, African Americans accounted for 45.1% of the sheltered homeless population that year. They represented 13.3% of the total U.S. population in 2016. Non-Hispanic whites accounted for an approximately equal share of the sheltered population, at 43.9% in 2016, while constituting 61.3% of the total U.S. population. Hispanics accounted for 23.3% of the sheltered population in 2016; this figure was somewhat higher than the proportion of Hispanics in the total U.S. population, which stood at 17.8% that year. The overrepresentation of African Americans in the sheltered homeless population was more pronounced among homeless families than among homeless individuals. Solari et al. indicate that in 2015 African Americans accounted for 50.1% of people in sheltered families and for 37.2% of sheltered individuals.

AGRM Survey Data

The AGRM's 2016 survey of 85 missions yielded demographic insights into the homeless population that broadly resemble those of HUD's 2016 HMIS data, while showing distinct differences. These differences were likely due to multiple factors, such as the fact that a portion of the AGRM client population was not homeless and that the religious orientation of gospel missions may have appealed to some homeless people more than others. In 2016 the AGRM determined that its client population was 72% male and 28% female. (See Table 5.1.) Out of the subset of clients that the AGRM identified as being part of family units, 58% were single women with children, 20% were couples with no children, 15% were couples with children, and 8% were single men with children. Children (6%) accounted for a far smaller proportion of the 2016 AGRM population than HUD's 2016 HMIS population, and whites (48%) accounted for a higher proportion of the AGRM population than the HUD HMIS population.

HOMELESS CHILDREN AND YOUTH

Homeless children have always received special attention from the public and welfare agencies. In the terminology of previous centuries, children are considered "worthy poor" (i.e., "worthy" of help from society) because they have no control over their financial circumstances. Homeless youth (those aged 18 to 24 years) are also often considered a population of particular concern. Both children and youth who find themselves homeless are considered at enhanced risk of sexual and physical abuse and other forms of violence. Additionally, the privations and stresses of homelessness can traumatize and scar young people in irreversible ways, leaving them more likely to be poor or homeless as adults.

HUD PIT Count Estimates

According to Henry et al., an estimated 120,819 children under the age of 18 years were homeless on one night in January 2016; 3,824 of these were living as unaccompanied individuals. Meanwhile, young people aged 18 to 24 years were much more likely to live unaccompanied than in families. Of the 50,001 homeless youths in that age group, 31,862 (63.7%) were living as unaccompanied individuals in 2016. (See Table 5.3.) Unaccompanied children and youth are among the most vulnerable of all homeless people, and their vulnerability is exacerbated by their disproportionate likelihood of living in unsheltered locations. As Figure 5.7 shows, 42% of unaccompanied children and 46.7% of unaccompanied youth were unsheltered in January 2016. By contrast, only 32.1% of the total homeless population was unsheltered during that same period.

NCHE and Related Estimates

The NCHE collects estimates of homeless children from public school districts and local education agencies. The data exclude infants as the HUD estimates do not, but the data include some children of preschool age.

FIGURE 5.6

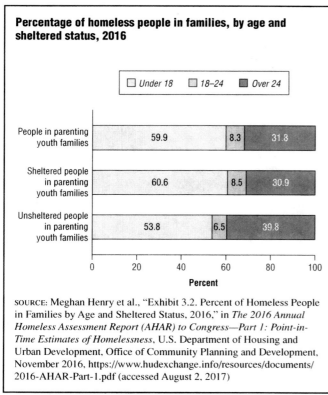

Percentage of homeless people in families, by age and sheltered status, 2016

SOURCE: Meghan Henry et al., "Exhibit 3.2. Percent of Homeless People in Families by Age and Sheltered Status, 2016," in *The 2016 Annual Homeless Assessment Report (AHAR) to Congress—Part 1: Point-in-Time Estimates of Homelessness*, U.S. Department of Housing and Urban Development, Office of Community Planning and Development, November 2016, https://www.hudexchange.info/resources/documents/2016-AHAR-Part-1.pdf (accessed August 2, 2017)

FIGURE 5.7

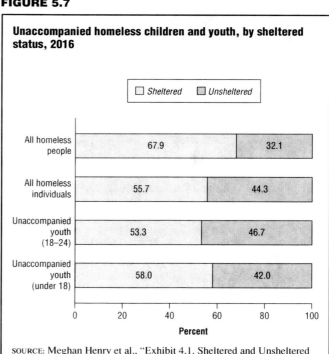

Unaccompanied homeless children and youth, by sheltered status, 2016

SOURCE: Meghan Henry et al., "Exhibit 4.1. Sheltered and Unsheltered Unaccompanied Homeless Youth by Sheltered Status, 2016," in *The 2016 Annual Homeless Assessment Report (AHAR) to Congress—Part 1: Point-in-Time Estimates of Homelessness*, U.S. Department of Housing and Urban Development, Office of Community Planning and Development, November 2016, https://www.hudexchange.info/resources/documents/2016-AHAR-Part-1.pdf (accessed August 2, 2017)

TABLE 5.2

Number and percentage of people experiencing homelessness, by selected characteristics and by sheltered status, 2016

Characteristic	All homeless people		Sheltered people		Unsheltered people	
	#	%	#	%	#	%
Total	549,928	100.0	373,571	100.0	176,357	100.0
Gender						
Female	217,268	39.5	165,780	44.4	51,488	29.2
Male	330,890	60.2	206,999	55.4	123,891	70.3
Transgender	1,770	0.3	792	0.2	978	0.6
Ethnicity						
Non-Hispanic	428,629	77.9	286,430	76.7	142,199	80.6
Hispanic	121,299	22.1	87,141	23.3	34,158	19.4
Race						
White	265,660	48.3	163,881	43.9	101,779	57.7
African American	215,177	39.1	168,623	45.1	46,554	26.4
Asian	5,603	1.0	3,476	0.9	2,127	1.2
Native American	15,229	2.8	7,880	2.1	7,349	4.2
Pacific Islander	8,734	1.6	4,499	1.2	4,235	2.4
Multiple races	39,525	7.2	25,212	6.8	14,313	8.1

SOURCE: Meghan Henry et al., "Exhibit 1.4. Demographic Characteristics of People Experiencing Homelessness, 2016," in *The 2016 Annual Homeless Assessment Report (AHAR) to Congress—Part 1: Point-in-Time Estimates of Homelessness*, U.S. Department of Housing and Urban Development, Office of Community Planning and Development, November 2016, https://www.hudexchange.info/resources/documents/2016-AHAR-Part-1.pdf (accessed August 2, 2017)

TABLE 5.3

Homeless youth, by age and sheltered status, 2016

	Total unaccompanied homeless youth		Sheltered unaccompanied youth		Unsheltered unaccompanied youth	
	#	%	#	%	#	%
Total homeless youth (under 25)	35,686	100.0	19,188	100.0	16,498	100.0
Homeless youth (under 18)	3,824	10.7	2,218	11.6	1,606	9.7
Homeless youth (18–24)	31,862	89.3	16,970	88.4	14,892	90.3

SOURCE: Meghan Henry et al., "Exhibit 4.2. Estimates of Unaccompanied Homeless Youth by Age and Sheltered Status, 2016," in *The 2016 Annual Homeless Assessment Report (AHAR) to Congress—Part 1: Point-in-Time Estimates of Homelessness*, U.S. Department of Housing and Urban Development, Office of Community Planning and Development, November 2016, https://www.hudexchange.info/resources/documents/2016-AHAR-Part-1.pdf (accessed August 2, 2017)

Also unlike HUD, the NCHE counts as homeless those students who are living doubled-up or in hotels and motels. Because it counts homeless students over the course of a school year and because it counts those who are doubled-up and living in hotels and motels, the NCHE arrives at a much larger estimate of the number of homeless children than do the HUD PIT counts. Nevertheless, in "Record Number of Homeless Children Enrolled in US Public Schools" (CSMonitor.com, September 23, 2014), Amanda Paulson indicates that the NCHE data are widely believed to undercount the school-aged population of homeless children. Besides the likelihood that a sizable proportion of homeless children (especially teenagers) are not enrolled in

school, it is also likely that some homeless children are not identified as such by school staff.

According to the NCHE, in *Federal Data Summary School Years 2012–13 to 2014–15: Education for Homeless Children and Youth* (December 2016, http://nche.ed.gov/downloads/data-comp-1213-1415.pdf), nearly 1.3 million homeless children were enrolled in public schools during the 2014–15 school year. (See Table 5.4.) According to the NCHE, in *Education for Homeless Children and Youth Program: Analysis of Data* (July 2008, http://center.serve.org/nche/downloads/data_comp_03-06.pdf), this total was nearly double the 679,724 homeless students tallied during the 2006–07 school year, prior to the onset of the Great Recession. As shown in Table 5.5, 7.3% of homeless children enrolled in public schools in 2016 (95,032 children) were living as unaccompanied individuals.

In *America's Youngest Outcasts: A Report Card on Child Homelessness* (November 2014, https://www.air.org/sites/default/files/downloads/report/Americas-Youngest-Outcasts-Child-Homelessness-Nov2014.pdf), Ellen L. Bassuk et al. of the National Center on Family Homelessness evaluate 2013 Census Bureau data to estimate the size of the child homeless population, including children not counted by the NCHE. The researchers calculate that 2.5 million children, or one out of every 30 U.S. children, were homeless at some point during that year.

In 2014–15, doubled-up housing arrangements accounted for 76% (958,495) of total homelessness among public school students and another 6.5% (82,159) of homeless students lived in hotels or motels. (See Table 5.4.) Many advocates for homeless children argue that children

TABLE 5.4

TABLE 5.5

Homeless student population, by primary nighttime residence, school years 2012–13, 2013–14, and 2014–15

Residence	2012–13	2013–14	2014–15
Total[a]	1,202,507	1,298,236	1,261,461
Shelters, transitional housing, awaiting foster care	174,715	186,265	181,386
Doubled-up[b]	919,370	989,844	958,495
Unsheltered[c]	39,243	42,003	39,421
Hotels/motels[d]	69,179	80,124	82,159

[a]The United States total includes District of Columbia and Puerto Rico Enrolled students includes those aged 3 through 5, Kindergarten through Grade 13, and Ungraded.
[b]i.e., living with others due to loss of housing, economic hardship, or a similar reason.
[c]i.e., cars, parks, campgrounds, temporary trailer, abandoned buildings, or other places not intended for human habitation.
[d]Due to the lack of alternate, adequate accommodations.

SOURCE: "Table 5. Number of Enrolled Homeless Students, by Primary Nighttime Residence: School Years 2012–13, 2013–14, and 2014–15," in *Federal Data Summary School Years 2012–13 to 2014–15: Education for Homeless Children and Youth*, National Center for Homeless Education, December 2016, http://nche.ed.gov/downloads/data-comp-1213-1415.pdf (accessed August 5, 2017)

Homeless students enrolled in public schools, by subgroup, school years 2012–13, 2013–14, and 2014–15

Subgroup	2012–13[a]	2013–14[b]	2014–15	Change over 3-year timeframe
Unaccompanied homeless youth[c]	78,654	88,966	95,032	21%
Migratory children/youth	16,231[d]	18,512	17,748	9%
Limited English Proficient (LEP) students	174,870	190,785	181,949	4%
Children with disabilities (IDEA)	191,259	220,405	216,477	13%

[a]Includes the District of Columbia and Puerto Rico; excludes students in Wisconsin for all subgroups except unaccompanied youth.
[b]Includes the District of Columbia and Puerto Rico; excludes Alabama LEAs that did not receive subgrants.
[c]Excludes California for SYs 2012–13 and 2013–14, Wyoming for 2014–15. New collection processes instituted in New Hampshire may have resulted in under reporting of students.
[d]Excludes Wyoming.

SOURCE: "Table 6. Number and Percentage Change in Enrolled Homeless Students, by Subgroup: School Years 2012–13, 2013–14, and 2014–15," in *Federal Data Summary School Years 2012–13 to 2014–15: Education for Homeless Children and Youth*, National Center for Homeless Education, December 2016, http://nche.ed.gov/downloads/data-comp-1213-1415.pdf (accessed August 5, 2017)

who are doubled-up or living in hotels and motels experience the same instability and emotional turmoil as those children that HUD classifies as homeless. According to this argument, these children are at a high risk of becoming homeless adults if they are not provided with assistance during their crucial childhood and adolescent years. Bipartisan legislation introduced in both houses of Congress in 2014 aimed to change the HUD definition of homelessness to include youth living in such circumstances. Rita Price reports in "Congress May Expand Who Counts as Homeless" (Dispatch.com, August 6, 2014) that such legislation was a long-standing priority of advocacy groups such as the National Association for the Education of Homeless Children and Youth. Critics of the proposed legislation included advocates for the homeless population as a whole, such as the NAEH, whose leadership felt the bill would expand the definition of homelessness to an impractical extent, given that the bill did not include any increased funding for the HUD programs that serve the homeless. The 113th Congress (2013 to 2015) took no action on the bill. It was reintroduced during the 114th Congress (2015 to 2017) in January 2015, but that iteration of the bill also resulted in no change. As of October 2017, no further versions of these bills had been introduced to Congress.

Regardless of their exact shelter situation, homeless children have less than optimal conditions for educational achievement. According to Bassuk et al., studies suggest that homeless children are sick more frequently than other children and they experience significant mental distress as a result of worries about whether they will continue to have food to eat and shelter at night and what will happen to their family. As a result, such children are more likely to demonstrate developmental delays and

mental health problems that require clinical intervention. They also miss school more frequently than other children, are more often required to repeat grades, and are more likely to drop out of school.

Lesbian, Gay, Bisexual, Transgender, and Queer Teens

In "The Forsaken: A Rising Number of Homeless Gay Teens Are Being Cast Out by Religious Families" (RollingStone.com, September 3, 2014), Alex Morris reports that lesbian, gay, bisexual, transgender, and queer (LGBTQ) young people account for only about 5% of the youth population, but they make up an estimated 40% of the homeless youth population. Research suggests that the number of homeless LGBTQ teens is rising and that a primary factor driving the phenomenon is the rejection such teens face in religious families. Buoyed by broad societal acceptance of LGBTQ people and by the ability to connect to like-minded people online and through social media, LGBTQ teens are more likely than in the past to come out to their family and friends while still dependent on their parents for housing and financial support. In many cases, however, the societal acceptance of LGBTQ people does not extend to the extremely religious, and religious parents often feel their beliefs require them to kick their children out of their home and to cut off financial support for them. As Figure 5.8 reveals, a survey by the Williams Institute found that well over half (55.3%) of homeless lesbian, gay, bisexual, and queer teens, and more than two-thirds (67.1%) of homeless transgender teens, had either been forced out of their homes by their families or had run away from home because of

FIGURE 5.8

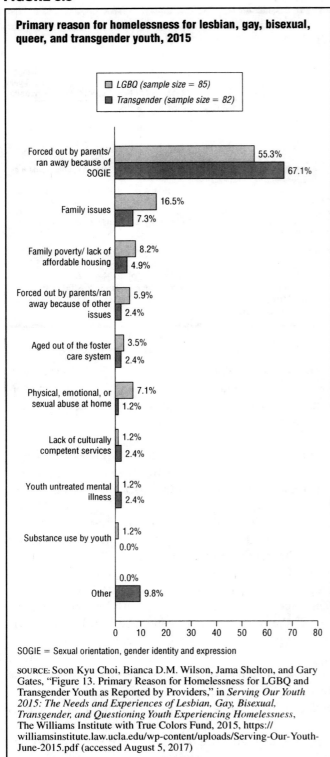

Primary reason for homelessness for lesbian, gay, bisexual, queer, and transgender youth, 2015

- ▢ LGBQ (sample size = 85)
- ▣ Transgender (sample size = 82)

Reason	LGBQ	Transgender
Forced out by parents/ran away because of SOGIE	55.3%	67.1%
Family issues	16.5%	7.3%
Family poverty/lack of affordable housing	8.2%	4.9%
Forced out by parents/ran away because of other issues	5.9%	2.4%
Aged out of the foster care system	3.5%	2.4%
Physical, emotional, or sexual abuse at home	7.1%	1.2%
Lack of culturally competent services	1.2%	2.4%
Youth untreated mental illness	1.2%	2.4%
Substance use by youth	1.2%	0.0%
Other	0.0%	9.8%

SOGIE = Sexual orientation, gender identity and expression

SOURCE: Soon Kyu Choi, Bianca D.M. Wilson, Jama Shelton, and Gary Gates, "Figure 13. Primary Reason for Homelessness for LGBQ and Transgender Youth as Reported by Providers," in *Serving Our Youth 2015: The Needs and Experiences of Lesbian, Gay, Bisexual, Transgender, and Questioning Youth Experiencing Homelessness,* The Williams Institute with True Colors Fund, 2015, https://williamsinstitute.law.ucla.edu/wp-content/uploads/Serving-Our-Youth-June-2015.pdf (accessed August 5, 2017)

TABLE 5.6

Percentage of homeless adults that are veterans, by sheltered status, 2016

	# of homeless veterans	# of homeless adults	% of homeless adults who are veterans
Total	**39,471**	**429,109**	**9.2**
Sheltered	26,404	264,705	10.0
Unsheltered	13,067	164,404	8.0

SOURCE: Meghan Henry et al., "Exhibit 5.2. Percent of Homeless Veterans by Sheltered Status, 2016," in *The 2016 Annual Homeless Assessment Report (AHAR) to Congress—Part 1: Point-in-Time Estimates of Homelessness,* U.S. Department of Housing and Urban Development, Office of Community Planning and Development, November 2016, https://www.hudexchange.info/resources/documents/2016-AHAR-Part-1.pdf (accessed August 2, 2017)

Morris that in the months after LGBTQ couples in New York won the right to marry, the number of homeless youth in need of shelter rose 40%.

HOMELESS MILITARY VETERANS

Homeless veterans are another group of particular concern to many Americans and policy makers. Many ordinary people and policy makers believe that some level of gratitude and support is owed to those who served in the military. Additionally, the trauma of combat and the difficulty of reintegrating into civilian life leave veterans at an increased risk of homelessness relative to the general population.

HUD and the VA work together to generate accurate estimates of the population of homeless veterans for each annual PIT count, and their estimates of veteran homelessness are believed to be among the most accurate estimates of any subpopulation in each *AHAR*. The homeless veteran population on a single night in January 2016 was an estimated 39,471 (9.2% of the adult homeless population). (See Table 5.6.) Veterans accounted for approximately the same proportion of both the sheltered and unsheltered adult population. Almost all homeless veterans experienced homelessness as individuals, and 90% of homeless veterans were men.

Combating both homelessness and chronic homelessness among veterans has been a concerted focus of HUD, the VA, and the other government agencies associated with the USICH. Homeless veterans, who have been disproportionately represented among the chronic homeless in most 21st-century PIT counts, have been a primary target of the efforts to expand the availability of PSH and to reduce the waiting and red tape previously associated with subsidized temporary and permanent housing. As a result of this and other efforts by USICH agencies and numerous private nonprofit organizations, the population of homeless veterans has fallen dramatically since 2009.

conflicts centered on their sexual or gender identity. Morris explains, "Tragically, every step forward for the gay-rights movement creates a false hope of acceptance for certain youth, and therefore a swelling of the homeless-youth population." Carl Siciliano, the founder of New York City's Ali Forney Center for homeless LGBTQ youth, told

FIGURE 5.9

Homeless veterans, by sheltered status, 2009–16

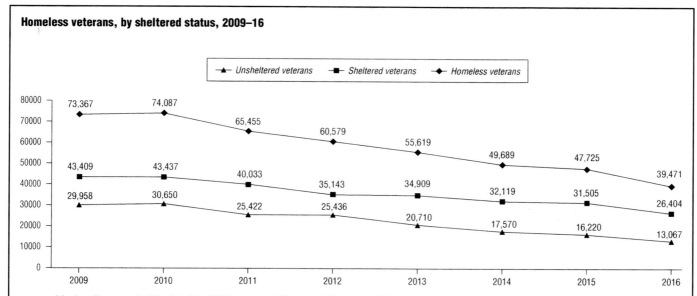

SOURCE: Meghan Henry et al., "Exhibit 5.1. PIT Estimates of Homeless Veterans by Sheltered Status, 2009–2016," in *The 2016 Annual Homeless Assessment Report (AHAR) to Congress—Part 1: Point-in-Time Estimates of Homelessness*, U.S. Department of Housing and Urban Development, Office of Community Planning and Development, November 2016, https://www.hudexchange.info/resources/documents/2016-AHAR-Part-1.pdf (accessed August 2, 2017)

In 2009, at the height of the Great Recession, there were an estimated 73,367 homeless veterans, and the following year saw a slight uptick in the population of homeless veterans, to 74,087. (See Figure 5.9.) Following the 2010 release of the USICH strategic plan, the numbers of homeless veterans declined steadily, to 65,445 in 2011, 60,579 in 2012, 55,619 in 2013, 49,689 in 2014, 47,725 in 2015, and 39,471 in 2016. Overall, the number of homeless veterans declined by 33,896 (46.2%) between 2009 and 2016. (See Table 5.7.) Initiatives to end veteran homelessness found particular success with unsheltered veterans, whose numbers decreased by 16,891 (56.4%) during this period.

THE GEOGRAPHY OF HOMELESSNESS

According to Henry et al., the January 2016 PIT count indicated that half of the U.S. homeless population lived in five states: California, New York, Florida, Texas, and Washington. (See Figure 5.10.) California alone had a homeless population of 118,142 people (22% of the national total). New York's homeless population was 86,352 (16% of the national total); Florida's, 33,559 (6%); Texas's, 23,122 (4%); and Washington's, 20,827 (4%). As Figure 5.11 shows, two-thirds (78,390, or 66.4%) of California's homeless population was unsheltered in 2016; by contrast, only 3,591 of the 86,352 homeless people in New York (4.2%) were unsheltered that year. Henry et al. report that the 25 states that each accounted for less than 1% of the national homeless population collectively accounted for less than 11% of the national homeless population.

TABLE 5.7

Change in the numbers of homeless veterans, by sheltered status, 2009–16

	2015–2016		2010–2016		2009–2016	
	#	%	#	%	#	%
Total veterans	**−8,254**	**−17.3**	**−34,616**	**−46.7**	**−33,896**	**−46.2**
Sheltered	−5,101	−16.2	−17,033	−39.2	−17,005	−39.2
Unsheltered	−3,153	−19.4	−17,583	−57.4	−16,891	−56.4

SOURCE: Meghan Henry et al., "Exhibit 5.4. Change in Numbers of Homeless Veterans by Sheltered Status, 2009–2016," in *The 2016 Annual Homeless Assessment Report (AHAR) to Congress—Part 1: Point-in-Time Estimates of Homelessness*, U.S. Department of Housing and Urban Development, Office of Community Planning and Development, November 2016, https://www.hudexchange.info/resources/documents/2016-AHAR-Part-1.pdf (accessed August 2, 2017)

Homelessness in the popular imagination is primarily an urban phenomenon, and the data support this view to a significant extent. Nearly half (49.3%) of the nation's homeless population in 2016 lived in major cities, while slightly over one-third (36.8%) lived in smaller cities. (See Figure 5.12.) As Table 5.8 shows, of the 86,352 homeless people living in the state of New York in 2016, 73,523 (85%) were in New York City alone. That year, more than half of California's total homeless population of 118,142 (66,043, or 55.9%) lived in the major metropolitan areas of Los Angeles, San Diego, San Francisco, and San Jose/Santa Clara. A comparable proportion of the homeless population in Washington (10,730 of 20,827, or 51.5%) lived in the Seattle/King County metropolitan area in 2016.

FIGURE 5.10

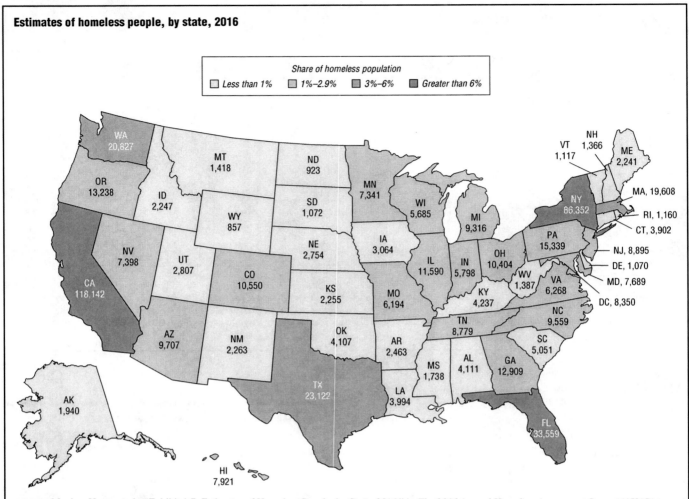

Estimates of homeless people, by state, 2016

Share of homeless population
☐ Less than 1% ☐ 1%–2.9% ☐ 3%–6% ☐ Greater than 6%

WA 20,827
OR 13,238
MT 1,418
ND 923
MN 7,341
WI 5,685
MI 9,316
VT 1,117
NH 1,366
ME 2,241
NY 86,352
MA, 19,608
ID 2,247
SD 1,072
WY 857
IA 3,064
IL 11,590
IN 5,798
OH 10,404
PA 15,339
RI, 1,160
CT, 3,902
NJ, 8,895
NV 7,398
UT 2,807
NE 2,754
CO 10,550
KS 2,255
MO 6,194
KY 4,237
WV 1,387
VA 6,268
DE, 1,070
MD, 7,689
DC, 8,350
CA 118,142
NC 9,559
AZ 9,707
NM 2,263
OK 4,107
AR 2,463
TN 8,779
SC 5,051
MS 1,738
AL 4,111
GA 12,909
TX 23,122
LA 3,994
AK 1,940
FL 33,559
HI 7,921

SOURCE: Meghan Henry et al., "Exhibit 1.7. Estimates of Homeless People, by State, 2016," in *The 2016 Annual Homeless Assessment Report (AHAR) to Congress—Part 1: Point-in-Time Estimates of Homelessness*, U.S. Department of Housing and Urban Development, Office of Community Planning and Development, November 2016, https://www.hudexchange.info/resources/documents/2016-AHAR-Part-1.pdf (accessed August 2, 2017)

Rural homelessness can differ from urban homelessness in numerous important ways. Rural communities are often less well equipped to serve and assess their homeless populations. There are fewer official shelters, and the transportation infrastructure necessary for the homeless to access services is often lacking. There are also fewer public places (e.g., heating grates, subways, or train stations) where the homeless can find temporary shelter or relief from the elements. Therefore, the rural homeless are more likely to live in a car or camper, or with relatives in overcrowded or rundown housing, than in shelters or in typical unsheltered locations. As a result, finding the rural homeless is more difficult for investigators of the problem, so it is possible that they are routinely undercounted in HUD and other surveys.

EMPLOYMENT AND THE HOMELESS

Barring significant assistance, finding a job is the only way for most people to escape homelessness. Unsympathetic views hold that people become homeless due to qualities such as laziness and an unwillingness to work. This belief is not supported by research. In "Employment, Day Labor, and Shadow Work among Homeless Assistance Clients in the United States" (*Journal of Poverty*, vol. 17, no. 3, 2013), Lei Lei of the University at Albany, State University of New York, notes that over 90% of homeless people express the desire to work and that approximately 80% have been found to be employed or looking for work. However, the homeless typically find it extremely difficult to find and keep good jobs.

In *Hunger and Homelessness Survey: A Status Report on Hunger and Homelessness in America's Cities, a 25-City Survey* (December 2014, https://www2.cortland.edu/dotAsset/655b9350-995e-4aae-acd3-298325093c34.pdf), the U.S. Conference of Mayors reports that between September 1, 2013, and August 31, 2014, 18% of homeless adults in its 25 survey cities were employed. This does not necessarily mean that all of these individuals were

FIGURE 5.11

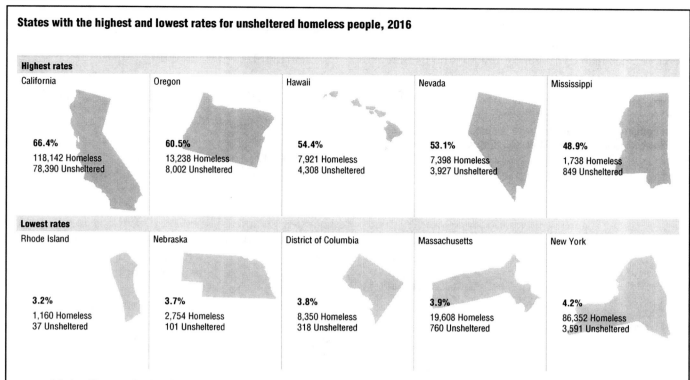

States with the highest and lowest rates for unsheltered homeless people, 2016

Highest rates

California	Oregon	Hawaii	Nevada	Mississippi
66.4%	**60.5%**	**54.4%**	**53.1%**	**48.9%**
118,142 Homeless	13,238 Homeless	7,921 Homeless	7,398 Homeless	1,738 Homeless
78,390 Unsheltered	8,002 Unsheltered	4,308 Unsheltered	3,927 Unsheltered	849 Unsheltered

Lowest rates

Rhode Island	Nebraska	District of Columbia	Massachusetts	New York
3.2%	**3.7%**	**3.8%**	**3.9%**	**4.2%**
1,160 Homeless	2,754 Homeless	8,350 Homeless	19,608 Homeless	86,352 Homeless
37 Unsheltered	101 Unsheltered	318 Unsheltered	760 Unsheltered	3,591 Unsheltered

SOURCE: Meghan Henry et al., "Exhibit 1.8. States with the Highest and Lowest Rates of Unsheltered Homeless People, 2016," in *The 2016 Annual Homeless Assessment Report (AHAR) to Congress—Part 1: Point-in-Time Estimates of Homelessness*, U.S. Department of Housing and Urban Development, Office of Community Planning and Development, November 2016, https://www.hudexchange.info/resources/documents/2016-AHAR-Part-1.pdf (accessed August 2, 2017)

involved in regular work, which is characterized by a permanent and ongoing relationship between employer and employee. Regular work does not figure significantly in the lives and routines of most homeless people, as it is usually unavailable or inaccessible. Homelessness makes getting and keeping regular work difficult because of the lack of a fixed address and means of communication, as well as, in many cases, the inability to get a good night's sleep, clean up, and dress appropriately. Studies find that the longer a person is homeless, the less likely he or she is to pursue wage labor and the more likely he or she is to engage in some other form of work.

In the absence of regular employment, homeless people earn money in a number of different ways, although their earnings are usually not sufficient to lift them out of homelessness. Some of the most common income-generating activities the homeless engage in are day labor, shadow work, and the distribution of street newspapers. Lei notes that studies in different U.S. locations and at different dates ranging between 1992 and 2009 have found that between 20% and 50% of homeless people engage in either regular work, day labor, or other kinds of informal work. Many homeless people also attempt to produce and sell street newspapers as a way of earning income.

Day Labor

Day labor (wage labor secured on a day-to-day basis, typically at lower wages and changing locations) is somewhat easier for the homeless to secure than regular work. According to Lei, studies indicate that homeless people account for up to 50% of the day-labor workforce nationwide. Day labor is often accessed through hiring agencies or in informal ways usually occurring in public open-air contexts. Also, employers looking for day laborers frequently hire individuals at homeless shelters. Over 80% of homeless day laborers do light industrial or warehouse work. Property owners also hire a substantial portion of the homeless day-laboring population, often for the purpose of doing lawn care and other maintenance work. Besides being more accessible to the homeless than regular employment, day laboring often appeals to the homeless because it involves immediate payment after the day's work is finished, employers do not require references or work experience, and most of those who hire day laborers provide transportation to and from the worksite.

However, there are many disadvantages to day laboring beyond low pay and a lack of prospects for the future. Acquiring a day-laboring job usually involves arriving at an agency or open-air market extremely early in the morning and waiting for long periods to see whether any work will be available. There is no guarantee that such efforts will be rewarded with paying work, and those who do obtain work are often exploited by bosses who deduct money from paychecks for transportation and cashing checks. Moreover, because day laboring involves no contractual

agreements beyond the day on which work is offered, such work opportunities are particularly susceptible to disappearing in challenging economic times. For example, Fernanda Santos reports in "In the Shadows, Day Laborers Left Homeless as Work Vanishes" (NYTimes.com, January 1, 2010) that during the Great Recession day-labor opportunities dried up considerably, leaving people who had depended on that work even more likely to become or remain homeless.

Shadow Work

Shadow work refers to income-earning opportunities that are outside the normal economy and distinct from ordinary wage-earning methods. Common forms of shadow work include peddling (selling various items), panhandling (asking passersby for money, food, or other goods without offering anything in return), prostitution, and stealing. Because the illegal forms of shadow work are difficult to research due to the obvious need for secrecy among its practitioners, most studies focus on peddling and panhandling. Lei notes that peddling practices vary depending on what individuals are able to acquire (often via recycling, the receiving of gifts, and stealing) and that common items sold by the homeless include "clothing, shoes, watches, rings, calculators, cigarettes, and beer." Peddling typically brings in very low sums of money because the extreme levels of need among the homeless mean that they often must sell at any price and because they often sell to other homeless people who have little money.

According to Lei, different studies show that between 5% and 40% of homeless people engage in panhandling. Panhandling is widely regarded as degrading by both those who engage in the activity and those who are targeted, and panhandlers are routinely ignored by their

FIGURE 5.12

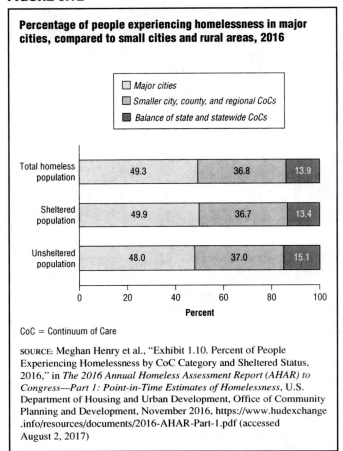

Percentage of people experiencing homelessness in major cities, compared to small cities and rural areas, 2016

CoC = Continuum of Care

SOURCE: Meghan Henry et al., "Exhibit 1.10. Percent of People Experiencing Homelessness by CoC Category and Sheltered Status, 2016," in *The 2016 Annual Homeless Assessment Report (AHAR) to Congress—Part 1: Point-in-Time Estimates of Homelessness*, U.S. Department of Housing and Urban Development, Office of Community Planning and Development, November 2016, https://www.hudexchange.info/resources/documents/2016-AHAR-Part-1.pdf (accessed August 2, 2017)

TABLE 5.8

Places with the largest numbers of people experiencing homelessness, 2016

Major city CoCs		Smaller city, county, and regional CoCs		Balance of State and state wide CoCs	
CoC	Total homeless	CoC	Total homeless	CoC	Total homeless
New York City, NY	73,523	Honolulu, HI	4,940	Texas Balance of State	6,048
Los Angeles City & County, CA	43,854	Santa Ana/Anaheim/Orange County, CA	4,319	Oregon Balance of State	5,710
Seattle/King County, WA	10,730	Nassau, Suffolk Counties/Babylon/Islip/Huntington, NY	3,960	Georgia Balance of State	5,575
San Diego City and County, CA	8,669	Salinas/Monterey, San Benito Counties, CA	3,022	Washington Balance of State	5,294
District of Columbia	8,350	Santa Rosa/Petaluma/Sonoma County, CA	2,906	Indiana Balance of State	3,711
San Francisco, CA	6,996	St. Petersburg/Clearwater/Largo/Pinellas Count, FL	2,777	Colorado Balance of State	3,520
San Jose/Santa Clara City & County, CA	6,524	Eastern Pennsylvania	2,599	Wisconsin Balance of State	3,445
Boston, MA	6,240	Springfield, MA	2,385	Ohio Balance of State	3,032
Las Vegas/Clark County, NV	6,208	Fort Pierce/St. Lucie, Indian River, Martin Counties, FL	2,382	Connecticut Balance of State	3,016
Philadelphia, PA	6,112	Ft. Lauderdale/Broward County, FL	2,302	Hawaii Balance of State	2,981

CoC = Continuum of Care

SOURCE: Meghan Henry et al., "Exhibit 1.11. CoCs with the Largest Numbers of People Experiencing Homelessness by CoC Category, 2016," in *The 2016 Annual Homeless Assessment Report (AHAR) to Congress—Part 1: Point-in-Time Estimates of Homelessness*, U.S. Department of Housing and Urban Development, Office of Community Planning and Development, November 2016, https://www.hudexchange.info/resources/documents/2016-AHAR-Part-1.pdf (accessed August 2, 2017)

targets, enhancing the level of degradation and making the activity an unreliable way of satisfying needs. Additionally, as Lei points out, since the 1970s many cities have passed ordinances restricting the legality of panhandling, in spite of the fact that the U.S. Supreme Court has ruled that it is protected by the First Amendment right to free speech. Thus, municipalities often pass laws that prohibit "aggressive panhandling," without defining what is meant by "aggressive." The effect is often to discourage even passive forms of panhandling, making the activity an even more difficult method of generating income than it has historically been.

Street Newspapers

In the United States, as well as in other countries, some homeless people write, publish, and sell their own newspapers, which typically focus on poverty, homelessness, and related issues. Besides providing income for homeless individuals and funding for homeless shelters and assistance agencies, street newspapers attempt to educate the public about homelessness and poverty. Many street newspapers formerly belonged to the North American Street Newspaper Association, which was organized in Chicago in 1996, but that organization was dissolved in 2013. Thereafter, street newspapers tended to be organized locally or regionally as part of nonprofit entities. Notable examples, as of 2017, included *Street Roots* (http://www.streetroots.org) of Portland, Oregon, and *Street Sense* (http://www.streetsense.org) of the District of Columbia. In "Real Change Comes to Bellevue as Homeless Sell, Make News" (SeattleTimes.com, November 19, 2013), Danny Westneat explains that one of the largest and most successful street newspapers is *Real Change* (http://www.realchangenews.org), a publication based in Seattle, Washington. According to Westneat, the

paper's expansion during the 1990s and through the early 21st century was a boon to the homeless, but it was also a grim sign of the spread of homelessness and poverty in the area. According to *Real Change*, in *2015 Real Change Annual Report* (2016, http://main.realchangenews.org/sites/default/files/RC%202015AnnualReport_03292016.pdf), more than a quarter of its total revenues in 2015 ($306,906 of $1.1 million, or 28.2%) came through circulation sales.

Although the income from selling street newspapers is unlikely, on its own, to provide a path back to permanent housing, it can provide people with crucial transitional funds as they prepare to embark on that path. Additionally, the activity of selling the newspapers can be a source of self-confidence, an aid in helping the homeless overcome the isolation they often feel, and a way to begin developing business skills. Many street newspapers accept submissions from the homeless themselves, including articles, letters, and artwork, offering an opportunity for self-expression that can further alleviate the feelings of marginalization common to many on the streets and in shelters. Finally, street newspapers dispel stereotypes about the homeless and offer a point of connection between them and the population at large.

Not all municipalities, however, welcome the vending of street newspapers. For example, in "Homeless Banned from Selling Newspapers on Major Roads?" (AlterNet.org, January 24, 2014), Tana Ganeva indicates that numerous cities in southern Florida have begun passing ordinances that prevent homeless-affiliated newspapers from being sold on major streets. These laws restrict the earning potential of many vendors for the Homeless Voice organization (http://www.homelessvoice.org), which operates numerous shelters in southern Florida and distributes street newspapers in Broward, Dade, and Palm Beach Counties.

CHAPTER 6

THE HOUSING PROBLEM

At one time a home was defined as a place where a family resided, but as American society changed, so did the definition of the term *home*. A home is now considered to be a place where one or more people live together, a private place to which they have legal right and where strangers may be excluded. It is the place where people keep their belongings and where they feel safe from the outside world. For housing to be considered a home, it should be permanent with an address. Furthermore, in the best of circumstances a home should not be substandard but should still be affordable. Many people would agree that a place to call home is a basic human right.

Those people who have no fixed address and no private space of their own are the homeless. The obvious solution to homelessness would be to find a home for everyone who needs one. There is enough housing available in the United States; as such, the problem lies in the affordability of that housing. Most of the housing in the United States costs far more than poor people can afford to rent or buy.

HIGH HOUSING COSTS AND HOMELESSNESS

Decades of research indicates that the primary cause of homelessness is the inability to pay for housing, which is itself caused by some combination of low income and high housing costs. Although many other factors may contribute to homelessness, such as a low level of educational achievement or mental illness, addressing such problems will seldom bring someone out of homelessness in the absence of attention to the problem of housing affordability.

Homeless people and homeless families are similar to other poor people. Given the disparity between incomes at the lowest strata of society and the costs of housing in the 21st century, most people living near or below the poverty line are at risk of becoming homeless at least periodically. Most of the homeless, in turn, do not stay homeless for long periods. These families and individuals are often able to return to permanent housing when they solve their income problems, such as by finding a job, or when they receive government or other assistance with housing.

For the chronically homeless, or those who experience long-term or repeated homelessness, other problems must often be addressed at the same time as housing affordability. The chronically homeless have higher rates of chronic disabilities, substance abuse disorders, physical disabilities, human immunodeficiency virus, and acquired immunodeficiency syndrome (AIDS). Because of these disabilities and diseases, combating chronic homelessness requires providing permanent housing that is linked to other supportive services that address the wide array of medical and social problems with which this population struggles.

Although government and nonprofit efforts to reduce chronic homelessness between 2007 and 2017 were unambiguously successful, as is discussed in Chapter 5, in the eyes of many experts the problem driving the majority of homelessness—a lack of affordable housing—was worsening rather than improving as of late 2017.

THE SCOPE OF THE HOUSING PROBLEM

The federal government establishes the official standard for low-income housing at 30% of a family's annual income. If a poor or near-poor household must spend more than 30% of its income on rent and utilities, its members risk being unable to afford other basic necessities. Low-income housing, then, is housing that is affordable to those in poverty based on this formula. In 2017 a family of two with an annual income of less than $16,240 was in poverty; a family of four was in poverty if its income was less than $24,600. (See Table 1.1 in Chapter 1.) Thus, in 2017 a single mother of one child generally qualified for low-income housing if her housing costs exceeded 30% of $16,240 annually, or more than $406 per month; a family of four qualified if its housing costs were more than 30% of $24,600 annually, or more than $615 per month.

However, qualifying for housing subsidies is much easier than obtaining them. Due to an insufficient supply of affordable housing as well as to limited government funding, many public housing programs have waiting lists on which applicants can expect to remain for years or even decades. Andrew Aurand et al. of the National Low Income Housing Coalition estimate in *Out of Reach 2017: The High Cost of Housing* (2017, http://nlihc.org/sites/default/files/oor/OOR_2017.pdf) that approximately three-quarters of extremely low-income (ELI; those who make less than 30% of an area's median income [the middle value; half of all renters earn less and half earn more]) renters fail to obtain housing assistance.

In the absence of housing assistance, the majority of low-income individuals and families are forced to acquire housing at market rates. The price of rental units has been on the rise since 1980, at the same time that the real income of renters has been declining. In *The State of the Nation's Housing 2017* (2017, http://www.jchs.harvard.edu/sites/jchs.harvard.edu/files/harvard_jchs_state_of_the_nations_housing_2017.pdf), the Joint Center for Housing Studies of Harvard University notes that the renters in the United States face an "affordability crisis." The share of renters considered cost-burdened (those who paid more than 30% of their income in rent) increased steadily between 2001 and 2011. This percentage declined slightly in the following years, but remained extremely high by historical standards, and there was significant variation from state to state. As Table 6.1 shows, 46.8% of renters in the United States were considered cost-burdened in 2015. The proportion was more than 50% in five states (California, Florida, Hawaii, New Jersey, and New York). It is no coincidence that the three states with the largest homeless populations (California, at 118,142; New York, at 86,352; and Florida, at 33,559) were among the states in which renters were most cost-burdened. (See Chapter 5 for homeless population estimates by state.)

According to the U.S. Census Bureau, the median monthly gross rent for renter-occupied housing units was $959 in 2015. (See Table 6.2.) Although this represented a yearly rental expense of approximately 21.4% of the 2015 national median household income of $53,889, the median income for renters is far lower. (See Table 6.3.) The median income for renter households was $33,784. A household earning the median renter income and paying the median rent would thus need to spend 34.1% of its income on housing.

Table 6.4 breaks down renter households by income level and rental costs as a share of income. In 2015 approximately 19.3 million renter households, or 45.8% of the total 42.2 million renter households, had an annual income of less than $35,000. Among these 19.3 million

TABLE 6.1

Percentage of renter-occupied units spending 30% or more of household income on rent and utilities, by state, 2015

Rank	Geographical area	Percent
	United States	46.8
1	California	52.9
1	Florida	52.9
3	Hawaii	52.4
4	New Jersey	50.5
5	New York	50.2
6	Connecticut	49.1
7	Oregon	48.2
8	Massachusetts	48.1
9	Colorado	48.0
10	Maryland	47.7
11	Nevada	46.8
12	Vermont	46.3
13	Michigan	46.1
14	Louisiana	46.0
14	Virginia	46.0
16	Georgia	45.8
17	District of Columbia	45.6
17	Illinois	45.6
19	Washington	45.4
20	New Mexico	45.3
21	Pennsylvania	45.2
22	Arizona	44.9
22	North Carolina	44.9
24	Maine	44.8
25	Rhode Island	44.6
26	Delaware	44.0
26	Minnesota	44.0
26	New Hampshire	44.0
29	Alaska	43.9
29	Indiana	43.9
29	Texas	43.9
32	South Carolina	43.8
33	Mississippi	43.6
34	Tennessee	43.5
35	Ohio	43.3
36	Wisconsin	43.0
37	Alabama	42.7
38	Idaho	42.5
39	Missouri	41.9
40	Arkansas	41.8
41	Utah	41.5
42	Kentucky	40.6
43	Montana	40.5
44	Iowa	40.1
45	Nebraska	39.7
45	Oklahoma	39.7
47	Kansas	38.9
48	West Virginia	38.7
49	South Dakota	37.2
50	North Dakota	36.2
51	Wyoming	35.9
	Puerto Rico	32.3

Notes: Data are based on a sample and are subject to sampling variability. While the 2015 American Community Survey (ACS) data generally reflect the February 2013 Office of Management and Budget (OMB) definitions of metropolitan and micropolitan statistical areas; in certain instances the names, codes, and boundaries of the principal cities shown in ACS tables may differ from the OMB definitions due to differences in the effective dates of the geographic entities. Estimates of urban and rural population, housing units, and characteristics reflect boundaries of urban areas defined based on Census 2010 data. As a result, data for urban and rural areas from the ACS do not necessarily reflect the results of ongoing urbanization.

SOURCE: Adapted from "GCT2515. Percent of Renter-Occupied Units Spending 30 Percent or More of Household Income on Rent and Utilities—United States—States; and Puerto Rico," in *2015 American Community Survey 1-Year Estimates*, U.S. Census Bureau, 2016, https://factfinder.census.gov/faces/tableservices/jsf/pages/productview.xhtml?pid=ACS_15_5YR_GCT2515.US01PR&prodType=table (accessed August 5, 2017)

TABLE 6.2

Median monthly housing costs for renter-occupied housing units, by state, 2015

Geographic area	Dollar
United States	959
Alabama	729
Alaska	1,163
Arizona	933
Arkansas	695
California	1,311
Colorado	1,111
Connecticut	1,108
Delaware	1,049
District of Columbia	1,417
Florida	1,046
Georgia	909
Hawaii	1,500
Idaho	770
Illinois	936
Indiana	758
Iowa	718
Kansas	782
Kentucky	702
Louisiana	800
Maine	792
Maryland	1,278
Massachusetts	1,164
Michigan	803
Minnesota	888
Mississippi	724
Missouri	763
Montana	763
Nebraska	750
Nevada	980
New Hampshire	1,017
New Jersey	1,214
New Mexico	783
New York	1,173
North Carolina	827
North Dakota	775
Ohio	746
Oklahoma	759
Oregon	943
Pennsylvania	868
Rhode Island	938
South Carolina	819
South Dakota	675
Tennessee	785
Texas	932
Utah	925
Vermont	923
Virginia	1,144
Washington	1,080
West Virginia	675
Wisconsin	792
Wyoming	815
Puerto Rico	433

Notes: Data are based on a sample and are subject to sampling variability. The degree of uncertainty for an estimate arising from sampling variability is represented through the use of a margin of error. The value shown here is the 90 percent margin of error. The margin of error can be interpreted roughly as providing a 90 percent probability that the interval defined by the estimate minus the margin of error and the estimate plus the margin of error (the lower and upper confidence bounds) contains the true value. In addition to sampling variability, the ACS estimates are subject to nonsampling error. The effect of nonsampling error is not represented in these tables.
While the 2015 American Community Survey (ACS) data generally reflect the February 2013 Office of Management and Budget (OMB) definitions of metropolitan and micropolitan statistical areas; in certain instances the names, codes, and boundaries of the principal cities shown in ACS tables may differ from the OMB definitions due to differences in the effective dates of the geographic entities.
Estimates of urban and rural population, housing units, and characteristics reflect boundaries of urban areas defined based on Census 2010 data. As a result, data for urban and rural areas from the ACS do not necessarily reflect the results of ongoing urbanization.

SOURCE: Adapted from "GCT2514. Median Monthly Housing Costs for Renter-Occupied Housing Units (Dollars)—United States—States; and Puerto Rico," in *2015 American Community Survey 1-Year Estimates*, U.S. Census Bureau, 2016, https://factfinder.census.gov/faces/tableservices/jsf/pages/productview.xhtml?pid=ACS_15_5YR_GCT2514.US01PR&prodType=table (accessed August 5, 2017)

TABLE 6.3

Median household income in the past 12 months, by housing type, 2015

	United States
	Estimate
Median household income in the past 12 months (in 2015 inflation-adjusted dollars)—	
Total:	**53,889**
Owner occupied (dollars)	68,797
Renter occupied (dollars)	33,784

Notes: Data are based on a sample and are subject to sampling variability.
While the 2011–2015 American Community Survey (ACS) data generally reflect the February 2013 Office of Management and Budget (OMB) definitions of metropolitan and micropolitan statistical areas; in certain instances the names, codes, and boundaries of the principal cities shown in ACS tables may differ from the OMB definitions due to differences in the effective dates of the geographic entities.
Estimates of urban and rural population, housing units, and characteristics reflect boundaries of urban areas defined based on Census 2010 data. As a result, data for urban and rural areas from the ACS do not necessarily reflect the results of ongoing urbanization.

SOURCE: Adapted from "B25119. Median Household Income in the Past 12 Months (in 2015 Inflation-Adjusted Dollars) by Tenure," in *2015 American Community Survey 1-Year Estimates*, U.S. Census Bureau, 2017, https://factfinder.census.gov/faces/tableservices/jsf/pages/productview.xhtml?pid=ACS_15_5YR_B25119&prodType=table (accessed August 7, 2017)

households, 11 million had an income of less than $20,000 per year and 8.3 million had an income of between $20,000 and $34,999. Roughly nine out of 10 (89%, or 9.8 million) renter households making less than $20,000 per year paid more than 30% of their annual income in rent, as did 74% (6.1 million) of renter households making between $20,000 and $34,999. Even at income levels placing all but the largest families well above the poverty line, those making $35,000 to $49,999, 41.9% (2.5 million) of households paid 30% or more of their annual income in rent.

Many households, especially those living in or near poverty, pay far more than 30% of their annual income in rent. As Table 6.5 shows, 3.4 million renter households living below the poverty line in 2013 paid 100% or more of their income in rent, and 1.3 million renter households in poverty paid between 70% and 99% of their income in rent. Overall, approximately 6.3 million, or 56.1% of the 11.1 million renter families living in poverty, paid more than half of their income in rent, and the median renter household in poverty paid 74% of its income in rent.

Aurand et al. introduce a metric called the "housing wage," which is the level of income needed to obtain

TABLE 6.4

Rent as a percentage of total household income, by income level of renter households, 2015

	United States Estimate
Total:	**116,926,305**
Renter-occupied housing units:	42,214,214
Less than $20,000:	11,030,046
Less than 20 percent	277,402
20 to 29 percent	935,932
30 percent or more	9,816,712
$20,000 to $34,999:	8,306,955
Less than 20 percent	482,609
20 to 29 percent	1,676,347
30 percent or more	6,147,999
$35,000 to $49,999:	6,068,516
Less than 20 percent	1,046,930
20 to 29 percent	2,481,407
30 percent or more	2,540,179
$50,000 to $74,999:	6,396,972
Less than 20 percent	2,519,055
20 to 29 percent	2,575,071
30 percent or more	1,302,846
$75,000 or more:	7,213,421
Less than 20 percent	5,105,618
20 to 29 percent	1,704,723
30 percent or more	403,080
Zero or negative income	953,352
No cash rent	2,244,952

Notes: Data are based on a sample and are subject to sampling variability. While the 2011–2015 American Community Survey (ACS) data generally reflect the February 2013 Office of Management and Budget (OMB) definitions of metropolitan and micropolitan statistical areas; in certain instances the names, codes, and boundaries of the principal cities shown in ACS tables may differ from the OMB definitions due to differences in the effective dates of the geographic entities.
Estimates of urban and rural population, housing units, and characteristics reflect boundaries of urban areas defined based on Census 2010 data. As a result, data for urban and rural areas from the ACS do not necessarily reflect the results of ongoing urbanization.

SOURCE: Adapted from "B25106. Tenure by Housing Costs as a Percentage of Household Income in the Past 12 Months," in *2015 American Community Survey 1-Year Estimates*, U.S. Census Bureau, 2017, https://factfinder.census.gov/faces/tableservices/jsf/pages/productview.xhtml?pid=ACS_15_5YR_B25106&prodType=table (accessed August 7, 2017)

adequate, affordable housing in the U.S. rental market. Using the 2017 fair market rent (FMR; the U.S. Department of Housing and Urban Development's [HUD] estimate of what a household seeking modest rental housing must expect to pay for rent and utilities) for a two-bedroom rental, the researchers determine that the hourly wage needed to pay for such an apartment while spending no more than 30% of one's income on rent was $21.21, more than 2.9 times the federal minimum wage of $7.25. Arnold et al. note that "in no state, metropolitan area, or county can a full-time minimum-wage worker afford a modest two-bedroom rental home."

Since 1991 HUD has released biannual reports to Congress on those renters who have what the agency calls "worst-case housing needs." Renters with worst-case needs are, according to the HUD definition, those with incomes below 50% of the area median income (the median income in the locality in which the individual lives) who receive no housing assistance from the government and who pay more than half of their income for housing, live in substandard conditions, or experience both of these housing problems. HUD's findings, which are reported by Barry L. Steffen et al. in *Worst Case Housing Needs: 2015 Report to Congress* (April 2015, https://www.huduser.gov/portal/Publications/pdf/WorstCaseNeeds_2015.pdf), support the dire assessments of the National Low Income Housing Coalition and other organizations.

HUD notes that between 2009 and 2011 the overall economy was slowly recovering from the Great Recession (which officially lasted from December 2007 to June 2009) and that by 2013 the benefits had begun reaching low-income renters. However, despite some improvement, the percentage of worst-case housing needs that year remained high compared with 2003 levels. "The number of worst case needs declined 9 percent since 2011, partially mitigating increases of 19 percent between 2009 and 2011 and 44 percent between 2007 and 2011," Steffen et al. note. "Nevertheless, the nation has 49 percent more worst case needs in 2013 than in 2003, or 2.54 million households. The percentage of U.S. households with worst case needs was 6.7 percent in 2013 compared with 4.9 percent in 2003."

Between 2007 and 2011 the number of renters with worst-case needs grew by an unprecedented 43.5%, from 5.9 million to 8.5 million. (See Figure 6.1.) Although this figure proceeded to fall to 7.7 million in 2013, it remained significantly higher than the total in 2007. HUD indicates that in 2013 less than 3% of those designated as having worst-case needs qualified for the designation because of the inadequacy of their housing; more than 97% qualified because they were paying more than half of their income for rent. The increase in worst-case housing needs affected virtually all household types and demographic groups. Among those with worst-case needs in 2013, there were 2.8 million households with children, 1.5 million elderly households, and 2.7 million nonfamily households (households consisting of unrelated people). Approximately 14% of households with worst-case housing needs in 2013 included a non-elderly disabled member, and such cases were rising dramatically. Between 2011 and 2013 the number of households including a disabled person and experiencing worst-case housing needs fell 17%, from 1.3 to 1.1 million.

FEDERALLY SUBSIDIZED HOUSING

The federal government, operating primarily through HUD, has a number of housing programs that help poor and low-income people. Subsidized housing, like other social welfare programs aimed specifically at low-income individuals and families, is means-tested, or based on income thresholds. The qualifying income level—much like the definition of poverty—changes over time. Beneficiaries of housing assistance never receive

TABLE 6.5

Housing costs of renters, by selected characteristics, 2013

[Numbers in thousands, except as indicated. Weighting consistent with Census 2010. Geography = United States.]

Characteristics	Total renter-occupied units	Household characteristics			
		Black alone	Hispanic	Elderly (65 years and over)	Below poverty level
Total	**40,218**	**8,542**	**7,783**	**5,151**	**11,140**
Monthly housing costs as percent of current income[a]					
Less than 5 percent	278	32	47	35	21
5 to 9 percent	1,140	185	154	109	32
10 to 14 percent	2,312	402	332	183	79
15 to 19 percent	3,609	618	586	323	120
20 to 24 percent	4,319	814	719	363	298
25 to 29 percent	4,178	876	852	575	522
30 to 34 percent	3,324	765	634	418	470
35 to 39 percent	2,471	579	534	327	360
40 to 49 percent	3,848	826	865	484	772
50 to 59 percent	2,412	528	623	302	799
60 to 69 percent	1,749	350	450	234	737
70 to 99 percent	2,570	604	562	405	1,322
100 percent or more[b]	4,339	1,076	845	817	3,397
Zero or negative income	1,594	477	302	75	1,387
No cash rent	2,076	409	277	501	825
Median (excludes 2 previous lines)(percent)	33%	36%	37%	39%	74%

[a]This item uses current income in its calculation.
[b]May reflect a temporary situation, living off savings, or response error.
Note: Monthly costs are calculated from yearly estimates.

SOURCE: Adapted from "C-10-R0. Housing Costs—Renter-Occupied Units (NATIONAL)," in *2013 American Housing Survey*, U.S. Census Bureau, 2014, http://factfinder2.census.gov/faces/tableservices/jsf/pages/productview.xhtml?pid=AHS_2013_C10RO&prodType=table (accessed August 7, 2017)

FIGURE 6.1

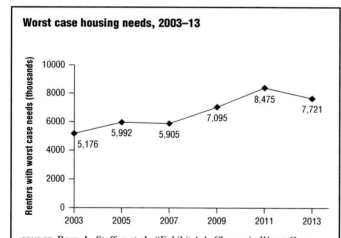

Worst case housing needs, 2003–13

SOURCE: Barry L. Steffen et al., "Exhibit 1-1. Change in Worst-Case Housing Needs, 2003–2013," in *Worst Case Housing Needs: 2015 Report to Congress*, U.S. Department of Housing and Urban Development, Office of Policy Development and Research, April 2015, https://www.huduser.gov/portal/Publications/pdf/WorstCaseNeeds_2015.pdf (accessed August 7, 2017)

cash outright. The benefits are therefore labeled "means-tested noncash benefits." According to the Census Bureau, in "American Housing Survey" (October 2017, https://www.census.gov/programs-surveys/ahs/data/interactive/ahstablecreator.html), of the 44.2 million rental households in the United States in 2015, 3.5 million (7.9%) qualified for some form of federal subsidy.

HUD operates many different kinds of subsidized-housing programs, but there are two basic forms of subsidies: vouchers and public housing. There are also two main types of voucher programs: tenant based and project based. In tenant-based programs the voucher stays with the tenant when the tenant moves to another qualifying unit. In project-based programs the voucher is attached to a particular housing project and remains available for a new tenant when a unit is vacant. Families are directed to participating projects after they qualify. Tenants cannot automatically transfer their voucher from one project-based dwelling to another, but they may qualify for another tenant-based voucher after they move. Tenant-based vouchers have increasingly become the most common mechanism for delivering federal housing subsidies.

In its 2018 budget estimate, HUD noted its intention to allocate approximately $19.8 billion of its total spending of $40.9 billion to tenant-based rental assistance. (See Table 6.6.) Another $10.9 billion was earmarked for project-based rental assistance. The agency planned to spend approximately $5.7 billion on public housing, $1.8 billion of which would go to the public housing capital fund and $3.9 billion of which would go to the public housing operating fund.

Vouchers

Voucher programs, which make up the bulk of HUD's efforts to provide housing for low-income Americans, pay a portion of the rent for qualifying families. Only low-income

TABLE 6.6

U.S. Department of Housing and Urban Development, budget outlays by program, fiscal years 2016–18

[Dollars in millions]

	2016 Actual	2017 Annualized CR	2018 Estimate
Discretionary programs			
Public and Indian housing			
Tenant-Based Rental Assistance	19,375	19,960	19,825
Housing Certificate Fund	188	219	152
Public Housing Capital Fund	2,116	1,819	1,791
Public Housing Operating Fund	4,386	4,377	3,894
Choice Neighborhoods	40	117	149
Revitalization of Severely Distressed Public Housing Projects	72	101	5
Family Self-Sufficiency	78	75	73
Native American Housing Block Grants	747	653	610
Native Hawaiian Housing Block Grants	12	4	5
Indian Housing Loan Guarantee Fund	6	5	4
Subtotal, public and Indian housing	**27,020**	**27,330**	**26,508**
Community planning and development			
Housing Opportunities for Persons with AIDS (HOPWA)	348	351	331
Community Development Fund	6,013	6,554	6,819
HOME Investment Partnerships Program	1,154	969	949
Self-Help Homeownership Opportunity/Habitat	54	50	48
Homeless Assistance Grants	1,886	2,124	2,267
Community Development Loan Guarantees	3	4	3
Permanent Supportive Housing	4	3	2
Brownfields Redevelopment Program	3	4	3
Rural Housing and Economic Development	1	2	2
Subtotal, community planning and development	**9,466**	**10,061**	**10,424**
Housing programs			
Project-Based Rental Assistance	10,667	10,764	10,941
Housing for the Elderly (Section 202)	721	694	661
Housing for Persons with Disabilities (Section 811)	171	185	175
Housing Counseling Assistance	37	43	44
Other Assisted Housing	217	175	133
Flexible Subsidy	(53)	(46)	(46)
FHA funds:			
Mutual Mortgage Ins. and Coop. Management Housing Ins. Funds:			
Program account	104	123	103
General Insurance and Special Risk Insurance Funds:			
Program account	—	—	—
Subtotal, FHA funds	**104**	**123**	**103**
Manufactured Housing Fees Trust Fund	12	12	12
Energy Innovation Fund	4	—	—
Subtotal, housing programs	**11,880**	**11,950**	**12,023**
Policy development and research			
Research and technology	62	64	68
Fair housing & equal opportunity			
Fair housing activities	63	66	67
Lead hazard control			
Lead Hazard Reduction	95	101	101
Management and administration			
Salaries and expenses, HUD	1,257	1,440	1,334
Salaries and expenses, OIG	127	123	126
Information Technology Fund	230	249	280
Working Capital Fund	43	—	—
Subtotal, management and administration	**1,657**	**1,812**	**1,740**
HUD transformation initiatives	39	23	19

families are eligible, specifically those with incomes lower than half of an area's median income. Under some circumstances, families with up to 80% of the local median income may also qualify; such cases may involve, for example, families that have been displaced by public housing demolition. The family pays 30% of its income toward the rent, and the voucher covers the remaining balance. Vouchers are issued by the local public housing agency (PHA), which executes assistance contracts with the landlord, who must also qualify.

TABLE 6.6

U.S. Department of Housing and Urban Development, budget outlays by program, fiscal years 2016–18 [CONTINUED]

[Dollars in millions]

	2016 Actual	2017 Annualized CR	2018 Estimate
Subtotal, HUD discretionary outlays (gross)	**50,282**	**51,407**	**50,950**
Deductions for offsetting receipts (discretionary)	(543)	(649)	(631)
Reclassification of MMI receipts	(9,185)	(11,191)	(7,111)
GNMA program account	(115)	(76)	(88)
GNMA reciepts	(1,415)	(1,243)	(1,623)
Total, HUD discretionary outlays (net)	**39,024**	**38,248**	**41,497**
Mandatory programs			
Indian Housing Loan Guarantee Fund	33	7	—
Native American Housing Block Grants	4	4	—
Community Development Loan Guarantees	—	1	—
Neighborhood Stabilization Program	32	99	71
Revolving Fund		1	1
Housing Trust Fund	—	18	65
FHA MMI Program Account	3,508	18,691	—
FHA MMI Liquidating	9	10	10
FHA MMI Capital Reserve Account	(15,567)	(1,842)	(198)
FHA GI/SRI Program	3,282	4,318	—
FHA GI/SRI Funds Liquidating	(194)	(119)	(180)
Home Ownership Preservation Equity Fund Program Account	(1)	—	—
Emergency Homeowners' Relief Fund	1	1	1
Rental Housing Assistance Fund	(2)	(2)	(2)
Housing for the Elderly or Handicapped Fund Liquidating Account	(352)	(294)	(250)
Guarantees of Mortgage-Backed Securities	190	100	100
Guarantees of Mortgage-Backed Securities Liquidating Account	(1)	1	1
Guarantees of Mortgage-Backed Securities Capital Reserve Account	(1,820)	(1,744)	(225)
Subtotal, HUD mandatory outlays (gross)	**(10,878)**	**19,250**	**(606)**
Deductions for offsetting receipts (mandatory)	(1,758)	(682)	(17)
Total, HUD mandatory outlays (net)	**(12,636)**	**18,568**	**(623)**
Total, HUD outlays	**26,388**	**56,816**	**40,874**

Notes: HUD = U.S. Department of Housing and Urban Development. FHA = Federal Housing Administration. OIG = Office of Inspector General. MMI = Mutual Mortgage Insurance. GNMA = Government National Mortgage Association. GI/SRI = General and Special Risk Insurance Fund. CR = Continuing Resolution.

SOURCE: "Department of Housing and Urban Development Budget Outlays by Program: Comparative Summary, Fiscal Years 2016–2018," in *HUD's Proposed 2018 Budget: Congressional Justifications*, U.S. Department of Housing and Urban Development, May 23, 2017, https://portal.hud.gov/hudportal/documents/huddoc?id=FY_18_CJS_COMBINED.PDF (accessed August 7, 2017)

Besides these two basic programs, HUD also has five other voucher programs. Conversion vouchers are used to help tenants relocate when public housing is demolished. Family unification vouchers are used to help families stay together. Homeownership vouchers assist families in purchasing a first home or another home if the family has not lived in a house in the past three years. Participants must be employed and have an income of at least minimum wage. Vouchers for people with disabilities and welfare-to-work vouchers assist the elderly or non-elderly disabled and families transitioning from welfare to work.

In all these programs the housing supplied is privately owned and operated, and the rents paid are at or below the FMR. HUD determines the FMR in every locality of the nation by an annual survey of new rental contracts that have been signed during the past 15 months. In most cities the FMR is set at the 40th percentile of rents paid, meaning that 40% of renters paid a lower rent and 60% paid a higher rent; in certain cities the FMR is calculated at the 50th percentile. HUD has chosen the 40th percentile to increase housing choices while keeping budgets at reasonable levels. Table 6.7 presents the FMRs that were used by HUD in a sample of small and large cities throughout the country in fiscal year 2017. Of the cities shown, San Francisco, California, had the highest average FMR for studio ($1,915; what is known as a 0-bedroom), one-bedroom ($2,411), two-bedroom ($3,018), three-bedroom ($3,927), and four-bedroom ($4,829) apartments. At the other end of the scale, the Cincinnati, Ohio, and Lexington-Fayette, Kentucky, metropolitan areas had FMR levels nearly four times lower than those of San Francisco.

According to HUD, in *Resident Characteristics Report* (October 24, 2017, https://pic.hud.gov/pic/RCRPublic/rcrmain.asp), 2.9 million households with 6.5 million individual members and an average annual income of $14,170 benefited from HUD programs between June 2016 and September 2017. Income data were unavailable for 70% of voucher recipients during that period, Approximately 20% of voucher recipients were classified as ELI, with incomes below 30% of their area's median; 6% were classified as very low income, with incomes below 50% of

TABLE 6.7

Fair market rental rates for selected metropolitan areas, fiscal year 2017

Area definition	0 bedroom	1 bedroom	2 bedroom	3 bedroom	4 bedroom
Bismark, ND	$636	$649	$859	$1,196	$1,514
Cincinnati, OH-KY-IN	$527	$613	$806	$1,125	$1,316
Lexington-Fayette, KY	$528	$605	$775	$1,108	$1,366
Kansas City, MO-KS	$609	$772	$946	$1,293	$1,463
Albuquerque, NM	$557	$716	$878	$1,278	$1,547
Salt Lake City, UT	$642	$795	$990	$1,425	$1,633
Memphis, TN-MS-AR	$631	$707	$835	$1,137	$1,331
Dallas, TX	$689	$837	$1,031	$1,390	$1,774
Minneapolis-St. Paul-Bloomington, MN-WI	$699	$862	$1,086	$1,538	$1,799
Charlotte-Concord-Gastonia, NC-SC	$703	$784	$907	$1,230	$1,560
Ann Arbor, MI	$797	$850	$1,025	$1,407	$1,765
New Orleans-Metairie, LA	$682	$796	$964	$1,234	$1,448
Atlanta-Sandy Springs-Roswell, GA	$818	$858	$990	$1,299	$1,599
Portland, ME	$911	$1,028	$1,301	$1,755	$1,906
Las Vegas-Henderson-Paradise, NV	$630	$769	$954	$1,389	$1,673
Gulfport-Biloxi, MS	$642	$673	$777	$1,066	$1,262
Orlando-Kissimmee-Sanford, FL	$766	$837	$1,002	$1,333	$1,604
Chicago-Joliet-Naperville, IL	$912	$1,055	$1,232	$1,569	$1,878
Flagstaff, AZ	$704	$835	$1,037	$1,309	$1,551
Anchorage, AZ	$888	$1,018	$1,293	$1,882	$2,278
Seattle-Bellevue, WA	$1,093	$1,249	$1,544	$2,240	$2,654
Philadelphia-Camden-Wilmington, PA-NJ-DE-MD	$845	$1,003	$1,211	$1,515	$1,686
Baltimore-Columbia-Towson, MD	$903	$1,097	$1,376	$1,769	$2,072
Los Angeles-Long Beach-Glendale, CA	$988	$1,195	$1,545	$2,079	$2,303
Boston-Cambridge-Quincy, MA-NH	$1,194	$1,372	$1,691	$2,116	$2,331
San Francisco, CA	$1,915	$2,411	$3,018	$3,927	$4,829
Washington-Arlington-Alexandria, DC-VA-MD	$1,440	$1,513	$1,746	$2,300	$2,855
New York, NY	$1,352	$1,419	$1,637	$2,102	$2,267
Honolulu, HI	$1,333	$1,492	$1,982	$2,885	$3,473

SOURCE: Adapted from *FY2017 Final Fair Market Rents Documentation System*, U.S. Department of Housing and Urban Development, 2017, https://www.huduser.gov/portal/datasets/fmr/fmrs/FY2017_code/select_Geography.odn (accessed August 7, 2017)

their area's median; and 3% were classified as low income, with incomes below 80% of their area's median. Roughly 1% were classified as above low income, with incomes above 81% of their area's median.

During the first decade of the 21st century there was a pronounced shift of the subsidized population from public housing toward voucher housing. This represented a major change in the direction of federal policy, and in the view of many analysts, it foreshadows a continued shift toward increased privatization of housing subsidies. Among voucher types, tenant-based programs are least dependent on nonmarket forces; they do not require the participation of developers, many of whom complain that the construction and maintenance of low-income housing is less profitable than other types of construction. Tenant-based vouchers also give low-income people choices in housing, allowing poor families to be more flexible in the pursuit of job opportunities. Tenant-based voucher recipients can move to areas with better opportunities and transportation options, and in the aggregate this offers possibilities to avoid one of the unintended negative effects of public housing and some project-based subsidies: the concentration and entrenchment of poverty in certain urban areas.

Public Housing

Although much maligned due to perceived failures in planning and upkeep—and not considered as central to

HUD's mission as in earlier decades—the agency's provision of public housing remained an important source of assistance to some of the poorest U.S. families and individuals as of 2017. According to the agency, in *Resident Characteristics Report*, 899,297 households with 1.9 million individual members and an average annual income of $14,639 benefited from HUD's public housing between June 2016 and September 2017. Approximately 64% of voucher recipients were classified as ELI, with incomes below 30% of their area's median; 21% were classified as very low income, with incomes below 50% of their area's median; and 9% were classified as low income, with incomes below 80% of their area's median. Roughly 3% were classified as above low income, with incomes above 81% of their area's median, and there were no income data in the report for 3% of voucher recipients.

The management of public housing is handled by PHAs that have been established by local governments to administer HUD housing programs. The U.S. Housing Act of 1937 required that PHAs submit annual plans to HUD and declared that it was the policy of the United States "to vest in public housing agencies that perform well, the maximum amount of responsibility and flexibility in program administration, with appropriate accountability to public housing residents, localities, and the general public."

Thus, PHAs operate under plans that are approved by HUD and under HUD supervision, and the HUD budget's allotment to public housing programs flows through these PHAs. However, the PHAs are also expected to operate with some independence and to be accountable to their residents, local (or state) government, and the public.

Not all PHAs have performed well, and HUD has been accused of lax supervision. PHAs and public housing generally reflect the distressed economic conditions of the population living in government-owned housing. Many PHAs have been charged with neglecting maintenance, tolerating unsafe living conditions for tenants, and conducting fraudulent or careless financial practices. In an effort to improve its accountability for the conditions of low-income housing, HUD implemented the Public Housing Assessment System (PHAS) in January 2000. The PHAS is used to measure the performance of PHAs. The assessment system consists of four primary components:

- Ensure, through physical inspection, that PHAs meet the minimum standard of being decent, safe, sanitary, and in good repair

- Oversee the finances of PHAs

- Evaluate the effectiveness of the management of PHAs

- Receive feedback from PHA residents on housing conditions

In *PHAS Made Simple... in 0 to 2.6 Seconds* (June 2005, https://www.hud.gov/sites/documents/DOC_14721 .PDF), HUD explains that individual PHAs are given a score for all four components. The first three components each account for 30% of the total score, and the fourth component (residents' feedback) accounts for 10%. The four component scores are combined for a total PHAS score, and the scores affect the PHAs' status with HUD. PHAs are classified as "high performers" when they score 90% or higher and score at least 60% in all four areas and as "standard performers" when they score between 60% and 90% and receive at least 60% on all but the residents' feedback. PHAs considered "substandard" receive 60% scores or higher on their overall PHAS but receive less than 60% on one of the subsections other than residents' feedback, and PHAs considered "troubled" receive less than 60% on their total PHAS score. Troubled PHAs are subject to increased HUD oversight and the possibility of being suspended or debarred if no improvement is made in two years.

PHAS scores are assembled and processed by HUD's Integrated Assessment Subsystem (NASS), a computer system that provides quality assurance, dissemination of scores to PHAs, and procedures for appeals and waiver requests. Because of the growing centrality of the NASS to the overall PHAS process, HUD increasingly refers to the assessment system as the NASS-PHAS.

Other Housing Assistance Programs

Besides its main voucher programs and public housing, HUD operates programs that offer subsidized housing for people living with AIDS, elderly people, Native Americans and Native Hawaiians, and people with disabilities. The Prisoner Reentry Initiative, begun in 2005, helps former prisoners find housing and receive job training and other services.

Other federal programs aim to increase privately owned low-income housing stock. HUD's Federal Housing Administration (FHA) offers mortgage insurance for multifamily projects, tax credits to housing developers who provide a portion of their projects at low rents, and a Community Development Block Grant program that is used to rehabilitate housing within urban communities that have people with low and moderate incomes.

HUD maintains demographic and income data only on participants in its major programs. For that reason, information on the characteristics of participants in many other HUD subsidy programs aimed at low-income people is unavailable.

Rural Housing Programs

The U.S. Department of Agriculture's (USDA) Rural Housing Service (RHS) administers a variety of rural housing programs. These programs make federal money available for housing in rural areas, which are considered places with populations of 50,000 or less. Eligibility for rural rental assistance is similar to that of subsidized urban programs. Other RHS programs include grants or low-interest loans to repair substandard housing, subsidized mortgages and down-payment assistance for low-income homeownership, and loans that help developers build multifamily housing for low-income residents. According to the USDA, in *USDA Rural Development 2016 Progress Report* (2017, https://www.rd.usda.gov/files/USDARDProgressReport2016.pdf), the RHS's multifamily housing programs served approximately 13,590 households through the construction or renovation of nearly 500 apartment developments in fiscal year 2016. In addition, in 2015 the RHS provided $1.4 billion in rental assistance to 306,970 very low-income and low-income rural residents.

Foreclosure Prevention Programs

With the collapse of the housing market during the Great Recession, millions of Americans saw the value of their homes drop below what they owed on their mortgages, making it difficult or impossible to refinance or sell their homes. Although the recession ended in mid-2009, many U.S. homeowners continued to struggle making their mortgage payments due to persistently high unemployment, and as a result foreclosure rates remained high for years afterward. The government responded by establishing a number of programs to help homeowners at risk of foreclosure.

The FHA put in place an early delinquency intervention program to help up to 400,000 homeowners avoid foreclosure. Through the agency, lenders could offer formal forbearance agreements (agreements that lending institutions will delay foreclosing on loans provided the borrowers perform certain agreed-on terms and conditions) to borrowers who were under 90 days in default of their loans. Loss mitigation (the process of attempting to collect past-due mortgage payments) programs were also created by the FHA to assist an additional 300,000 homeowners. Mortgage modifications, pre-foreclosure sales, and special forbearance agreements were also offered by the early delinquency intervention program.

A joint program offered by HUD and the U.S. Department of the Treasury, the Making Home Affordable (MHA) program, was aimed at helping homeowners refinance or modify mortgages to make them more affordable. Part of the program was designed to specifically assist borrowers who owed more on their mortgage than their home was worth. In addition, HUD reoriented its free counseling programs that had previously helped consumers make well-informed decisions about taking on mortgages. By fiscal year 2010 most counseling services were geared toward helping homeowners avoid foreclosure. In the press release "Obama Administration Extends Application Deadline for the Making Home Affordable Program" (May 30, 2013, https://www.treasury.gov/press-center/press-releases/Pages/jl1959.aspx), HUD and the Department of the Treasury note that approximately 1.3 million homeowners had received direct assistance through the program between March 2009 and May 2013 and that the median amount of savings these homeowners obtained was $546 per month. The MHA program was set to expire on December 31, 2013, but the continued difficulties faced by homeowners led the agencies to extend the program through December 31, 2015. The program was subsequently extended for another year, before finally expiring on December 31, 2016.

DIFFICULTIES IN MEETING HOUSING NEEDS

Aurand et al. report that more than one out of four renter households (11.4 million out of 43.3 million, or 26.3%) was considered ELI in 2016. Of the 7.5 million affordable rental homes in the U.S. market in 2016, roughly 3.5 million (46.7%) remained unavailable to ELI renters. Aurand et al. note, "In the private market, the poorest renters compete with higher income households for rental homes." As a result, the majority of ELI renters spend considerably more on housing than they can afford. For such households to have even a basic level of health and stability, they would need to pay no

more than $523 per month in rent, and yet the national one-bedroom FMR stood at $892 in 2016.

Although households in such situations theoretically qualify for rent subsidies, obtaining housing assistance can in reality be very challenging. In large part this problem is tied to inadequate funding. Aurand et al. explain that "federal funding for housing assistance programs that serve the lowest income households, including Housing Choice Vouchers, Public Housing, Section 8 Project-Based Rental Assistance, Housing for the Elderly, and Housing for Persons with Disabilities, declined by 3.3% between 2010 and 2017." Furthermore, as Aurand et al. report, more than half (53%) of all waiting lists for Housing Choice Vouchers were closed to new applicants in 2016.

The situation for applicants is particularly dire among large city housing agencies. For example, Lolly Bowean reports in "Chicago Housing Authority Opens Wait Lists for Public Housing, Vouchers" (ChicagoTribune.com, October 27, 2014) that in 2014 the Chicago Housing Authority allowed the city's residents to enter into a lottery to be added to one of three waiting lists for public housing (one for public housing, one for vouchers, and one for privately owned subsidized housing). The waiting lists had been closed for more than four years, and the Chicago Housing Authority expected more than 250,000 families to apply for spots on the waiting lists. Selection in the lottery did not mean a family would receive a voucher or apartment; it simply meant that the family would be added to a list on which it could expect to wait for years, at the end of which it would be screened for eligibility to receive vouchers or subsidized housing.

According to the New York City Housing Authority, in "NYCHA 2017 Fact Sheet" (April 13, 2017, https://www1.nyc.gov/assets/nycha/downloads/pdf/factsheet.pdf), on March 6, 2017, there were 257,143 families on the waiting list for public housing, 146,808 families on the waiting list for vouchers (or Section 8 housing, as the main HUD voucher program is often called, in reference to the relevant section of the Housing Act of 1937), and 15,096 families on both lists. At that time, there were 176,066 total apartments in the city's traditional public housing developments, more than 81,000 fewer than the number of applicants, and the turnover rate in 2016 (the rate at which apartments became available to people on the waiting list) was 2.6%. Assuming that approximately 2.6% of apartments would become available in 2017, an estimated 4,578 of the families, or 1.8% of the families on the public housing waiting list, might be able to move into an apartment that year. At that rate it would take decades to exhaust the waiting list. The waiting list for Section 8 housing (146,808) exceeded the number of Section 8 apartments currently rented (86,194) by a similar proportion.

Reasons for the Shortage of Affordable Housing

In December 2000 Congress established the bipartisan Millennial Housing Commission to examine the role of the federal government in meeting the nation's housing needs. In *Meeting Our Nation's Housing Challenges* (May 30, 2002, http://permanent.access.gpo.gov/lps19766/www.mhc.gov/mhcfinal.pdf), the commission states that "there is simply not enough affordable housing. The inadequacy of supply increases dramatically as one moves down the ladder of family earnings. The challenge is most acute for rental housing in high-cost areas, and the most egregious problem is for the very poor."

Steffen et al. indicate in *Worst Case Housing Needs* that the supply of affordable housing for those renters at the lowest end of the income scale remained relatively unchanged between 2009 and 2013. (See Table 6.8.) In 2013 only 65.2 units of adequate and affordable rental housing were available for every 100 very low-income renters, and only 39 such units were available for every 100 ELI renters. This scarcity was most extreme in central cities and suburbs. HUD notes that the major causes of the increases in worst-case needs among very low-income renters were shrinking incomes due to unemployment, a growing lack of federal rental assistance, and competition for affordable units. HUD further observes that competition for rental units increased primarily due to the foreclosure crisis and the high rate of unemployment, both of which persisted well beyond the end of the Great Recession. Although most of those who lost their homes were not at the lowest end of the income scale, almost all of them subsequently entered the rental market, increasing the competition and, as a consequence, the prices for rental homes and apartments. Likewise, many of those who lost their job during the recession went from being a homeowner to being a renter.

Although real estate developers are constantly adding housing units to the nation's supply, it is almost always less profitable to build affordable housing for low-income families and individuals than to build housing for those at the middle and upper portions of the income scale. To provide incentives to developers, the 1986 Low-Income Housing Tax Credit (LIHTC) program gave the states $1.25 per capita (per person) in tax credits toward the private development of low-income housing. In "A New Era for Affordable Housing" (NREIOnline.com, March 1, 2003), H. Lee Murphy reports on data from the National Council of State Housing Agencies indicating that construction hit a high in 1994, when 117,100 apartment units were built with the credits. Skyrocketing construction costs brought a decline in new construction, which reached a low of 66,900 units in 2000. In 2001 Congress raised the per capita allotment to $1.75, and beginning in 2003 the allotment was adjusted each year to account for inflation. HUD reports in "Low-Income Housing Tax Credits" (July 10, 2017, https://www.huduser.gov/portal/datasets/lihtc.html) that between 1995 and 2015 an average of 1,460 projects and roughly 110,000 housing units per year were built because of the tax credit.

This rate of construction, however, is not keeping pace with the demand for affordable housing. Besides the decay and demolition of older public housing units, a perpetual issue in maintaining the current stock of subsidized housing is the expiration of contracts between government agencies such as HUD and the private owners of buildings who offer voucher-based assistance. When such contracts expire, building owners are typically free to offer the apartments to renters on the open market, and many owners find it advantageous to remove their buildings from the subsidized marketplace, renovate them to suit the tastes of more affluent families, and either rent them on the open market or sell them as condominiums.

The Joint Center for Housing Studies notes in *State of the Nation's Housing 2017* that an estimated 500,000 units in properties available through the LIHTC program were set to expire by 2027. Additionally, the LIHTC's provision of tax credits to developers who build and preserve affordable housing are likewise in effect for

TABLE 6.8

Supply of affordable rental units for very low-income and extremely low-income renters, 2009–13

| | Rental Units per 100 Renters | | | | |
| | | | | Change | |
Income Category	2009	2011	2013	2009 to 2011	2011 to 2013
Extremely low-income renters (0–30% AMI)					
Affordable	61.0	58.2	65.3	− 2.8	7.1
Affordable and available	35.7	35.8	39.0	0.2	3.2
Very low-income renters (0–50% AMI)					
Affordable	98.7	92.4	97.2	− 6.3	4.8
Affordable and available	67.2	64.6	65.2	− 2.6	0.6

AMI = Area Median Income

SOURCE: Barry L. Steffen et al., "Exhibit 2-7. Trend in Rental Housing Stock by Income Category, 2007 to 2013," in *Worst Case Housing Needs: 2015 Report to Congress*, U.S. Department of Housing and Urban Development, Office of Policy Development and Research, April 2015, https://www.huduser.gov/portal/Publications/pdf/WorstCaseNeeds_2015.pdf (accessed August 7, 2017)

finite periods. Once owners of these properties reach the end of their compliance periods, they are allowed to apply for tax credits again, continue to offer affordable housing without receiving subsidies in the form of tax credits, or convert their affordable housing to market-rate units. The Joint Center for Housing Studies indicates that although most LIHTC property owners elect to continue offering affordable housing after their compliance periods end, those owned by for-profit companies in high-cost housing markets are oftentimes converted to market-rate housing. Furthermore, LIHTC buildings that reach the end of their compliance period typically require substantial repairs and renovations before the owners can qualify for another round of tax credits. These extensive repairs provide a further incentive for owners to remove their buildings from the affordable housing stock when their local housing market is capable of supporting a profitable conversion to market-rate housing.

Besides these complex factors, a comparatively simple force often stands in the way of new construction of low-income housing: community resistance based on the stigma conventionally associated with the occupants of public and subsidized housing. Many middle- and upper-income people resist the introduction of low-income housing in their communities out of a traditional "not in my backyard" mentality, believing that such developments will bring rising crime, falling property values, and overcrowded classrooms, dragging down living standards for existing residents.

WHERE THE HOMELESS LIVE

When faced with high rents and low housing availability, many poor people become homeless. What happens to them? Where do they live? Research shows that after becoming homeless, many people move around, staying in one place for a while, then moving on to another place. Many homeless people take advantage of homeless shelters at some point. Such shelters may be funded by the federal government, by religious organizations, or by other private homeless advocates.

Emergency Shelters, Transitional Housing, and Permanent Supportive Housing

Typically, emergency shelters provide dormitory-style sleeping accommodations and bathing facilities, with varying services for laundry, telephone calls, and other needs. Residents are often limited in the length of their stay and must leave the shelters during the day under most circumstances. These shelters are often run by nonprofit groups. Some groups are local chapters of national organizations, such as the Salvation Army, whereas others are standalone local nonprofits that serve a single community. As is noted in Chapter 5, shelters in many localities are operated by churches or Christian organizations affiliated with the Association of Gospel Rescue Missions (AGRM). The

AGRM has more than 300 missions that can be searched by region at the association's website (http://www.agrm .org/agrm/Locate_a_Mission.asp). For example, as of October 2017, the AGRM listed 47 shelters in its directory for the Sierra region, an area that included Arizona, California, Hawaii, Nevada, and Utah. Thirty-three of these shelters were in California, which has the largest homeless population in the country.

By contrast, transitional housing is intended to bridge the gap between the shelter or street and permanent housing, with appropriate services to move the homeless into independent living. It may be a room in a hotel or motel, or it may be a subsidized apartment in a development where services are accessible on-site. Like emergency shelters, transitional housing typically depends on federal funding through HUD, which often takes the form of grants to developers who build or convert buildings into such housing and vouchers that provide rental subsidies to occupants. Although federal funding agencies have begun shifting resources from transitional housing to permanent supportive housing, numerous transitional housing programs continue to serve pressing needs, often when a specific homeless subpopulation's needs align more closely with long-term but temporary housing than with permanent housing. One example is the Transitional Housing Assistance Grants for Victims of Domestic Violence, Dating Violence, Stalking, or Sexual Assault Program, which is funded through the U.S. Department of Justice's Office on Violence against Women. In "Grant Programs" (June 22, 2017, http://www.justice.gov/ovw/ grant-programs), the Department of Justice indicates that these grants are awarded to state and local governments as well as to organizations that have a proven ability to serve this specific subpopulation. Similarly, the Family and Youth Services Bureau (FYSB) of the U.S. Department of Health and Human Services funds transitional housing for homeless youth through its Transitional Living Program. The FYSB notes in "Transitional Living Program Fact Sheet" (June 24, 2016, https://www.acf.hhs .gov/fysb/resource/tlp-fact-sheet) that in 2014 it awarded $43.6 million to state and local government agencies and nonprofit groups that served nearly 3,000 homeless youth aged 16 to 22 years with housing.

Permanent supportive housing is the emerging paradigm for housing the chronically homeless, as is discussed at length in Chapters 5 and 7. Typically constructed or developed in the same way as transitional housing, with linked services and with federal funding, and operated by local nonprofit groups or public-private partnerships, there are no time limits on occupancy or service utilization. As Figure 5.1 in Chapter 5 shows, between 2007 and 2016 the number of emergency shelter beds increased significantly, from 211,205 to 264,629; the number of transitional housing beds decreased significantly, from 211,205 to 144,749; and the number of permanent supportive housing beds increased dramatically, from 188,636 to 340,906.

Illegal Occupancy

Poor neighborhoods are usually full of abandoned buildings. Often, falling real estate prices or the high costs of renovation leave landlords unable to maintain their properties without losing money, so they let their buildings deteriorate or simply walk away, leaving the fate of the building and its residents in the hands of the government. Despite overcrowding and unsafe conditions, many homeless people move into dilapidated buildings illegally, glad for what shelter they can find. Municipal governments, which are overwhelmed by long waiting lists for public housing, by a lack of funds and personnel, and by an inadequate supply of emergency shelter beds, are often unable or unwilling to strictly enforce housing laws, allowing the homeless to become squatters rather than forcing them into the streets. Some deliberately turn a blind eye to the problem, knowing they have no better solution for the homeless.

The result is a multitude of housing units with deplorable living conditions—tenants bedding down in illegal boiler basements, sharing beds with children or in-laws, or sharing bathrooms with strangers. The buildings may have leaks and rot, rusted fire escapes, and rat and roach infestations. Given the alternative, many homeless people feel lucky to be sheltered at all.

As a result of the housing crisis that began in 2008, some homeless people began turning to foreclosed homes in their search for shelter. According to the article "Some Homeless Turn to Foreclosed Homes" (Associated Press, February 17, 2008), many homeless began moving into these vacant homes and became squatters. The article notes that "foreclosed homes often have an advantage over boarded-up and dilapidated houses that have been abandoned because of rundown conditions: Sometimes the heat, lights and water are still working." The article "Activist Moves Homeless into Foreclosures" (Associated Press, December 1, 2008) explains that in 2008 homeless people were squatting in foreclosed homes in southern Florida with the help of the national organization Take Back the Land. This group finds empty foreclosed properties, arranges to have the utilities turned on, and becomes a pseudo landlord. Taryn Wobbema reports in "City Foreclosures Open Space for Squatters" (MNDaily.com, March 4, 2009) that in Minneapolis, Minnesota, the Poor People's Economic Human Rights Campaign places homeless people in empty homes illegally.

In "Homeless Squatting in Foreclosed City Homes" (13WHAM.com, December 20, 2010), Rachel Barnhart indicates that in 2010 homeless squatters were moving into some of the 3,000 empty houses in Rochester, New York. The squatters were helped by Take Back the Land.

Similar actions were taking place around the country. Take Back the Land explains in "Cathy Lennon Takes Back Her Home after Being Evicted" (May 9, 2011, http://takebackroc.rocus.org/node/51) that in March 2011 it staged a two-week-long community eviction defense by physically blocking authorities from removing Catherine Lennon and 10 extended family members from her Rochester home, which had been foreclosed. Eventually, the police were ordered to forcibly evict Lennon and her family. Intense media scrutiny led Representative Louise McIntosh Slaughter (1929–; D-NY) to intervene and ask the federal authorities to negotiate with Lennon. Although Bank of America and the Federal National Mortgage Association, a federally subsidized mortgage-backed securities company, continued to press their foreclosure case, the negative publicity eventually led them to pursue a settlement that allowed Lennon and her family to stay in the home.

Tent Cities

The Great Recession also saw an increase in the number of homeless people living in "tent cities"—mass encampments that in many cases grew large enough to become communities in their own right. Although overall levels of homelessness declined between 2010 and 2017, according to HUD's annual point-in-time counts, the situation varied by state and locality. Many individual tent cities continued to grow larger during this time, and the phenomenon of tent cities attracted increased media attention. In *Welcome Home: The Rise of Tent Cities in the United States* (March 2014, http://nlchp.org/documents/WelcomeHome_TentCities), Julie Hunter et al. analyze local and national media accounts of tent cities across the United States between 2008 and 2013 and also convey the results of firsthand research that was conducted at select tent cities treated as "case studies." The researchers document the existence of more than 100 tent communities in 46 states and the District of Columbia, and their interviews with tent city residents led them to isolate a number of factors that are believed to be driving the tent city trend:

- A general lack of availability of shelter space compared to the number of homeless individuals in need of shelter.

- Inadequacies with the shelter system in certain locations, including safety concerns, a lack of a sense of community or participation, and logistical problems that hamper homeless individuals' ability to seek employment or to carry out daily life activities.

- A pattern of criminalizing behaviors, such as public urination and sleeping in public, that homeless individuals engage in of necessity, because of their lack of access to shelter, with enforcement usually focused on driving homeless individuals out of the central city or other highly visible areas.

- An approach to the problem of homelessness focused not on solving the problem of homelessness but instead aimed largely at decreasing the visibility of homeless individuals and communities.

- A lack of attentiveness by service providers and state and local governments to the participation of homeless individuals in creating the solutions that are offered to them.

- A lack of political will to devote sufficient resources to addressing the problem in a long-term, sustainable manner, and a focus instead on short-term solutions that take homeless people off the streets but are not responsive to the needs of homeless people themselves or, indeed, to longer term community interests.

Like many media outlets reporting on the phenomenon, Hunter et al. note that tent cities offer homeless people an alternative to emergency shelters that in some cases provide for increased feelings of safety and a sense of belonging to a community. However, levels of comfort and functionality vary by location. According to Blake Ellis, in "America's Homeless: The Rise of Tent City, USA" (CNN.com, May 16, 2014), "Some have 'mayors' who determine the rules of the camp and who can and can't join, others are a free-for-all. Some are overflowing with trash, old food, human waste and drug paraphernalia, others are relatively clean and drug-free." Hunter et al. determine that of the 100 or so camps that existed between 2008 and 2013, eight were allowed to exist legally, 10 were not legally authorized but were allowed to go on existing while city or county authorities looked the other way, and most of the rest were dismantled and the occupants evicted.

CHAPTER 7
DEALING WITH THE PROBLEM OF HOMELESSNESS

THE CHANGING RESPONSE TO HOMELESSNESS

In "The New Approach: The Emergence of a Better Way to Address Homelessness" (November 18, 2014, http://b.3cdn.net/naeh/f022a3e40771e1eea8_6nm6iyueq .pdf), the National Alliance to End Homelessness (NAEH) notes that prior to the 1980s the phenomenon of mass homelessness during times when the economy was otherwise operating at or near capacity was unprecedented. After a period of high unemployment and inflation (the devaluation of a country's currency, which causes people to become poorer even when the amount of money they earn or possess remains the same) during the early 1980s, the U.S. economy rebounded strongly later in that decade, but the homeless population did not decline. Numerous government programs and nonprofit attempts to address the problem of homelessness emerged, many of which emphasized the construction of emergency shelters, transitional housing, and services intended to help the homeless until they were capable of becoming self-sufficient. The model for helping an individual escape homelessness typically involved a move from emergency housing to transitional housing, where one had to abide by rules meant to address addiction, promote mental health, develop productive routines, and build employment skills. Transitional housing often proved successful for those who were able to abide by the restrictions placed on them, but a large proportion of chronically homeless people left such programs before completion and returned to the streets.

The homeless population continued to grow through the late 1990s in spite of a growing economy and the many government and nonprofit efforts to address the population's needs. This situation led many advocates for the homeless to call for a shift in tactics. Rather than continue to support the homeless until they became self-sufficient, numerous advocacy groups and local governments began experimenting with programs to end homelessness first and then consider the potential for individuals and families

to become self-sufficient. Local governments and non-profit agencies pioneered these types of programs between the late 1990s and the onset of the Great Recession (which officially lasted from December 2007 to June 2009).

Pioneering Change at the Local Level

Individual programs varied, but many of the most successful ones shared an emphasis on what is called "housing first," an approach that calls for providing the homeless with permanent housing as quickly as possible. Housing-first approaches represent an alternative to the other major programs that offer federally subsidized housing, which are discussed in Chapter 6. Whereas traditional subsidized housing, including temporary housing, is typically available on a first-come first-serve or lottery basis and often involves an extended waiting period before housing becomes available, housing-first programs seek to place the homeless in houses immediately, with a minimal application process and regardless of their eligibility for other government services. After housing is secured, these programs then address clients' needs for services.

The housing-first approach varies by type of homelessness. Those who are chronically homeless, often because of disabilities or conditions that prevent them from becoming self-sufficient, are best served by permanent supportive housing. Permanent supportive housing includes immediate placement in a permanent home as well as the provision of services that will allow clients to remain in their home permanently. There are no time limits on the assistance that the formerly homeless receive through permanent supportive housing.

For families and individuals who become homeless due to temporary crises, rapid rehousing represents a cost-effective intervention. Like permanent supportive housing, rapid rehousing involves quickly getting the homeless into a permanent home and supplying them with the services they need to remain housed. However, unlike permanent supportive housing, rapid rehousing does not involve permanent subsidies and services. Aimed at those who need temporary help to escape homelessness, the program seeks to return clients to self-sufficiency so that they can eventually pay rent and expenses on their own.

Other successful programs pioneered at the local level include efforts to prevent people from becoming homeless in the first place. Prevention programs are often geared toward families, whose homelessness is frequently a result of unforeseen crises, such as abrupt increases in household expenses, job loss, or illness. Prevention can take many forms, including cash assistance, housing subsidies, and other short-term services that allow families to weather periods of acute financial stress.

Housing First at the National Level

The federal government, along with numerous nonprofit groups, attempted to adapt local successes on a national scale during the administrations of George W. Bush (1946–) and Barack Obama (1961–). Besides the demonstrated success of local programs, the housing-first approach found support at the national level because it did not involve an increase in government funding. Instead, the U.S. Department of Housing and Urban Development (HUD) reallocated funding from transitional housing and other programs and grants were increasingly awarded to local service providers based on their adoption of a housing-first approach.

These efforts gained momentum during the Great Recession, when homelessness became increasingly visible, as foreclosures, job losses, and other financial difficulties pushed large numbers of people into homelessness, including many whose earnings had previously been well above the poverty line. A key element in the federal push to expand housing-first programs was passage of the Homeless Emergency Assistance and Rapid Transition to Housing (HEARTH) Act of 2009, which altered the structure of HUD's main homeless assistance programs to focus on permanent supportive housing and rapid rehousing and which required the U.S. Interagency Council on Homelessness (USICH) to create a national strategic plan to end homelessness. That plan, *Opening Doors: Federal Strategic Plan to Prevent and End Homelessness* (June 2015, https://www.usich.gov/resources/uploads/asset_library/USICH_OpeningDoors_Amendment 2015_FINAL.pdf), codified the housing-first approaches to chronic and veteran homelessness that were already under way and set a target for ending chronic homelessness by 2017.

The large-scale effort to implement housing-first policies was not, however, strictly a government endeavor. Housing-first programs, like most programs that serve the homeless, are typically operated locally, by government agencies and nonprofit organizations that receive grants from HUD, the U.S. Department of Veterans Affairs (VA), or other federal agencies. One of the leading forces in the effort to take the housing-first approach national was the nonprofit organization Community Solutions, which launched the 100,000 Homes campaign. Josh Leopold and Helen Ho of the Urban Institute explain in *Evaluation of the 100,000 Homes Campaign* (February 2015, https://www.urban.org/sites/default/files/publication/44391/2000148-Evaluation-of-the-100000-Homes-Campaign .pdf) that when the program launched in July 2010, the average participating community was placing 1.3% of its chronically homeless population into housing every month. By April 2014 this rate had risen to 4.7%. Working through a wide range of local agencies and organizations, participating communities employed a methodology that involved getting to know every homeless person in a community by name and evaluating his or her individual needs. The resulting profiles of individual homeless people were then entered in a database that allowed the participating community organizations to prioritize housing for those who needed it most and to locate the available government subsidies that could be used to pay for housing. This proactive approach to screening and application allowed the organizations affiliated with 100,000 Homes to place the chronically homeless into homes much more rapidly than was typical of government assistance programs. According to Leopold and Ho, the campaign exceeded its goal, successfully generating 105,580 homes for homeless people nationwide in the four years of its existence.

A housing-first approach is not only successful in reducing homelessness, it is also believed to offer substantial cost savings relative to a "management" approach to homelessness. Christina Scotti reports in "How Housing for the Chronically Homeless May Save Taxpayers Money" (FOXBusiness.com, July 7, 2014) that Community Solutions claimed the 100,000 Homes campaign's success at placing the chronically homeless in permanent housing saved taxpayers approximately $1.3 billion annually, or $13,000 annually per each chronically homeless person. Although the costs of subsidizing housing and services (which are typically paid by the federal government) rise in a housing-first approach, the costs to the many organizations and institutions that deal with the problems of the chronically homeless, including incarceration and treatment in emergency departments, fall precipitously.

Despite the success of the 100,000 Homes campaign, no national housing placement initiatives of a comparable scale had been launched as of October 2017.

Persistent Problems

The success of housing-first and other efforts was offset to a large degree by a worsening shortage of affordable housing during the first decade of the 21st century. In most major cities and suburbs real estate prices rose rapidly prior to the Great Recession, but wages, especially for those at the lower end of the income scale, did not rise comparably. In *Out of Reach 2017: The High Cost of Housing* (2017, http://nlihc.org/sites/default/files/oor/OOR_2017.pdf), Andrew Aurand et al. of the National Low Income Housing Coalition note that the national "housing wage" (the hourly wage a full-time worker would need to afford adequate two-bedroom housing, as established by HUD's fair market rents) was $21.21 in 2017, more than 2.9 times higher than the federal minimum wage of $7.25. Additionally, the National Law Center on Homelessness and Poverty (NLCHP) observes in *No Safe Place: The Criminalization of Homelessness in U.S. Cities* (July 2014, https://www.nlchp.org/documents/No_Safe_Place) that decreased funding for federal housing subsidies led to the loss of approximately 12.8% of the United States' overall supply of low-income housing between 2001 and 2014. The NLCHP estimates that three-quarters of those who qualify for federal housing subsidies fail to receive assistance due to the supply shortage. Many families and individuals remain on waiting lists for years or even decades before receiving housing assistance.

Thus, critics of housing first sometimes characterize the approach as a last resort generated in response to wider government failures. For example, in "Housing First Doesn't Work: The Homeless Need Community Support" (HuffingtonPost.com, January 16, 2014), Pat LaMarche quotes Ralph DaCosta Nunez, the president and chief executive officer of the Institute for Children, Poverty, and Homelessness, who described housing first as "all that's left after the other poverty fighting programs have been underfunded or eliminated." Nunez argued that housing first is a one-size-fits-all approach that addresses the need for housing but does not adequately address corresponding problems such as mental illness, domestic violence victimization, and a lack of education, all of which affect sizable proportions of the homeless population.

Although housing enjoys widespread support at the federal level and has been lauded in numerous national and local media stories, most homeless advocacy organizations stress the need to focus on many fronts in the attempt to end homelessness. In its "Five Fundamentals to Prevent and End Homelessness," which were issued in 2007, the National Coalition for the Homeless (NCH; January 25, 2012, http://www.nationalhomeless.org/publications/fivefundamentals/index.html) identified what it considered the keys to solving the problem. The first fundamental concerned the reauthorization of key federal funding under the McKinney-Vento Homeless Assistance Act, which was accomplished with the passage of the HEARTH Act in 2009. The other four fundamentals remain works in progress: a dramatic increase in the supply of affordable housing; access to health care, education, and social services for all who need them; a better match between personal income and living expenses; and ending discrimination against the homeless.

Similarly, the NAEH lists "The Ten Essentials" (2017, http://www.hmissummit.net/coc/10%20Year%20Plans/tenessentials.pdf) that communities must address if they are to find permanent solutions to homelessness. These 10 strategies for ending homelessness include not only permanent supportive housing and rapid rehousing but also the prevention of homelessness (both in emergency situations and in cases where individuals are transitioning out of institutions such as jails and the foster care system), systematic planning, data collection that allows full understanding of the problem, outreach to homeless families and individuals to guide them out of homelessness, an emphasis on shortening the period that any given person or family spends without a home, connecting the homeless with government services, and ensuring that people exiting homelessness have income.

FEDERAL PROGRAMS TO ASSIST THE HOMELESS

Since 1860 the federal government has been actively involved with the housing industry, specifically the low-income housing industry. In 1860 the government conducted the first partial census of housing—by counting slave dwellings. Twenty years later the U.S. census counted the living quarters of the rest of the population in its first full housing census. Prior to the rise of homelessness during the 1980s the federal government played an increasingly larger role in combating housing problems in the United States. Major expansions of federal authority over issues related to low-income housing include:

- 1937—the U.S. Housing Act established the Public Housing Administration (which was later merged into the Federal Housing Administration and HUD) to create low-rent housing programs across the country through the establishment of local public housing agencies.

- 1949—the Housing Act set the goals of "a decent home and a suitable environment" for every family and authorized an 810,000-unit public housing program over the next six years. Title I of the act created the Urban Renewal Program, and Title V created the basic rural housing program under the Federal Housing Administration, which put the federal government directly into the mortgage business.

- 1965—Congress established HUD. Its goal was to create a new rent supplement program for low-income households in private housing.

- 1974—the Housing and Community Development Act created a new leased-housing program that included a certificate (voucher) program, expanding housing choices for low-income tenants. The voucher program soon became known as Section 8, after the section of the act that established it.

The McKinney-Vento Homeless Assistance Act

Widespread public outcry over the plight of the homeless during the early 1980s prompted Congress to pass the Stewart B. McKinney Homeless Assistance Act of 1987. Congress renamed the act the McKinney-Vento Homeless Assistance Act in 2000 to honor the U.S. representative Bruce F. Vento's (1940–2000; D-MN) service to the homeless. The range and reach of the act has broadened over the years. Most of the money authorized by the act went, initially, toward the funding of emergency and transitional homeless shelters. Amendments to the act later enabled funding and other services to support permanent housing and other programs to help the homeless. Throughout the act's history, HUD has been the lead funding agency for homeless assistance.

In May 2009 President Obama signed the HEARTH Act, ushering in a new era of homeless assistance under McKinney-Vento. The act consolidated a number of HUD homeless assistance programs, expanded the definition of homelessness, added new funds in areas including emergency shelter needs and rural housing, and codified the shift toward a goal of ending rather than managing homelessness, as described earlier.

HUD Homeless Assistance Programs

By far the largest homeless assistance program among HUD's homeless assistance efforts is the Continuum of Care (CoC) Program. The program is competitively funded; that is, nonprofit groups, as well as state and local governments, apply for grants in competition with one another. HUD explains in "Continuum of Care (CoC) Program" (2017, https://www.hudexchange.info/programs/coc/) that the program is "designed to promote communitywide commitment to the goal of ending homelessness; provide funding for efforts by nonprofit providers, and State and local governments to quickly rehouse homeless individuals and families while minimizing the trauma and dislocation caused to homeless individuals, families, and communities by homelessness; promote access to and effect utilization of mainstream programs by homeless individuals and families; and optimize self-sufficiency among individuals and families experiencing homelessness."

Originally the vehicle for providing much of the funding for emergency and transitional shelters, the CoC Program has increasingly emphasized housing-first efforts, in keeping with the trends described earlier. Also, HUD notes in "Homeless Emergency Assistance and Rapid Transition to Housing: Continuum of Care Program" (*Federal Register*, vol. 77, no. 147, July 31, 2012) that the HEARTH Act consolidated three programs for combating homelessness under the umbrella of the CoC Program:

- Supportive Housing Program—provides funding for the purchasing, renovation, leasing, and construction of housing for homeless people; for supportive services such as case management, outreach, and behavioral health care; for the development and maintenance of the Homeless Management Information Systems; and for administrative costs related to such projects.

- Shelter Plus Care Program—funds rent subsidies for permanent supportive housing aimed at homeless people with serious mental illness, chronic substance abuse problems, and diseases such as the human immunodeficiency virus or the acquired immunodeficiency syndrome.

- Section 8 Moderate Rehabilitation for Single Room Occupancy Dwellings—provides funding to public housing agencies and nonprofit groups that provide single room occupancy housing with supportive services for homeless individuals.

Table 7.1 outlines the categories of homeless people and services that qualify for funding under the CoC Program.

Another major component of HUD's homeless assistance efforts is the Emergency Solutions Grants (ESG) Program, which was established by the HEARTH Act as the successor of the Emergency Shelter Grants Program. In "Emergency Solutions Grants (ESG) Program" (July 27, 2017, https://www.hudexchange.info/resources/documents/EmergencySolutionsGrantsProgramFactSheet.pdf), HUD indicates that the ESG Program is aimed at promoting housing-first approaches as well as homelessness prevention and emergency shelters by providing funding to states, large cities, urban counties, and U.S. territories. These local and state governments do not compete for funding; rather, eligible governments apply for and receive funding based on formulas that calculate the funding levels necessary to meet the needs of their communities. These jurisdictions then distribute funds at their discretion to the local government agencies or nonprofit groups that are best positioned to provide assistance to the homeless population or to specific subpopulations, such as veterans, victims of domestic violence, unaccompanied youth, or families. HUD requires recipients of ESG funds to coordinate with the CoC Program in their area to determine optimal funding allocations. Table 7.2

TABLE 7.1

Eligibility requirements for U.S. Department of Housing and Urban Development Continuum of Care homeless assistance

Eligibility by component

Supportive services only

Individuals and families defined as homeless under the following categories are eligible for assistance in Supportive Services Only projects:
- Category 1—Literally homeless
- Category 2—Imminent risk of homeless
- Category 3*—Homeless under other federal statutes
- Category 4—Fleeing/attempting to flee domestic violence

Safe havens

Individuals defined as homeless under the following categories are eligible for assistance in Safe Havens projects:
- Category 1—Literally homeless

SH projects have the following additional Notice of Funding Availability (NOFA) limitations on eligibility within Category 1:
- Must serve individuals only
- Individual must have a severe mental illness
- Individual must be living on the streets and unwilling or unable to participate in supportive services

Transitional housing

Individuals and families defined as homeless under the following categories are eligible for assistance in Transitional Housing projects:
- Category 1—Literally homeless
- Category 2—Imminent risk of homeless
- Category 3*—Homeless under other federal statutes
- Category 4—Fleeing/attempting to flee domestic violence

Permanent supportive housing

Individuals and families defined as homeless under the following categories are eligible for assistance in Permanent Supportive Housing projects:
- Category 1—Literally homeless
- Category 4—Fleeing/attempting to flee domestic violence

Permanent Supportive Housing projects have the following additional NOFA limitations on eligibility within Category 1:
- Individuals and families coming from Transitional Housing must have originally come from the streets or emergency shelter
- Individuals and families must also have an individual family member with a disability

Projects that are dedicated chronically homeless projects, including those that were originally funded as Samaritan Bonus Initiative Projects must continue to serve chronically homeless persons exclusively.

*Projects must be located within a CoC that has received HUD approval to serve this category.
Notes: HUD = Department of Housing and Urban Development.

SOURCE: Adapted from "The Homeless Definition and Eligibility for SHP, SPC, and ESG," U.S. Department of Housing and Urban Development, May 2012, https://www.hudexchange.info/resources/documents/HomelessDefEligibility%20_SHP_SPC_ESG.pdf (accessed August 25, 2017)

TABLE 7.2

Eligibility requirements for U.S. Department of Housing and Urban Development Emergency Solutions Grants homeless assistance

Eligibility by component

Street outreach

Individuals defined as homeless under the following categories are eligible for assistance in street outreach:
- Category 1—Literally homeless
- Category 4—Fleeing/attempting to flee domestic violence (where the individual or family also meets the criteria for Category 1)

Street outreach projects have the following additional limitations on eligibility within Category 1:
- Individuals and families must be living on the streets (or other places not meant for human habitation) and be unwilling or unable to access services in emergency shelter

Emergency shelter

Individuals and families defined as homeless under the following categories are eligible for assistance in emergency shelter projects:
- Category 1—Literally homeless
- Category 2—Imminent risk of homeless
- Category 3—Homeless under other federal statutes
- Category 4—Fleeing/attempting to flee domestic violence

Rapid re-housing

Individuals defined as homeless under the following categories are eligible for assistance in rapid re-housing projects:
- Category 1—Literally homeless
- Category 4—Fleeing/attempting to flee domestic violence (where the individual or family also meets the criteria for category 1)

Homelessness prevention

Individuals and families defined as homeless under the following categories are eligible for assistance in homelessness prevention projects:
- Category 2—Imminent risk of homeless
- Category 3—Homeless under other federal statutes
- Category 4—Fleeing/attempting to flee domestic violence

Individuals and families who are defined as at risk of homelessness are eligible for assistance in homelessness prevention projects.

Homelessness prevention projects have the following additional limitations on eligibility with homeless and at risk of homeless:
- Must only serve individuals and families that have an annual income below 30% of area median income

SOURCE: Adapted from "The Homeless Definition and Eligibility for SHP, SPC, and ESG," U.S. Department of Housing and Urban Development, May 2012, https://www.hudexchange.info/resources/documents/HomelessDefEligibility%20_SHP_SPC_ESG.pdf (accessed August 25, 2017)

outlines the categories of homeless people and services that qualify for funding under the ESG Program. In fiscal year (FY) 2017, HUD allocated $310 million in ESG funding.

HUD manages two more homeless assistance programs in collaboration with other federal agencies. The HUD–Veterans Affairs Supportive Housing Program, which is administered in partnership with the VA, combines the targeting of tenant-based rental vouchers with supportive services for homeless veterans. The supportive services, including case management, medical services, and mental health care, are provided primarily through VA medical centers and clinics and their personnel. HUD also operates the Base Realignment and Closure Program, a partnership with the U.S. Department of Defense, which enables homeless assistance providers to house and serve the homeless in the buildings and on the grounds of decommissioned military bases.

In FY 2016 HUD spent $1.9 billion on homeless assistance programs. (See Table 6.6 in Chapter 6.) This amount increased to $2.1 billion in FY 2017, and was projected to approach $2.3 billion in FY 2018. According to HUD, in "FY 2017 CoC Program NOFA" (August 2017, https://www.hudexchange.info/resource/5419/fy-2017-coc-program-nofa/), approximately $2 billion of the agency's total FY 2017 homeless assistance funding was dedicated to the CoC Program.

VA Homeless Assistance Programs

After HUD, the VA is the most important federal funder of assistance to the homeless. As is noted in Chapter 5, U.S. military veterans have historically been disproportionately represented among the homeless. In the fact sheet "Supportive Services for Veteran Families (SSVF) Program" (November 23, 2010, http://www.va.gov/HOMELESS/docs/Prevention_Fact_Sheet_11-22-10.pdf), the VA notes that there were an estimated 313,000 homeless veterans on one night in 2003. In the years that followed, widespread public and bipartisan outrage at the fact of veteran homelessness led to an intense focus on this subpopulation. Since then, veteran homelessness has been rapidly reduced. A result of the same trends that have led to rapid decreases in the chronic homeless population, the progress in ending veteran homelessness is attributable to a number of VA programs in addition to the HUD programs that fund local homeless assistance efforts. By 2016 the number of homeless veterans on one night in January had fallen to 39,471. (See Table 5.6 in Chapter 5.)

As noted earlier, homeless veterans often access permanent supportive housing through the HUD–Veterans Affairs Supportive Housing Program. HUD supplies the housing subsidies through its voucher programs, and the VA supplies supportive services. According to the

USICH, in *The President's 2016 Budget: Fact Sheet on Homelessness Assistance* (February 5, 2015, https://www.usich.gov/resources/uploads/asset_library/2016_Budget_Fact_Sheet_on_Homelessness_Assistance.pdf), there are four main VA programs that provide support for homeless veterans:

- Supportive Services for Veteran Families—provides funding to nonprofit groups that focus on providing the supportive services that enable veterans and their families to make the transition to permanent housing

- Homeless Providers Grant and Per Diem Program—provides funding to community organizations that aid homeless veterans through transitional housing and related services

- Domiciliary Care for Homeless Veterans Program—provides around-the-clock in-home rehabilitation and treatment to homeless veterans with severe health problems

- Healthcare for Homeless Veterans Program—funds outreach to homeless veterans undertaken by VA social workers and clinicians, with the goal of helping veterans access the health care services they need to escape homelessness, and additionally funds in-home treatment and long-term case management

According to the USICH, the FY 2016 federal budget allocated $1.4 billion toward homeless assistance programs administered by the VA. Of this amount, $300 million was earmarked for Supportive Services for Veteran Families, $201 million for the Homeless Providers Grant and Per Diem Program, $183 million for the Domiciliary Care for Homeless Veterans Program, and $155 million for the Healthcare for Homeless Veterans Program.

Programs Administered by Other Government Agencies

A number of other federal agencies also provide services to the homeless. Many of these programs dovetail with the HUD and VA efforts described in this chapter, whereas others are attempts to address individual issues or subpopulations, in keeping with the given agency's mandate.

U.S. DEPARTMENT OF EDUCATION. At the time of the original McKinney Homeless Assistance Act's passage in 1987, only an estimated 57% of homeless children were enrolled in school. The act thus included an Education for Homeless Children and Youth Program, which is overseen by the U.S. Department of Education under the terms of the updated McKinney-Vento Act. The program ensures that homeless children and youth have equal access to the same free, appropriate education that is provided to other children. School systems are run by the individual states, so the Education for Homeless

Children and Youth Program provides funding to states to maintain an office to coordinate homeless education, to develop and execute a state plan for educating homeless children, and to make subgrants to individual school districts that serve homeless students. The USICH notes in *President's 2016 Budget* that the Department of Education requested $71.5 million for the program in FY 2016—a level of funding that was slightly higher than the $65 million the program received in both FYs 2014 and 2015.

As is discussed in Chapter 5, the National Center for Homeless Education (NCHE), which assists the Department of Education in data collection mandated under the Education for Homeless Children and Youth Program, employs a broader definition of homelessness than that used by HUD. Taking into account those students who are doubled-up and living in temporary quarters such as motels and hotels, the NCHE finds that homelessness among children has been increasing steadily since the Great Recession. The NCHE notes in *Education for Homeless Children and Youth Program: Analysis of Data* (July 2008, http://center.serve.org/nche/downloads/data_comp_03-06.pdf) that there were 679,724 homeless students during the 2006–07 school year. In *Federal Data Summary School Years 2012–13 to 2014–15: Education for Homeless Children and Youth* (December 2016, http://nche.ed.gov/downloads/data-comp-1213-1415.pdf), the NCHE reports that by the 2014–15 school year this number had increased to nearly 1.3 million. This trend was cause for alarm among many homeless advocates, and it sized up the challenge faced by states and school districts that had seen their funding for homeless education remain flat during these years.

U.S. DEPARTMENT OF HEALTH AND HUMAN SERVICES. In *President's 2016 Budget*, the USICH indicates that the U.S. Department of Health and Human Services (HHS) manages five main programs for assisting the homeless. The Health Care for the Homeless Program, provisionally budgeted at $371 million in FY 2016, delivers a range of health care and related services to the homeless, including primary care, substance abuse treatment, emergency care, referrals for in-patient hospital and other care, outreach, and help determining eligibility for government benefits and housing. The agency's Runaway and Homeless Youth Program, budgeted at $123 million in FY 2016, funds hundreds of local government, nonprofit, and faith-based organizations that serve runaway children and homeless youth. The HHS's Projects for Assistance in Transition from Homelessness, budgeted at $65 million in FY 2016, funds state programs that serve homeless people with mental illness or co-occurring mental illness and substance abuse. Treatment Systems for Homelessness, a program budgeted at $41 million in FY 2016 and administered by the Substance Abuse and Mental Health Services Administration (SAMHSA), funds local public and nonprofit entities that serve homeless people with mental illness or co-occurring mental illness and substance abuse. SAMHSA's Homeless Prevention and Housing Programs, budgeted at $33 million in FY 2016, supplies funding to individuals and families that need mental health and addiction treatment to escape homelessness.

According to the USICH, the U.S. Departments of Justice and Labor also manage programs that serve the homeless. The Department of Justice funds local programs that help people who have become homeless as a result of sexual assault, domestic violence, dating violence, or stalking; and the Department of Labor awards competitive grants to organizations that assist homeless veterans who want to reintegrate into the labor force.

The Role of Private Nonprofit Groups

As outlined earlier, the majority of all federal funding to combat homelessness is channeled into local government agencies and nonprofit groups that serve the homeless populations and subpopulations in their communities. Nonprofit groups in particular often have the flexibility to undertake projects that are tailored to their individual communities and to experiment with new methods for serving the homeless. Indeed, the housing-first approach that has become the preferred federal approach to homelessness has its roots in the work of one local nonprofit group. Deborah K. Padgett notes in "Choices, Consequences and Context: Housing First and Its Critics" (*European Journal of Homelessness*, vol. 7, no. 2, December 2013) that one of the most influential models for the housing-first approach was the work of the "tiny upstart" group Pathways to Housing, which began operating in New York City in 1992 with a philosophy that housing is a fundamental human right. Ignoring then-prevailing notions that substance abuse and mental health treatment should precede the effort to find housing for the homeless, Sam Tsemberis, the founder of Pathways, conducted rigorous studies that demonstrated the effectiveness of a housing-first approach relative to the existing models, and by around 2005 his work was beginning to transform opinions at the highest levels of government in the United States, Canada, and elsewhere.

Another nonprofit pioneer is the Downtown Emergency Service Center (DESC; http://www.desc.org/), which was founded in 1979 in Seattle, Washington. The DESC's permanent supportive housing program, 1811 Eastlake, targets homeless people with chronic alcoholism, a group known to impose enormous costs on the public in the form of jail time, hospital visits, publicly funded alcohol treatment, and Medicaid usage. In "Health Care and Public Service Use and Costs before and after Provision of Housing for Chronically Homeless

Persons with Severe Alcohol Problems" (*Journal of the American Medical Association*, vol. 301, no. 13, April 1, 2009), Mary E. Larmer et al. report on a study that compared the homeless people served by 1811 Eastlake's housing-first approach with a comparable group of homeless people who were waitlisted for temporary housing. The study showed that 1811 Eastlake participants on average cost the public $2,449 less per person per month, excluding the costs of housing.

Besides deriving their funding from federal agencies, nonprofit organizations also frequently collaborate with local government agencies. For example, the Community Shelter Board (CSB), a public-private organization (a group that includes both government and private nonprofit involvement), partnered with the local Young Women's Christian Association (YWCA) in Columbus, Ohio, to form Coordinated Entry (http://cohhio.org/member-services-2/boscoc/coordinated-entry/) as a way of coordinating emergency shelter access communitywide. Prior to 1999, families that needed housing had to contact numerous shelters to determine which one(s) had vacancies, and they frequently had to move from shelter to shelter. By establishing the YWCA as a central access point for all homeless families, the CSB was able to reduce the volatility of the experience of family homelessness and to provide a means of accessing a range of homeless assistance. Families that obtained shelter through the YWCA were also provided information about how to access transitional and permanent housing and services. Eventually, the CSB established a parallel system for homeless individuals, and it transitioned to a phone-based central access point through which individuals and families could enter the homeless assistance system. This program has since become a model for homeless assistance at the national level.

There are thousands of similar nonprofit groups and initiatives intent on transforming the experience of homelessness in the United States. Any community that has a sizable homeless population is likely to have nonprofit organizations devoted to serving the homeless. No successful effort to combat homelessness in the United States is conceivable without the involvement of these groups.

THE CRIMINALIZATION OF HOMELESSNESS

Although local governments often lead the fight to combat homelessness in their communities, they are also subject to pressures from the nonhomeless population, many of whom feel threatened by the sight of impoverished people going about their lives in public spaces. Many people believe that providing space for the homeless to sleep, eat, or even sit will attract more homeless people, straining the capacity of public resources and leading to a deterioration of the quality of life in the area.

Furthermore, the influential "broken windows" theory of the criminologists James Q. Wilson (1931–2012) and George L. Kelling (1935–), as detailed in "Broken Windows" (Atlantic.com, March 1982), is used to support homeless criminalization efforts. Wilson and Kelling argue that allowing indications of disorder, such as a broken window or street people, to remain unaddressed shows a loss of public order and control, as well as apathy in a neighborhood, which breeds more serious criminal activity. Therefore, keeping a city neat and orderly should help prevent crime.

Motivated by such rationales, city and county governments in the 21st century have increasingly passed laws that make it a crime to engage in many of the daily activities associated with homelessness. Advocates for the homeless contend that these laws deny the homeless their most basic human, legal, and political rights. Furthermore, most experts argue that the criminalization of homelessness defers and even exacerbates the problem rather than solving it.

In *No Safe Place*, the NLCHP finds that although few cities had sufficient affordable housing and shelter space for their homeless populations in 2014, 34% of cities imposed citywide bans on public camping and 57% imposed camping bans in certain locations. The NLCHP notes that laws prohibiting camping are typically written broadly and are used to prohibit all outdoor sleeping. Many cities also had laws that specifically outlawed outdoor sleeping. Nearly one out of five (18%) of the surveyed cities imposed citywide bans on sleeping in public and more than a quarter (27%) imposed sleeping bans in certain locations. In 43% of cities the homeless were prohibited from sleeping in their own vehicle.

Likewise, one of the homeless population's only means of deriving income, begging or panhandling, was prohibited citywide in 24% of municipalities in 2014; and 76% of cities prohibited the activity in certain locations. Even being present in a public place, which is a necessity for homeless people who by definition have no private place to go, is frequently illegal—33% of surveyed cities had laws prohibiting loitering in public anywhere in the city and 65% prohibited loitering in certain locations. Similarly, sitting or lying down in certain public locations was prohibited in 53% of cities.

Meanwhile, numerous media reports pointed out a new development in the trend toward criminalizing homelessness: the criminalization of attempts to feed the homeless in public places where they are known to gather, such as parks and streets. The NCH reports in *Share No More: The Criminalization of Efforts to Feed People in Need* (http://nationalhomeless.org/wp-content/uploads/2014/10/Food-Sharing2014.pdf) that as of October 2014, 57 U.S. cities had passed legislation that outlawed the practice of sharing food with the homeless. The

NCH further observes that 21 of these restrictive ordinances had been introduced since January 2013, suggesting that this trend is gaining momentum. Those who attempt to feed the homeless, often members of small faith-based or nonprofit organizations, are subject to citations and arrest under these ordinances. According to the NCH, serving food to the homeless in the locations where they are present is often the only way of ensuring that those with disabilities and a lack of transportation can meet their basic survival needs.

The NCH explains that cities outlaw the feeding of the homeless through multiple methods. The most common methods are restrictions on the use of public property that mandate permits, often limited in number, for which fees sometimes totaling hundreds of dollars must be paid. These costs can be prohibitive for many of the small organizations that engage in attempts to feed the homeless. Furthermore, permits to feed the homeless often include detailed guidelines, the violation of which can be used as grounds for revocation of the right to engage in the activity. Other cities have outlawed food-sharing by subjecting the activity to food-service regulations such as those that apply to restaurants, which are frequently difficult, if not impossible, to satisfy in the outdoor settings where food-sharing often takes place.

Violating Rights

In *No Safe Place*, the NLCHP notes that many laws criminalizing the activities of the homeless have been found to violate First Amendment rights to freedom of speech and assembly, Eighth Amendment rights to freedom from cruel and unusual punishment, and 14th Amendment rights to due process. According to the United Nations Human Rights Committee, laws criminalizing homelessness also violate international human rights treaties that the U.S. government has signed, including the International Covenant on Civil and Political Rights.

The USICH, speaking on behalf of the federal government, has made public its opposition to the criminalization of homelessness. In "We Still Believe in Human Rights" (December 10, 2014, http://dev2.usich.gov/news/we-still-believe-in-human-rights1), Maria Foscarinis and Laura Green Zeilinger report that since 2010 the USICH has been advising the Department of Justice to take a human rights approach to the issue of criminalizing homeless behavior and that it is involved in ongoing efforts to persuade local and state governments, as well as other federal agencies, to adopt alternatives to criminalization.

Increasing Costs and Inefficiencies

The NLCHP maintains in *No Safe Place* that "criminalization is the most expensive and least effective way of addressing homelessness." The center points to numerous research studies that compare the cost of a "management"

approach to homelessness that includes criminalization with the cost of a housing-first approach. For example, in 2013 the Utah Housing and Community Development Division found that the average homeless person in the state of Utah cost taxpayers $16,670 annually in hospital bills and jail expenses, compared with an average annual cost of $11,000 for providing a homeless person with an apartment and a social worker. Similarly, the University of New Mexico's Institute for Social Research found that a housing-first program in Albuquerque cut jail expenses related to the homeless by 64%.

Exacerbating the Problem

In *No Safe Place*, the NLCHP states that criminalizing homelessness fails to address the root causes of homelessness, such as a lack of affordable housing and job availability, and instead exacerbates the problem by burdening homeless individuals and families. Those who are arrested for going about the daily activities associated with being homeless typically spend a short amount of time in jail and then return to the streets; their preexisting burdens are amplified by the disruption and the inability to pay the fines and court fees they have often incurred in the process. Additionally, the criminal records that homeless people accumulate as a result of restrictive ordinances sometimes ruin their prospects for housing, employment, and government aid programs. Thus, criminalization can have the perverse effect of guaranteeing that the homeless will remain homeless.

Alternatives to Criminalization

The USICH suggests in *Searching out Solutions: Constructive Alternatives to the Criminalization of Homelessness* (2012, http://dev2.usich.gov/resources/uploads/asset_library/RPT_SoS_March2012.pdf) three key strategies to replace efforts at criminalization:

- Creation of comprehensive and seamless systems of care—in an effort to address gaps in service delivery, many local organizations partner to coordinate housing and services, creating systems of care. These systems of care enable long-term reductions in street homelessness and connect individuals with benefits and services that improve housing stability.

- Collaboration between law enforcement, behavioral health, and social service providers—collaboration between service providers and law enforcement regarding outreach to individuals and specialized crisis intervention training can limit the number of arrests for nonviolent offenses. This partnership can also help link individuals experiencing homelessness with the system of care and permanent, supportive housing.

- Alternative justice system strategies—strategies that provide alternatives to prosecution and incarceration and offer reentry planning for individuals show an increase in the likelihood that people will connect to permanent housing and employment. This solution includes the use of specialty courts, citation dismissal programs, holistic public defenders offices, and reentry programs.

RAISING AWARENESS

The 1980s and 1990s saw a number of mainstream media events that were designed to raise awareness of homelessness as a national problem as well as to raise money to aid in the fight against homelessness. The Hands across America fund-raiser, held in 1986, involved approximately 6.5 million people who locked hands to form a 4,150-mile (6,680 km) human chain across the country. That same year the comedians Robin Williams (1951–2014), Whoopi Goldberg (1955–), and Billy Crystal (1948–) hosted the HBO comedy special *Comic Relief* to help raise money for the homeless. The show was a success and became an annual event through 1996.

New installments of *Comic Relief* appeared sporadically through the late 1990s and the early 2000s, but the prominence of later iterations faded. No comparable high-profile events have emerged to supplant the show, but numerous small organizations and individuals continue to experiment with ways of making the problem of homelessness matter to ordinary Americans. One prominent example is Street Soccer USA (http://streetsoccerusa.org), a group that organizes soccer practices and games among the homeless in urban areas nationwide. As of 2017, there were Street Soccer USA programs in 14 U.S. cities, including men's and women's teams as well as programs for homeless youth. Each year the organization selects national men's, women's, boys', and girls' teams from the rosters of the local teams. The adult teams travel to the annual Homeless World Cup (held in a different international city each year since 2003), where they represent the United States in competition against other countries' national homeless teams. The youth teams represent the United States in the Street Child World Cup, which is held in advance of each quadrennial Fédération Internationale de Football Association World Cup.

Another innovative approach to raise awareness about homelessness was established in 2014 by NearShot (https://www.facebook.com/pg/NearShot/about/?ref= page_internal), a digital media company in San Francisco, whose first project was called Homeless GoPro (later Homeless POV). In an attempt to help homeless people tell their own stories and build emotional connections with people in their communities, NearShot equips homeless San Franciscans with GoPro wearable digital video cameras, which are small devices that can be affixed to the body or head and that are typically used by adventure-sports enthusiasts to document their activities as they experience them. The homeless people wear the cameras and document daily life as they live it. The videos are then edited into short films and posted online. In "Homeless GoPro Offers 1st-Hand Look on S.F. Homeless" (SFGate.com, April 15, 2014), Kevin Fagan quotes Kevin Adler, a sociologist and founder of the project, who said, "This project is about building empathy. We walk by the homeless every day, and sometimes we smile, sometimes we give a dollar, sometimes we do nothing. But what do most people really know about those they are walking by?"

Meanwhile, in July 2015 HUD released *Family Options Study: Short-Term Impacts of Housing and Services Interventions for Homeless Families* (July 2015, https://www.huduser.gov/portal/portal/sites/default/files/pdf/FamilyOptionsStudy_final.pdf), a landmark report investigating the effectiveness of existing homelessness prevention strategies. In the study, HUD focused on three prevalent forms of homeless interventions: voucher programs, rapid rehousing, and project-based transitional housing. According to Alana Semuels, in "The Best Way to End Homelessness" (Atlantic.com, July 11, 2015), midway through the three-year study, HUD found that families participating in voucher programs experienced fewer physical and mental health problems, reported fewer incidences of domestic violence, and spent less time in shelters than participants in other programs. Although the monthly costs associated with the voucher program typically accumulate over a longer period than other interventions, HUD suggests that providing stable housing to the homeless could prove to be the most effective way of ending long-term dependence on government assistance. Semuels notes that the access to "permanent housing" provided by voucher programs "can allow families to get back on their feet, find work, and get off subsidies."

CHAPTER 8

HEALTH CARE

HEALTH OF POOR PEOPLE

Connection between Poor Health and Poverty

Adults in poverty are more likely than other adults to have health problems and to be uninsured, and on average they have shorter life spans than the nonpoor. Likewise, children in poverty have elevated risks for poor health and teen pregnancy and are more likely than nonpoor children to be uninsured.

Although the correlation between poverty and health problems is well established, less consensus exists about the specific nature of the cause and effect relationship. Low levels of education, low income, marginal employment status, and poor health reinforce one another in numerous ways. Those with low levels of education are more likely to have low-paying and low-status jobs or to be unemployed. Low-paying and low-status jobs can pose health risks that higher-status jobs do not, and because they are less likely to provide health insurance benefits, they correlate with lower access to preventive health care, including vaccinations. Additionally, low levels of education, which are common among the impoverished, can result in a lack of awareness about the health effects of certain lifestyle choices. These characteristics, which are often discussed together as measures of socioeconomic status (SES), correlate with behaviors that adversely affect health, including tobacco use and physical inactivity. In addition, low-SES children and adults often live in low-income neighborhoods that are lacking in resources for promoting healthy lifestyles. For example, Tara Culp-Ressler explains in "Restaurants Located in Poor Areas Tend to Offer Unhealthy Food" (ThinkProgress.org, April 22, 2014) that the prevalence of fast-food restaurants near public housing developments can lead residents to consume diets that are high in calories and fat, while lacking in vegetables and nutritious grains. Both the poor and the near-poor (those whose incomes are below 200% of the poverty level) are more likely to be uninsured than those in higher economic brackets, and therefore they

often seek medical care only when health issues have reached a crisis stage. Furthermore, low-SES women are less likely to use contraception to prevent pregnancy than are high-SES women, and when pregnant, they are less likely to receive satisfactory prenatal care.

ADULTS. In *Health, United States, 2016: With Chartbook on Long-Term Trends in Health* (May 2017, https://www.cdc.gov/nchs/data/hus/hus16.pdf), the National Center for Health Statistics (NCHS), a department within the Centers for Disease Control and Prevention, highlights some specific health challenges that are common among low-income adults. As Table 8.1 shows, the likelihood that an adult will have a disability increases as income decreases. In 2015, 42.8% of adults with incomes below the federal poverty threshold ($24,600 for a family of four) and 41% of adults whose incomes ranged from 100% to 199% of the poverty line had at least one difficulty that affected basic actions such as movement, sensory functioning (e.g., hearing or vision), emotions, or cognition. By comparison, 32.4% of adults whose incomes ranged from 200% to 399% of poverty, and 22.1% of adults at 400% or more of poverty, had difficulties that affected their basic actions. This pattern held among working-age adults as well as among adults aged 65 years and older. Similarly, low-income adults were more likely than higher-income adults to suffer from one or more limitations that affected their ability to perform complex actions such as self-care or daily living activities, social interactions, or work.

The poor and the near-poor are similarly more likely than higher-income adults to experience mental health difficulties categorized by the NCHS as "serious psychological distress." For *Health, United States, 2016*, the agency determined levels of psychological distress by studying the frequency with which survey respondents felt "so sad that nothing could cheer you up," "nervous," "restless or fidgety," "hopeless," "that everything was an effort," or "worthless." In 2014–15 adults living below the poverty line were six times more likely (8.3%) to be living with serious psychological distress than adults living at 400% or more of poverty (1.3%). (See Table 8.2.) Although adults living at 100% to 199% of poverty (5.3%) were less likely than adults in poverty to describe experiencing serious psychological distress, they were four times more likely to do so than adults with incomes equaling 400% or more of poverty. These percentages had changed only slightly since 1997–98.

The relationship between income and the prevalence of chronic health conditions (arthritis, asthma, cancer, diabetes, heart disease, hepatitis, hypertension, obstructive pulmonary disease, stroke, and weak or failing kidneys) was similar. The likelihood that an adult had no chronic health conditions or one chronic health condition increased in direct proportion to income in 2015 as in prior years, and the likelihood that an adult had two to three chronic health conditions or four or more

TABLE 8.1

Percentage of adults with at least one disability, by poverty level, selected years 1997–2015

[Data are based on household interviews of a sample of the civilian noninstitutionalized population]

Characteristic	18 years and over				18–64 years				65 years and over			
	1997	2000	2010[a]	2015[a]	1997	2000	2010[a]	2015[a]	1997	2000	2010[a]	2015[a]
					At least one basic actions difficulty[b]							
Percent of poverty level[d]					Percent							
Below 100%	41.9	38.4	40.6	42.8	36.2	31.9	36.3	37.8	74.1	71.6	72.7	76.8
100%–199%	38.2	37.1	38.7	41.0	29.2	26.5	30.5	33.3	66.6	69.4	69.5	69.0
200%–399%	28.4	28.2	31.1	32.4	22.0	22.1	24.1	24.6	56.1	53.9	58.9	60.5
400% or more	21.0	19.4	23.0	22.1	18.2	16.8	19.3	17.5	45.5	44.7	47.0	43.7
					At least one complex activity limitation[c]							
Percent of poverty level[d]												
Below 100%	30.0	26.0	27.5	29.3	25.2	22.0	24.0	25.5	56.9	46.7	54.5	55.6
100%–199%	23.3	22.0	23.7	24.2	16.7	15.1	18.4	19.7	43.9	42.8	43.7	40.6
200%–399%	13.3	12.8	14.5	16.1	9.3	9.2	10.8	11.2	30.6	27.5	29.3	33.5
400% or more	7.3	6.4	7.7	8.3	5.8	5.0	5.8	5.8	20.2	19.6	19.8	19.8

[a]Starting with 2007 data (shown in spreadsheet version), the hearing question, a component of the basic actions difficulty measure, was revised. Consequently, data for basic actions difficulty prior to 2007 are not comparable with 2007 data and beyond.
[b]A basic actions difficulty is defined as having difficulties in one or more of the following areas of functioning: movement, emotional, sensory (seeing or hearing), or cognitive. Starting with 2007 data, the hearing question, a component of basic actions difficulty, was revised. Consequently, data prior to 2007 are not comparable with data for 2007 and beyond.
[c]A complex activity limitation is defined as having one or more of the following limitations: maintaining independence (performing activities of daily living or instrumental activities of daily living), socializing, or working.
[d]Percent of poverty level is based on family income and family size and composition using U.S. Census Bureau poverty thresholds. Missing family income data were imputed for 1997 and beyond.

SOURCE: Adapted from "Table 42. Disability Measures among Adults Aged 18 and over, by Selected Characteristics: United States, Selected Years 1997–2015," in *Health, United States, 2016: With Chartbook on Long-Term Trends in Health*, Centers for Disease Control and Prevention, National Center for Health Statistics, May 2017, https://www.cdc.gov/nchs/data/hus/hus16.pdf (accessed August 25, 2017)

TABLE 8.2

Percentage of adults with serious psychological distress in the past 30 days, by poverty level, selected years 1997–2015

[Data are based on household interviews of a sample of the civilian noninstitutionalized population]

Characteristic	1997–1998	1999–2000	2001–2002	2004–2005	2010–2011	2014–2015[a]
Percent of poverty level[b, c]						
Below 100%	9.1	6.8	8.4	8.6	8.2	8.3
100%–199%	5.0	4.4	5.2	5.0	5.0	5.3
200%–399%	2.5	2.3	2.8	2.5	2.9	2.8
400% or more	1.3	1.2	1.3	1.1	1.2	1.3

[a]Starting in 2013, the six psychological distress questions were moved to the adult selected items section of the sample adult questionnaire. Observed differences between the 2012 and earlier estimates and the 2013 and later estimates may be partially or fully attributable to this change in question placement within the sample adult questionnaire.
[b]Estimates are age-adjusted to the year 2000 standard population using five age groups: 18–44 years, 45–54 years, 55–64 years, 65–74 years, and 75 years and over.
[c]Percent of poverty level is based on family income and family size and composition using U.S. Census Bureau poverty thresholds. Missing family income data were imputed for 1997 and beyond.

SOURCE: Adapted from "Table 46. Serious Psychological Distress in the Past 30 Days among Adults Aged 18 and over, by Selected Characteristics: United States, Average Annual, Selected Years 1997–1998 through 2014–2015," in *Health, United States, 2016: With Chartbook on Long-Term Trends in Health*, Centers for Disease Control and Prevention, National Center for Health Statistics, May 2017, https://www.cdc.gov/nchs/data/hus/hus16.pdf (accessed August 25, 2017)

chronic health conditions increased as income fell. (See Table 8.3.) People with more than one chronic condition present particular complications to health care professionals, increasing both the amount of treatment typically required and the expense of that treatment. The correlation between income and the likelihood that an adult would have one of the deadliest of chronic health conditions (heart disease, cancer, or stroke) varied slightly by condition. (See Table 8.4.) The poor and near-poor are more likely than higher earners to have heart disease and stroke, whereas the percentage of adults with cancer does not meaningfully vary by income. This may reflect the fact that heart disease and stroke are linked not only to genetics

but also to environmental and lifestyle factors (such as diet, smoking, alcohol and drug use, and stress levels), whereas cancer is less strongly linked to such factors.

CHILDREN. NCHS data also show that children in low-income households fare consistently worse on measures of health and well-being than children in higher-income households. Rates of current asthma as well as the prevalence of asthma attacks over the preceding year were noticeably higher among children living in poverty, and rates of attention-deficit/hyperactivity disorder (ADHD) and serious emotional or behavioral difficulties were dramatically higher for children in poverty than for

TABLE 8.3

Number of chronic conditions among adults, by poverty level, selected years 2002–15

[Data are based on household interviews of a sample of the civilian noninstitutionalized population]

	Number of respondent-reported chronic conditions from 10 selected conditions[a]											
	0–1 chronic conditions				2–3 chronic conditions				4 or more chronic conditions			
Characteristic	2002	2010	2013	2015	2002	2010	2013	2015	2002	2010	2013	2015
Percent of poverty level[b, c]					Percent distribution							
Below 100%	71.9	69.2	69.7	68.1	21.3	22.7	21.9	23.3	6.8	8.1	8.4	8.6
100%–199%	76.4	72.6	73.6	73.3	18.6	21.0	20.7	20.6	5.0	6.4	5.7	6.1
200%–399%	77.8	75.6	76.9	76.6	18.9	19.9	18.9	18.9	3.3	4.5	4.2	4.5
400% or more	81.2	78.3	80.0	80.5	15.9	18.7	17.5	16.6	2.8	3.0	2.5	2.9

[a]Adults were categorized as having 0–1, 2–3, or 4 or more of the following chronic conditions: hypertension, coronary heart disease, stroke, diabetes, cancer, arthritis, hepatitis, weak or failing kidneys, chronic obstructive pulmonary disease, or current asthma. Data from the National Health Interview Survey capture 10 of 20 chronic conditions used in a standardized approach for defining chronic conditions in the United States. Thus, these estimates are conservative in nature.
[b]Estimates are age-adjusted to the year 2000 standard population using five age groups: 18–44 years, 45–54 years, 55–64 years, 65–74 years, and 75 years and over.
[c]Percent of poverty level is based on family income and family size and composition using U.S. Census Bureau poverty thresholds. Missing family income data were imputed.

SOURCE: Adapted from "Table 39. Number of Respondent-Reported Chronic Conditions from 10 Selected Conditions among Adults Aged 18 and over, by Selected Characteristics: United States, Selected Years 2002–2015," in *Health, United States, 2016: With Chartbook on Long-Term Trends in Health*, Centers for Disease Control and Prevention, National Center for Health Statistics, May 2017, https://www.cdc.gov/nchs/data/hus/hus16.pdf (accessed August 25, 2017)

TABLE 8.4

Percentage of adults with heart disease, cancer, and stroke, by poverty level, selected years 1997–2015

[Data are based on household interviews of a sample of the civilian noninstitutionalized population]

	Heart disease[a]				Cancer[b]				Stroke[c]			
Characteristic	1997–1998	1999–2000	2010–2011	2014–2015	1997–1998	1999–2000	2010–2011	2014–2015	1997–1998	1999–2000	2010–2011	2014–2015
Percent of poverty level[d, e]					Percent of adults							
Below 100%	15.3	13.6	13.9	13.7	4.9	4.9	5.3	5.8	4.3	3.7	4.6	4.3
100%–199%	13.2	12.0	12.3	12.0	4.8	5.3	5.9	5.5	3.1	3.2	3.7	3.6
200%–399%	11.5	11.0	11.3	10.7	4.9	5.1	6.2	5.9	2.1	2.1	2.5	2.4
400% or more	11.0	10.2	9.8	9.5	5.2	5.1	6.2	6.2	1.6	1.5	1.5	1.4

[a]Heart disease is based on self-reported responses to questions about whether respondents had ever been told by a doctor or other health professional that they had coronary heart disease, angina (angina pectoris), a heart attack (myocardial infarction), or any other kind of heart disease or heart condition.
[b]Cancer is based on self-reported responses to a question about whether respondents had ever been told by a doctor or other health professional that they had cancer or a malignancy of any kind. Excludes squamous cell and basal cell carcinomas.
[c]Stroke is based on self-reported responses to a question about whether respondents had ever been told by a doctor or other health professional that they had a stroke.
[d]Estimates are age-adjusted to the year 2000 standard population using five age groups: 18–44 years, 45–54 years, 55–64 years, 65–74 years, and 75 years and over. Age-adjusted estimates in this table may differ from other age-adjusted estimates based on the same data and presented elsewhere if different age groups are used in the adjustment procedure.
[e]Percent of poverty level is based on family income and family size and composition using U.S. Census Bureau poverty thresholds. Missing family income data were imputed for 1997–1998 and beyond.

SOURCE: Adapted from "Table 38. Respondent-Reported Prevalence of Heart Disease, Cancer, and Stroke among Adults Aged 18 and over, by Selected Characteristics: United States, Average Annual, Selected Years 1997–1998 through 2014–2015," in *Health, United States, 2016: With Chartbook on Long-Term Trends in Health*, Centers for Disease Control and Prevention, National Center for Health Statistics, May 2017, https://www.cdc.gov/nchs/data/hus/hus16.pdf (accessed August 25, 2017)

TABLE 8.5

Health conditions among children, by percentage of poverty level, selected years 1997–2015

[Data are based on household interviews of a sample of the civilian noninstitutionalized population]

Characteristic	Current asthma[a]				Asthma attack in the past 12 months[b]			
	1997–1999	2000–2002	2003–2005	2013–2015	1997–1999	2000–2002	2003–2005	2013–2015
Percent of poverty level[c]								
Below 100%	—	—	10.4	10.9	6.1	7.1	6.5	6.2
100%–199%	—	—	8.6	8.5	5.3	5.4	5.2	4.4
200%–399%	—	—	8.3	7.9	5.0	5.3	5.2	4.0
400% or more	—	—	7.9	6.9	5.2	5.5	4.9	3.7

Characteristic	Attention-deficit/hyperactivity disorder[d]				Serious emotional or behavioral difficulties[e]			
Percent of poverty level[c]								
Below 100%	7.2	8.2	8.4	12.7	—	—	7.4	8.1
100%–199%	6.7	7.5	7.8	10.9	—	—	5.4	6.1
200%–399%	6.2	7.7	7.8	9.4	—	—	4.9	4.9
400% or more	6.1	7.1	6.9	9.2	—	—	3.7	4.3

—Data not available.

[a]Based on parent or knowledgeable adult responding to both questions, "Has a doctor or other health professional ever told you that your child had asthma?" and "Does your child still have asthma?"

[b]Based on parent or knowledgeable adult responding to both questions, "Has a doctor or other health professional ever told you that your child had asthma?" and "During the past 12 months, did your child have an episode of asthma or an asthma attack?"

[c]Percent of poverty level is based on family income and family size and composition using U.S. Census Bureau poverty thresholds. Missing family income data were imputed for 1997 and beyond.

[d]Based on parent or knowledgeable adult responding to the question, "Has a doctor or health professional ever told you that your child had attention-deficit/hyperactivity disorder (ADHD) or attention deficit disorder (ADD)?"

[e]Based on parent or knowledgeable adult responding to the question, "Overall, do you think that [child] has difficulties in any of the following areas: emotions, concentration, behavior, or being able to get along with other people?"

SOURCE: Adapted from "Table 35. Health Conditions among Children under Age 18, by Selected Characteristics: United States, Average Annual, Selected Years 1997–1999 through 2013–2015," in *Health, United States, 2016: With Chartbook on Long-Term Trends in Health*, Centers for Disease Control and Prevention, National Center for Health Statistics, May 2017, https://www.cdc.gov/nchs/data/hus/hus16.pdf (accessed August 25, 2017)

children in higher-income brackets. (See Table 8.5.) For example, in the period 2013 to 2015, 12.7% of poor children had been diagnosed with ADHD, compared with 9.2% of children in families that had an income of 400% or more of poverty. In addition, 8.1% of poor children had serious emotional or behavioral difficulties, nearly double the rate (4.3%) for children in homes with an income of 400% or more of poverty.

Poverty and Access to Health Care

One of the major factors in low-income adults' negative health outcomes relative to higher-income adults is their inability to afford medical care. As Table 8.6 shows, the likelihood that an adult had to delay or forgo necessary medical treatment due to cost was directly correlated with income levels between 1997 and 2015. Among all income groups, the likelihood of delays or nonreceipt of care rose between 1997 and 2010, before falling sharply in 2015. In 2015 as in prior years, the percentage of those living in poverty that had to delay or forgo care (16.6%) was almost identical to the percentage living at 100% to 199% who had to delay or forgo care (15.9%). Just over one out of 10 (10.8%) of those living at 200% to 399% of poverty also had to delay or forgo care in 2015, a fact that underscores how expensive comprehensive health care was during this period. By comparison, 4.2% of those

living at 400% or more of poverty delayed or did not receive needed treatment during these years.

Oral health is strongly linked to overall health, as the Mayo Clinic reports in "Oral Health: A Window to Your Overall Health" (2017, http://www.mayoclinic.org/healthy-living/adult-health/in-depth/dental/art-20047475). Research suggests that oral health issues can affect, be caused by, or contribute to a number of diseases and conditions, including endocarditis (an infection in the heart), cardiovascular disease, premature birth and low birth weight, diabetes, human immunodeficiency virus (HIV)/acquired immunodeficiency syndrome (AIDS), osteoporosis, and Alzheimer's disease, among other conditions. Good oral hygiene and regular dental care are accordingly considered important components of overall health, but low-income adults are much more likely than other adults to be unable to afford dental care. More than one out of five of those living in poverty (21.2%) and at 100% to 199% of poverty (20.9%) had to forgo dental care in 2015 because of cost, compared with 12.9% of those whose incomes reached 200% to 399% of poverty and 4% of those at 400% or more of poverty. (See Table 8.6.)

Disparities in access to health care were less dramatic among children during this period, in large part due to Medicaid (a state and federal health care coverage

TABLE 8.6

Delay or nonreceipt of needed medical or dental care due to cost in past 12 months, by percentage of poverty level, 1997–2015

[Data are based on household interviews of a sample of the civilian noninstitutionalized population]

Characteristic	Delay or nonreceipt of needed medical care due to cost[a]				Nonreceipt of needed prescription drugs due to cost[b]				Nonreceipt of needed dental care due to cost[c]			
	1997	2005	2010	2015	1997	2005	2010	2015	1997	2005	2010	2015
Percent of poverty level[d]												
Below 100%	19.6	20.0	23.4	16.6	14.8	19.5	21.5	12.9	19.4	24.4	30.4	21.2
100%–199%	17.9	18.9	24.0	15.9	11.6	16.3	18.4	12.7	18.3	21.0	29.2	20.9
200%–399%	10.5	11.8	15.2	10.8	5.5	9.5	11.4	7.0	10.2	13.7	17.3	12.9
400% or more	4.6	5.0	6.8	4.2	1.7	3.3	3.9	2.3	4.5	5.9	7.0	4.0

— Data not available.

[a]Based on persons responding to the questions, "During the past 12 months was there any time when person needed medical care but did not get it because person couldn't afford it?" and "During the past 12 months has medical care been delayed because of worry about the cost?"

[b]Based on persons responding to the question, "During the past 12 months was there any time when person needed prescription medicine but didn't get it because person couldn't afford it?"

[c]Based on persons responding to the question, "During the past 12 months was there any time when person needed dental care (including checkups) but didn't get it because person couldn't afford it?"

[d]Percent of poverty level is based on family income and family size and composition using U.S. Census Bureau poverty thresholds. Missing family income data were imputed for 1997 and beyond.

SOURCE: Adapted from "Table 63. Delay or Nonreceipt of Needed Medical Care, Nonreceipt of Needed Prescription Drugs, or Nonreceipt of Needed Dental Care during the Past 12 Months Due to Cost, by Selected Characteristics: United States, Selected Years 1997–2015," in *Health, United States, 2016: With Chartbook on Long-Term Trends in Health*, Centers for Disease Control and Prevention, National Center for Health Statistics, May 2017, https://www.cdc.gov/nchs/data/hus/hus16.pdf (accessed August 25, 2017)

program for which all children in poverty are eligible) and the Children's Health Insurance Program (CHIP), for which many low-income children who are above the poverty level are eligible. In 1993–94, 7.7% of children had no usual source of health care, and by 2014–15 the percentage of children with no regular source of care had fallen to 4%. (See Table 8.7.) Nevertheless, children in low-income households remained more likely than those in higher-income households to have no usual source of care. In 2014–15, 6.5% of children living in poverty and 5.4% of those at 100% to 199% of poverty had no usual source of care, compared with 3.4% of children in households with an income at 200% to 399% of poverty and 1.4% of those at 400% or more of poverty. Furthermore, with the expiration of CHIP funding on September 30, 2017, it appeared almost certain that this disparity would grow even more pronounced. As of October 2017, Congress had not yet passed a bill that extended funding for CHIP.

The percentage of children who made no health care visits to an office or clinic in the course of a given year declined significantly during this period as well. As Table 8.8 shows, in 1997–98, 12.8% of all children made no office or clinic visits, and in 2014–15, 8.5% of children made no office or clinic visits. The percentage of children in families with an income below 200% of poverty who made no office or clinic visits (10.3% of children below poverty and 10.4% of children at 100% to 199% of poverty) was approximately twice the percentage of children at 400% or more of poverty who made no office or clinic visits. Children aged six to 17 years were twice as likely than children under the age of six years to make no office or clinic visits in all years and at all income levels.

HEALTH INSURANCE AND HEALTH CARE REFORM

An Overview of the Health Insurance Landscape

U.S. health care is extremely expensive by world standards and in relation to American incomes, and few people can afford to pay for care at retail prices. Health insurance policies allow individuals and families to obtain care at reduced prices because insurance companies share the cost of treatments, drugs, and other services. Thus, the health of most Americans depends to a large extent on their ability to obtain and keep insurance coverage.

The overwhelming majority of U.S. residents obtain health insurance either through their employers or through the federal and state governments. In the U.S. Census Bureau's survey of health care coverage among U.S. residents, *Health Insurance Coverage in the United States: 2015* (September 2016, https://www.census.gov/content/dam/Census/library/publications/2016/demo/p60-257.pdf), Jessica C. Barnett and Marina S. Vornovitsky report that in 2015, 289.9 million Americans, or 90.9% of the total U.S. population, had health insurance. (See Table 8.9.) Among insured people, 214.2 million (67.2%) had private insurance policies and 118.4 million (37.1%) had coverage through the government. Approximately 29 million people, who constituted 9.1% of the total U.S. population, were uninsured in 2015.

Most people who go without insurance typically do so for one or more of the following reasons: their employers do not offer coverage, they do not qualify for government-funded insurance, and/or they cannot afford to purchase individual policies directly from companies. Those who obtain employment-based insurance typically share the

TABLE 8.7

Percentage of children with no usual source of health care, by selected characteristics, selected years 1993–2015

[Data are based on household interviews of a sample of the civilian noninstitutionalized population]

Characteristic	Under 18 years			Under 6 years			6–17 years		
	1993–1994[a]	1999–2000	2014–2015	1993–1994[a]	1999–2000	2014–2015	1993–1994[a]	1999–2000	2014–2015
	Percent of children without a usual source of health care[b]								
All children[c]	**7.7**	**6.9**	**4.0**	**5.2**	**4.6**	**2.7**	**9.0**	**8.0**	**4.6**
Sex									
Male	8.1	6.7	3.9	5.3	4.5	2.4	9.6	7.8	4.6
Female	7.3	7.1	4.1	5.0	4.7	3.0	8.5	8.2	4.6
Race[d]									
White only	7.0	6.3	3.7	4.7	4.4	2.4	8.3	7.2	4.3
Black or African American only	10.3	7.7	4.8	7.6	4.4	4.0	11.9	9.1	5.1
American Indian or Alaska Native only	9.3*	9.4*	*	*	*	*	8.7*	9.4*	*
Asian only	9.7	10.0	5.0	3.4*	5.8*	4.2*	13.5	12.2	5.4
Native Hawaiian or Other Pacific Islander only	—	*	*	—	*	*	—	*	*
2 or more races	—	4.9*	4.8	—	*	3.3*	—	7.2*	5.8
Hispanic origin and race[d]									
Hispanic or Latino	14.3	14.2	6.2	9.3	9.0	3.9	17.7	17.2	7.5
Not Hispanic or Latino	6.7	5.5	3.3	4.4	3.6	2.3	7.8	6.3	3.7
White only	5.7	4.7	2.6	3.7	3.3	1.7	6.7	5.4	3.0
Black or African American only	10.2	7.6	4.5	7.7	4.5	3.8	11.6	9.0	4.8
Percent of poverty level[e]									
Below 100%	13.9	13.1	6.5	9.4	7.6	4.4	16.8	16.2	7.6
100%–199%	9.8	10.6	5.4	6.7	7.5	3.7	11.6	12.2	6.2
200%–399%	3.7	4.8	3.4	1.9	3.2	2.3	4.5	5.6	3.9
400% or more	3.7	2.6	1.4	1.6*	1.5	0.8*	5.0	3.0	1.7
Hispanic origin and race and percent of poverty level[d, e]									
Hispanic or Latino:									
Below 100%	19.6	19.4	7.6	12.7	11.6	4.8*	24.8	24.5	9.3
100%–199%	15.3	17.1	6.9	9.9	11.3	4.0*	18.9	20.4	8.3
200%–399%	5.2	8.3	5.0	*	5.0*	3.5*	6.7	10.1	5.8
400% or more	*	3.8*	2.4*	*	*	*	*	5.0*	3.0*
Not Hispanic or Latino:									
White only:									
Below 100%	10.2	10.7	4.9	6.5	6.3*	*	12.7	13.1	5.4
100%–199%	8.7	7.8	4.0	6.3	5.7	3.2*	10.1	8.8	4.5
200%–399%	3.3	4.0	2.6	1.6	2.7	1.3*	4.0	4.6	3.3
400% or more	4.0	2.3	1.1	1.7*	1.5*	*	5.4	2.6	1.4
Black or African American only:									
Below 100%	13.7	9.4	5.0	10.9	4.7*	4.8*	15.5	11.8	5.1
100%–199%	9.1	9.7	5.3	6.0*	6.4*	*	10.8	11.2	6.1
200%–399%	5.0	5.0	4.1*	*	*	*	6.2	5.7	4.2*
400% or more	*	3.5*	*	*	*	*	*	4.0*	*
Health insurance status at the time of interview[f]									
Insured	5.0	3.9	2.8	3.3	2.6	2.1	5.9	4.5	3.1
Private	3.8	3.4	2.1	1.9	2.2	1.5	4.6	3.9	2.3
Medicaid	8.9	5.3	3.7	6.4	3.5	2.8	11.3	6.7	4.3
Uninsured	23.5	29.3	27.9	18.0	20.8	20.3	26.0	32.9	30.3
Health insurance status prior to interview[f]									
Insured continuously all 12 months	4.6	3.6	2.5	3.1	2.3	1.9	5.5	4.2	2.8
Uninsured for any period up to 12 months	15.3	15.0	13.5	10.9	12.5	10.8	18.1	16.4	14.8
Uninsured more than 12 months	27.6	35.8	34.9	21.4	26.8	23.5*	30.0	39.1	37.5

expense of their coverage with their employers, and their employers can, additionally, secure better pricing from insurance companies for group coverage (coverage offered to an entire employee pool) than can be secured for individual coverage (coverage purchased directly from insurance companies by individuals). Employment-based insurance is typically a perk available to salaried workers in middle- and upper-income jobs. As Table 8.9 shows, 177.5 million people, or 55.7% of the U.S. population, had employment-based insurance in 2015.

TABLE 8.7

Percentage of children with no usual source of health care, by selected characteristics, selected years 1993–2015 [CONTINUED]

[Data are based on household interviews of a sample of the civilian noninstitutionalized population]

Characteristic	Under 18 years			Under 6 years			6–17 years		
	1993–1994[a]	1999–2000	2014–2015	1993–1994[a]	1999–2000	2014–2015	1993–1994[a]	1999–2000	2014–2015
	Percent of children without a usual source of health care[b]								
Percent of poverty level and health insurance status prior to interview[e, f]									
Below 100%:									
Insured continuously all 12 months	8.6	5.7	4.0	5.8	2.7*	2.9	10.7	7.5	4.5
Uninsured for any period up to 12 months	21.7	19.8	20.8	18.0	16.0*	*	23.7	21.9	21.5
Uninsured more than 12 months	31.2	42.7	47.9	25.5	31.0	*	33.4	47.1	49.8
100%–199%:									
Insured continuously all 12 months	5.6	5.2	3.0	3.7	3.7	2.4	6.7	6.0	3.3
Uninsured for any period up to 12 months	14.5	15.4	14.8	9.7*	14.4*	11.3*	18.0	15.9	16.6
Uninsured more than 12 months	27.6	34.4	34.6	21.4	26.4	*	30.2	37.4	36.0
200%–399%:									
Insured continuously all 12 months	2.8	3.2	2.3	1.5	2.1	1.9	3.4	3.7	2.5
Uninsured for any period up to 12 months	9.1	11.1	9.4	*	8.4*	*	11.6	12.7	11.4*
Uninsured more than 12 months	18.2	27.1	26.5	9.7*	20.3*	*	21.0	29.4	30.1
400% or more:									
Insured continuously all 12 months	3.1	2.0	1.2	*	1.2*	*	4.3	2.4	1.5
Uninsured for any period up to 12 months	*	10.3*	*	*	*	*	*	*	*
Uninsured more than 12 months	*	30.0*	*	*	*	*	*	33.3*	*
Geographic region									
Northeast	4.1	2.8	1.7	2.9	2.3	1.4*	4.8	3.0	1.8
Midwest	5.2	5.3	3.5	4.1	3.7	2.7	5.9	6.0	3.8
South	10.9	8.5	4.5	7.3	5.8	3.0	12.7	9.8	5.3
West	8.6	9.7	5.1	5.3	5.7	3.1	10.6	11.7	6.1
Location of residence[g]									
Within MSA	7.7	6.8	4.0	5.0	4.7	2.7	9.2	7.8	4.7
Outside MSA	7.8	7.4	3.8	6.0	4.2	3.1	8.7	8.7	4.1

*Estimates are considered unreliable.
—Data not available.
[a]Data prior to 1997 are not strictly comparable with data for later years due to the 1997 questionnaire redesign.
[b]Persons who report the emergency department as their usual source of care are defined as having no usual source of care.
[c]Includes all other races not shown separately and unknown health insurance status.
[d]The race groups, white, black, American Indian or Alaska Native, Asian, Native Hawaiian or Other Pacific Islander, and 2 or more races, include persons of Hispanic and non-Hispanic origin. Persons of Hispanic origin may be of any race. Starting with 1999 data, race-specific estimates are tabulated according to the 1997 Revisions to the Standards for the Classification of Federal Data on Race and Ethnicity and are not strictly comparable with estimates for earlier years. The five single-race categories plus multiple-race categories shown in the table conform to the 1997 Standards. Starting with 1999 data, race-specific estimates are for persons who reported only one racial group; the category 2 or more races inlcudes persons who reported more than one racial group. Prior to 1999, data were tabulated according to the 1977 Standards with four racial groups, and the Asian only category included Native Hawaiian or Other Pacific Islander. Estimates for single-race categories prior to 1999 included persons who reported one race or, if they reported more than one race, identified one race as best representing their race. Starting with 2003 data, race responses of other race and unspecified multiple race were treated as missing, and then race was imputed if these were the only race responses. Almost all persons with a race response of other race were of Hispanic origin.
[e]Percent of poverty level is based on family income and family size and composition using U.S. Census Bureau poverty thresholds. Missing family income data were imputed starting in 1993.
[f]Health insurance categories are mutually exclusive. Persons who reported both Medicaid and private coverage are classified as having private coverage. Medicaid includes other public assistance through 1996. Starting with 1997 data, state-sponsored health plan coverage is included as Medicaid coverage. Starting with 1999 data, coverage by the Children's Health Insurance Program (CHIP) is included with Medicaid coverage. In addition to private and Medicaid, the insured category also includes military, other government, and Medicare coverage. Persons not covered by private insurance, Medicaid, CHIP, public assistance (through 1996), state-sponsored or other government-sponsored health plans (starting in 1997), Medicare, or military plans are considered to have no health insurance coverage. Persons with only Indian Health Service coverage are considered to have no health insurance coverage. Health insurance status was unknown for 8%–9% of children in1993–1996 and about 1% in 1997–2015.
[g]MSA is metropolitan statistical area. Starting with 2005–2006 data, MSA status is determined using 2000 census data and the 2000 standards for defining MSAs.

SOURCE: "Table 61. No Usual Source of Health Care among Children under Age 18, by Selected Characteristics: United States, Average Annual, Selected Years 1993–1994 through 2014–2015," in *Health, United States, 2016: With Chartbook on Long-Term Trends in Health*, Centers for Disease Control and Prevention, National Center for Health Statistics, May 2017, https://www.cdc.gov/nchs/data/hus/hus16.pdf (accessed August 25, 2017)

Most low-income workers, including those who do hourly work for large corporations, those who work for very small businesses, and those who are self-employed, do not have access to employer-based coverage. To obtain private insurance coverage, such people must purchase policies directly from companies. These policies have historically been unaffordable for low- and even middle-income workers. Only 52.1 million people, or 16.3% of the population, had direct-purchase insurance in 2015 (see Table 8.9); and as Barnett and Vornovitsky point out, a

majority of these people (58.1%) had some other type of health insurance, which indicates that such plans may more often be purchased to supplement other plan types (such as Medicare or employer-provided coverage) than to serve the full range of a policyholder's health needs.

In 2015 many adults and all children living below the poverty level were eligible for Medicaid, a form of free health insurance coverage funded by the federal and state governments; and many children above the poverty level

TABLE 8.8

Percentage of children who made no health care visits to an office or clinic within the past 12 months, by selected characteristics, selected years 1997–2015

[Data are based on household interviews of a sample of the civilian noninstitutionalized population]

Characteristic	Under 18 years			Under 6 years			6–17 years		
	1997–1998	2001–2002	2014–2015	1997–1998	2001–2002	2014–2015	1997–1998	2001–2002	2014–2015
	Percent of children without a health care visit[a]								
All children[b]	12.8	12.1	8.5	5.7	6.3	5.1	16.3	14.9	10.2
Sex									
Male	12.9	12.3	8.5	4.9	6.4	5.0	16.8	15.1	10.2
Female	12.7	11.9	8.5	6.5	6.1	5.2	15.8	14.6	10.2
Race[c]									
White only	12.2	11.5	8.2	5.5	6.4	5.0	15.5	13.9	9.7
Black or African American only	14.3	13.3	9.8	6.5	5.9	6.1	18.1	16.8	11.6
American Indian or Alaska Native only	13.8	18.6	15.6	*	*	*	17.6*	23.0*	20.0
Asian only	16.3	15.6*	9.6	5.6*	6.8*	6.0*	22.1	20.5	11.5
Native Hawaiian or other Pacific Islander only	—	*	*	—	*	*	—	*	*
2 or more races	—	8.3	6.5	—	3.3*	*	—	12.4	9.2
Hispanic origin and race[c]									
Hispanic or Latino	19.3	18.8	11.3	9.7	9.6	5.9	25.3	24.0	14.2
Not Hispanic or Latino	11.6	10.6	7.6	4.8	5.4	4.8	14.9	13.0	8.9
White only	10.7	9.7	6.8	4.3	5.3	4.6	13.7	11.7	7.9
Black or African American only	14.5	13.4	9.7	6.5	6.0	6.2	18.3	16.8	11.3
Percent of poverty level[d]									
Below 100%	17.6	17.3	10.3	8.1	9.1	6.7	23.6	21.8	12.3
100%–199%	16.2	14.8	10.4	7.2	7.4	5.9	20.8	18.7	12.6
200%–399%	11.7	11.2	8.8	4.9	5.4	5.3	14.8	13.8	10.5
400% or more	7.4	7.7	5.2	3.0	4.1	2.6	9.5	9.3	6.3
Hispanic origin and race and percent of poverty level[c, d]									
Hispanic or Latino:									
Below 100%	23.2	22.1	11.1	11.7	10.4	6.8	31.1	29.4	13.7
100%–199%	20.9	21.3	13.3	9.7	12.3	6.5	28.1	26.2	16.5
200%–399%	15.7	15.5	11.3	8.0	7.3*	5.9	19.7	20.0	14.1
400% or more	7.8	9.7	6.2	*	*	*	9.3	12.5	8.9
Not Hispanic or Latino:									
White only:									
Below 100%	14.0	13.2	8.3	5.6*	8.6*	6.6*	19.7	15.6	9.2
100%–199%	14.1	11.8	8.7	6.0	6.0	6.5	18.0	14.8	9.8
200%–399%	10.9	10.2	7.5	4.3	4.8	4.8	13.9	12.5	8.9
400% or more	7.2	7.4	4.8	2.8*	4.2	2.5*	9.1	8.6	5.8
Black or African American only:									
Below 100%	15.8	16.1	10.5	7.6	7.8*	7.1*	20.5	20.3	12.4
100%–199%	16.4	13.3	9.1	7.7*	4.4*	*	20.4	17.5	11.4
200%–399%	13.3	12.2	10.6	4.9*	6.5*	*	16.7	14.6	11.6
400% or more	8.3	8.9	6.5*	*	*	*	10.7	11.5	6.7*
Health insurance status at the time of interview[e]									
Insured	10.4	9.8	7.5	4.5	4.7	4.8	13.4	12.3	8.9
Private	10.4	9.5	7.2	4.3	4.3	4.0	13.1	11.8	8.6
Medicaid	10.1	10.3	7.9	5.0	5.5	5.4	14.4	13.3	9.3
Uninsured	28.8	31.9	27.1	14.6	21.0	13.1	34.9	36.3	31.6
Health insurance status prior to interview[e]									
Insured continuously all 12 months	10.3	9.5	7.3	4.4	4.6	4.7	13.2	12.0	8.7
Uninsured for any period up to 12 months	15.9	17.7	14.6	7.7	10.3	8.1*	20.9	21.9	17.8
Uninsured more than 12 months	34.9	41.4	35.1	19.9	30.2	18.2*	40.2	45.3	39.0

were eligible for either Medicaid or CHIP, which offers free or reduced-price coverage to families whose incomes are too high to qualify for Medicaid but too low to enable the purchase of insurance. Elderly Americans are eligible for subsidized health insurance coverage under the federally funded Medicare program. As Table 8.9 shows, 62.4 million people, or 19.6% of the population, obtained health care coverage through Medicaid in 2015; and 51.9 million, or 16.3% of the population, obtained coverage through Medicare.

TABLE 8.8

Percentage of children who made no health care visits to an office or clinic within the past 12 months, by selected characteristics, selected years 1997–2015 [CONTINUED]

[Data are based on household interviews of a sample of the civilian noninstitutionalized population]

Characteristic	Under 18 years			Under 6 years			6–17 years		
	1997–1998	2001–2002	2014–2015	1997–1998	2001–2002	2014–2015	1997–1998	2001–2002	2014–2015
Percent of poverty level and health insurance status prior to interview[d, e]	Percent of children without a health care visit[a]								
Below 100%:									
Insured continuously all 12 months	12.6	11.7	8.8	5.7	6.1	6.1	17.6	14.9	10.3
Uninsured for any period up to 12 months	19.9	21.8	18.4	9.9*	14.4*	*	26.1	26.6	20.4
Uninsured more than 12 months	39.9	48.2	36.2	24.9	28.0*	*	45.2	55.7	40.1
100%–199%:									
Insured continuously all 12 months	12.6	10.9	8.3	4.8	4.2	4.9	16.7	14.5	10.0
Uninsured for any period up to 12 months	15.6	18.9	15.8	8.7*	10.7*	8.0*	20.2	23.2	19.7
Uninsured more than 12 months	33.7	41.3	39.0	21.3	35.4	31.0*	37.9	43.6	40.3
200%–399%:									
Insured continuously all 12 months	10.5	10.0	7.9	4.5	4.6	5.2	13.2	12.4	9.3
Uninsured for any period up to 12 months	12.8	14.5	11.5	*	7.1*	*	17.2	18.7	14.7
Uninsured more than 12 months	29.9	30.8	31.1	11.8*	24.2*	*	36.5	32.9	36.0
400% or more:									
Insured continuously all 12 months	7.0	7.2	4.9	2.9	3.9	2.6	8.8	8.7	5.9
Uninsured for any period up to 12 months	10.8*	11.4*	10.7*	*	*	*	15.1*	14.1*	*
Uninsured more than 12 months	28.8*	38.4*	*	*	*	*	37.7*	40.3*	*
Geographic region									
Northeast	7.0	6.0	5.1	3.1	3.9	3.2*	8.9	6.9	6.0
Midwest	12.2	10.3	7.5	5.9	5.1	4.9	15.3	12.8	8.8
South	14.3	14.0	9.2	5.6	7.0	6.0	18.5	17.4	10.7
West	16.3	16.0	10.5	7.9	8.1	5.0	20.7	20.0	13.3
Location of residence[f]									
Within MSA	12.3	11.7	8.2	5.4	6.1	5.1	15.9	14.5	9.8
Outside MSA	14.6	13.5	10.2	6.9	6.9	5.3	17.9	16.3	12.6

*Estimates are considered unreliable.

—Data not available.

[a]Respondents were asked how many times a doctor or other health care professional was seen in the past 12 months at a doctor's office, clinic, or some other place. Excluded are visits to emergency rooms, hospitalizations, home visits, and telephone calls. Starting with 2000 data, dental visits were also excluded.

[b]Includes all other races not shown separately and unknown health insurance status.

[c]The race groups, white, black, American Indian or Alaska Native, Asian, Native Hawaiian or Other Pacific Islander, and 2 or more races, include persons of Hispanic and non-Hispanic origin. Persons of Hispanic origin may be of any race. Starting with 1999 data, race-specific estimates are tabulated according to the 1997 Revisions to the Standards for the Classification of Federal Data on Race and Ethnicity and are not strictly comparable with estimates for earlier years. The five single-race categories plus multiple-race categories shown in the table conform to the 1997 standards. Starting with 1999 data, race-specific estimates are for persons who reported only one racial group; the category 2 or more races includes persons who reported more than one racial group. Prior to 1999, data were tabulated according to the 1977 Standards with four racial groups, and the Asian only category included Native Hawaiian or Other Pacific Islander. Estimates for single-race categories prior to 1999 included persons who reported one race or, if they reported more than one race, identified one race as best representing their race. Starting with 2003 data, race responses of other race and unspecified multiple race were treated as missing, and then race was imputed if these were the only race responses. Almost all persons with a race response of other race were of Hispanic origin.

[d]Percent of poverty level is based on family income and family size and composition using U.S. Census Bureau poverty thresholds. Missing family income data were imputed starting in 1997.

[e]Health insurance categories are mutually exclusive. Persons who reported both Medicaid and private coverage are classified as having private coverage. Starting with 1997 data, state-sponsored health plan coverage is included as Medicaid coverage. Starting with 1999 data, coverage by the Children's Health Insurance Program (CHIP) is included with Medicaid coverage. In addition to private and Medicaid, the insured category also includes military, other government, and Medicare coverage. Persons not covered by private insurance, Medicaid, CHIP, state-sponsored or other government-sponsored health plans (starting in 1997), Medicare, or military plans are considered to have no health insurance coverage. Persons with only Indian Health Service coverage are considered to have no health insurance coverage.

[f]MSA is metropolitan statistical area. Starting with 2005–2006 data, MSA status is determined using 2000 census data and the 2000 standards for defining MSAs.

SOURCE: "Table 64. No Health Care Visits to an Office or Clinic within the Past 12 Months among Children under Age 18, by Selected Characteristics: United States, Average Annual, Selected Years 1997–1998 through 2014–2015," in *Health, United States, 2016: With Chartbook on Long-Term Trends in Health*, Centers for Disease Control and Prevention, National Center for Health Statistics, May 2017, https://www.cdc.gov/nchs/data/hus/hus16.pdf (accessed August 25, 2017)

The Uninsured

Figure 8.1 shows the uninsured rate between 2008 and 2015. This figure is based on information from the Census Bureau's American Community Survey (ACS). It provides a slightly different, although consistent, picture of the uninsured than do other tables and figures in this chapter (including Table 8.9) that are based on data from the Census Bureau's Current Population Survey (CPS).

(When not otherwise noted, Census Bureau data in this chapter are derived from the CPS.) Based on ACS data, the percentage of the population that was uninsured fluctuated between 13% and 16% between 2008 and 2013, before falling dramatically, to 9.4%, in 2015. The decline in the uninsured rate was likely caused by two main factors: the country's emergence from the Great Recession (which officially lasted from December

TABLE 8.9

Number and percentage of people, by health insurance status, 2013–15

[Numbers in thousands, margins of error in thousands or percentage points as appropriate. Population as of March of the following year.]

Coverage type	2013				2014				2015				Change			
													2015 less 2014		2015 less 2013	
	Number	MOE[a] (±)	Rate	MOE[a] (±)	Number	MOE[a] (±)	Rate	MOE[a] (±)	Number	MOE[a] (±)	Rate	MOE[a] (±)	Number	Rate	Number	Rate
Any health plan	**271,606**	**636**	**86.7**	**0.2**	**283,200**	**568**	**89.6**	**0.2**	**289,903**	**650**	**90.9**	**0.2**	**6,702***	**1.3***	**18,297***	**4.3***
Any private plan[b, c]	201,038	1,140	64.1	0.4	208,600	1,221	66.0	0.4	214,238	1,118	67.2	0.4	5,639*	1.2*	13,201*	3.0*
Employment-based[b]	174,418	1,160	55.7	0.4	175,027	1,188	55.4	0.4	177,540	1,229	55.7	0.4	2,513*	0.3	3,122*	Z
Direct-purchase[b]	35,755	615	11.4	0.2	46,165	798	14.6	0.3	52,057	916	16.3	0.3	5,891*	1.7*	16,302*	4.9*
Any government plan[b, d]	108,287	1,115	34.6	0.4	115,470	1,035	36.5	0.3	118,395	1,067	37.1	0.3	2,924*	0.6*	10,107*	2.6*
Medicare[b]	49,020	377	15.6	0.1	50,546	339	16.0	0.1	51,865	308	16.3	0.1	1,319*	0.3*	2,845*	0.6*
Medicaid[b]	54,919	969	17.5	0.3	61,650	931	19.5	0.3	62,384	917	19.6	0.3	734	0.1	7,465*	2.0*
Military health care[b, e]	14,016	595	4.5	0.2	14,143	568	4.5	0.2	14,849	626	4.7	0.2	706	0.2	833	0.2
Uninsured[f]	**41,795**	**614**	**13.3**	**0.2**	**32,968**	**561**	**10.4**	**0.2**	**28,966**	**634**	**9.1**	**0.2**	**−4,002***	**21.3***	**−12,829***	**−4.3***

MOE = margin of error

*Changes between the estimates are statistically different from zero at the 90 percent confidence level.

Z Represents or rounds to zero.

[a]A margin of error (MOE) is a measure of an estimate's variability. The larger the MOE in relation to the size of the estimate, the less reliable the estimate. This number, when added to and subtracted from the estimate, forms the 90 percent confidence interval. MOEs shown in this table are based on standard errors calculated using replicate weights.

[b]The estimates by type of coverage are not mutually exclusive; people can be covered by more than one type of health insurance during the year.

[c]Private health insurance includes coverage provided through an employer or union, coverage purchased directly by an individual from an insurance company, or coverage through someone outside the household.

[d]Government health insurance coverage includes Medicaid, Medicare, TRICARE, CHAMPVA (Civilian Health and Medical Program of the Department of Veterans Affairs), and care provided by the Department of Veterans Affairs and the military.

[e]Military health care includes TRICARE and CHAMPVA (Civilian Health and Medical Program of the Department of Veterans Affairs), as well as care provided by the Department of Veterans Affairs and the military.

[f]Individuals are considered to be uninsured if they do not have health insurance coverage for the entire calendar year.

SOURCE: Jessica C. Barnett and Marina S. Vornovitsky, "Table 1. Coverage Numbers and Rates by Type of Health Insurance: 2013 to 2015," in *Health Insurance Coverage in the United States: 2015*, U.S. Census Bureau, September 2016, https://www.census.gov/content/dam/Census/library/publications/2016/demo/p60-257.pdf (accessed August 25, 2017)

FIGURE 8.1

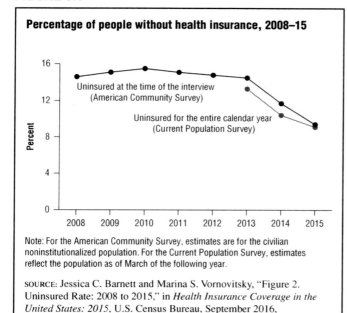

Percentage of people without health insurance, 2008–15

Uninsured at the time of the interview
(American Community Survey)

Uninsured for the entire calendar year
(Current Population Survey)

Note: For the American Community Survey, estimates are for the civilian noninstitutionalized population. For the Current Population Survey, estimates reflect the population as of March of the following year.

SOURCE: Jessica C. Barnett and Marina S. Vornovitsky, "Figure 2. Uninsured Rate: 2008 to 2015," in *Health Insurance Coverage in the United States: 2015*, U.S. Census Bureau, September 2016, https://www.census.gov/content/dam/Census/library/publications/2016/demo/p60-257.pdf (accessed August 25, 2017)

2007 to June 2009), a period when millions of people had lost their jobs and, in many cases, the health insurance benefits that were tied to those jobs; and the implementation of the Patient Protection and Affordable Care Act, which was passed in 2010 but not fully instated until 2014.

Although the percentage of people nationwide who had no health insurance in 2015 was 9.1% according to the CPS and 9.4% according to the ACS, the percentage varied significantly by state. Some of the states with the highest uninsured rates also had very large populations, as Figure 8.2 (based on data from the ACS) shows. In 2015 approximately 14% or more of the populations of Texas (the nation's second-largest state by population) and Alaska were uninsured; in five states (Florida, Georgia, Mississippi, Oklahoma, and Nevada) the uninsured accounted for between 12% and 13.9% of the total population; and in 12 states (Alabama, Arizona, Idaho, Louisiana, Montana, New Mexico, North Carolina, South Carolina, South Dakota, Tennessee, Utah, and Wyoming) the uninsured rate hovered between 10% and 11.9% of the total population. Table 8.10 (also based on data from the ACS) shows that 4.6 million people in Texas, 3.3 million people in California, 2.7 million people in Florida, 1.4 million people in Georgia, 1.4 million people in New York, and 1.1 million in North Carolina were without health insurance coverage in 2015.

Because most low- and middle-income children were eligible for health insurance through Medicaid or CHIP in 2015, and because all people aged 65 years and older were

eligible for health insurance through Medicare, the uninsured population at that time primarily consisted of those between the ages of 19 and 64 years old. (See Figure 8.3.) The percentage of the population without insurance climbed between ages 19 and 23, peaked through age 26, and then fell more or less steadily through age 64. This is consistent with overall career patterns: as people move through their prime working years, they tend to advance in both pay and benefit levels, making it more likely that they will have access to employer-based insurance or the employer-based insurance of a spouse or partner. As Table 8.11 shows, in 2015 people became steadily more likely to have private insurance the older they were. Roughly six out of 10 (62.3%) of those under the age of 18 years were covered by private insurance, and just over four out of 10 (43%) were covered by government-funded insurance. The private insurance rate rose for those between ages 19 and 25 (69.9%) and for those between ages 26 and 34 (69.6%), the years that people are most likely to be uninsured. Past age 35 people were significantly more likely than younger adults to have private insurance. Almost all of those aged 65 years and older had government health insurance through Medicare. Nonetheless, 52.1% of those aged 65 years and older retained private insurance, usually in addition to Medicare.

Unsurprisingly, the likelihood that an individual will be uninsured or receive insurance through the government is directly proportional to household income levels. As Table 8.12 shows, those living in households making less than $25,000 in 2015 were the most likely group to receive insurance through the government (66.6% did so), but they were also the group most likely to be uninsured (14.8%). Both the percentage of those with government health insurance (50.8%) and with no insurance (12.5%) were slightly lower for individuals in households making between $25,000 and $49,999; and these percentages were lower again in households making $50,000 to $74,999 (34.6% and 9.6%), $75,000 to $99,999 (27.2% and 7.3%), and $100,000 or more (19.1% and 4.5%).

The likelihood that one will be uninsured varies significantly by other demographic characteristics as well. By race and Hispanic origin, non-Hispanic whites and Asian Americans were less likely to be uninsured than other groups. (See Figure 8.4.) A dramatically higher percentage of the adult Hispanic population, and a significantly higher percentage of the child Hispanic population, were uninsured than were adults and children of other racial and ethnic groups. This might be because many Hispanics in the United States are not citizens, and 28.9% of adult noncitizens and 17.4% of child noncitizens were uninsured in 2015.

FIGURE 8.2

Percentage of population without health insurance, by state, 2015

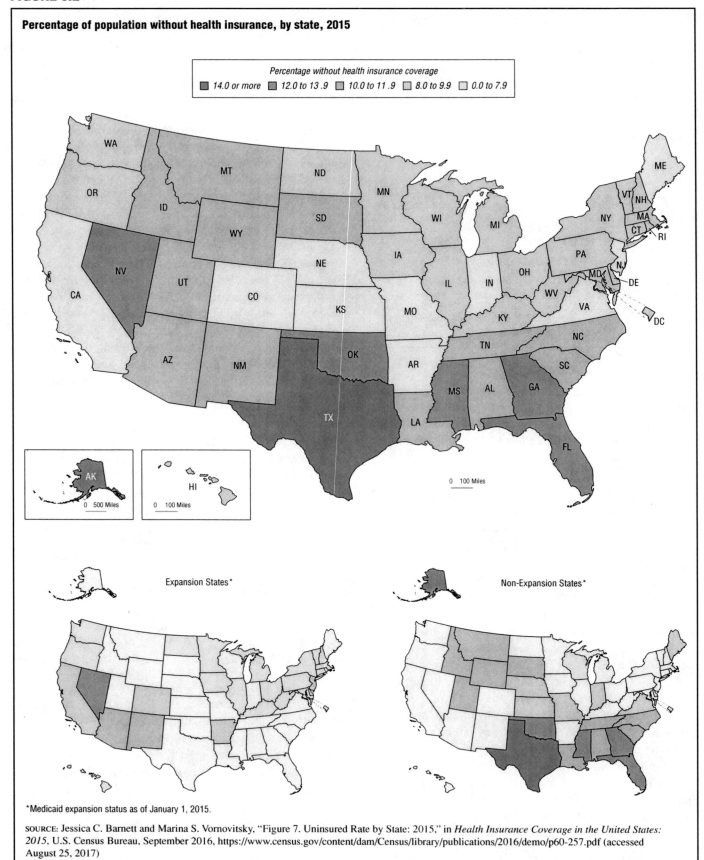

*Medicaid expansion status as of January 1, 2015.

SOURCE: Jessica C. Barnett and Marina S. Vornovitsky, "Figure 7. Uninsured Rate by State: 2015," in *Health Insurance Coverage in the United States: 2015*, U.S. Census Bureau, September 2016, https://www.census.gov/content/dam/Census/library/publications/2016/demo/p60-257.pdf (accessed August 25, 2017)

TABLE 8.10

Number and percentage of population without health insurance, by state, 2013–15

[Numbers in thousands. Civilian noninstitutionalized population.]

State	Medicaid expansion state? Yes (Y) or No (N)[a]	2013 uninsured		2014 uninsured		2015 uninsured		Difference in uninsured (2015 less 2014)		Difference in uninsured (2015 less 2013)	
		Number	Percent	Number	Percent	Number	Percent	Number	Percent	Number	Percent
United States		45,181	14.5	36,670	11.7	29,578	9.4	−6,913*	−2.3*	−15,423*	−5.1*
Alabama	N	645	13.6	579	12.1	484	10.1	−95*	−2.0*	−161*	−3.4*
Alaska	N	132	18.5	122	17.2	106	14.9	−16*	−2.3*	−26*	−3.7*
Arizona	Y	1,118	17.1	903	13.6	728	10.8	−175*	−2.8*	−390*	−6.3*
Arkansas	Y	465	16.0	343	11.8	278	9.5	−66*	−2.3*	−187*	−6.5*
California	Y	6,500	17.2	4,767	12.4	3,317	8.6	−1,449*	−3.9*	−3,183*	−8.6*
Colorado	Y	729	14.1	543	10.3	433	8.1	−110*	−2.2*	−297*	−6.0*
Connecticut	Y	333	9.4	245	6.9	211	6.0	−35*	−1.0*	−122*	−3.4*
Delaware	Y	83	9.1	72	7.8	54	5.9	−17*	−1.9*	−29*	−3.3*
District of Columbia	Y	42	6.7	34	5.3	25	3.8	−9*	−1.5*	−17*	−2.9*
Florida	N	3,853	20.0	3,245	16.6	2,662	13.3	−584*	−3.2*	−1,191*	−6.7*
Georgia	N	1,846	18.8	1,568	15.8	1,388	13.9	−180*	−2.0*	−458*	−5.0*
Hawaii	Y	91	6.7	72	5.3	55	4.0	−18*	−1.3*	−36*	−2.8*
Idaho	N	257	16.2	219	13.6	180	11.0	−38*	−2.5*	−77*	−5.1*
Illinois	Y	1,618	12.7	1,238	9.7	900	7.1	−338*	−2.6*	−718*	−5.6*
Indiana	N	903	14.0	776	11.9	628	9.6	−148*	−2.3*	−275*	−4.3*
Iowa	Y	248	8.1	189	6.2	155	5.0	−34*	−1.1*	−93*	−3.1*
Kansas	N	348	12.3	291	10.2	261	9.1	−31*	−1.1*	−88*	−3.1*
Kentucky	Y	616	14.3	366	8.5	261	6.0	−105*	−2.4*	−355*	−8.3*
Louisiana	N	751	16.6	672	14.8	546	11.9	−126*	−2.8*	−206*	−4.7*
Maine	N	147	11.2	134	10.1	111	8.4	−23*	−1.7*	−37*	−2.8*
Maryland	Y	593	10.2	463	7.9	389	6.6	−74*	−1.3*	−204*	−3.6*
Massachusetts	Y	247	3.7	219	3.3	189	2.8	−29*	−0.5*	−57*	−0.9*
Michigan	Y[b]	1,072	11.0	837	8.5	597	6.1	−240*	−2.5*	−475*	−4.9*
Minnesota	Y	440	8.2	317	5.9	245	4.5	−72*	−1.4*	−195*	−3.7*
Mississippi	N	500	17.1	424	14.5	372	12.7	−53*	−1.8*	−128*	−4.4*
Missouri	N	773	13.0	694	11.7	583	9.8	−111*	−1.9*	−190*	−3.3*
Montana	N	165	16.5	143	14.2	119	11.6	−25*	−2.6*	−46*	−4.8*
Nebraska	N	209	11.3	179	9.7	154	8.2	−25*	−1.4*	−55*	−3.1*
Nevada	Y	570	20.7	427	15.2	351	12.3	−76*	−2.9*	−219*	−8.4*
New Hampshire	Y[b]	140	10.7	120	9.2	83	6.3	−37*	−2.8*	−57*	−4.4*
New Jersey	Y	1,160	13.2	965	10.9	771	8.7	−194*	−2.2*	−389*	−4.5*
New Mexico	Y	382	18.6	298	14.5	224	10.9	−74*	−3.6*	−158*	−7.7*
New York	Y	2,070	10.7	1,697	8.7	1,381	7.1	−316*	−1.6*	−689*	−3.6*
North Carolina	N	1,509	15.6	1,276	13.1	1,103	11.2	−173*	−1.9*	−406*	−4.5*
North Dakota	Y	73	10.4	57	7.9	57	7.8	1	−0.1	−16*	−2.6*
Ohio	Y	1,258	11.0	955	8.4	746	6.5	−209*	−1.8*	−511*	−4.5*
Oklahoma	N	666	17.7	584	15.4	533	13.9	−51*	−1.5*	−133*	−3.8*
Oregon	Y	571	14.7	383	9.7	280	7.0	−102*	−2.7*	−291*	−7.6*
Pennsylvania	Y[b]	1,222	9.7	1,065	8.5	802	6.4	−263*	−2.1*	−420*	−3.4*
Rhode Island	Y	120	11.6	77	7.4	59	5.7	−18*	−1.7*	−61*	−5.9*
South Carolina	N	739	15.8	642	13.6	523	10.9	−118*	−2.7*	−216*	−4.9*
South Dakota	N	93	11.3	82	9.8	86	10.2	4	0.4	−7	−1.1*
Tennessee	N	887	13.9	776	12.0	667	10.3	−109*	−1.8*	−219*	−3.6*
Texas	N	5,748	22.1	5,047	19.1	4,615	17.1	−432*	−2.0*	−1,133*	−5.0*
Utah	N	402	14.0	366	12.5	311	10.5	−54*	−2.1*	−91*	−3.5*
Vermont	Y	45	7.2	31	5.0	24	3.8	−7*	−1.1*	−21*	−3.4*
Virginia	N	991	12.3	884	10.9	746	9.1	−137*	−1.7*	−244*	−3.2*
Washington	Y	960	14.0	643	9.2	468	6.6	−175*	−2.6*	−492*	−7.4*
West Virginia	Y	255	14.0	156	8.6	108	6.0	−48*	−2.6*	−147*	−8.0*
Wisconsin	N	518	9.1	418	7.3	323	5.7	−95*	−1.7*	−195*	−3.5*
Wyoming	N	77	13.4	69	12.0	66	11.5	−2	−0.4	−11*	−1.9*

*Statistically different from zero at the 90 percent confidence level.
[a]Medicaid expansion status as of January 1, 2015.
[b]Expanded Medicaid eligibility between January 1, 2014, and January 1, 2015.
Note: Differences are calculated with unrounded numbers, which may produce different results from using the rounded values in the table.

SOURCE: Adapted from Jessica C. Barnett and Marina S. Vornovitsky, "Table A-1. Population without Health Insurance Coverage by State: 2013 to 2015," in *Health Insurance Coverage in the United States: 2015*, U.S. Census Bureau, September 2016, https://www.census.gov/content/dam/Census/library/publications/2016/demo/p60-257.pdf (accessed August 25, 2017).

The Patient Protection and Affordable Care Act

The health care reform effort spearheaded by the administration of President Barack Obama (1961–) took the form of the Patient Protection and Affordable Care Act (typically referred to as the Affordable Care Act [ACA], or Obamacare). The ACA, which was signed into law in

FIGURE 8.3

Percentage of population without health insurance, by age, 2013–15

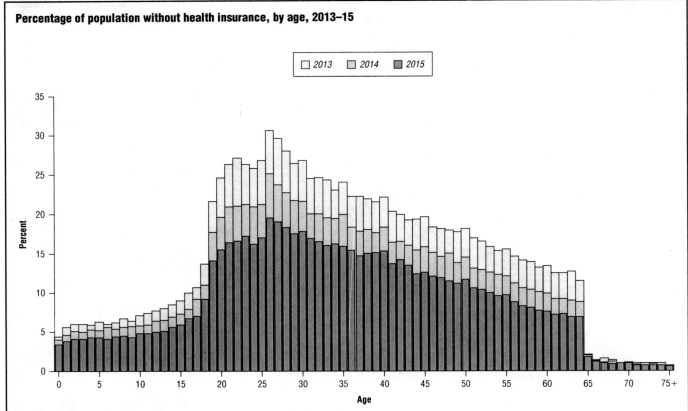

SOURCE: Jessica C. Barnett and Marina S. Vornovitsky, "Figure 4. Uninsured Rate by Single Year of Age: 2013 to 2015," in *Health Insurance Coverage in the United States: 2015*, U.S. Census Bureau, September 2016, https://www.census.gov/content/dam/Census/library/publications/2016/demo/p60-257.pdf (accessed August 25, 2017)

2010 and fully implemented over the next four years, sought to make insurance more affordable for low- and middle-income workers who did not receive coverage through their employers. It also sought to expand the number of low-income people who receive coverage through Medicaid. This was accomplished by extending to most households making less than 400% of poverty subsidies that could be used to purchase individual insurance through websites run by either state governments or the federal government. The ACA's expansion of Medicaid involved raising the income thresholds used to determine eligibility so that coverage would be available to all adults living below 138% of poverty, whereas Medicaid in most states had previously covered only certain adults with dependent children. Between the provision of subsidies to those purchasing individual policies and the expansion of Medicaid, near-universal health care coverage was considered an attainable eventuality.

Opponents of the ACA, however, mounted a two-part legal challenge to the law's constitutionality, and their case was eventually heard by the U.S. Supreme Court in *National Federation of Independent Business v. Sebelius* (567 U.S.___ [2012]). The Kaiser Family Foundation

(KFF) explains in "A Guide to the Supreme Court's Affordable Care Act Decision" (July 2012, http://kaiser familyfoundation.files.wordpress.com/2013/01/8332.pdf) that the plaintiffs in the case were in reality a combined set of plaintiffs from two separate lawsuits originally filed in Florida immediately after the law's passage. One group consisted of the state of Florida and 25 other states whose attorneys general opposed the law, and the other group consisted of the National Federation of Independent Business (a conservative lobbying group that advances the interests of small business owners), along with individuals who did not have insurance coverage. Both groups named Kathleen Sebelius (1948–), the secretary of the U.S. Department of Health and Human Services (the federal agency responsible for implementing the ACA), as the defendant in their cases. The U.S. Supreme Court heard both cases together and issued its ruling in June 2012.

One legal challenge to the ACA centered on the so-called individual mandate, a law that required all U.S. residents who did not receive health insurance through their employers or through public programs to purchase an individual policy or pay a fine. The purpose of the individual mandate was to add young and healthy people to the pool of individuals who bought their coverage

TABLE 8.11

Type of health insurance, by age, 2014 and 2015

[Numbers in thousands, margins of error in percentage points. Population as of March of the following year.]

Characteristic	Total Number 2014	Total Number 2015	Any health insurance Percent 2014	Any health insurance Percent 2015	Change (2015 less 2014)[a,*]	Private health insurance[b] Percent 2014	Private health insurance[b] Percent 2015	Change (2015 less 2014)[a,*]	Government health insurance[c] Percent 2014	Government health insurance[c] Percent 2015	Change (2015 less 2014)[a,*]	Uninsured[d] Percent 2014	Uninsured[d] Percent 2015	Change (2015 less 2014)[a,*]
Total	316,168	318,868	89.6	90.9	1.3*	66.0	67.2	1.2*	36.5	37.1	0.6*	10.4	9.1	−1.3*
Age														
Under age 65	270,174	271,322	88.0	89.5	1.5*	68.2	69.8	1.6*	26.8	27.2	0.4	12.0	10.5	−1.5*
Under age 18	73,920	74,062	94.0	94.8	0.8*	60.6	62.3	1.6*	43.1	43.0	−0.1	6.0	5.2	−0.8*
Under age 19[e]	78,119	78,182	93.8	94.7	0.9*	61.0	62.6	1.6*	42.6	42.6	Z	6.2	5.3	−0.9*
Aged 18 to 64	196,254	197,260	85.8	87.5	1.7*	71.1	72.7	1.6*	20.7	21.3	0.6*	14.2	12.5	−1.7*
Aged 19 to 64	192,055	193,140	85.7	87.4	1.7*	71.1	72.7	1.6*	20.4	21.0	0.6*	14.3	12.6	−1.7*
Aged 19 to 25[f]	30,508	30,475	82.9	85.5	2.6*	67.5	69.9	2.4*	22.1	23.0	1.0	17.1	14.5	−2.6*
Aged 26 to 34	38,415	38,960	81.8	83.7	1.9*	67.2	69.6	2.4*	20.3	20.1	−0.3	18.2	16.3	−1.9*
Aged 35 to 44	39,919	40,005	84.6	86.3	1.7*	71.5	72.7	1.2*	18.2	19.3	1.2*	15.4	13.7	−1.7*
Aged 45 to 64	83,213	83,701	89.0	90.4	1.3*	74.1	75.3	1.2*	20.9	21.4	0.5	11.0	9.6	−1.3*
Aged 65 and older	45,994	47,547	98.6	98.9	0.3*	52.8	52.1	−0.7	93.6	93.8	0.2	1.4	1.1	−0.3*

*Changes between the estimates are statistically different from zero at the 90 percent confidence level.
Z Represents or rounds to zero.
[a]Details may not sum to totals because of rounding.
[b]Private health insurance includes coverage provided through an employer or union, coverage purchased directly by an individual from an insurance company, or coverage through someone outside the household.
[c]Government health insurance coverage includes Medicaid, Medicare, TRICARE, CHAMPVA (Civilian Health and Medical Program of the Department of Veterans Affairs), and care provided by the Department of Veterans Affairs and the military.
[d]Individuals are considered to be uninsured if they do not have health insurance coverage for the entire calendar year.
[e]Children under the age of 19 are eligible for Medicaid/CHIP.
[f]This age is of special interest because of the Affordable Care Act's dependent coverage provision. Individuals aged 19 to 25 may be eligible to be a dependent on a parent's health insurance plan.
Note: The estimates by type of coverage are *not* mutually exclusive; people can be covered by more than one type of health insurance during the year.

SOURCE: Adapted from Jessica C. Barnett and Marina S. Vornovitsky, "Table 2. Percentage of People by Type of Health Insurance Coverage by Age: 2014 and 2015," in *Health Insurance Coverage in the United States: 2015*, U.S. Census Bureau, September 2016, https://www.census.gov/content/dam/Census/library/publications/2016/demo/p60-257.pdf (accessed August 25, 2017)

directly from insurers, which was a necessary development if the individual insurance market was to become affordable enough for a majority of potential purchasers.

Prior to the ACA's implementation, the market for individual coverage included a disproportionate number of older people and those with existing health problems. Such policies have historically been costly because insurers raise premiums (the monthly amount paid by the customer to obtain coverage) to account for the high costs of insuring those who need extensive medical care. An influx of young and healthy policyholders would, according to the ACA's architects, balance out the overall pool of individual policyholders, allowing insurance companies to lower rates to an entire state's pool of individual applicants regardless of their individual health status.

The logic of the individual mandate mirrored the logic of group coverage offered by businesses, which similarly spreads risk (the risk that any one individual will need high-cost medical treatment) among a group of people. Companies offer coverage to the whole group at rates lower than would be obtainable by the sickest members of the group if they were purchasing it on their own. In many cases the healthiest members of a group pay more than they might if coverage were based on their level of health. Nonetheless, because all people will experience worsening health over time, everyone eventually benefits from the spreading of risk. The individual mandate extended this concept to the state level.

The second key challenge to the ACA in *National Federation of Independent Business v. Sebelius* centered on the Medicaid expansion. Medicaid is a joint federal-state program, whereby the federal and state governments share costs and the states oversee administration. Prior to the ACA, Medicaid eligibility varied by state, with eligibility standards set in relation to the federal poverty level. Some states offered coverage to adults at or even above the poverty line, but many states restricted eligibility to adults with dependent children in households making half or less of poverty. By expanding eligibility to almost all Americans under the age of 65 years whose incomes were below 138% of poverty, the ACA was expected to result in the extension of health coverage to approximately 17 million low-income people.

National Federation of Independent Business v. Sebelius challenged both the individual mandate and the Medicaid expansion on constitutional grounds. The plaintiffs argued that the government had no authority to force individuals to purchase a product or service from a company and that the federal government's insistence that

TABLE 8.12

Type of health insurance, by household income and poverty level, 2014 and 2015

[Numbers in thousands, margins of error in percentage points. Population as of March of the following year.]

Characteristic	Total Number		Any health insurance			Private health insurance[b]			Government health insurance[c]			Uninsured		
			Percent		Change (2015 less 2014)[a,*]	Percent		Change (2015 less 2014)[a,*]	Percent		Change (2015 less 2014)[a,*]	Percent		Change (2015 less 2014)[a,*]
	2014	2015	2014	2015		2014	2015		2014	2015		2014	2015	
Total	316,168	318,868	89.6	90.9	1.3*	66.0	67.2	1.2*	36.5	37.1	0.6*	10.4	9.1	−1.3*
Household income														
Less than $25,000	55,212	51,999	83.4	85.2	1.7*	30.1	30.8	0.7	65.3	66.6	1.3*	16.6	14.8	−1.7*
$25,000 to $49,999	67,311	65,289	85.9	87.5	1.6*	52.6	53.2	0.6	48.6	50.8	2.2*	14.1	12.5	−1.6*
$50,000 to $74,999	55,664	55,131	89.3	90.4	1.1*	70.6	70.4	−0.2	32.9	34.6	1.7*	10.7	9.6	−1.1*
$75,000 to $99,999	41,294	43,123	92.0	92.7	0.7*	79.4	79.7	0.3	25.4	27.2	1.9*	8.0	7.3	−0.7*
$100,000 or more	96,687	103,328	94.7	95.5	0.8*	87.4	87.4	Z	18.5	19.1	0.6	5.3	4.5	−0.8*
Income-to-poverty ratio														
Below 100 percent of poverty	46,657	43,123	80.7	82.6	2.0*	26.8	28.6	1.8*	61.3	62.1	0.8	19.3	17.4	−2.0*
Below 138 percent of poverty	68,885	64,711	81.9	83.6	1.8*	30.5	32.1	1.6*	60.5	61.4	0.9	18.1	16.4	−1.8*
Between 100 and 199 percent of poverty	58,686	57,770	84.9	86.4	1.5*	46.5	46.5	Z	52.2	53.8	1.6*	15.1	13.6	−1.5*
Between 200 and 299 percent of poverty	51,451	49,668	88.3	90.2	1.8*	67.3	66.9	−0.4	35.9	38.8	3.0*	11.7	9.8	−1.8*
Between 300 and 399 percent of poverty	40,822	41,691	91.6	92.7	1.1*	77.2	78.3	1.1*	28.0	29.8	1.8*	8.4	7.3	−1.1*
At or above 400 percent of poverty	118,187	126,202	95.2	95.5	0.3*	86.8	86.4	−0.4	22.1	22.6	0.5	4.8	4.5	−0.3*

*Changes between the estimates are statistically different from zero at the 90 percent confidence level.

Z Represents or rounds to zero.

[a]Details may not sum to totals because of rounding.

[b]Private health insurance includes coverage provided through an employer or union, coverage purchased directly by an individual from an insurance company, or coverage through someone outside the household.

[c]Government health insurance coverage includes Medicaid, Medicare, TRICARE, CHAMPVA (Civilian Health and Medical Program of the Department of Veterans Affairs), and care provided by the Department of Veterans Affairs and the military.

Note: The estimates by type of coverage are *not* mutually exclusive; people can be covered by more than one type of health insurance during the year.

SOURCE: Adapted from Jessica C. Barnett and Marina S. Vornovitsky, "Table 4. Percentage of People by Type of Health Insurance Coverage by Household Income and Income-to-Poverty Ratio: 2014 and 2015," in *Health Insurance Coverage in the United States: 2015*, U.S. Census Bureau, September 2016, https://www.census.gov/content/dam/Census/library/publications/2016/demo/p60-257.pdf (accessed August 25, 2017).

states expand their Medicaid coverage (which would ultimately create new costs and administrative responsibilities for the states, although the federal government would initially pay for 100% of the costs of expansion) represented an unconstitutionally coercive act by the federal government.

As the KFF notes, in a 5–4 decision written by Chief Justice John Roberts (1955–), the Supreme Court upheld the constitutionality of the individual mandate, ruling that the fines imposed on those who refused to purchase insurance represented an acceptable form of taxation. By a 7–2 majority, the court ruled that the Medicaid expansion was, as the plaintiffs had argued, an unconstitutionally coercive act by the federal government. However, the same 5–4 majority that upheld the individual mandate ruled that the coercive nature of the Medicaid expansion could be remedied by allowing the states to decide for themselves whether or not to participate. The implementation of the ACA thus proceeded over the following year and a half, taking full effect in 2014.

Medicaid

Medicaid, which is authorized under Title XIX of the Social Security Act, is a federal-state program that provides free medical insurance for low-income people. Within federal guidelines, each state designs and administers its own program. For this reason, there may be considerable differences from state to state as to who is covered, what type of coverage is provided, and how much is paid for medical services. As noted earlier, some states have historically gone beyond the minimum eligibility requirements established by the federal government, and some continue to extend eligibility above the income threshold of 138% established by the ACA.

As a result of the Medicaid portion of the Supreme Court's ACA ruling, a number of states chose not to participate in the Medicaid expansion. According to the KFF, in "Status of State Action on the Medicaid Expansion Decision" (https://www.kff.org/health-reform/state-indicator/state-activity-around-expanding-medicaid-under-the-affordable-care-act), as of January 1, 2017, the District of Columbia and 31 states had adopted the Medicaid

FIGURE 8.4

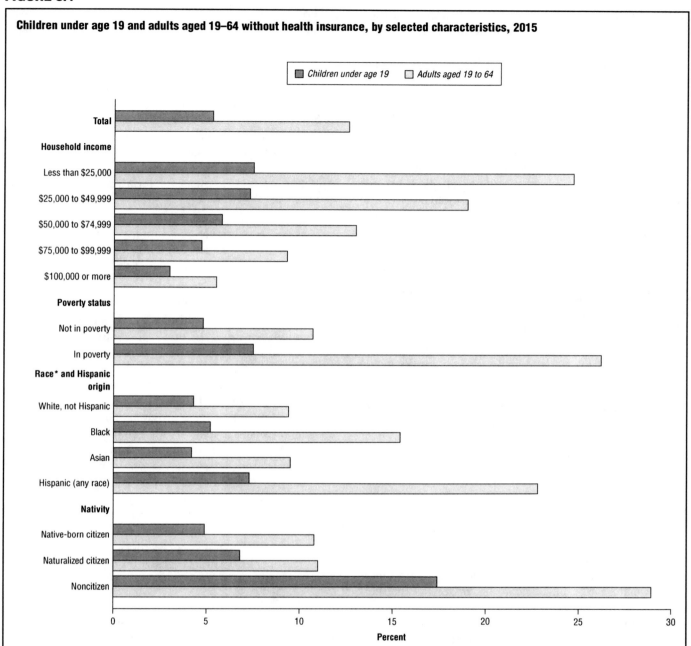

Children under age 19 and adults aged 19–64 without health insurance, by selected characteristics, 2015

□ Children under age 19   □ Adults aged 19 to 64

Total

Household income

Less than $25,000

$25,000 to $49,999

$50,000 to $74,999

$75,000 to $99,999

$100,000 or more

Poverty status

Not in poverty

In poverty

Race* and Hispanic origin

White, not Hispanic

Black

Asian

Hispanic (any race)

Nativity

Native-born citizen

Naturalized citizen

Noncitizen

Percent

*Federal surveys give respondents the option of reporting more than one race. This figure shows data using the race-alone concept. For example, Asian refers to people who reported Asian and no other race.

SOURCE: Jessica C. Barnett and Marina S. Vornovitsky, "Figure 6. Children under Age 19 and Adults Aged 19 to 64 Years without Health Insurance Coverage by Selected Characteristics: 2015," in *Health Insurance Coverage in the United States: 2015*, U.S. Census Bureau, September 2016, https://www.census .gov/content/dam/Census/library/publications/2016/demo/p60-257.pdf (accessed August 25, 2017)

expansion: Alaska, Arizona, Arkansas, California, Colorado, Connecticut, Delaware, Hawaii, Illinois, Indiana, Iowa, Kentucky, Louisiana, Maryland, Massachusetts, Michigan, Minnesota, Montana, Nevada, New Hampshire, New Jersey, New Mexico, New York, North Dakota, Ohio, Oregon, Pennsylvania, Rhode Island, Vermont, Washington, and West Virginia. There was no time limit for opting into the Medicaid expansion, so states that had thus far abstained from doing so may reverse course in the future.

Mandatory federal guidelines on eligibility for children and pregnant women apply even in states that have opted not to expand Medicaid under the ACA. The Center on Budget and Policy Priorities explains in "Introduction to Medicaid" (August 16, 2016, http:// www.cbpp.org/files/policybasics-medicaid.pdf) that to receive federal funding, states are required to cover all children under the age of 18 years in families whose incomes fall below 138% of poverty and all pregnant women whose incomes are below 138% of poverty. States are also required to cover most of those disabled and elderly people who receive benefits under the Supplemental Security Income program. Additionally, states are obliged to continue paying benefits to parents whose incomes met eligibility guidelines before the implementation of welfare reform.

Nevertheless, in many of the states that have thus far chosen not to expand Medicaid, very few adults are eligible for coverage, no matter how poor they are. Typically, these states provide no Medicaid coverage at all for adults without children, and they set eligibility for parents of dependent children at a threshold well below the poverty level. For example, the KFF notes in "Medicaid Income Eligibility Limits for Adults as a Percent of the Federal Poverty Level" (http://kff.org/health-reform/state-indicator/medicaid-income-eligibility-limits-for-adults-as-a-percent-of-the-federal-poverty-level) that, as of January 1, 2017, Alabama and Texas provided Medicaid only to parents of dependent children with incomes of 18% of the federal poverty level or less. Other states that provided no coverage for adults without children and that set exceptionally low income thresholds for adults were Missouri, which limited eligibility to parents of dependent children in households with an income of 22% of the federal poverty level, Idaho (26%), Mississippi (27%), Florida (33%), Georgia (37%), Kansas (38%), Virginia (38%), North Carolina (44%), Oklahoma (44%), Utah (44%), South Dakota (51%), Wyoming (56%), Nebraska (63%), and South Carolina (67%).

Additionally, in those states that have not expanded Medicaid, low-income adults (those making 138% or less of the federal poverty level) are not eligible for the subsidized private insurance plans that are available to middle-income individuals in all states. Because the Supreme Court upheld the constitutionality of the individual mandate (the mechanism that underpins the marketplace for subsidized individual policies), all states provide subsidized insurance policies for people making between 138% and 399% of the federal poverty level. Therefore, in those states that have not expanded Medicaid, the poorest adults are typically ineligible for government-funded health insurance, while comparatively wealthier adults are eligible for assistance.

January Angeles and Matthew Broaddus of the Center on Budget and Policy Priorities note in "Federal Government Will Pick Up Nearly All Costs of Health Reform's Medicaid Expansion" (March 28, 2012, http://www.cbpp.org/files/4-20-10health2.pdf) that since the inception of Medicaid, the federal government has paid, on average, 57% of the costs of the program, with states contributing the remainder. Under the ACA, the federal government agreed to pay 100% of the costs of covering newly eligible Medicaid enrollees for the first three years of the expansion (2014 to 2016), and then the federal share of the expansion costs was scheduled to fall slightly. By 2020 the federal government would pay 90% of the costs of all newly eligible individuals, and it would continue to pay this share of the expansion costs indefinitely.

In "Estimates of Eligibility for ACA Coverage among the Uninsured in 2016" (October 18, 2016, https://www.kff.org/health-reform/issue-brief/estimates-of-eligibility-for-aca-coverage-among-the-uninsured-in-2016), Rachel Garfield et al. of the KFF estimate that in 2016 approximately 3.8 million low-income adults and 2.6 million low-income children remained uninsured but eligible for Medicaid under the terms of the ACA. These included people who were eligible under the ACA but whose states had chosen not to adopt the expansion, as well as people who were eligible for Medicaid (either in states that had expanded eligibility or in states that had not expanded eligibility) but who had not enrolled.

Children's Health Insurance Program

The Children's Health Insurance Program (CHIP) was introduced in 1997 in an effort to provide health coverage to uninsured children in families with incomes too high to qualify for Medicaid but too low to afford private health insurance. Authorized under Title XXI of the Social Security Act, CHIP is structured like Medicaid, as a joint federal-state program. The federal government contributes a majority of funding, and the states provide the remainder of funding as well as administration. The federal share of costs typically exceeds that of Medicaid by approximately 15 percentage points. Thus, in a state where the federal government pays the national average of 57% of Medicaid costs, the federal government typically pays 72% of CHIP costs. States may use this money to expand their Medicaid programs, design new child health insurance programs, or create a combination of the two.

The Children's Health Insurance Program Reauthorization Act (CHIPRA) was signed into law by President Obama in February 2009, extending and expanding CHIP. The ACA maintained current levels of CHIP funding through October 1, 2015, after which point the federal share of CHIP funding was scheduled to increase dramatically, to an average of 93% of total costs in each state.

As with Medicaid, states have the ability to set their own eligibility standards for CHIP. However, states must enroll children who meet Medicaid's eligibility requirements in Medicaid rather than in CHIP. Thus, CHIP eligibility typically picks up at the income thresholds where Medicaid cuts off, and it rises above 300% of poverty in some states. According to the KFF, in "Where Are States Today? Medicaid and CHIP Eligibility Levels for Children, Pregnant Women, and Adults" (March 15, 2017, https://www.kff.org/medicaid/fact-sheet/where-are-states-today-medicaid-and-chip/), as of January 2017, only two states—Idaho and North Dakota—had income cutoffs below 200% of the federal poverty level; 30 states had income limits between 200% and 300% of poverty; and 19 states set income requirements greater than 300% of the federal poverty level. States have the option to determine how much, if any, costs are shared by applicant families. Generally, cost-sharing requirements cannot rise above 5% of a family's annual income, and cost-sharing is prohibited for certain services, such as well-baby and well-child visits, which are free to all families enrolled in the program.

ACA Enrollment Statistics

As of late 2017, the ACA had succeeded in substantially reducing the uninsured population, in keeping with its design and in spite of the limitations placed on it by those states that had opted not to expand Medicaid. Sarah R. Collins, Munira Z. Gunja, and Michelle M. Doty of the Commonwealth Fund report in "Following the ACA Repeal-and-Replace Effort, Where Does the U.S. Stand on Insurance Coverage? Findings from the Commonwealth Fund Affordable Care Act Tracking Survey, March–June 2017" (September 7, 2017, http://www.commonwealth fund.org/Publications/Issue-Briefs/2017/Sep/Post-ACA-Repeal-and-Replace-Health-Insurance-Coverage) that during the year following the ACA's initial open enrollment in 2013, the proportion of uninsured Americans between the ages of 19 and 64 years fell from 19.9% to 14.8%. This figure continued to fall over the next two years, to 13.3% in 2015 and 12.7% in 2016, before increasing to 14% in 2017. Collins, Gunja, and Doty note that the uninsured rate was significantly higher in states that declined to expand Medicaid. In states without expanded Medicaid benefits, 19% of adults between the ages of 19 and 64 years were uninsured in 2017, compared with only 11% of adults in that age group living in states that had accepted the Medicaid expansion. Of the roughly 27 million uninsured adults aged 19 to 64 years in 2017, nearly half (48%) had an income below 400% of the poverty threshold, making them eligible for federal subsidies to purchase health insurance.

In the months following the inauguration of President Donald Trump (1946–) in January 2017, the Republican-led Congress made a concerted effort to repeal and replace the ACA. The initial repeal effort came in May of that year, when the U.S. House of Representatives passed the American Health Care Act. That same month the U.S. Senate drafted an alternative bill, the Better Care Reconciliation Act (BCRA). However, Mitch McConnell (1942–; R-KY), the Senate majority leader, was ultimately forced to postpone a vote on the BCRA after the Congressional Budget Office issued a report stating that the proposed bill would increase the number of uninsured Americans by

15 million in 2018. Over the course of the summer Republicans introduced several alternative bills aimed at repealing and replacing the ACA, although all failed to receive the necessary votes to become law.

In October 2017 President Trump signed an executive order that terminated the federal subsidies used to fund health coverage for low-income Americans under the ACA. According to the article "19 States File Lawsuit against Trump over Decision to Halt Obamacare Subsidies" (Associated Press, October 15, 2017), Trump's decision prompted attorneys general from 19 states to file a lawsuit in federal court, on the grounds that halting the subsidies violated the ACA. At the same time, the U.S. senators Lamar Alexander (1940–; R-TN) and Patty Murray (1950–; D-WA) of the Senate Committee on Health, Education, Labor, and Pensions drafted a bipartisan agreement aimed at continuing federal funding for ACA subsidies through an act of Congress. As of October 2017, lawmakers had yet to vote on the proposal.

HEALTH OF THE HOMELESS

The rates of both chronic (long-term) and acute (severe or intense) health problems are disproportionately high among the homeless population. Except for obesity, strokes, and cancer, homeless people are more likely than housed people to suffer from every category of chronic health problems. Other serious illnesses, such as tuberculosis (TB), are almost exclusively associated with the unhealthy living conditions brought on by poverty, and homeless people are especially vulnerable to them. In general, experts agree that homeless individuals suffer from more types of illnesses, for longer periods, and with more harmful consequences than housed people. Meanwhile, delivery of health care is complicated by a patient's homeless status, making management of chronic diseases such as diabetes, HIV, and hypertension more difficult.

Street living comes with a set of health conditions that living in a home does not. Homeless people fall prey to parasites, frostbite, leg ulcers, and infections. They are also at greater risk of physical and psychological trauma resulting from muggings, beatings, and rape. With no safe place to store belongings, the proper storage or administration of medications becomes difficult. In addition, some homeless people with mental disorders may use drugs or alcohol to self-medicate, and those with addictive disorders are more susceptible to HIV and other communicable diseases.

Homeless people may also lack the ability to access some of the basic rituals of self-care: bed rest, adequate nutrition, and good personal hygiene. Infections that are easy to prevent among those able to clean themselves thoroughly and frequently can pose persistent threats to the homeless. Additionally, the ability to rest and recuperate, which is often essential for the recovery process, is almost impossible for homeless people. Not only must they spend time locating places to sleep and food to eat, in many cities it is illegal for them to rest in public, as is discussed in Chapter 7.

Melissa Gambatese et al. note in "Programmatic Impact of 5 Years of Mortality Surveillance of New York City Homeless Populations" (*American Journal of Public Health*, suppl. 2, vol. 103, no. S2, 2013) that homeless individuals' risk of death ranges from 1.5 to 11.5 times greater than that of the population at large. The researchers further report on a study of the causes of death among New York City's homeless population between 2005 and 2010 and find that the leading causes of death were heart disease, drug overdose, accidents, alcohol abuse, and assault/homicide. Heart disease is the leading cause of death for the U.S. population at large, but New York City's homeless population, like homeless people generally, appear much more likely than the general population to die from alcohol and drug-related causes as well as from violence and other external factors.

In "Psychiatric Disorders and Mortality among People in Homeless Shelters in Denmark: A Nationwide Register-Based Cohort Study" (*Lancet*, vol. 377, no. 9784, June 25, 2011), a Danish study of 32,711 homeless people over the course of a decade (1999 to 2009), Sandra Feodor Nielsen et al. assess the degree to which homeless health outcomes differ from those of the general population, particularly in relation to mental health and substance abuse issues. The researchers find that 62.4% of homeless men and 58.2% of homeless women had psychiatric disorders and that 49% of homeless men and 36.9% of homeless women had substance abuse diagnoses. During the 10 years of research, 16.7% of the male study cohort and 9.8% of the female cohort died, and external causes accounted for 27.9% of the deaths for which a cause could be established. Nielsen et al. also find that for homeless men aged 15 to 24 years, life expectancy was 21.6 years lower than that of the corresponding age group in the population at large, and for homeless women aged 15 to 24 years, life expectancy was 17.4 years lower than that of the corresponding age group in the population at large.

Many studies have focused on the rates of prevalence of specific diseases among the homeless. Bonnie D. Kerker et al. find in "A Population-Based Assessment of the Health of Homeless Families in New York City" (*American Journal of Public Health*, vol. 101, no. 3, March 2011) that rates of TB infection among homeless families were three times higher than among housed low-income families. According to Lillian Gelberg et al., in "Prevalence, Distribution, and Correlates of Hepatitis C Virus Infection among Homeless Adults in Los Angeles" (*Public Health Reporter*, vol. 127, no. 4, July–August 2012), 26.7% of homeless people sampled in Los Angeles, California, tested positive for hepatitis C. The researchers

note that the most recent national data at the time of publication indicated a prevalence rate of 1.6% among the population at large. They also note that despite the extremely high rate of infection among the homeless population, approximately half of the cases were unknown and almost all were untreated.

In "Housing Status and the Health of People Living with HIV/AIDS" (*Current HIV/AIDS Report*, vol. 9, no. 4, December 2012), Michael-John Milloy et al. conduct an exhaustive analysis of major academic studies on the subject of HIV/AIDS as it relates to housing status. They note that studies of people living with HIV/AIDS (PLWHA) find that a substantial portion are homeless or living in marginal housing situations such as shelters or hotel rooms. For example, a study of PLWHA in New York City found that 33% were homeless or marginally housed and that during the study 70% of study participants reported housing needs ranging from homelessness to eviction threats to fears of physical violence. A study of PLWHA in Los Angeles found that 13% were homeless or living in marginal housing. A survey of research on the subject found that homeless individuals living with HIV/AIDS consistently receive suboptimal treatment for the disease, which is typically highly treatable through antiretroviral therapy. A study of patients in a public health clinic in Florida found that homeless HIV/AIDS patients were nearly 10 times more likely to die from the disease than HIV/AIDS patients who were housed. A study of 1,661 PLWHA in New York City isolated housing need as a reliable predictor of patients' likelihood of receiving appropriate HIV treatment or any medical care at all. A study conducted in Los Angeles also found that homelessness was the strongest factor predicting whether or not a PLWHA had unmet treatment needs.

Ulla Beijer, Achim Wolf, and Seena Fazel similarly review published research on the correlation of homelessness and disease in "Prevalence of Tuberculosis, Hepatitis C Virus, and HIV in Homeless People: A Systematic Review and Meta-Analysis" (*Lancet Infectious Diseases*, vol. 12, no. 11, November 2012). In 43 studies that together surveyed a total homeless population of 63,812, the prevalence rates for TB ranged from 0.2% to 7.7%, the prevalence rates for hepatitis C ranged from 3.9% to 36.2%, and the prevalence rates for HIV infection ranged from 0.3% to 21.1%. The homeless were thus 34 to 452 times more likely than the general population to have TB, four to 70 times more likely to have hepatitis C, and one to 77 times more likely to be infected with HIV.

Mental Illness and Substance Abuse

Before the 1960s people with chronic mental illness were often committed involuntarily to state psychiatric hospitals. The development of medications that could control the symptoms of mental illness coincided with a growing belief that involuntary hospitalization was warranted only when a mentally ill person posed a threat to him- or herself or to others. Gradually, large numbers of mentally ill people were discharged from hospitals and other treatment facilities. Because the community-based treatment centers that were supposed to take the place of state hospitals were often either inadequate or nonexistent, many of these people ended up living on the streets.

Experts debate the rate of mental disorders among homeless populations, but they generally agree that it is greater among the homeless than the general population. In "The Prevalence of Mental Disorders among the Homeless in Western Countries: Systematic Review and Meta-regression Analysis" (*PLoS Medline*, vol. 5, no. 12, December 2, 2008), Seena Fazel et al. analyze data from 29 surveys of the homeless in Western countries to find the prevalence of mental disorders in this population. The researchers find that the most common mental disorders were alcohol and drug dependence. The prevalence rates of psychosis and depression ranged from 2.8% to 42.3%. Fazel et al. conclude that the prevalence of substance abuse disorder, psychotic disorders, and depression are higher among the homeless population than among the general population.

Mentally ill homeless people present special problems for health care workers. They may not be as cooperative and motivated as other patients. Because of their limited resources, they may have difficulty getting transportation to treatment centers. They frequently forget to show up for appointments or to take medications. The addition of substance abuse can make them unruly or unresponsive. Among people with severe mental disorders, those at greatest risk of homelessness are both the most severely ill and the most difficult to help.

The National Alliance on Mental Illness explains in "Dual Diagnosis" (August 2017, https://www.nami.org/Learn-More/Mental-Health-Conditions/Related-Conditions/Dual-Diagnosis) that mental illness and substance abuse frequently occur together; clinicians call this dual diagnosis. The alliance notes that certain groups, including men, individuals of low SES, military veterans, and people who are frequently ill, are more likely than the general population to abuse drugs and/or alcohol. Each of these groups overlaps considerably with the homeless population.

Traumatic Stress

In "Trauma and Trauma-Informed Care" (March 22, 2017, https://www.samhsa.gov/homelessness-housing/trauma-informed-care), the Substance Abuse and Mental Health Services Administration (SAMHSA) notes that the prevalence of traumatic stress (negative psychological states brought about by having witnessed or been the victim of violence or loss) is high among the homeless. Traumatic stress is particularly damaging for children,

whose early exposure to trauma is one of the most influential links to difficulties in later life. Sarah L. Cristofaro et al. observe in "Measuring Trauma and Stressful Events in Childhood and Adolescence among Patients with First-Episode Psychosis: Initial Factor Structure, Reliability, and Validity of the Trauma Experiences Checklist" (*Psychiatry Research*, vol. 210, no. 2, December 15, 2013) that exposure to traumatic stress has been firmly linked to a multitude of poor mental health and other outcomes, including homelessness and many mental health conditions prevalent among the homeless. Additionally, homelessness itself raises the likelihood that one will experience or witness traumatic incidents.

Violence

VIOLENCE TOWARD HOMELESS WOMEN. In "Correlates of Adult Assault among Homeless Women" (*Journal of Health Care for the Poor and Underserved*, vol. 21, no. 4, November 2010), Angela L. Hudson et al. find that some homeless women are more likely than others to experience violence. Noting that "homeless women are highly susceptible to victimization," the authors cite research that finds that one-third of homeless women reported experiencing sexual assault within the past year and another one-third reported being physically assaulted within the past year. Hudson et al. studied homeless women in Los Angeles to uncover relationships among homeless women's psychological functioning, past victimization, and the likelihood of adult victimization. They determine that mental illness and low self-esteem were important risk factors for physical and sexual victimization among the homeless women in their study. Physical victimization was also associated with a history of physical abuse as a child, and sexual victimization was associated with a history of sexual abuse as a child. Current and previous substance abuse as well as involvement in the sex trade placed homeless women at great risk for physical and sexual victimization.

Suzanne L. Wenzel et al. find in "Sexual Risk among Impoverished Women: Understanding the Role of Housing Status" (*AIDS and Behavior*, vol. 11, supplement 6, November 2007) that impoverished women who are homeless or who have been recently victimized are also more likely to engage in risky sexual behavior that can lead to HIV infection. The researchers indicate that homeless African American and Hispanic women had from two to five times greater odds of engaging in risky sexual behavior than women who were housed.

HATE CRIMES. In *No Safe Street: A Survey of Hate Crimes and Violence Committed against Homeless People in 2014 and 2015* (July 2016, http://nationalhomeless.org/wp-content/uploads/2016/07/HCR-2014-151.pdf), the National Coalition for the Homeless notes that between 1999 and 2015, 1,657 acts of violence against the homeless were reported and that 428 victims of such violence died. Hate crimes against the homeless tend to be committed by males under the age of 30 years, and the targets are also typically male. In 2015, 73% of all homeless hate-crime perpetrators were under 30 years old and 90% were male, whereas 57% of victims were aged 40 years and older and 77% were male. Of the 77 reported hate crimes against homeless people in 2015, 27 resulted in the victim's death.

HEALTH CARE FOR THE HOMELESS

The homeless share the same barriers to health care that low-income housed people do, with the added constraints that come with the instability of life on the streets or in shelters. Prior to the implementation of the ACA, homeless children and some homeless adults had access to health care through Medicaid, and homeless veterans had access to care through the U.S. Department of Veterans Affairs. By attempting to expand Medicaid eligibility to all adults making less than 138% of poverty, the ACA offered the chance to improve health outcomes for the homeless dramatically. This opportunity was limited by the refusal of many states to expand Medicaid, but preliminary data indicate that in states that expanded the program, the homeless were already receiving significantly improved care as of late 2014.

In *Early Impacts of the Medicaid Expansion for the Homeless Population* (November 2014, http://files.kff .org/attachment/early-impacts-of-the-medicaid-expansion-for-the-homeless-population-issue-brief), Barbara DiPietro, Samantha Artiga, and Alexandra Gates of the KFF report on the findings of focus groups that were conducted with administrators, providers, and those helping to enroll the homeless in Medicaid at five homeless-serving organizations across the country. Four of these organizations were located in cities whose state governments had gone forward with the Medicaid expansion (Albuquerque, New Mexico; Baltimore, Maryland; Chicago, Illinois; and Portland, Oregon), and one was located in a city whose state government had not (Jacksonville, Florida). DiPietro, Artiga, and Gates note that the Albuquerque, Baltimore, and Portland organizations reported dramatic increases in the percentage of their homeless clients who had health coverage, whereas the Chicago organization reported significant but less dramatic coverage gains and the Jacksonville organization reported no change in the number of homeless people covered.

The four homeless health care providers in Medicaid expansion states also reported that the acquisition of coverage allowed patients to access "life-saving or life-changing surgeries or treatments," including health interventions that allowed individuals to work and remain housed following their receipt of care. Also, the providers reported that the Medicaid expansion allowed them to practice medicine more effectively, because the funding of care gave them increased options for treatment, whereas prior to the expansion they had to decide on treatment based on what could be done for free (based on resources provided through charity efforts) or at discounted prices. Increased funding of these homeless health care services allowed providers to increase staff size and better allocate resources. The Jacksonville provider of health care to the homeless reported no change in the quality of coverage that it was able to provide. Furthermore, that site was facing increasing financial challenges given the absence of Medicaid funding and a decline in funding from other sources.

Beyond providing care to the homeless through Medicaid and the Department of Veterans Affairs (which funds health care for all veterans, including those who are homeless), the federal government funds homeless health efforts by providing assistance to local organizations under the Health Care for the Homeless (HCH) program, authorized under Title VI of the McKinney-Vento Homeless Assistance Act, which was signed into law in 1987. The Department of Health and Human Services (2017, https://bphc.hrsa.gov/uds/datacenter.aspx ?q=t4&year=2016&state=&fd=ho) indicates that in 2016 it served 886,576 homeless people under the program. The HCH program's goal is to improve the health of homeless individuals and families by improving access to primary health care and substance abuse services. The program provides outreach, counseling to clients explaining available services, case management, and referrals to services such as mental health treatment, housing, benefits, and other critical supports. Access to around-the-clock emergency services is available, as is help in establishing eligibility for assistance and obtaining services under entitlement programs.

IMPORTANT NAMES
AND ADDRESSES

Association of Gospel Rescue Missions
7222 Commerce Center Dr., Ste. 120
Colorado Springs, CO 80919
(719) 266-8300
1-800-473-7283
FAX: (719) 266-8600
E-mail: info@agrm.org
URL: http://www.agrm.org/

Center on Budget and Policy Priorities
820 First St. NE, Ste. 510
Washington, DC 20002
(202) 408-1080
FAX: (202) 408-1056
E-mail: center@cbpp.org
URL: https://www.cbpp.org/

Child Care Aware of America
1515 N. Courthouse Rd., Second Floor
Arlington, VA 22201
1-800-424-2246
URL: http://www.childcareaware.org/

Children's Defense Fund
25 E St. NW
Washington, DC 20001
1-800-233-1200
E-mail: cdfinfo@childrensdefense.org
URL: http://www.childrensdefense.org/

Community Solutions
125 Maiden Ln., Ste. 16C
New York, NY 10038
(646) 797-4370
URL: https://www.community.solutions/

Innocenti Research Centre
United Nations Children's Fund
Piazza SS. Annunziata, 12
Florence, 50122 Italy
(011-39-055) 20330
FAX: (011-39-055) 2033220
E-mail: florence@unicef.org
URL: https://www.unicef-irc.org/

Joint Center for Housing Studies
Harvard University
One Bow St., Ste. 400
Cambridge, MA 02138
(617) 495-7908

FAX: (617) 496-9957
E-mail: jchs@harvard.edu
URL: http://www.jchs.harvard.edu/

Kaiser Family Foundation
2400 Sand Hill Rd.
Menlo Park, CA 94025
(650) 854-9400
FAX: (650) 854-4800
URL: https://www.kff.org/

National Alliance on Mental Illness
3803 N. Fairfax Dr., Ste. 100
Arlington, VA 22203
(703) 524-7600
URL: https://www.nami.org/

National Alliance to End Homelessness
1518 K St. NW, Second Floor
Washington, DC 20005
(202) 638-1526
FAX: (202) 638-4664
E-mail: info@naeh.org
URL: https://endhomelessness.org/

National Center for Children in Poverty
215 W. 125th St., Third Floor
New York, NY 10027
(646) 284-9600
FAX: (646) 284-9623
E-mail: info@nccp.org
URL: http://www.nccp.org/

National Center for Homeless Education
SERVE
5900 Summit Ave., Ste. 201
Browns Summit, NC 27214
1-800-308-2145
FAX: (336) 315-7457
E-mail: homeless@serve.org
URL: http://center.serve.org/nche/

National Center on Family Homelessness
American Institutes for Research
1000 Thomas Jefferson St. NW
Washington, DC 20007
(202) 403-5000
FAX: (885) 459-6213
URL: http://www.air.org/center/national-center-family-homelessness/

National Coalition for the Homeless
2201 P St. NW
Washington, DC 20037
(202) 462-4822
E-mail: info@nationalhomeless.org
URL: http://www.nationalhomeless.org/

National Law Center on Homelessness and Poverty
2000 M St. NW, Ste. 210
Washington, DC 20036
(202) 638-2535
FAX: (202) 628-2737
E-mail: email@nlchp.org
URL: https://www.nlchp.org/

National Low Income Housing Coalition
1000 Vermont Ave., Ste. 500
Washington, DC 20005
(202) 662-1530
FAX: (202) 393-1973
URL: http://www.nlihc.org/

Organisation for Economic Co-operation and Development
2 rue André Pascal
Paris, 75775 CEDEX 16 France
(011-33-1) 45-24-82-00
FAX: (011-33-1) 45-24-85-00
URL: http://www.oecd.org/

Southern Education Foundation
135 Auburn Ave. NE, Second Floor
Atlanta, GA 30303
(404) 523-0001
FAX: (404) 523-6904
E-mail: info@southerneducation.org
URL: http://www.southerneducation.org/

Urban Institute
2100 M St. NW
Washington, DC 20037
(202) 833-7200
URL: https://www.urban.org/

U.S. Conference of Mayors
1620 Eye St. NW
Washington, DC 20006
(202) 293-7330
URL: https://www.usmayors.org/

RESOURCES

The federal government is the premier source of facts on many issues related to social welfare, including poverty, employment, the welfare system, housing, and homelessness. A variety of government agencies and departments provide detailed data related to these issues in the form of reports, websites, and searchable databases.

Data gathered by the U.S. Census Bureau was central to compiling this book. The Census Bureau's searchable web portal American FactFinder was particularly helpful, as were the following reports: *Custodial Mothers and Fathers and Their Child Support: 2013* (Timothy Grall, January 2016), *Income and Poverty in the United States: 2015* (Bernadette D. Proctor, Jessica L. Semega, and Melissa A. Kollar, September 2016), *Dynamics of Economic Well-Being: Poverty, 2009–2011* (Ashley N. Edwards, January 2014), *Health Insurance Coverage in the United States: 2015* (Jessica C. Barnett and Marina S. Vornovitsky, September 2016), and *The Supplemental Poverty Measure: 2015* (Trudi Renwick and Liana Fox, September 2016).

The U.S. Department of Labor's Bureau of Labor Statistics (BLS) provides valuable data on wages and work patterns in its searchable web portal Databases, Tables & Calculators by Subject and its Labor Force Statistics from the Current Population Survey, on which it collaborates with the Census Bureau. The BLS also offers details about low-income workers in *A Profile of the Working Poor, 2015* (April 2017) and about minimum-wage workers in *Characteristics of Minimum Wage Workers, 2016* (April 2017). The Department of Labor's Employment and Training Administration offers data on unemployment compensation claims in *Unemployment Insurance Data Summary* (2017) and detailed historical data pertaining to the recipients of unemployment compensation in *UI Benefits Study: Recent Changes in the Characteristics of Unemployed Workers* (Marios Michaelides, August 2009).

The U.S. Department of Housing and Urban Development (HUD) is the source for much valuable data on homelessness, housing affordability, and subsidized housing programs. Among the HUD publications used in this book are *The 2016 Annual Homeless Assessment Report (AHAR) to Congress—Part 1: Point-in-Time Estimates of Homelessness* (Meghan Henry et al., November 2016), *The 2015 Annual Homeless Assessment Report (AHAR) to Congress—Part 2: Estimates of Homelessness in the United States* (Claudia D. Solari et al., October 2016), *HUD's Proposed 2018 Budget: Congressional Justifications* (May 2017), and *Worst Case Housing Needs: 2015 Report to Congress* (Barry L. Steffen et al., April 2015).

Important data on federal nutrition programs came from the U.S. Department of Agriculture's (USDA) Food and Nutrition Service, which provides detailed tables about the National School Lunch Program, the School Breakfast Program, the Supplemental Nutrition Assistance Program, and the Special Supplemental Nutrition Program for Women, Infants, and Children. Additionally, the USDA's Economic Research Service provides data on those Americans whose food needs either go unmet or are in danger of going unmet in *Household Food Security in the United States in 2015* (Alisha Coleman-Jensen et al., September 2016).

Other valuable data came from the U.S. Department of Health and Human Services' (HHS) Office of Family Assistance, in particular the report *Temporary Assistance for Needy Families Program (TANF): Eleventh Report to Congress* (April 2016). The Centers for Disease Control and Prevention (CDC), which is also a part of HHS, was a valuable source of data on health care and illness. The CDC's National Center for Health Statistics report *Health, United States, 2016: With Chartbook on Long-Term Trends in Health* (May 2017) offers particularly useful insights into the connections between poverty and health.

Many different organizations study the poor and homeless. Notable among them for their many studies on poverty and homelessness are the Urban Institute (UI) and the Center on Budget and Policy Priorities (CBPP). The UI publications used in preparing this volume include *TANF Recipients with Barriers to Employment* (Dan Bloom, Pamela J. Loprest, and Sheila R. Zedlewski, July 2011), *How Has the TANF Caseload Changed over Time?* (Pamela J. Loprest, March 2012), *SNAP's Role in the Great Recession and Beyond* (Sheila Zedlewski, Elaine Waxman, and Craig Gundersen, July 2012), *Evaluation of the 100,000 Homes Campaign* (Josh Leopold and Helen Ho, February 2015), and *Welfare Rules Databook: State TANF Policies as of July 2015* (Elissa Cohen et al., September 2016). The CBPP publications that were useful in compiling this book include *Chart Book: TANF at 20* (August 2016), *A Guide to Statistics on Historical Trends in Income Inequality* (Chad Stone et al., September 2017), *How States Use Funds under the TANF Block Grant* (Liz Schott and Ife Finch, January 2017), and *Contrary to "Entitlement Society" Rhetoric, over Nine-Tenths of Entitlement Benefits Go to Elderly, Disabled, or Working Households* (Arloc Sherman, Robert Greenstein, and Kathy Ruffing, February 2012), and the "Policy Basics" features on its website provide up-to-date overviews of all major federal public assistance programs.

Additional information on poverty, homelessness, and related issues came from a variety of organizations, including the Association of Gospel Rescue Missions, the National Center for Homeless Education, the National Alliance to End Homelessness, the National Coalition for the Homeless, the National Law Center on Homelessness and Poverty, the U.S. Conference of Mayors, the Joint Center for Housing Studies of Harvard University, the Kaiser Family Foundation, and the Innocenti Research Centre of the United Nations Children's Fund.

INDEX

military veterans homelessness, 110t
minimum wage, 73t
minimum wage workers, 74t
official poverty measure vs.
Supplemental Poverty Measure, 11t, 12t
official poverty measure vs.
Supplemental Poverty Measure, by age, 12f
opposite-sex unmarried couples, demographic characteristics of, 37t–38t
permanent supportive housing beds inventory, 103(f5.2)
poverty, by age, 7f, 9f
poverty, by demographic characteristics, 8t
poverty, by employment status, 47t
poverty, by family status, 4t–5t, 32t
poverty and labor market problems of workers, 51t
poverty guidelines, 3t
poverty of custodial parents, 46f
psychological distress, by poverty level, 142(t8.2)
rental housing costs, 118t, 119(t6.2), 120t, 121t
single-parent families, demographics of, 40t–42t
Special Supplemental Nutrition Program for Women, Infants, and Children, 71t
Supplemental Nutrition Assistance Program benefits, by state, 64t
Supplemental Nutrition Assistance Program eligibility income thresholds, 66t
Supplemental Nutrition Assistance Program maximum allotments, 85t
Supplemental Nutrition Assistance Program participant demographics, 86f, 89t, 90t, 91t
Supplemental Nutrition Assistance Program participation and costs, 67t
Supplemental Security Income, 96t, 97t
tax relief, 76t
Temporary Assistance for Needy Families benefits, by state, 62f, 63t
Temporary Assistance for Needy Families participants, 79t, 80f, 81t–82t, 83t, 84f
unemployment, 6t, 95t
unemployment insurance, 93t
uninsured persons, 151f, 152f, 153t, 154f, 157f
working poor, 48t, 49t, 50t
worst-case housing needs, 121f
Stewart B. McKinney Homeless Assistance Act. See McKinney-Vento Homeless Assistance Act
Street newspapers, 115
Street Soccer USA, 140
Stress and homelessness, 161
Students, homeless, 107–109, 109t, 136–137

Subsidies, housing, 120–126
Substance abuse, 137, 160–161
Substance Abuse and Mental Health Services Administration (SAMHSA), 137, 161
Suburban areas, 31, 127
Supplemental Nutrition Assistance Program (SNAP)
average monthly benefit, by state, 64t
effectiveness, 78
eligibility and benefits, 61, 66, 66t
employment and poverty status of recipients, 86f
maximum benefits, 85t
participation and costs, 67t
Personal Responsibility and Work Opportunity Reconciliation Act, 60
poverty guidelines, 2
recipients, 84–86, 88, 90–92, 90t, 91t
Supplemental Poverty Measure, 11–12, 11t, 12f, 12t, 31
Supplemental Security Income (SSI)
eligibility and benefits, 74–75
Medicaid, 158
Personal Responsibility and Work Opportunity Reconciliation Act, 56
recipients, 94–95, 96t, 97t
Supplemental Nutrition Assistance Program, 66
Temporary Assistance for Needy Families, 65
Supportive Housing Program, 134
Supportive Services for Veteran Families, 136
Survey of Income and Program Participation (SIPP), 51–52
Surveys, food insecurity, 85–88
Systems of care, 139

T

Take Back the Land, 129
TANF. See Temporary Assistance for Needy Families
Tanner, Michael, 84–85
Tax credits, low-income housing, 127–128
Tax Reform Act, 75
Taxes and tax relief, 10, 11, 75, 76t, 78, 156
Technology revolution, 16
Teenaged parents, 56
Temporary Assistance for Needy Families (TANF)
employment rate of recipients, 84f
maximum benefits, by state, 62f, 63t
provisions, 56, 60–61
recipients, 78–84, 83t
Supplemental Nutrition Assistance Program, 66, 90
welfare reform, 1–2, 55
welfare-to-work concept, 61–66
Tenant-based housing vouchers, 124
Tennessee, 151
Tent cities, 129–130

Texas, 151
Thrifty Food Plan, 60, 66
Transgender youth homelessness. See Lesbian, gay, bisexual, transgender, and queer youth homelessness
Transitional housing, 101, 128
Transportation issues, 65–66
Trauma and homelessness, 161
Treaties and international agreements, 139
Trump, Donald, 61, 159
Tsemberis, Sam, 137
Tuberculosis, 160
Turkey, 28, 30

U

Undocumented immigrants, 60
Unemployment
demographic characteristics, 95t
Great Depression, 1
homelessness, 101
poverty, 3, 24t–25t, 46
rate statistics, 6t
Supplemental Nutrition Assistance Program recipients, 85t
unemployment insurance, 70–72, 78, 92–94
Unemployment insurance, 70–72, 78, 92–94, 93t
UNICEF (United Nations Children's Fund), 28, 30
Uninsured persons
by age, 154f
demographic characteristics, 157f
Medicaid eligibility, 158
rates of, 149, 151, 151f
by state, 152f, 153t
United Nations Children's Fund (UNICEF), 28, 30
United Nations Human Rights Committee, 139
University of New Mexico, 139
Urban areas
affordable housing shortages, 127
homelessness, 111, 114f
panhandling ordinances, 115
poverty, 31
rental housing costs, 123, 124t
U.S. Bureau of Labor Statistics, 92
U.S. Census Bureau
accuracy of poverty measures, 7
food insecurity survey, 85–88
homelessness measures, 18
poverty guidelines, 2
rental housing costs, 118
Supplemental Poverty Measure, 31
Survey of Income and Program Participation, 51–52
uninsured population, 149, 151
U.S. Department of Agriculture (USDA)
rural housing programs, 125

174   Index

Social Welfare

school meal programs, 68
Supplemental Nutrition Assistance Program, 60, 66, 85
U.S. Department of Education, 136–137
U.S. Department of Health and Human Services (HHS), 2, 63–64, 137
U.S. Department of Housing and Urban Development (HUD)
affordable housing shortages, 127
anti-homelessness programs, 21
budget outlays, by program, 122*t*–123*t*
Family Options Study, 140
foreclosure prevention programs, 126
HEARTH Act, 132
homeless assistance programs, 134, 135*t*, 136
homeless children and youth, 107–108, 109
homeless military veterans, 11
homelessness estimates, 18, 99–100
housing vouchers, 121–124
public housing, 124–125
worst-case housing needs, 120
U.S. Department of Justice, 137, 139
U.S. Department of Labor, 137
U.S. Department of the Treasury, 126
U.S. Department of Veterans Affairs, 110, 136, 162
U.S. Housing Act, 124, 133

U.S. Interagency Council on Homelessness (USICH), 101, 110–111, 132, 136, 137, 139
U.S. Interagency Technical Working Group, 11
USDA. *See* U.S. Department of Agriculture
Utah, 63, 151, 158
Utah Housing and Community Development Division, 139

V

Vento, Bruce F., 134
Vermont, 75, 157
Veterans, homeless, 110–111, 110*t*, 111*f*, 111*t*, 136, 162
Victimization of the homeless, 161–162
Vocational education, 63
Vouchers, housing, 121–124, 126, 134, 140

W

Wages. *See* Income and earnings
Waivers, welfare-to-work, 63–64
War on Poverty, 2, 3, 12, 19–21
Washington (state), 115, 157
Wealth inequality, 16
Welfare assistance
family status and household composition of recipients, 57*t*–59*t*

history, 1–2
minimum wage workers, 73
school meal programs, 66–68
unemployment insurance, 92–94, 93*t*
welfare-to-work concept, 61–66
See also specific programs
Welfare reform, 1–2, 55
West Virginia, 157
White-collar unemployment, 94
WIC program (Special Supplemental Nutrition Program for Women, Infants, and Children), 2, 68–70
Williams, Robin, 140
Wilson, James Q., 138
Winship, Scott, 20
Wisconsin, 61
Wise, Terrance, 73–74
Women, homeless, 161
Workforce Investment Act, 2
Works Progress Administration, 1
World Bank, 12–13
Worst-case housing needs, 120, 121*f*
Wyoming, 151, 158

Y

Young Women's Christian Association (YWCA), 138
Youth. *See* Children and youth

CPSIA information can be obtained
at www.ICGtesting.com
Printed in the USA
FFOW04n0001140518
46624902-48683FF